The

BOOK OF WORSHIP

for

Church and Home

The
BOOK OF WORSHIP
for
Church and Home

With Orders for the Administration of the
Sacraments and Other Rites and
Ceremonies According to the
Use of

THE METHODIST CHURCH

FOR VOLUNTARY AND OPTIONAL USE

THE METHODIST PUBLISHING HOUSE
Founded 1789

THE General Conference of The Methodist Church, meeting in Kansas City, Missouri, April 26–May 6, 1944, authorized the publication of THE BOOK OF WORSHIP FOR CHURCH AND HOME for "optional and voluntary use by Methodist churches and Methodist people."

We "instruct the Commission on Ritual and Orders of Worship and the Book Editor to make such editorial changes as shall be necessary to avoid all infelicities of expression, and to assure uniformity in spelling and the use of the Scripture."

—Proceedings of the General Conference, p. 142

PREFACE

THIS Book of Worship for Church and Home is published at the direction of the General Conference of The Methodist Church. It is designed to help people in their worship of God. It makes available in one volume not only the historic offices and Ritual of The Methodist Church, but also a wealth of devotional material in the form of prayers, scriptural readings, and orders of worship which may be used as need may require. Private worship, with forms to guide the individual and family in daily devotion, has been given foremost attention in this volume.

Methodism has never been considered a liturgical church, but it always has had fixed forms to guide it in its recurrent acts of public worship. During the greater part of John Wesley's life Methodists in England worshiped in their parish churches. Methodist meetings were usually held at times that did not conflict with the stated services of worship in the churches. When the Methodist societies met, they followed a simple pattern, singing hymns—mostly those of Charles and John Wesley —reading Scripture, engaging in extempore prayer, and preaching the Word. It was assumed that members of the societies had already shared in public worship according to the order of the Book of Common Prayer.

When the time came for American Methodism to be set off from the parent societies in England, after the American Revolution, John Wesley sent over to America an abridgment of the Book of Common Prayer for the use of Methodists here. This abridgment he called *The Sunday Service for the Methodists of North America.* It was a book that contained much of what we now call our Ritual, together with a great many other forms and offices of the old Prayer Book. But the *Sunday Service* was never very widely used in America, being supplanted in a few years by American Methodism's own distinctive book, the Dis-

v

cipline. In the Discipline, from 1792 to the present, there have always appeared and been preserved the Offices of the Church which John Wesley sent to this country. These were: The Sacrament of the Lord's Supper, the offices for Infant and Adult Baptism, Matrimony, Burial of the Dead, and forms for the Ordination of a Ministry. These offices were together termed "The Ritual" and are to be found in an appropriate place in this book, as are certain other offices which the later church has added to them through the years.

Methodism has thus a twofold tradition of worship—both liturgical and free. It is liturgical in conducting its recurrent stated services with reverence according to officially adopted forms; it is free in its ability to use extempore prayer, to bend each service to the glorifying of God and to the bringing of his saving grace unto men.

During recent years there has developed among Methodist people a desire to have more readily available the rich inheritance which the Christian Church has preserved in its ancient and modern treasures of devotion. Therefore, following the union of Methodist churches in 1939, at the first General Conference in 1940, there was appointed a Commission on Ritual and Orders of Worship. This commission was specifically requested to provide forms and orders of worship which would "draw upon richer and wider sources than those that have been available up to the present time."

Pursuant to this mandate a commission was appointed as follows: Bishop Ivan Lee Holt (chairman), Bishop Charles Wesley Flint (vice-chairman), Oscar Thomas Olson (secretary), Fred Winslow Adams, Charles Wesley Caldwell, Clarence T. Craig, W. F. Dunkle, Jr., C. E. Forlines, Luther L. Gobbel, Nolan B. Harmon, Jr., Jerome C. Hixson, James R. Houghton, Lindsay B. Longacre, Edgar A. Love, Robert G. McCutchan, Charles Nelson Pace, Paul W. Quillian, J. N. R. Score, J. S. Ladd Thomas, William J. Williams. At the General Conference of 1944, the following persons were added to the commission to replace those who were deceased or retired:

A. L. Baner, Fred G. Holloway, Amos Thornburg, Oscar P. Bennett, Roy H. McVicker.

Throughout the better part of four years the members of the commission labored, gathering from many sources and putting together with earnest care and reverent skill the materials which are to be found in this book. The volume was duly presented to the General Conference of 1944 and with some slight changes was adopted by that body and recommended to all Methodist people for optional use. The Ritual which this book contains is of course official and is to be invariably used.

The wealth of devotional acts which is the noble heritage of the Universal Church has been freely drawn upon in the making of this book. The language of Scripture and Christian devotion throughout the centuries is used. The characteristic expression of evangelical experience which is native to Methodism is recognized. It is hoped that these aids will inspire adoring hearts to worship God in spirit and in truth, will bring a sense of real penitence to our day, will arouse a faith that lays hold of the life that is eternal, and will result in the dedication of men, women, and children to the Kingdom of righteousness, peace, and good will of Jesus Christ our Lord.

If we, a body of people called Methodists, can find for our day the resources of God through the disciplined experience of common prayer and devoted service, we shall find ourselves at the place where we can claim the fulfillment of the gracious promise of God: "Then shall ye call upon me, and ye shall go and pray unto me, and I will hearken unto you. And ye shall seek me, and find me, when ye shall search for me with all your heart."

August 1, 1945

NOTE

CONGREGATIONAL use of this volume requires that all copies have the same page numbers, so that the worshipers may locate selections without confusion. Accordingly the new orders added to the Ritual by the General Conference have been placed as Addenda at the end of the book, where they will not disarrange the paging of material appearing in the first edition. Since the new orders will rarely be used in a local church, and other revisions in the Ritual involve only sentences spoken by the minister, congregations may continue to use their copies of the first edition, replacing only those which become worn or damaged.

CONTENTS

ORDERS OF WORSHIP FOR GENERAL USE

ORDERS OF WORSHIP FOR OCCASIONAL USE
Suggested for Festival Observances of the Christian Year

CONTENTS

x

CONTENTS

THE MINISTRY TO THE SICK

ADDENDA

CONTENTS

The Pattern for the Orders of Worship

AN order of worship should move with unity and meaning. There is a fourfold aspect to an order of worship. Four attitudes of the devout worshipper are presented in ascending movements—adoration, confession, affirmation, and dedication. They imply the divinely descending movements of vision, pardon, illumination, and fruition.

While this pattern allows for wide variety of content, it at the same time possesses such unity that, if it is generally followed by our churches, a Methodist will feel at home in any Methodist church. This is because the things we are most used to always come in the same order. For example, the Lord's Prayer, the Responsive Reading, and the Creed are always found in the same place, as are the Call to Worship and the Benediction.

I. THE ADORATION OF GOD

The congregation should be called to worship at the opening of every service by a hymn of praise and adoration.

PRELUDE

CALL TO WORSHIP

HYMN

INVOCATION

COLLECT

II. THE CONFESSION OF SIN

If through our adoration we come to a vision of God, we naturally feel the need of confessing our sins.

PRAYER OF CONFESSION

SILENT MEDITATION

WORDS OF ASSURANCE

1

PRAYER FOR PARDON or WORDS OF FORGIVENESS

THE LORD'S PRAYER

III. THE AFFIRMATION OF FAITH

The experience of forgiveness should bring a mood of exaltation, in which we can affirm our faith through music, scripture, and creed, all moving toward the Pastoral Prayer.

ANTHEM

THE RESPONSIVE READING

GLORIA PATRI

AFFIRMATION OF FAITH

THE LESSONS: Old Testament, New Testament

PASTORAL PRAYER

IV. THE DEDICATION OF LIFE

All that follows the Pastoral Prayer, from Offertory to Benediction, should be in a mood of dedication, which is centralized in the Sermon. The goal of all worship is the dedication of ourselves, in the name of Christ, to his Church and Kingdom.

OFFERTORY

HYMN

THE SERMON

AN INVITATION TO CHRISTIAN DISCIPLESHIP

HYMN

SILENT PRAYER

BENEDICTION

POSTLUDE

This order is arranged for regular morning worship. The pattern may be considerably varied on Christmas or Easter or other festival occasions.

An Order of Worship

Let the service of worship begin at the time appointed. Let the people kneel or bow in silent prayer upon entering the sanctuary.

PRELUDE *The people in devout meditation.*

HYMN *The people standing.*

SCRIPTURE SENTENCES, INVOCATION, or PRAYER OF CONFESSION

ANTHEM

THE RESPONSIVE READING *Here let the people stand and remain standing during the singing of the* Gloria Patri.

GLORIA PATRI

THE SCRIPTURE LESSON

PASTORAL PRAYER *Followed by the Lord's Prayer. The people seated and bowed or kneeling.*

OFFERTORY *The dedication of gifts and tithes. An offertory sentence may be said or sung.*

HYMN

THE SERMON

PRAYER

AN INVITATION TO CHRISTIAN DISCIPLESHIP

HYMN or DOXOLOGY *The people standing.*

SILENT PRAYER

BENEDICTION

POSTLUDE

An Order of Worship for Morning I

Let the service of worship begin at the time appointed. Let the people kneel or bow in silent prayer upon entering the sanctuary.

PRELUDE *The people in devout meditation.*

CALL TO WORSHIP

Minister: Know ye that the Lord he is God: it is he that hath made us, and not we ourselves.

People: **We are his people, and the sheep of his pasture.**

Minister: Enter into his gates with thanksgiving, and into his courts with praise.

People: **We give thanks unto him, and bless his name: for the Lord is good. Amen.**

HYMN *The people standing. If the hymn be a processional, let it precede the Call to Worship.*

INVOCATION *The minister.*

Let us pray.

Almighty God, from whom every good prayer cometh, and who pourest out on all who desire it the spirit of grace and supplication; deliver us, when we draw nigh to thee, from coldness of heart and wanderings of mind, that with steadfast thoughts and kindled affections we may worship thee in spirit and in truth; through Jesus Christ our Lord. **Amen.**

PRAYER OF CONFESSION *Here let the people unite with the minister in prayer.*

Have mercy upon us, O God, according to thy lovingkindness: according to the multitude of thy tender mercies blot out our transgressions. Wash us thoroughly from our iniquities, and cleanse us from our sins. For we acknowledge our transgressions, and our sin

is ever before us. Create in us clean hearts, O God, and renew a right spirit within us; through Jesus Christ our Lord. Amen.

SILENT MEDITATION

THE LORD'S PRAYER

Our Father who art in heaven, hallowed be thy name; thy kingdom come; thy will be done on earth as it is in heaven. Give us this day our daily bread. And forgive us our trespasses, as we forgive those who trespass against us. And lead us not into temptation, but deliver us from evil. For thine is the kingdom, and the power, and the glory, forever. Amen.

ANTHEM

THE RESPONSIVE READING *Here let the people stand and remain standing during the singing of the* Gloria Patri.

GLORIA PATRI

THE LESSONS *From the Old and New Testament Scriptures.*

PASTORAL PRAYER *The people seated and bowed, or kneeling.*

OFFERTORY *The dedication of gifts and tithes. An offertory sentence may be said or sung.*

HYMN

THE SERMON *Which may be followed by prayer.*

AN INVITATION TO CHRISTIAN DISCIPLESHIP

HYMN or DOXOLOGY *The people standing.*

SILENT PRAYER

BENEDICTION

POSTLUDE

An Order of Worship for Morning II

Let the service of worship begin at the time appointed. Let the people kneel or bow in silent prayer upon entering the sanctuary.

PRELUDE *The people in devout meditation.*

CALL TO WORSHIP *Which may be said or sung.*

Minister: The Lord is in his holy temple.

People: **Let all the earth keep silence before him.**

Minister: He is not far from any one of us.

People: **Let us worship him in spirit and in truth. Amen.**

HYMN *The people standing. If the hymn be a processional, let it precede the Call to Worship.*

PRAYER OF CONFESSION *Here let the people unite with the minister in prayer.*

Almighty and most merciful Father, we have erred and strayed from thy ways like lost sheep. We have followed too much the devices and desires of our own hearts. We have offended against thy holy laws. We have left undone those things which we ought to have done, and we have done those things which we ought not to have done. But thou, O Lord, have mercy upon us. Spare thou those, O God, who confess their faults. Restore thou those who are penitent, according to thy promises declared unto mankind in Christ Jesus our Lord. And grant, O most merciful Father, for his sake, that we may hereafter live a godly, righteous, and sober life; to the glory of thy holy name. Amen.

SILENT MEDITATION

WORDS OF ASSURANCE *The minister.*

Hear what assuring words our Saviour Christ saith unto all

that truly turn to him: Come unto me, all ye that labor and are heavy laden, and I will give you rest.

Hear also the words from St. John's Gospel: God so loved the world, that he gave his only-begotten Son, that whosoever believeth in him should not perish, but have everlasting life.

PRAYER FOR PARDON *The minister.*

O Lord, we beseech thee, absolve thy people from their offenses, that through thy bountiful goodness we may be delivered from the bonds of those sins which by our frailty we have committed. Grant this, O heavenly Father, for Jesus Christ's sake, our blessed Lord and Saviour. **Amen.**

THE LORD'S PRAYER

Our Father who art in heaven, hallowed be thy name; thy kingdom come; thy will be done on earth as it is in heaven. Give us this day our daily bread. And forgive us our trespasses, as we forgive those who trespass against us. And lead us not into temptation, but deliver us from evil. For thine is the kingdom, and the power, and the glory, forever. Amen.

ANTHEM or CHANT

THE RESPONSIVE READING *Here let the people stand and remain standing until after the Affirmation of Faith.*

GLORIA PATRI

AFFIRMATION OF FAITH *Here let the people, following the exhortation of the minister, unite with him in the creed.*

Where the Spirit of the Lord is, there is the one true Church, apostolic and universal, whose holy faith let us now reverently and sincerely declare.

I believe in God the Father Almighty, Maker of heaven and earth; and in Jesus Christ his only Son our Lord; who was conceived by the Holy Spirit, born of the Virgin Mary, suffered under Pontius Pilate, was crucified, dead, and buried; the third day he rose from

the dead; he ascended into heaven, and sitteth at the right hand of God the Father Almighty; from thence he shall come to judge the quick and the dead. I believe in the Holy Spirit, the holy catholic Church, the communion of saints, the forgiveness of sins, the resurrection of the body, and the life everlasting. Amen.

THE LESSONS *From the Old and New Testament Scriptures.*

PASTORAL PRAYER *The people seated and bowed, or kneeling.*

OFFERTORY *The dedication of gifts and tithes. An offertory sentence may be said or sung.*

HYMN

THE SERMON *Which may be followed by prayer.*

AN INVITATION TO CHRISTIAN DISCIPLESHIP

HYMN or DOXOLOGY *The people standing.*

SILENT PRAYER

BENEDICTION

POSTLUDE

An Order of Worship for Morning III

Let the service of worship begin at the time appointed. Let the people kneel or bow in silent prayer upon entering the sanctuary.

PRELUDE *The people in devout meditation.*

PROCESSIONAL HYMN *The people standing. If there be no processional, let the first hymn follow the Call to Worship.*

CALL TO WORSHIP

Minister: This is the day which the Lord hath made; let us rejoice and be glad in it.

People: **This is none other than the house of God, and this is the gate of heaven.**

Minister: Enter into his gates with thanksgiving, and into his courts with praise.

People: **For the hour cometh, and now is, when the true worshipers shall worship the Father in spirit and in truth. Amen.**

Here let the people be seated.

INVOCATION *The minister.*

Let us pray.

Almighty God, author of eternal light; illumine our hearts by the light of thy grace, that our lips may praise thee, that our lives may bless thee, that our worship may glorify thee; through Jesus Christ our Lord. **Amen.**

COLLECT *Here let the people unite with the minister in prayer.*

Almighty God, unto whom all hearts are open, all desires known, and from whom no secrets are hid; cleanse the thoughts of our hearts by the inspiration of thy Holy Spirit, that we may perfectly love thee, and worthily magnify thy holy name; through Christ our Lord. Amen.

9

PRAYER OF CONFESSION

Almighty and eternal God, who searchest the hearts of men; we acknowledge and confess that we have sinned against thee in thought, word, and deed; that we have not loved thee with all our heart and soul, with all our mind and strength; and that we have not loved our neighbor as ourselves. Forgive us our transgressions, and help us to amend our ways, and of thine eternal goodness direct what we shall be, so that we may henceforth walk in the way of thy commandments, and do those things which are worthy in thy sight; through Jesus Christ our Lord. Amen.

SILENT MEDITATION

WORDS OF ASSURANCE *The minister.*

Rest in the LORD, and wait patiently for him. Commit your ways unto him. Come unto him, all ye that labor and are heavy laden, and he will give you rest.

WORDS OF FORGIVENESS *The minister.*

May Almighty God, who caused light to shine out of darkness, shine in your hearts, cleansing you from all your sins, and restoring you to the light of the knowledge of his glory in the face of Jesus Christ. **Amen.**

THE LORD'S PRAYER

Our Father who art in heaven, hallowed be thy name; thy kingdom come; thy will be done on earth as it is in heaven. Give us this day our daily bread. And forgive us our trespasses, as we forgive those who trespass against us. And lead us not into temptation, but deliver us from evil. For thine is the kingdom, and the power, and the glory, forever. Amen.

Minister: O Lord, open thou our lips.

People: **And our mouth shall show forth thy praise.**

Minister: Praise ye the Lord.

People: **The Lord's name be praised.**

ANTHEM or CHANT

THE RESPONSIVE READING *Here let the people stand and remain standing until after the Affirmation of Faith.*

GLORIA PATRI

AFFIRMATION OF FAITH *Here let the people, following the exhortation of the minister, unite with him in the Affirmation of Faith.*

Where the Spirit of the Lord is, there is the one true Church, apostolic and universal, whose holy faith let us now reverently and sincerely declare.

We believe in God the Father, infinite in wisdom, power, and love, whose mercy is over all his works, and whose will is ever directed to his children's good.

We believe in Jesus Christ, Son of God and Son of man, the gift of the Father's unfailing grace, the ground of our hope, and the promise of our deliverance from sin and death.

We believe in the Holy Spirit as the divine presence in our lives, whereby we are kept in perpetual remembrance of the truth of Christ, and find strength and help in time of need.

We believe that this faith should manifest itself in the service of love as set forth in the example of our blessed Lord, to the end that the Kingdom of God may come upon the earth. Amen.

THE LESSON FROM THE OLD TESTAMENT *Which may be preceded by the* Gloria Deo.

THE LESSON FROM THE NEW TESTAMENT *Which may be followed by the* Gratia Tibi.

CALL TO PRAYER

Minister: The Lord be with you.

People: **And with thy spirit.**

Minister: Let us pray.

Here let the people kneel or be seated and bow in prayer.

Minister: O Lord, show thy mercy upon us.

People: **And grant us thy salvation.**

Minister: O God, make clean our hearts within us.

People: **And take not thy Holy Spirit from us.**

PASTORAL PRAYER *Which may be followed by a choral response.*

OFFERTORY *The dedication of gifts and tithes. An offertory sentence may be said or sung.*

HYMN

THE SERMON *Which may be followed by prayer.*

AN INVITATION TO CHRISTIAN DISCIPLESHIP

HYMN or DOXOLOGY *The people standing.*

SILENT PRAYER

BENEDICTION *Which may be followed by a choral response.*

POSTLUDE

An Order of Worship for Evening I

Let the service of worship begin at the time appointed. Let the people kneel or bow in silent prayer upon entering the sanctuary.

PRELUDE *The people in devout meditation.*

SENTENCES *The minister.*

From the rising of the sun unto the going down of the same the LORD's name is to be praised.

The day goeth away, for the shadows of the evening are stretched out. But it shall come to pass, that at evening time it shall be light.

HYMN *The people standing. If the hymn be a processional, let it precede the Sentences.*

COLLECT FOR PURITY *Here let the people unite with the minister in prayer.*

Almighty God, unto whom all hearts are open, all desires known, and from whom no secrets are hid; cleanse the thoughts of our hearts by the inspiration of thy Holy Spirit, that we may perfectly love thee, and worthily magnify thy holy name; through Christ our Lord. Amen.

RESPONSIVE PRAYER

Search me, O God, and know my heart.

Try me, and know my thoughts.

And see if there be any wicked way in me.

And lead me in the way everlasting.

LORD, lift thou up the light of thy countenance upon us.

Out of the depths have I cried unto thee, O LORD.

Lord, hear my voice.

Let thine ears be attentive to the voice of my supplications.

13

If thou, LORD, shouldest mark iniquities, O Lord, who shall stand?

But there is forgiveness with thee, that thou mayest be feared. Amen.

SILENT MEDITATION

THE LORD'S PRAYER

Our Father who art in heaven, hallowed be thy name; thy kingdom come; thy will be done on earth as it is in heaven. Give us this day our daily bread. And forgive us our trespasses, as we forgive those who trespass against us. And lead us not into temptation, but deliver us from evil. For thine is the kingdom, and the power, and the glory, forever. Amen.

ANTHEM

THE MAGNIFICAT *Which may be sung, or read responsively. If it be read responsively, let the people stand.*

My soul doth magnify the Lord.

And my spirit hath rejoiced in God my Saviour.

For he hath regarded the low estate of his handmaiden: for, behold, from henceforth all generations shall call me blessed.

For he that is mighty hath done to me great things; and holy is his name.

His mercy is on them that fear him from generation to generation.

He hath showed strength with his arm; he hath scattered the proud in the imagination of their hearts.

He hath put down the mighty from their seats, and exalted them of low degree.

He hath filled the hungry with good things; and the rich he hath sent empty away.

He hath given help to his servant Israel, in remembrance of his mercy;

As he spake to our fathers, to Abraham, and to his seed forever.

GLORIA PATRI

THE SCRIPTURE LESSON

PASTORAL PRAYER *The people seated and bowed, or kneeling.*

OFFERTORY *The dedication of gifts and tithes. An offertory sentence may be said or sung.*

HYMN

THE SERMON

INTERCESSION *Here let the people unite with the minister in prayer.*

O God, with whom there is no darkness, but the night shineth as the day; keep and defend us, and all thy people, in soul and body during the coming night. May we rest in the consciousness of thy favor, in the peace of a good conscience, in the hope of a better life, in the faith of thy providence, in the love of thy Spirit. May we rise up again to labor in our several callings, to do thy work while it is day, seeing the night cometh in which no man can work. And whether we wake or sleep, may we live together with Jesus Christ our Lord. Amen.

AN INVITATION TO CHRISTIAN DISCIPLESHIP

HYMN *Which may be a recessional.*

SILENT PRAYER

BENEDICTION

POSTLUDE

An Order of Worship for Evening II

Let the service of worship begin at the time appointed. Let the people kneel or bow in silent prayer upon entering the sanctuary.

PRELUDE *The people in devout meditation.*

HYMN *The people standing.*

SENTENCES *The minister.*

The day goeth away, for the shadows of the evening are stretched out. But it shall come to pass, that at evening time it shall be light.

Let my prayer be set forth before thee as incense; and the lifting up of my hands as the evening sacrifice.

The sacrifices of God are a broken spirit: a broken and a contrite heart, O God, thou wilt not despise.

Let the words of my mouth, and the meditation of my heart, be acceptable in thy sight, O Lord, my strength, and my redeemer.

INVOCATION *The minister.*
Let us pray.

Almighty God, our heavenly Father; receive us in this evening hour as we offer ourselves anew to thee in body, soul, and spirit. Let not thy holy day pass except it leave its benediction with us. Give to us the still and quiet heart. Speak to us thy truth, that we may glorify thee; through Jesus Christ our Lord. **Amen.**

SUPPLICATION *Here let the people unite with the minister in prayer.*
Send thy peace into our hearts, O Lord, that we may be contented with thy mercies of this day, and confident of thy protection for this night; and now, having forgiven others, even as thou dost forgive us, may we have a pure comfort and a healthful rest within

16

the shelter of thy love; through Jesus Christ our Lord. **Amen.**

AN EVENING HYMN

RESPONSIVE READING *Here let the people stand and remain standing during the singing of the* Gloria Patri.

My heart shall indite a good matter: I will bless the Lord, who giveth me light.

I will say to the sorrowful, Be comforted, and to them that wait for the morning, Be glad of heart.

For the glory of the Lord is risen upon the earth; the day breaketh, and the shadows flee away.

Lo, the Master calleth his servants; be ready to meet him, O my soul;

Who forgiveth all thy sins, who healeth all thine infirmities,

Who openeth thy way into the kingdom of heaven, who maketh thee heir of eternal life.

O Lord our God, lift up the light of thy countenance upon us.

In thy light we shall see light; and thou wilt lead us to thy holy hill,

And dwell with us, and be our God; and the days of our lamentation shall be ended.

And all tribes shall be gathered together, and thy spirit poured out upon all flesh.

The old men shall dream dreams, and the young men shall see visions.

Then shall the earth clothe her in beautiful raiment; she shall shine as the daughter of the Great King.

The houses of mourning shall be full of light, and the rod of the oppressor shall be broken forever.

And men shall rejoice in the work of his hands, and the habitations of darkness shall be no more.

Be glad, O ye nations, and shout for joy: be strong and of a good courage, ye servants of the Lord.

For the living God is our helper: he that sitteth above the heavens shall bring it to pass.

Glory to him that hath his throne in the heavens, and his kingdom in the heart of his servants.

His kingdom is an everlasting kingdom; of his dominion there shall be no end.

GLORIA PATRI

THE SCRIPTURE LESSON

Minister: O Lord, open thou our lips.

People: **And our mouth shall show forth thy praise.**

Minister: Praise ye the Lord.

People: **The Lord's name be praised.**

ANTHEM

EVENING PRAYER *The Minister.*

O God, before whose face the generations rise and pass away; age after age the living seek thee and find that of thy faithfulness there is no end. Our fathers in their pilgrimage walked by thy guidance, and rested on thy compassion; still to their children be thou the cloud by day, the fire by night. Where but in thee have we a covert from the storm, or shadow from the heat of life? In our manifold temptations thou alone knowest and art ever nigh; in sorrow thy pity reviveth the fainting soul; in our prosperity and ease it is thy Spirit only that can wean us from our pride and keep us humble. O thou only source of peace and righteousness, take now the veil from every heart, and join us in one communion with thy prophets and saints, who have trusted in thee and were not ashamed. Not of our worthiness but of thy tender mercy hear our prayer; through Jesus Christ our Lord. **Amen.**

OFFERTORY *The dedication of gifts and tithes. An offertory sentence may be said or sung.*

HYMN

THE SERMON *Which may be followed by prayer.*

AN INVITATION TO CHRISTIAN DISCIPLESHIP

HYMN or **DOXOLOGY** *The people standing.*

SILENT PRAYER

BENEDICTION

POSTLUDE

An Order of Worship for Evening III

Let the service of worship begin at the time appointed. Let the people kneel or bow in silent prayer upon entering the sanctuary.

PRELUDE *The people in devout meditation.*

HYMN *The people standing.*

CALL TO WORSHIP

    Minister: Praise ye the Lord, to whom all praise is due.

    People: **Praised be the Lord, to whom all praise is due for ever and ever. Amen.**

Here let the people be seated.

INVOCATION *The minister.*

Let us pray.

Praised be thou, O Lord our God, Ruler of the world, by whose law the shadows of evening fall and the gates of morn are opened. In wisdom thou hast established the changes of times and seasons, and ordered the ways of the stars in their heavenly courses. Creator of heaven and earth, O living God, rule thou over us forever. Praised be thou, O Lord, for the day and its work and for the night and its rest. **Amen.**

AN EVENING HYMN

A MEDITATION ON THE ORDERING OF OUR PERSONAL LIVES *To be said responsively by the minister and the people.*

Be ye not shaped to the pattern of this world, but be ye transformed for the service of the world by the renewing of your minds, so that ye may prove what is the good and acceptable and perfect will of God.

Let us examine our lives in the light of those ideals which, according to the teaching of Jesus, belong to the Kingdom of God.

Jesus said: Blessed are the poor in spirit: for theirs is the kingdom of heaven.

We humbly beseech thee, O Lord, that thou wouldest give us the true spirit of detachment in our lives, that we may not become enslaved by our possessions, or entangled in any interests which cannot be consecrated to thee.

That it may please thee to deliver us from pride and self-complacency, and make us ever willing to confess that we cannot walk in our own strength, or by ourselves live good and useful lives.

That it may please thee to keep us always awake to the vast possibilities of Christian saintship and Christian endeavor, lest we should ever feel that we had already attained.

Blessed are the poor in spirit: for theirs is the kingdom of heaven.

Jesus said: Blessed are they that mourn: for they shall be comforted.

Give us, O Lord, sorrow for our sins, and for the sins of the world; that through our sorrow there may be joy in the presence of the angels of God.

Give us, O Lord, the spirit of thy Son, that, being well and glad and strong, we may never lack sympathy for those who suffer and are sad.

Give us, O Lord, the power when we suffer pain to look into thy face, and learn from thee how to bear it patiently for thy sake.

Blessed are they that mourn: for they shall be comforted.

Jesus said: Blessed are the meek: for they shall inherit the earth.

Teach us, O Lord, to think less of our own importance; help us to overcome our desire to push ourselves forward at the expense of others; and grant that we may never glory in our achievements, but in thine.

Make us, O Lord, willing to learn to be thy servants, through whom thou mayest achieve thy perfect will, and so fill us with the spirit of service, that we shall not merely wait to be called, but be instant to help others.

Give us, O Lord, such a realization of our sonship to thee, that we may look upon all this wonderful world, its beauty and its treasures, as thy gift, and so recognize always that all we have must be used in accordance with thy will.

Blessed are the meek: for they shall inherit the earth.

Jesus said: Blessed are they that hunger and thirst after righteousness: for they shall be filled.

Give to each one of us, O Lord, a reverence for the truth, a desire both to think and to speak honestly; and save us from ever being afraid of that which is just and true.

Increase in us, O Lord, the desire to see justice established among men, and to hasten that day when love shall rule in our social and industrial life, and none shall enrich himself at others' expense, or live indifferent to others' needs and claims.

Blessed are they that hunger and thirst after righteousness: for they shall be filled.

Jesus said: Blessed are the merciful: for they shall obtain mercy.

Help us, O Lord, to see the good in others and not the evil only, and always to strive to understand before we hastily condemn.

Save us, O Lord, from the spirit of resentment; make us quick to forgive, as men who know how greatly we stand in need of others' forgiveness and of thine.

Help us, O Lord, to remember how often men do wrong through want of thought rather than lack of love, and how cunningly are woven the snares that trip men's feet; make us worthy to pray that we may be forgiven in the measure in which we forgive.

Blessed are the merciful: for they shall obtain mercy.

Jesus said: Blessed are the pure in heart: for they shall see God.

Teach us to reverence our bodies as temples of the Holy Spirit, and grant that we may ever strive to be pure in thought, word, and deed.

Grant, O Lord, that we may think clean, generous, humble thoughts, and harbor none which stain the mind and dim our vision of thee.

Help us, O Lord, so to fix our minds on thy love, thy purpose, and thy power, that we may be delivered from pride and from morbid occupation with ourselves.

Blessed are the pure in heart: for they shall see God.

Jesus said: Blessed are the peacemakers: for they shall be called the sons of God.

Help us, O Lord, to keep open the windows of our souls to thee in prayer, and renew us ever by thy grace; that, through all the restlessness and complexity of life, we may possess the peace of those whose minds are stayed on thee.

Keep us, O Lord, from embittering our earthly relationships, and give us to reveal a courteous and forbearing spirit, that so we may be makers of peace.

Finally, O Lord, grant that we may never rest content with a divided and embittered Church; save us from factiousness and division, and grant that, in opposing evil and maintaining our faith, we may never forget the law of love.

Blessed are the peacemakers: for they shall be called the sons of God.

O Lord, hear our prayer.

And let our cry come unto thee.

SILENT MEDITATION

Then let the minister and the people unite in saying:

Grant, we beseech thee, O Christ, that as we all share in one life, being members of thy body, so we may all use thy gifts for the perfecting of the saints, unto the work of ministering, unto the building up of thy body, till we attain unto the unity of the faith, and of the knowledge of thee, unto a full-grown man, unto the measure of the stature of thy fullness, to whom be all praise and glory now and for evermore. Amen.

HYMN

THE SERMON *Which may be followed by prayer.*

AN INVITATION TO CHRISTIAN DISCIPLESHIP

ANTHEM

OFFERTORY *The dedication of gifts and tithes. An offertory sentence may be said or sung.*

HYMN or DOXOLOGY *The people standing.*

SILENT PRAYER

BENEDICTION

POSTLUDE

An Order of Worship for Morning or Evening I

Let the service of worship begin at the time appointed. Let the people kneel or bow in silent prayer upon entering the sanctuary.

PRELUDE *The people in devout meditation.*

CALL TO WORSHIP *Which may be said or sung.*

HYMN *If a processional, the hymn shall precede the Call to Worship, and the people shall then rise at the second stanza and join in singing.*

PRAYER OF CONFESSION *To be said by all, the people seated and bowed, or kneeling. The following, or other prayer of confession, may be said:*

Our heavenly Father, who by thy love hast made us, and through thy love hast kept us, and in thy love wouldest make us perfect; we humbly confess that we have not loved thee with all our heart and soul and mind and strength, and that we have not loved one another as Christ hath loved us. Thy life is within our souls, but our selfishness hath hindered thee. We have resisted thy Spirit. We have neglected thine inspirations. Forgive what we have been; help us to amend what we are; and in thy Spirit direct what we shall be; that thou mayest come into the full glory of thy creation, in us and in all men; through Jesus Christ our Lord. Amen.

SILENT MEDITATION *The people seated and bowed, or kneeling.*

WORDS OF ASSURANCE *The minister.*

THE LORD'S PRAYER *Which may be said or sung.*

ANTHEM *or* CHANT *Which may be the* Venite *or the* Te Deum.

THE RESPONSIVE READING *The people to stand and remain standing until after the Affirmation of Faith.*

GLORIA PATRI

AFFIRMATION OF FAITH *To be said by the minister and people.*

THE LESSON FROM THE HOLY SCRIPTURES *The Old and New Testaments.*

PASTORAL PRAYER *The people seated and bowed, or kneeling.*

OFFERTORY *The dedication of offerings, with prayer or offertory sentences.*

HYMN *The people standing.*

THE SERMON

PRAYER *The people seated and bowed, or kneeling.*

AN INVITATION TO CHRISTIAN DISCIPLESHIP

HYMN or DOXOLOGY *The people standing. The closing hymn may be a recessional.*

BENEDICTION *The people seated and bowed, or kneeling.*

SILENT PRAYER

POSTLUDE

An Order of Worship for Morning or Evening II

Let the service of worship begin at the time appointed. Let the people kneel or bow in silent prayer upon entering the sanctuary.

PRELUDE

CALL TO WORSHIP

INVOCATION

HYMN

AFFIRMATION OF FAITH

I believe in God the Father Almighty, Maker of heaven and earth; and in Jesus Christ his only Son our Lord; who was conceived by the Holy Spirit, born of the Virgin Mary, suffered under Pontius Pilate, was crucified, dead, and buried; the third day he rose from the dead; he ascended into heaven, and sitteth at the right hand of God the Father Almighty; from thence he shall come to judge the quick and the dead. I believe in the Holy Spirit, the holy catholic Church, the communion of saints, the forgiveness of sins, the resurrection of the body, and the life everlasting. Amen.

ANTHEM

THE RESPONSIVE READING

GLORIA PATRI

THE LESSON FROM THE HOLY SCRIPTURES

SILENT MEDITATION

PASTORAL PRAYER

THE LORD'S PRAYER

27

OFFERTORY *The dedication of offerings, with prayer or offertory sentences.*

HYMN

THE SERMON

PRAYER

AN INVITATION TO CHRISTIAN DISCIPLESHIP

HYMN

BENEDICTION

POSTLUDE

An Order of Worship for Morning or Evening III

Let the service of worship begin at the time appointed. Let the people kneel or bow in silent prayer upon entering the sanctuary.

PRELUDE *The people in devout meditation.*

CALL TO WORSHIP *Which may be said or sung.*

HYMN *If a processional, the hymn shall precede the call to worship, and the people shall then rise at the second stanza and join in singing.*

PRAYER OF CONFESSION *To be said by all, the people seated and bowed, or kneeling. The following, or other prayer of confession, may be said:*

Almighty God, from whom every good prayer cometh, and who pourest out, on all who desire it, the spirit of grace and supplication; deliver us, when we draw nigh to thee, from coldness of heart and wanderings of mind, that with steadfast thoughts, and kindled affections, we may worship thee in spirit and in truth; through Jesus Christ our Lord. Amen.

SILENT MEDITATION *The people seated and bowed, or kneeling.*

THE LORD'S PRAYER *Which may be said or sung.*

ANTHEM

THE LESSON FROM THE HOLY SCRIPTURES *If a responsive reading is used, it should be followed by the* Gloria Patri, *the people standing.*

PASTORAL PRAYER *The people seated and bowed, or kneeling.*

PRESENTATION OF OFFERINGS

HYMN *The people standing.*

THE SERMON

AN INVITATION TO CHRISTIAN DISCIPLESHIP

HYMN or DOXOLOGY *The people standing.*

SILENT PRAYER

BENEDICTION *The people seated and bowed, or kneeling.*

POSTLUDE

An Order for Morning or Evening Prayer

Adapted from the Sunday Service of
JOHN WESLEY

Suggested for Occasional Use

Let the service of worship begin at the time appointed. Let the people kneel or bow in silent prayer upon entering the sanctuary.

PRELUDE *The people in devout meditation.*

SENTENCES *One or more of them to be read by the minister, the people standing.*

The LORD is in his holy temple: let all the earth keep silence before him.

Let the words of my mouth, and the meditation of my heart, be acceptable in thy sight, O LORD, my strength, and my redeemer.

This is the day which the LORD hath made, we will rejoice and be glad in it.

The hour cometh, and now is, when the true worshipers shall worship the Father in spirit and in truth.

The sacrifices of God are a broken spirit: a broken and a contrite heart, O God, thou wilt not despise.

HYMN *If a processional, the hymn should precede the Sentences, and the people shall then rise and join in singing.*

CALL TO CONFESSION *By the minister, the people standing.*

Dearly beloved, the Scripture moveth us to acknowledge and confess our sins before Almighty God our heavenly Father with a humble, lowly, penitent, and obedient heart, to the end that we may obtain forgiveness by his infinite goodness and mercy. Wherefore I pray and beseech you, as

31

many as are here present, to accompany me with a pure heart and a humble voice unto the throne of the heavenly grace.

Let us pray.

GENERAL CONFESSION *To be said by all, the people seated and bowed, or kneeling.*

Almighty and most merciful Father, we have erred and strayed from thy ways like lost sheep. We have followed too much the devices and desires of our own hearts. We have offended against thy holy laws. We have left undone those things which we ought to have done, and we have done those things which we ought not to have done. But thou, O Lord, have mercy upon us. Spare thou those, O God, who confess their faults. Restore thou those who are penitent, according to thy promises declared unto mankind in Christ Jesus our Lord. And grant, O most merciful Father, for his sake, that we may hereafter live a godly, righteous, and sober life; to the glory of thy holy name. Amen.

PRAYER FOR PARDON *The minister.*

O Lord, we beseech thee, absolve thy people from their offenses, that through thy bountiful goodness we may be delivered from the bonds of those sins which by our frailty we have committed. Grant this, O heavenly Father, for Jesus Christ's sake, our blessed Lord and Saviour. **Amen.**

The people shall answer here, and at the end of all other prayers, **Amen.**

THE LORD'S PRAYER *To be said by all.*

Minister: O Lord, open thou our lips.
People: **And our mouth shall show forth thy praise.**
Minister: Praise ye the Lord.
People: **The Lord's name be praised.**

VENITE *To be said or sung by all, the people standing.*

PSALTER *To be said by all, the people standing.*

GLORIA PATRI *To be said or sung by all, the people standing.*

THE LESSON FROM THE OLD TESTAMENT

TE DEUM *To be said or sung by all, the people standing.*

THE LESSON FROM THE NEW TESTAMENT

JUBILATE DEO *To be said or sung by all, the people standing.*

AFFIRMATION OF FAITH *Here shall be said the Apostles' Creed.*

Minister: The Lord be with you.
People: **And with thy spirit.**
Minister: Let us pray.

COLLECT FOR PEACE *To be said by all, the people seated and bowed, or kneeling.*

O God, who art the author of peace and lover of concord, in knowledge of whom standeth our eternal life, whose service is perfect freedom; defend us thy humble servants in all assaults of our enemies, that we, surely trusting in thy defense, may not fear the power of any adversaries, through the might of Jesus Christ our Lord. Amen.

COLLECT FOR GRACE

O Lord, our heavenly Father, almighty and everlasting God, who hast safely brought us to the beginning of this day; defend us in the same with thy mighty power; and grant that this day we fall into no sin, neither run into any kind of danger, but that all our doings may be ordered by thy governance, to do always that which is righteous in thy sight; through Jesus Christ our Lord. Amen.

PRAYER *Then may the minister offer a prayer, ending with:*

The grace of our Lord Jesus Christ, and the love of God, and the communion of the Holy Spirit, be with us all. **Amen.**

OFFERTORY *Then may be sung an anthem, and an offering may be received.*

THE SERMON *When the service is followed by a sermon or the Holy Communion, the minister shall make use of appropriate hymns and prayers. Otherwise, the service may close with a hymn and the following benediction.*

BENEDICTION

The peace of God, which passeth all understanding, keep your hearts and minds in the knowledge and love of God, and of his Son Jesus Christ our Lord; and the blessing of God Almighty, the Father, the Son, and the Holy Spirit, be among you, and remain with you always. **Amen.**

POSTLUDE

When this order of worship is to be used for Evening Prayer, the following changes shall be made:

The Magnificat *shall be used in place of the* Te Deum.

The Nunc Dimittis *shall be used in place of the* Jubilate Deo.

In place of the Collect for Grace shall be said the following collects:

Lighten our darkness, we beseech thee, O Lord; and by thy great mercy defend us from all perils and dangers of this night; for the love of thine only Son, our Saviour Jesus Christ. Amen.

Direct us, O Lord, in all our doings, with thy most gracious favor, and further us with thy continual help, that in all our works, begun, continued, and ended in thee, we may glorify thy holy name, and finally, by thy mercy, obtain everlasting life; through Jesus Christ our Lord. Amen.

THESE orders of worship are intended as guides to point out the variety and richness of material that may be used to aid in deepening the spiritual life and interpreting the Christian message.

An Order of Worship for Advent

Let the service of worship begin at the time appointed. Let the people kneel or bow in silent prayer upon entering the sanctuary.

PRELUDE *The people in devout meditation.*

HYMN *The people standing.*

CALL TO WORSHIP

> *Minister:* O praise the Lord, all ye nations: praise him, all ye people.
>
> *People:* **His merciful kindness is great toward us.**
>
> *Minister:* Blessed be he that cometh in the name of the Lord.
>
> *People:* **Blessed be the name of the Lord for evermore. Amen.**

Here let the people be seated.

INVOCATION *The minister.*

Let us pray.

O God, who hast set before us the great hope that thy Kingdom shall come on earth, and hast taught us to pray for its coming; make us ever ready to thank thee for the signs of its dawning, and to pray and work for that perfect day when thy will shall be done on earth as it is in heaven; through Jesus Christ our Lord. **Amen.**

COLLECT FOR ADVENT *Here let the people unite with the minister in prayer.*

Almighty God, who in thy providence hast made all

[1] For a calendar of the Christian Year see pages 209-12.

ages a preparation for the kingdom of thy Son; we beseech thee to make ready our hearts for the brightness
of thy glory and the fullness of thy blessing in Jesus
Christ our Lord. Amen.

PRAYER OF CONFESSION

Almighty God, our heavenly Father, who didst cause
light to shine out of darkness in the advent of our
Lord Jesus Christ, to take away the sins of the world;
we humbly confess our transgressions and implore thy
forgiveness. We are ashamed of that within us which
maketh neither for good will to others nor for growth
in goodness in our own lives. We beseech thee that the
Spirit of Christ may be born anew within us, and that
we may glorify his nativity with hearts of compassion,
deeds of kindly service, and the spirit of good will toward all mankind; through Jesus Christ our Lord.
Amen.

SILENT MEDITATION

WORDS OF ASSURANCE *The minister.*

The Lord is at hand. In nothing be anxious; but in everything by prayer and supplication with thanksgiving let your
requests be made known unto God. And the peace of God,
which passeth all understanding, shall keep your hearts and
minds through Christ Jesus.

PRAYER FOR PARDON *The minister.*

O Lord, we beseech thee, absolve thy people from their
offenses, that through thy bountiful goodness we may be
delivered from the bonds of those sins which by our frailty
we have committed. Grant this, O heavenly Father, for Jesus
Christ's sake, our blessed Lord and Saviour. **Amen.**

THE LORD'S PRAYER

Our Father who art in heaven, hallowed be thy name;
thy kingdom come; thy will be done on earth as it is in
heaven. Give us this day our daily bread. And forgive

us our trespasses, as we forgive those who trespass against us. And lead us not into temptation, but deliver us from evil. For thine is the kingdom, and the power, and the glory, forever. Amen.

ANTHEM or CHANT

THE RESPONSIVE READING *Here let the people stand and remain standing until after the Affirmation of Faith.*

GLORIA PATRI

AFFIRMATION OF FAITH *Here let the people, following the exhortation of the minister, unite with him in the creed.*

Where the Spirit of the Lord is, there is the one true Church, apostolic and universal, whose holy faith let us now reverently and sincerely declare.

I believe in one God the Father Almighty, Maker of heaven and earth, and of all things visible and invisible:

And in one Lord Jesus Christ, the only-begotten Son of God, begotten of his Father before all worlds, God of God, Light of Light, very God of very God, begotten, not made, being of one substance with the Father, by whom all things were made; who for us men and for our salvation came down from heaven, and was incarnate by the Holy Ghost of the Virgin Mary, and was made man, and was crucified also for us under Pontius Pilate; he suffered and was buried, and the third day he rose again according to the Scriptures, and ascended into heaven, and sitteth on the right hand of the Father; and he shall come again with glory, to judge both the quick and the dead, whose kingdom shall have no end.

And I believe in the Holy Ghost, the Lord and Giver of life, who proceedeth from the Father and the Son, who with the Father and the Son together is worshiped and glorified, who spake by the prophets. And I believe one catholic and apostolic Church. I acknowledge one baptism for the remission of sins. And I look for

the resurrection of the dead, and the life of the world to come. Amen.

THE LESSONS *From the Old and New Testament Scriptures.*

OUR LORD'S SUMMARY OF THE LAW *The responses may be said or sung. Let the people be bowed.*

Our Lord Jesus Christ said: The first of all the commandments is, Hear, O Israel; The Lord our God is one Lord: and thou shalt love the Lord thy God with all thy heart, and with all thy soul, and with all thy mind, and with all thy strength: this is the first commandment.

Lord, have mercy upon us, and incline our hearts to keep this law.

And the second is like, namely this, Thou shalt love thy neighbor as thyself.

Lord, have mercy upon us, and incline our hearts to keep this law.

A new commandment I give unto you, That ye love one another; as I have loved you, that ye also love one another.

Lord, have mercy upon us, and write all these thy laws in our hearts, we beseech thee. Amen.

PASTORAL PRAYER

OFFERTORY *The dedication of gifts and tithes. An offertory sentence may be said or sung.*

HYMN

THE SERMON *Which may be followed by prayer.*

AN INVITATION TO CHRISTIAN DISCIPLESHIP

HYMN or DOXOLOGY *The people standing.*

SILENT PRAYER

BENEDICTION

POSTLUDE

An Order of Worship for Christmas Sunday

PRELUDE

QUIET MOMENTS *Let the people kneel or bow in silent prayer upon entering the sanctuary and devoutly meditate on the following words.*

SCRIPTURE SENTENCES

The LORD hath made known his salvation: his righteousness hath he openly showed in the sight of the nations.

The angel said, Behold, I bring you good tidings of great joy, which shall be to all people. For unto you is born this day in the city of David a Saviour, which is Christ the Lord.

In this was manifested the love of God toward us, because that God sent his only-begotten Son into the world, that we might live through him.

For God, who commanded the light to shine out of darkness, hath shined in our hearts, to give the light of the knowledge of the glory of God in the face of Jesus Christ.

A PRAYER AT CHRISTMASTIME

We beseech thee, O God, let our hearts be graciously enlightened by the radiance of the dayspring from on high, that we may escape the darkness of this world, and by thy guidance attain to the country of eternal brightness; through Jesus Christ our Lord. Amen.

A CHRISTMAS MEDITATION

As we commemorate the holy nativity of our Lord, let us remember:

His lowly toil and his lonely way,
The gracious words of his lips and the deep compassion of his heart,
His friendship for the defeated and his care for the outcast,

The crown of thorns and the cruel cross,
His victory over death and his promised peace to
all men,
The presence of his spirit and the assurance of
eternal life.

As we celebrate Christmas, let us rejoice:
For the light that shines on our pathway,
For the great redemption revealed in the coming
of Jesus Christ,
For the fellowship of faith in the beloved com-
munity of the Church.

PROCESSIONAL HYMN *The people standing. If there be no processional, let the first hymn follow the Call to Worship.*

CALL TO WORSHIP

Minister: Behold, I bring you good tidings of great joy,
which shall be to all people. For unto you is born
a Saviour, which is Christ the Lord.

People: **This child is set for the fall and rising again
of many.**

Minister: Let us with the wise men, lowly shepherds, and all
the heavenly host, worship the Holy Babe.

People: **O come, let us adore him, Christ the Lord.
Amen.**

Here let the people be seated.

INVOCATION *The minister.*

Let us pray.

O God our Father, who hast brought us again to the glad
season when we commemorate the birth of thy Son Jesus
Christ our Lord; grant that his Spirit may be born anew in
our hearts this day and that we may joyfully welcome him
to reign over us. Open our ears that we may hear again
the angelic chorus of old; open our lips that we too may
sing with uplifted hearts, Glory to God in the highest, and
on earth peace, good will toward men. **Amen.**

COLLECT FOR CHRISTMAS *Here let the people unite with the minister in prayer.*

O Father, who hast declared thy love to men by the birth of the holy Child at Bethlehem; help us to welcome him with gladness and to make room for him in our common days, so that we may live at peace with one another and in good will with all thy family; through Jesus Christ our Lord. Amen.

Minister: O Lord, open thou our lips.

People: **And our mouth shall show forth thy praise.**

Minister: Praise ye the Lord.

People: **The Lord's name be praised.**

ANTHEM

CHRISTMAS LITANY *The minister, the people responding.*

Let us pray.

Glory to God in the highest.

And on earth peace, good will toward men.

O God, thou art our salvation; we will trust, and not be afraid. Thou art our strength and our song.

Therefore with joy shall we draw water out of the wells of salvation.

We thank thee for the birth of Jesus, that thy Spirit was upon him, that he was anointed to preach good tidings to the poor, to proclaim release to the captives, the recovering of sight to the blind, to set at liberty them that are bruised.

Help us to make our present time the acceptable year of the Lord.

O God, enable us, as we worship thee, to kindle with the joy of simple shepherds long ago at the thought of all that came to the world in the birth of the child Jesus.

Cast out our sin, and enter in; be born in us today.

Help us, O God, in the light of the shining star to realize the wastes and desolations of the world, to feel the weight of the world's sorrow and need, to be made aware of the power of evil, to see what spiritual loss is caused by man's hatred and sins.

Help us with the spirit of Jesus to build the old wastes and to raise up the former desolations.

Forgive us, O God, for our weariness of heart through great conflict and exertion. Suffer us not to become creatures and nations of selfishness, of narrow, foolish pride; marred with hardness of heart, and weakened by fear and suspicion.

Grant unto us that we being delivered out of the hand of our enemies may serve thee without fear.

Over the face of the ancient earth, weary and torn with strife, the passing generations have come and are gone, and have not seen the triumph of good will among men; yet we give thanks for the unceasing renewal of life born to new hopes and strong to achieve new victories of good.

For unto us a child is born, unto us a son is given: and the government shall be upon his shoulder.

In the light of the shining star that giveth happiness to little children and cheer to all, help us to renew our zeal for that good time when none shall be far off or forgotten, but shall live within the circle of the blessed life.

May the dayspring from on high visit us, to give light to them that sit in darkness, to guide our feet into the way of peace. Amen.

GLORIA PATRI

THE LESSON

Comfort ye, comfort ye my people, saith your God. Speak ye comfortably to Jerusalem, and cry unto her, that her warfare is accomplished, that her iniquity is pardoned.

The voice of him that crieth in the wilderness, Prepare ye the way of the LORD, make straight in the desert a highway for our God.

Every valley shall be exalted, and every mountain and hill shall be made low : and the crooked shall be made straight, and the rough places plain.

And the glory of the LORD shall be revealed, and all flesh shall see it together : for the mouth of the LORD hath spoken it.

Thus saith the LORD of hosts, Yet once, it is a little while, and I will shake the heavens, and the earth, and the sea, and the dry land ; and I will shake all nations, and the desire of all nations shall come.

The Lord, whom ye seek, shall suddenly come to his temple, even the messenger of the covenant, whom ye delight in : behold, he shall come, saith the LORD of hosts.

But who may abide the day of his coming, and who shall stand when he appeareth ?

For he is like a refiner's fire.

And he shall purify the sons of Levi, that they may offer unto the LORD an offering in righteousness.

Behold, a virgin shall conceive, and bear a son, and shall call his name Immanuel, God with us.

O thou that tellest good tidings to Zion, get thee up into the high mountain ; O thou that tellest good tidings to Jerusalem, lift up thy voice with strength ; lift it up, be not afraid ; say unto the cities of Judah, Behold your God !

Arise, shine ; for thy light is come, and the glory of the LORD is risen upon thee.

For, behold, the darkness shall cover the earth, and gross darkness the people : but the LORD shall arise upon thee, and his glory shall be seen upon thee. And the nations shall come to thy light, and kings to the brightness of thy rising.

The people that walked in darkness have seen a great light : they that dwell in the land of the shadow of death, upon them hath the light shined.

For unto us a child is born, unto us a son is given : and the government shall be upon his shoulder : and his name shall be called Wonderful, Counselor, The Mighty God, The Everlasting Father, The Prince of Peace.

There were shepherds abiding in the field, keeping watch over their flocks by night.

And, lo, the angel of the Lord came upon them, and the glory of the Lord shone round about them; and they were sore afraid.

And the angel said unto them, Fear not: for, behold, I bring you good tidings of great joy, which shall be to all people.

For unto you is born this day in the city of David a Saviour, which is Christ the Lord.

And suddenly there was with the angel a multitude of the heavenly host praising God, and saying,

Glory to God in the highest, and on earth peace, good will toward men.

Rejoice greatly, O daughter of Zion; shout, O daughter of Jerusalem: behold, thy King cometh unto thee.

He is the righteous Saviour, and he shall speak peace unto the nations.

Then the eyes of the blind shall be opened, and the ears of the deaf shall be unstopped. Then shall the lame man leap as an hart, and the tongue of the dumb sing.

He shall feed his flock like a shepherd: he shall gather the lambs with his arm, and carry them in his bosom, and shall gently lead those that are with young.

Come unto him, all ye that labor and are heavy laden, and he will give you rest.

Take his yoke upon you, and learn of him; for he is meek and lowly in heart: and ye shall find rest unto your souls.

His yoke is easy, and his burden is light.

Hallelujah! For the Lord God omnipotent reigneth. The kingdoms of this world are become the kingdoms of our Lord, and of his Christ; and he shall reign for ever and ever. King of kings, and Lord of lords. Hallelujah!

—*From* The Messiah: *Isa. 40:1-5; Hag. 2:6-7; Mal. 3:1-3; Isa. 7:14; 40:9; 60:1-3; 9:2, 6; Luke 2:8-11, 13-14; Zech. 9:9; Isa. 35:5-6; 40:11; Matt. 11:28-30; Rev. 19:6; 11:15; 19:6.*

CAROLS

MEDITATION

> Let all mortal flesh keep silence,
> And with fear and trembling stand;
> Ponder nothing earthly minded,
> For with blessing in his hand,
> Christ our God to earth descendeth,
> Our full homage to demand. Amen.

PASTORAL PRAYER *Which may be followed by a choral response.*

OFFERTORY *The dedication of gifts and tithes.*

ACT OF CONSECRATION *Here let the people rise and sing.*

> **Praise God, from whom all blessings flow;**
> **Praise him, all creatures here below;**
> **Praise him above, ye heavenly host:**
> **Praise Father, Son, and Holy Ghost. Amen.**

HYMN OF PREPARATION

THE CHRISTMAS SERMON

AN INVITATION TO CHRISTIAN DISCIPLESHIP

HYMN *The people standing.*

SILENT PRAYER

BENEDICTION and CHORAL AMEN

POSTLUDE

The Order of Worship for Such as Would Enter into or Renew Their Covenant with God

For Use in a Watch-Night Service or on the First Sunday of the New Year

"ON December 25, 1747, John Wesley strongly urged the Methodists to renew their Covenant with God. His first Covenant Service was held in the French Church at Spitalfields on August 11, 1755, when he recited the words of 'that blessed man Richard Alleine,' which he published that year in the 'Christian Library.' Wesley issued this as a pamphlet in 1780, and the form was used without alteration for nearly a century. Various modifications were then made, till a form was prepared which gave the people a larger share in the devotions. That form has now been revised with a deep sense of the importance of a service which has been a fruitful source of blessing to Methodism ever since 1755."—*The Book of Offices, The Methodist Church of Great Britain and Ireland.*

The covenant hymn, "Come, let us use the grace divine," was written for this service by Charles Wesley.

Let the service of worship begin at the time appointed. Let the people kneel or bow in silent prayer upon entering the sanctuary.

PRELUDE *The people in devout meditation.*

HYMN *The people standing.*

COLLECT FOR PURITY *Here let the people unite with the minister in prayer.*

Almighty God, unto whom all hearts are open, all desires known, and from whom no secrets are hid; cleanse the thoughts of our hearts by the inspiration of thy Holy Spirit, that we may perfectly love thee, and worthily magnify thy holy name; through Christ our Lord. Amen.

THE LORD'S PRAYER

Our Father who art in heaven, hallowed be thy name; thy kingdom come; thy will be done on earth as it is in heaven. Give us this day our daily bread. And forgive us our trespasses, as we forgive those who trespass against us. And lead us not into temptation, but deliver us from evil. For thine is the kingdom, and the power, and the glory, forever. Amen.

THE SCRIPTURE LESSON *Here may be read John 15:1-8 or the responsive reading for Watch Night.*

HYMN *The people standing.*

THE INVITATION *The minister. Let the people remain standing.*

Dearly beloved, the Christian life, to which we are called, is a life in Christ, redeemed from sin by him, and through him consecrated to God. Upon this life we have entered, having been admitted into that new covenant of which our Lord Jesus Christ is mediator, and which he sealed with his own blood, that it might stand forever.

On one side the covenant is God's promise that he will fulfill in and through us all that he declared in Jesus Christ, who is the author and perfecter of our faith. That his promise still stands we are sure, for we have known his goodness and proved his grace in our lives day by day.

On the other side we stand pledged to live no more unto ourselves, but to him who loved us and gave himself for us and called us to serve him that the purposes of his coming be fulfilled.

From time to time we renew our vows of consecration, especially when we gather at the table of the Lord; but on this day we meet expressly, as generations of our fathers have met, that we may joyfully and solemnly renew the covenant which bound them and binds us to God.

Let us then, remembering the mercies of God and the hope of his calling, examine ourselves by the light of his Spirit, that we may see wherein we have failed or fallen short in faith and practice and, considering all that this covenant means, may give ourselves anew to God.

Let us pray.

THE ACT OF ADORATION *The minister, the people responding. Here let the people kneel or be seated and bow.*

Let us adore the Father, the God of love who created us;

Who every moment preserves and sustains us;

Who has loved us with an everlasting love, and given us the light of the knowledge of his glory in the face of Jesus Christ.

We praise thee, O God; we acknowledge thee to be the Lord.

Let us glory in the grace of our Lord Jesus Christ;

Who, though he was rich, yet for our sakes became poor;

Who went about doing good and preaching the gospel of the kingdom;

Who was tempted in all points like as we are, yet without sin;

Who became obedient unto death, even the death of the cross;

Who was dead, and liveth for evermore;

Who opened the kingdom of heaven to all believers;

Who sitteth at the right hand of God in the glory of the Father.

Thou art the King of Glory, O Christ.

Let us rejoice in the fellowship of the Holy Spirit, the Lord and Giver of life, by whom we are born into the family of God, and made members of the Body of Christ;

Whose witness confirms us;

Whose wisdom teaches us;

Whose power enables us;

Who waits to do for us exceeding abundantly above all that we ask or think.

All praise to thee, O Holy Spirit. Amen.

ANTHEM Gloria in Excelsis.

Glory be to God on high, and on earth, peace, good will toward men. We praise thee, we bless thee, we worship thee, we glorify thee, we give thanks to thee for thy great glory, O Lord God, heavenly King, God the Father Almighty!

O Lord, the only-begotten Son Jesus Christ; O Lord God, Lamb of God, Son of the Father, that takest away the sins of the world, have mercy upon us. Thou that takest away the sins of the world, have mercy upon us. Thou that takest away the sins of the world, receive our prayer. Thou that sittest at the right hand of God the Father, have mercy upon us. For thou only art holy; thou only art the Lord; thou only, O Christ, with the Holy Ghost, art most high in the glory of God the Father. Amen.

THE ACT OF THANKSGIVING *The minister, the people responding.*

Let us rise and give thanks to God for his manifold mercies.

Here let the people stand.

O God our Father, the fountain of all goodness, who hast been gracious to us through all the years of our life; we give thee thanks for thy lovingkindness which hath filled our days and brought us to this time and place.

We praise thy holy name, O Lord.

Thou hast given us life and reason, and set us in a world which is full of thy glory. Thou hast comforted us with kindred and friends, and ministered to us through the hands and minds of our fellows.

We praise thy holy name, O Lord.

Thou hast set in our hearts a hunger for thee, and given us thy peace. Thou hast redeemed us and called us to a high calling in Christ Jesus. Thou hast given us a place in the fellowship of thy Spirit and the witness of thy Church.

We praise thy holy name, O Lord.

In darkness thou hast been our light, in adversity and temptation a rock of strength, in our joys the very spirit of joy, in our labors the all-sufficient reward.

We praise thy holy name, O Lord.

Thou hast remembered us when we have forgotten thee, followed us even when we fled from thee, met us with forgiveness when we turned back to thee. For all thy long-suffering and the abundance of thy grace,

We praise thy holy name, O Lord. Amen.

ANTHEM or HYMN

THE ACT OF CONFESSION *The minister, the people responding.*

Let us now examine ourselves before God, humbly confessing our sins and watching our hearts, lest by self-deceit we shut ourselves out from his presence.

Let us pray.

Here let all kneel or bow.

O God our Father, who hast set forth the way of life for us in thy beloved Son; we confess with shame our slowness to learn of him, our reluctance to follow him. Thou hast spoken and called, and we have not given heed; thy beauty hath shone forth, and we have been blind; thou hast stretched out thy hands to us through our fellows, and we have passed by. We have taken great benefits with little thanks; we have been unworthy of thy changeless love.

Have mercy upon us and forgive us, O Lord.

Forgive us, we beseech thee, the poverty of our worship, the formality and selfishness of our prayers, our inconstancy and unbelief, our neglect of fellowship and of the means of grace, our hesitating witness for Christ, our false pretenses, and our willful ignorance of thy ways.

Have mercy upon us and forgive us, O Lord.

Forgive us wherein we have wasted our time or misused our gifts. Forgive us wherein we have excused our own wrongdoing or evaded our responsibilities. Forgive us that we have been unwilling to overcome evil with good, that we have drawn back from the cross.

Have mercy upon us and forgive us, O Lord.

Forgive us that so little of thy love hath reached others through us, and that we have borne so lightly wrongs and sufferings that were not our own. Forgive us wherein we have cherished the things that divide us from others, and wherein we have made it hard for them to live with us, and wherein we have been thoughtless in our judgments, hasty in condemnation, grudging in forgiveness.

Have mercy upon us and forgive us, O Lord.

If we have made no ventures in fellowship, if we have kept in our heart a grievance against another, if we have not sought reconciliation, if we have been eager for the punishment of wrongdoers and slow to seek their redemption,

Have mercy upon us and forgive us, O Lord.

Let each of us in silence make confession to God.

SILENT MEDITATION

Then let the minister and the people unite in saying:

Have mercy upon me, O God, according to thy lovingkindness; according unto the multitude of thy tender mercies blot out my transgressions. Wash me thoroughly from mine iniquity, and cleanse me from my sin. Create in me a clean heart, O God; and renew a right spirit within me. Amen.

THE WORDS OF ASSURANCE *Then, the people still kneeling or bowed, let the minister rise and say:*

This is the message which we have heard of him, and declare unto you, that God is light, and in him is no darkness at all. If we walk in the light, as he is in the light, we have fellowship one with another, and the blood of Jesus Christ his Son cleanseth us from all sin. If we say that we have no sin, we deceive ourselves, and the truth is not in us. If we confess our sins, he is faithful and just to forgive us our sins, and to cleanse us from all unrighteousness.

COVENANT HYMN 540 *"Come let us use the grace divine." The people standing.*

THE COVENANT *Let the people remain standing.*

And now, beloved, let us bind ourselves with willing bonds to our covenant God, and take the yoke of Christ upon us.

This taking of his yoke upon us means that we are heartily content that he appoint us our place and work, and that he alone be our reward.

Christ has many services to be done; some are easy, others are difficult; some bring honor, others bring reproach; some are suitable to our natural inclinations and temporal interests, others are contrary to both. In some we may please Christ and please ourselves; in others we cannot please Christ except by denying ourselves. Yet the power to do all these things is assuredly given us in Christ, who strengtheneth us.

Therefore let us make the covenant of God our own. Let us engage our heart to the Lord, and resolve in his strength never to go back.

Being thus prepared, let us now, in sincere dependence on his grace and trusting in his promises, yield ourselves anew to him.

Let us pray.

THE COVENANT PRAYER *Here let the people kneel or bow.*

O Lord God, holy Father, who hast called us through Christ to be partakers in this gracious covenant; we take upon ourselves with joy the yoke of obedience, and engage ourselves, for love of thee, to seek and do thy perfect will. We are no longer our own, but thine.

Here let the minister and the people unite in saying:

I am no longer my own, but thine. Put me to what thou wilt, rank me with whom thou wilt; put me to

doing, put me to suffering; let me be employed for thee or laid aside for thee, exalted for thee or brought low for thee; let me be full, let me be empty; let me have all things, let me have nothing; I freely and heartily yield all things to thy pleasure and disposal.

And now, O glorious and blessed God, Father, Son and Holy Spirit, thou art mine, and I am thine. So be it. And the covenant which I have made on earth, let it be ratified in heaven. Amen.

THE SURSUM CORDA and SANCTUS *Here let the people stand and join in singing or saying the responses.*

Lift up your hearts.

We lift them up unto the Lord.

Let us give thanks unto the Lord.

It is meet and right so to do.

It is very meet, right, and our bounden duty that we should at all times and in all places give thanks unto thee, O Lord, holy Father, almighty, everlasting God.

Therefore with angels and archangels, and with all the company of heaven, we laud and magnify thy glorious name, evermore praising thee, and saying: Holy, holy, holy, Lord God of hosts, heaven and earth are full of thy glory. Glory be to thee, O Lord most high! Amen.

HYMN OF DEDICATION *Here may follow the Holy Communion, beginning with the Prayer of Consecration; or here may follow a sermon.*

BENEDICTION

POSTLUDE

An Order of Worship for Epiphany

Let the service of worship begin at the time appointed. Let the people kneel or bow in silent prayer upon entering the sanctuary.

PRELUDE *The people in devout meditation.*

HYMN *The people standing.*

CALL TO WORSHIP

Minister: God is light, and in him is no darkness at all.

People: **If we walk in the light, as he is in the light, we have fellowship one with another.**

Minister: O magnify the Lord with me, and let us exalt his name together.

People: **For with him is the fountain of life: in his light shall we see light. Amen.**

RESPONSE

Father of lights, in whom there is no shadow,
    Giver of every good and perfect gift,
With one accord we seek thy holy presence,
    Gladly our hearts to thee in praise we lift. Amen.

INVOCATION *The minister.*

Let us pray.

From the rising of the sun even unto the going down of the same, thy name, O God, shall be great among the Gentiles; and in every place incense shall be offered unto thy name, and a pure offering; for thy name shall be great among the nations; through Jesus Christ our Lord. **Amen.**

COLLECT FOR EPIPHANY *Here let the people unite with the minister in prayer.*

Father of lights and giver of all good, we praise thee that thou callest us to share as thine own sons and daughters the life of freedom, truth, and love. Grant,

we pray thee, that in purity of heart we may receive and manifest the blessings of thy light and life; through Jesus Christ our Lord. Amen.

PRAYER OF CONFESSION *Here let the people kneel or be seated and with bowed heads unite with the minister in prayer.*

O most merciful Father, we confess before thee that we have done little to forward thy Kingdom in the world, and to advance thy glory. We would humble ourselves before thee for our past neglects, and seek for mercy and forgiveness. Pardon our shortcomings. Give us greater zeal for thy glory. Make us more ready and diligent, by our prayers, by our gifts, and by our examples, to spread abroad the knowledge of thy truth and to enlarge the boundaries of thy Kingdom. May the love of Christ constrain us, and may we do all to thy glory; through Jesus Christ our Lord. Amen.

SILENT MEDITATION

WORDS OF ASSURANCE *The minister.*

The LORD is my light and my salvation; whom shall I fear? the LORD is the strength of my life; of whom shall I be afraid? Wait on the LORD: be of good courage, and he shall strengthen thine heart: wait, I say, on the LORD.

WORDS OF FORGIVENESS *The minister.*

May Almighty God, who caused light to shine out of darkness, shine in your hearts, cleansing you from all your sins, and restoring you to the light of the knowledge of his glory in the face of Jesus Christ our Lord. Amen.

THE LORD'S PRAYER

Our Father who art in heaven, hallowed be thy name; thy kingdom come; thy will be done on earth as it is in heaven. Give us this day our daily bread. And forgive us our trespasses, as we forgive those who trespass against us. And lead us not into temptation, but deliver us from evil. **For thine is the kingdom, and the power, and the glory, forever. Amen.**

HYMN

RESPONSIVE READING *Here let the people stand and remain standing during the singing of the* Gloria Patri.

Arise, shine; for thy light is come, and the glory of the Lord is risen upon thee.

For behold, darkness shall cover the earth, and gross darkness the people.

But the Lord shall rise upon thee, and his glory shall be seen upon thee.

And the nations shall come to thy light, and kings to the brightness of thy rising.

The sun shall be no more thy light by day; neither for brightness shall the moon give light unto thee.

But the Lord shall be unto thee an everlasting light, and thy God thy glory.

Thy sun shall no more go down; neither shall thy moon withdraw itself.

For the Lord shall be thine everlasting light, and the days of thy mourning shall be ended.

GLORIA PATRI

THE LESSON FROM THE NEW TESTAMENT *Matthew 2:1-12.*

THE LITANY *The minister, the people responding.*

Let us pray.

Blessed be the Lord God for his tender mercy, whereby the dayspring from on high hath visited us,

To give light to them that sit in darkness and in the shadow of death, and to guide our feet into the way of peace.

Jesus said: They shall come from the east, and from the

west, and from the north, and from the south, and shall sit down in the kingdom of God.

Thanks be to thee, O Christ, for thy holy gospel.

Other sheep I have, which are not of this fold: them also I must bring, and they shall hear my voice; and there shall be one fold, and one shepherd.

Thanks be to thee, O Christ, for thy holy promise.

Go ye therefore, and teach all nations, baptizing them in the name of the Father, and of the Son, and of the Holy Spirit: teaching them to observe all things whatsoever I have commanded you.

Thanks be to thee, O Christ, for thy holy word.

Ye shall receive power after that the Holy Spirit is come upon you: and ye shall be witnesses unto me both in Jerusalem, and in all Judaea, and in Samaria, and unto the uttermost part of the earth.

Thanks be to thee, O Christ, for thy Holy Spirit.

We beseech thee to hear us, O Lord, that thou wouldest stir up the hearts of thy faithful people to greater obedience, and unite thy Church to face the world's great need. That thou wouldest send forth laborers into thy harvest,

Hear us, we beseech thee.

That those who have gone forth may be supported by thy presence, guided by thy counsel, and filled with thy power,

Hear us, we beseech thee.

Then let the minister and the people unite in saying:

Accept the devotion of our hearts, till we all come in the unity of the faith, and of the knowledge of thee, unto a perfect man, unto the measure of the stature of thy fullness. Amen.

OFFERTORY *The dedication of gifts and tithes. An offertory sentence may be said or sung.*

ANTHEM

HYMN

THE SERMON *Which may be followed by prayer.*

AN INVITATION TO CHRISTIAN DISCIPLESHIP

HYMN or DOXOLOGY *The people standing.*

SILENT PRAYER

BENEDICTION

POSTLUDE

An Order of Worship for Lent

Let the service of worship begin at the time appointed. Let the people kneel or bow in silent prayer upon entering the sanctuary.

PRELUDE *The people in devout meditation.*

INTROIT *Which may be said or sung.*

> Before Jehovah's awe-full throne,
> Ye nations, bow with sacred joy;
> Know that the Lord is God alone,
> He can create, and he destroy.
>
> His sov'reign pow'r, without our aid,
> Made us of clay, and form'd us men;
> And, when like wand'ring sheep we stray'd,
> He brought us to his fold again.
>
> Wide as the world is his command;
> Vast as eternity his love;
> Firm as a rock his truth shall stand,
> When rolling years shall cease to move. Amen.

CALL TO WORSHIP

Minister: Wherewith shall I come before the Lord, and bow myself before the high God?

People: **He hath showed thee, O man, what is good; and what doth the Lord require of thee, but to do justly, and to love mercy, and to walk humbly with thy God?**

Minister: The hour cometh, and now is, when the true worshipers shall worship the Father in spirit and in truth; for the Father seeketh such to worship him.

People: **Give unto the Lord the glory due unto his name; worship the Lord in the beauty of holiness. Amen.**

59

INVOCATION *The minister.*

Let us pray.

Almighty and everlasting God, who hatest nothing that thou hast made, and dost forgive the sins of all those who are penitent; create and make in us new and contrite hearts, that we, truly lamenting our sins and acknowledging our wickedness, may obtain of thee, the God of all mercy, perfect remission and forgiveness; through Jesus Christ our Lord. **Amen.**

HYMN *The people standing. If the hymn be a processional, let it precede the Introit.*

PRAYER OF CONFESSION *Here let the people kneel or be seated and with bowed heads unite with the minister in prayer.*

Almighty God, Father of our Lord Jesus Christ, Maker of all things, Judge of all men; we acknowledge our manifold sins and wickedness, which we have committed by thought, word, and deed. We do earnestly repent, and are heartily sorry for these our misdoings. Have mercy upon us, most merciful Father; forgive us all that is past; and grant that we may ever hereafter serve and please thee in newness of life; through Jesus Christ our Lord. Amen.

WORDS OF ASSURANCE *The minister.*

The sacrifices of God are a broken spirit: a broken and a contrite heart, O God, thou wilt not despise.

If we confess our sins, he is faithful and just to forgive us our sins, and to cleanse us from all unrighteousness.

WORDS OF FORGIVENESS *The minister.*

Let the wicked forsake his way, and the unrighteous man his thoughts: and let him return unto the LORD, and he will have mercy upon him; and to our God, for he will abundantly pardon.

THE LORD'S PRAYER

Our Father who art in heaven, hallowed be thy name;

thy kingdom come; thy will be done on earth as it is in heaven. Give us this day our daily bread. And forgive us our trespasses, as we forgive those who trespass against us. And lead us not into temptation, but deliver us from evil. For thine is the kingdom, and the power, and the glory, forever. Amen.

HYMN

RESPONSIVE READING *Here let the people stand and remain standing during the singing of the* Gloria Patri.

Out of the depths have I cried unto thee, O LORD.

Lord, hear my voice: let thine ears be attentive to the voice of my supplications.

If thou, LORD, shouldest mark iniquities, O Lord, who shall stand?

But there is forgiveness with thee, that thou mayest be feared.

I wait for the LORD, my soul doth wait, and in his word do I hope.

My soul waiteth for the Lord more than they that watch for the morning: I say, more than they that watch for the morning.

Let Israel hope in the LORD: for with the LORD there is mercy, and with him is plenteous redemption.

And he shall redeem Israel from all his iniquities.

GLORIA PATRI

THE LESSONS *From the Old and New Testament Scriptures.*

PRAYER *The minister and the people.*

Almighty God, who hast shown us in the life and teaching of thy Son the true way of blessedness; thou hast also showed us in his suffering and death that the path of love may lead to the cross, and the reward of faithfulness may be a crown of thorns. Give us grace to learn these hard lessons. May we take up our cross and follow Christ, in the strength and patience and the constancy of faith; and may we have such fellowship with him in his sorrow that we may know the secret of his strength and peace, and see, even in our darkest hour of trial and anguish, the shining of the eternal light. Amen.

PASTORAL PRAYER.

OFFERTORY *The dedication of gifts and tithes. An offertory sentence may be said or sung.*

HYMN

THE SERMON *Which may be followed by prayer.*

AN INVITATION TO CHRISTIAN DISCIPLESHIP

HYMN or DOXOLOGY *The people standing.*

SILENT PRAYER

BENEDICTION

POSTLUDE

An Order of Worship for Good Friday

A Three-Hour Service of Devotion

THIS order of worship is for use on Good Friday from twelve o'clock noon to three o'clock—the traditional hours for the commemoration of the crucifixion of our Lord.

PRELUDE

QUIET MOMENTS *Let the people kneel or bow in silent prayer upon entering the sanctuary and devoutly meditate upon the following words.*

SCRIPTURE SENTENCES

The Spirit itself beareth witness with our spirit, that we are the children of God; and if children, then heirs; heirs of God, and joint-heirs with Christ; if so be that we suffer with him, that we may be also glorified together.

God forbid that I should glory, save in the cross of our Lord Jesus Christ.

Let us run with patience the race that is set before us, looking unto Jesus the author and finisher of our faith; who for the joy that was set before him endured the cross, despising the shame, and is set down at the right hand of the throne of God.

God commendeth his love toward us, in that, while we were yet sinners, Christ died for us.

Whosoever will come after me, let him deny himself, and take up his cross, and follow me. For whosover will save his life shall lose it; but whosoever shall lose his life for my sake and the gospel's, the same shall save it.

PRAYER

Help us, Almighty God, to bear with patience whatever cross now rests upon our shoulders, knowing that in so doing we shall, with Christ, overcome the world and vanquish

63

our last enemies; through the same Jesus Christ our Lord. Amen.

12:00

HYMN 134 *"O come and mourn with me awhile."*

CALL TO WORSHIP

Minister: Is it nothing to you, all ye that pass by?

People: **Behold, and see if there be any sorrow like unto his sorrow.**

Minister: God commendeth his love toward us, in that, while we were yet sinners, Christ died for us.

People: **Behold the Lamb of God, which taketh away the sin of the world. Amen.**

Here let the people be seated.

INVOCATION *The minister.*

Let us pray.

O God our Father, we come beseeching thee mercifully to guide us in these our meditations, supplications, and prayers, and to dispose the minds and hearts of all men toward the attainment of everlasting salvation; through Jesus Christ our Lord. **Amen.**

COLLECT FOR GOOD FRIDAY *Here let the people unite with the minister in prayer.*

Almighty God, we beseech thee graciously to behold this thy family, for which our Lord Jesus Christ was content to be betrayed, and given up into the hands of wicked men, and to suffer death upon the cross; who now liveth and reigneth with thee and the Holy Spirit, ever one God, world without end. Amen.

Minister: O Lord, open thou our lips.

People: **And our mouth shall show forth thy praise.**

Minister: Praise ye the Lord.

People: **The Lord's name be praised.**

ANTHEM *"God So Loved the World."*

God ,so loved the world, that he gave his only-begotten Son, that whosoever believeth in him should not perish, but have everlasting life. For God sent not his Son into the world to condemn the world; but that the world through him might be saved.

PRAYER OF CONFESSION *The minister, the people responding.*

Let us pray.

O God, in this hour of solemn remembrance we acknowledge with sorrow and shame that our sins are such as sent our blessed Lord to the cross.

Lord, have mercy upon us.

We confess with penitence that we have been slow to accept that forgiveness of sins and cleansing from all unrighteousness which, by his death, he sealed for us as the free gift of God.

Lord, have mercy upon us.

We have not always entered into the fellowship of his sufferings, and have charged thee with indifference to sorrow and pain.

Lord, have mercy upon us. Amen.

WORDS OF FORGIVENESS *The minister.*

May the Lamb of God, who taketh away the sins of the world, loose you from all your sins by his blood, for the sake of his wounds pardon all your transgressions, and by his stripes grant you healing, both of body and of mind. **Amen.**

THE LORD'S PRAYER

Our Father who art in heaven, hallowed be thy name; thy kingdom come; thy will be done on earth as it is in heaven. Give us this day our daily bread. And forgive us our trespasses, as we forgive those who trespass against us. And lead us not into temptation, but deliver us from evil. For thine is the kingdom, and the power, and the glory, forever. Amen.

HYMN 137 *"O Love divine, what hast thou done!"*

12:15

THE FIRST WORD *Luke 23:34.*

Father, forgive them; for they know not what they do.

HYMN 144 *"Beneath the cross of Jesus."*

SILENT MEDITATION

PRAYERS *The minister.*

Let us pray.

Almighty and everlasting God, grant us so to celebrate the mysteries of our Lord's passion, that we, obtaining pardon through his precious blood, may come with joy to the commemoration of that sacrifice by which thou hast been pleased to redeem us; through the same thy Son our Saviour Jesus Christ. **Amen.**

The minister and the people.

O Lord, we beseech thee, absolve thy people from their offenses, that through thy bountiful goodness we may be delivered from the bonds of those sins which by our frailty we have committed. May all who have sinned in ignorance, or are this day sincerely sorry for their sins, be given pardon and amendment of life. Grant this, O heavenly Father, for Jesus Christ's sake, our blessed Lord and Saviour. Amen.

ANTHEM

12:40

THE SECOND WORD *Luke 23:43.*

Today shalt thou be with me in paradise.

HYMN 146 *"Never further than thy cross."*

SILENT MEDITATION

PRAYERS *The minister.*

Let us pray.

O Lord, we beseech thee, mercifully hear our prayers, and spare all those who confess their sins unto thee, that they whose consciences by sin are accused, by thy merciful pardon may be absolved; through Christ our Lord. Amen.

The minister and the people.

O Thou who art love, and who seest all the suffering, injustice, and misery which reign in this world; have pity, we implore thee, on the work of thy hands. Look mercifully upon the poor, the oppressed, and all who are heavy laden with error, labor, and sorrow. Fill our hearts with deep compassion for those who suffer, and hasten the coming of thy kingdom of justice and truth; through Jesus Christ our Lord. Amen.

1:00

THE THIRD WORD *John 19:26-27.*

Woman, behold thy son! . . . Behold thy mother!

HYMN 138 *"Near the cross her vigil keeping."*

SILENT MEDITATION

PRAYERS *The minister.*

Let us pray.

Infinite and eternal Spirit, our God and our Father, author of all good, and never far from any of thy children; we draw near to thee that in fellowship with thee we may receive of thy Spirit. May all the bonds of love and ties of friendship be made stronger and sweeter through him who in his mortal agony was not forgetful that we need one another's love, even Jesus Christ our Lord. Amen.

The minister and the people.

O eternal God, who alone makest men to be of one mind in a house; help us, the members of this house-

hold, faithfully to fulfill our duties to thee and to each other. Put far from us all unkind thoughts, anger, and evil speaking. Give us tender hearts, full of affection and sympathy toward all. Grant us grace to feel the sorrows and trials of others as our own, and to bear patiently with their imperfections. Preserve us from selfishness, and grant that, day by day, walking in love, we may grow up into the likeness of thy Son Jesus Christ our Lord. Amen.

1:20

THE FOURTH WORD *Matthew 27:46.*

My God, my God, why hast thou forsaken me?

HYMN 274 *"In the hour of trial."*

SILENT MEDITATION

PRAYERS *The minister.*

Let us pray.

O Almighty God, who art a most strong tower to all those who put their trust in thee, to whom all things in heaven, in earth, and under the earth do bow and obey; be now and evermore our defense, and make us know and feel that there is none other name under the heaven given to man, in whom and through whom we may receive health and salvation, but only the name of thy Son our Lord Jesus Christ. **Amen.**

The minister and the people.

Thou knowest, Lord, the secrets of our hearts; shut not thy merciful ears to our prayer; but spare us, Lord most holy, O God most mighty, O holy and merciful Saviour, thou most worthy Judge eternal, suffer us not, at our last hour, for any pains of death, to fall from thee. May we not feel forsaken of thee, or shut out from thy love; but save us in all our mortal strife; through Jesus Christ our Lord. Amen.

ANTHEM

1:50

THE FIFTH WORD *John 19:28.*

I thirst.

HYMN 273 *"O Love divine, that stooped to share."*

SILENT MEDITATION

PRAYERS *The minister.*

Let us pray.

Almighty God, whose most dear Son went not up to joy but first he suffered pain, and entered not into glory before he was crucified; mercifully grant that we, walking in the way of the cross, may find it none other than the way of life and peace; through Jesus Christ our Lord. **Amen.**

The minister and the people.

O Lord, increase our faith, renew our courage, and by thy Spirit make us victors over the things that beset us by giving our utmost to the highest. May thy blessing rest upon all who give cups of cold water to others because they belong to Christ. Show us that in every woe thou art still with us, that in every sorrow thou art still loving us, even unto the uttermost. And may our faith stand firm in thy faithfulness; through Jesus Christ our Lord. Amen.

2:10

THE SIXTH WORD *John 19:30.*

It is finished.

HYMN 139 *"It is finished!"*

SILENT MEDITATION

PRAYERS *The minister.*

Let us pray.

Thou Forgiver of sin, Healer of sorrow, Vanquisher of death; draw us unto thyself, who art our salvation and our all-conquering hope. Make us citizens of thy Kingdom, men of invincible good will, builders of a world where righteousness shall reign and the law of love shall triumph over hate and strife. Hasten the day when thou shalt take unto thyself thy great power and reign. Increase in us true devotion unto thyself; nourish us with all goodness; and of thy great mercy keep us steadfast; through Jesus Christ our Lord. **Amen.**

The minister and the people.

Almighty God, we thank thee for the good examples of all those thy servants who, having finished their course in faith, do now rest from their labors. And we beseech thee that we, with all those who are departed in the true faith of thy holy name, may have our perfect consummation and bliss in thy eternal and everlasting glory; through Jesus Christ our Lord. Amen.

2:30

THE SEVENTH WORD *Luke 23:46.*

Father, into thy hands I commend my spirit.

HYMN 148 *"When I survey the wondrous cross."*

SILENT MEDITATION

ANTHEM

PRAYERS *The minister.*

Let us pray.

O Father of mercies, whose beloved Son was, as on this day, crucified for us, the just for the unjust, to bring us to thee; give grace, we beseech thee, to every member of this family to look in faith upon that cross, and to crucify himself upon it to every impure desire and unchristian temper. May we learn in humble devotion to our Master's service to deny ourselves daily, for his sake, and for one another's sake, that we may follow him. Remove from us every corrupt and unfaithful affection. May we never be afraid to do right and never dare to do wrong. And so out of the good treasure of the heart may we ever be bringing forth good things to the praise and glory of thy name; through Jesus Christ our Lord. Amen.

The minister and the people.

O Lord, our heavenly Father, we offer and present unto thee ourselves, our souls and bodies, to be a reasonable, holy, and living sacrifice unto thee. Take us as we are and make us more fit for thy service. Use us for thyself and for the edification of thy Church. We are not our own, but thine, bought with a price; therefore claim us as thy right, keep us as thy charge, and use us as thou wilt, to the glory of thy holy name and the good of our fellow men; through Jesus Christ our Lord. Amen.

HYMN 147 *"Ask ye what great thing I know?"*

PRAYER

BENEDICTION

POSTLUDE

The offerings for this service may be received in the plates at the door as the worshipers leave.

Those who find it necessary to leave the service before its close should leave during the singing of the hymns.

An Order of Worship for Good Friday Evening

THIS service may be used on any other evening during Holy Week.

Let the service of worship begin at the time appointed. Let the people kneel or bow in silent prayer upon entering the sanctuary.

PRELUDE *The people in devout meditation.*

HYMN 144 *"Beneath the cross of Jesus."*

CALL TO WORSHIP

Minister: God so loved the world, that he gave his only-begotten Son, that whosoever believeth in him should not perish, but have everlasting life.

People: **Christ hath once suffered for sins, the just for the unjust, that he might bring us to God.**

Minister: God spared not his own Son, but delivered him up for us all.

People: **Greater love hath no man than this, that a man lay down his life for his friends. Amen.**

INVOCATION *The minister.*

Let us pray.

Almighty and most merciful God, whose will is that all men should be saved, and who didst give thy Son our Lord Jesus Christ to be the propitiation for the sins of the whole world; we bow in adoration before thy throne and praise thee for this thy unspeakable gift. **Amen.**

ASCRIPTION *Here let the people unite with the minister in prayer.*

Unto him that loved us, and washed us from our sins in his own blood, and hath made us kings and priests unto God and his Father; to him be glory and dominion for ever and ever. Worthy is the Lamb that was slain to

72

receive power, and riches, and wisdom, and strength, and honor, and glory, and blessing. Amen.

ANTHEM

RESPONSIVE READING *Here let the people stand and remain standing during the singing of the* Gloria Patri.

He is despised and rejected of men; a man of sorrows, and acquainted with brief.

Surely he hath borne our griefs, and carried our sorrows.

He was wounded for our transgressions, he was bruised for our iniquities.

The chastisement of our peace was upon him; and with his stripes we are healed.

All we like sheep have gone astray; we have turned every one to his own way.

And the Lord hath laid on him the iniquity of us all.

He was oppressed, and he was afflicted, yet he opened not his mouth.

He is brought as a lamb to the slaughter, and as a sheep before her shearers is dumb, so he openeth not his mouth.

He was taken from prison and from judgment: and who shall declare his generation?

For he was cut off out of the land of the living: for the transgression of my people was he stricken.

Yet it pleased the Lord to bruise him; he hath put him to grief.

He shall see of the travail of his soul, and shall be satisfied.

GLORIA PATRI

THE LESSON FROM THE NEW TESTAMENT

ADORATION AT THE CROSS *Here let the people kneel or bow in prayer, and sing the responses.*

God forbid that I should glory, save in the cross of our Lord Jesus Christ, by whom the world is crucified unto me, and I unto the world.

Silent Meditation

Hymn 149

In the cross of Christ I glory,
    Towering o'er the wrecks of time;
All the light of sacred story
    Gathers round its head sublime.

Who his own self bare our sins in his own body on the tree.

Silent Meditation

Hymn 137

O Love divine, what hast thou done!
    Th' incarnate God hath died for me!
The Father's coeternal Son
    Bore all my sins upon the tree!
        The Son of God for me hath died:
        My Lord, my Love, is crucified.

Ye were not redeemed with corruptible things, as silver and gold, but with the precious blood of Christ, as of a lamb without blemish and without spot.

Silent Meditation

Hymn 141

O sacred Head, now wounded,
    With grief and shame weighed down,
Now scornfully surrounded
    With thorns, thine only crown;
How pale thou art with anguish,
    With sore abuse and scorn!
How does that visage languish
    Which once was bright as morn!

Christ hath once suffered for sins, the just for the unjust, that he might bring us to God.

Silent Meditation

Hymn 148

See, from his head, his hands, his feet,
  Sorrow and love flow mingled down:
Did e'er such love and sorrow meet,
  Or thorns compose so rich a crown?

We see Jesus, because of the suffering of death, crowned with glory and honor.

Silent Meditation

Hymn 147

Ask ye what great thing I know
That delights and stirs me so?
What the high reward I win?
Whose the name I glory in?
  Jesus Christ, the Crucified.

Who defeats my fiercest foes?
Who consoles my saddest woes?
Who revives my fainting heart,
Healing all its hidden smart?
  Jesus Christ, the Crucified.

Who is life in life to me?
Who the death of death will be?
Who will place me on his right,
With the countless hosts of light?
  Jesus Christ, the Crucified.

Here let the people stand.

This is that great thing I know;
This delights and stirs me so:
Faith in him who died to save,
Him who triumphed o'er the grave,
  Jesus Christ, the Crucified. Amen.

INTERCESSION *Here let the people kneel or be seated and with bowed heads join in prayer for the conversion of all men.*

O merciful God, who hast made all men, and hatest nothing that thou hast made, and willest not the death of a sinner, but rather that he should be converted and live; have mercy upon all who have not known thee, or who deny the faith of Christ crucified. Take from them all ignorance, hardness of heart, and contempt of thy word; and so bring them home, blessed Lord, to thy fold, that we may be made one flock under one shepherd, Jesus Christ our Lord, who liveth and reigneth with thee and the Holy Spirit, one God, world without end. Amen.

THE LORD'S PRAYER

Our Father who art in heaven, hallowed be thy name; thy kingdom come; thy will be done on earth as it is in heaven. Give us this day our daily bread. And forgive us our trespasses, as we forgive those who trespass against us. And lead us not into temptation, but deliver us from evil. For thine is the kingdom, and the power, and the glory, forever. Amen.

OFFERTORY *The dedication of gifts and tithes. An offertory sentence may be said or sung.*

HYMN 207 *"By thy birth and by tears."*

THE SERMON

PRAYER

AN INVITATION TO CHRISTIAN DISCIPLESHIP

HYMN 135 *"There is a green hill far away."*

SILENT PRAYER

BENEDICTION

POSTLUDE

An Order of Worship for Easter Day

PRELUDE

QUIET MOMENTS *Let the people kneel or bow in silent prayer upon entering the sanctuary and devoutly meditate on the following words.*

SCRIPTURE SENTENCES

We look not at the things which are seen, but at the things which are not seen: for the things which are seen are temporal; but the things which are not seen are eternal.

The ransomed of the LORD shall return with songs and everlasting joy upon their heads; they shall obtain joy and gladness, and sorrow and sighing shall flee away.

There is a natural body, and there is a spiritual body. As we have borne the image of the earthy, we shall also bear the image of the heavenly.

Awake thou that sleepest, and arise from the dead, and Christ shall give thee light. If ye then be risen with Christ, seek those things which are above.

MEDITATION

This festival day celebrates the triumph of the great hope of everlasting life that shines through the gospel. As the eternal Christ rose triumphant over the bitter pain of the cross and the darkness of the tomb, we have the assurance that enables us to look beyond the things of earth that pass away to find our joy and peace in God's infinite love. We hold this festival of praise in gratitude for the everlasting hopes that arise within the human heart, and for the gospel which has brought life and immortality to light.

PRAYER

Almighty and everlasting God, who on Easter Day didst turn the despair of the disciples into triumph by the resurrection of Christ, who had been crucified; give us faith to

77

believe that every good which hath seemed to be overcome by evil, and every love which hath seemed to be buried in darkness and in death, shall rise again to life immortal; through Jesus Christ, who liveth with thee for evermore. Amen.

PROCESSIONAL HYMN

A HYMN OF ADORATION

CALL TO WORSHIP

Minister: He is risen!

People: **The Lord is risen indeed!**

Minister: He shall reign!

People: **Hallelujah!**

Minister: And he shall reign forever!

People: **Hallelujah! Hallelujah!**

Minister: And he shall reign, King of kings and Lord of lords, for ever and ever!

People: **Hallelujah! Hallelujah! Hallelujah!**

Here let the people be seated.

INVOCATION *The minister.*

Let us pray.

O God, our Father in heaven, we consecrate ourselves anew to thee this Easter Day. Grant us loyalty to thy Church, and gladness in thy service. Fill us with the spirit of reverence and humility that we are permitted to sing thy praises. Keep us in the blessed remembrance that we are thy children and in thy presence, and make us faithful in our duty and worthy of thy love; through Jesus Christ our Lord. **Amen.**

COLLECT FOR EASTER DAY *Here let the people unite with the minister in prayer.*

O God, who for our redemption didst give thine only-begotten Son to the death of the cross, and by his glorious resurrection hast delivered us from the power of our enemy; grant us to die daily from sin, that we

may evermore live with him in the joy of his resurrection; through Jesus Christ our Lord. Amen.

THE LORD'S PRAYER

Our Father who art in heaven, hallowed be thy name; thy kingdom come; thy will be done on earth as it is in heaven. Give us this day our daily bread. And forgive us our trespasses, as we forgive those who trespass against us. And lead us not into temptation, but deliver us from evil. For thine is the kingdom, and the power, and the glory, forever. Amen.

Minister: O Lord, open thou our lips.

People: **And our mouth shall show forth thy praise.**

Minister: Praise ye the Lord.

People: **The Lord's name be praised.**

ANTHEM

RESPONSIVE READING FOR EASTER DAY *Here let the people stand and remain standing until after the Scripture Lesson.*

O LORD, thou art my God; I will exalt thee, I will praise thy name.

For thou hast done wonderful things; thy counsels of old are faithfulness and truth.

For thou hast been a stronghold to the poor, a strength to the needy in his distress,

A refuge from the storm, a shadow from the heat, when the blast of the terrible ones is as a storm against the wall.

And he will destroy in this mountain the covering that is cast over the face of the peoples,

And the veil that is spread over the nations.

He hath swallowed up death forever; and the Lord GOD will wipe away tears from off all faces.

The reproach of his people shall he take away from off the earth: for the LORD hath spoken it.

And it shall be said in that day, Lo, this is our God; we have waited for him, and he will save us.

This is the LORD; we have waited for him, we will be glad and rejoice in his salvation.

Thou wilt keep him in perfect peace, whose mind is stayed on thee: because he trusteth in thee.

Trust ye in the LORD forever: for in the LORD Jehovah is everlasting strength. Amen.

GLORIA PATRI

AFFIRMATION OF FAITH *Here let the people, following the exhortation of the minister, unite with him in the creed.*

Where the Spirit of the Lord is, there is the one true Church, apostolic and universal, whose holy faith let us now reverently and sincerely declare.

I believe in God the Father Almighty, Maker of heaven and earth; and in Jesus Christ his only Son our Lord; who was conceived by the Holy Spirit, born of the Virgin Mary, suffered under Pontius Pilate, was crucified, dead, and buried; the third day he rose from the dead; he ascended into heaven, and sitteth at the right hand of God the Father Almighty; from thence he shall come to judge the quick and the dead. I believe in the Holy Spirit, the holy catholic Church, the communion of saints, the forgiveness of sins, the resurrection of the body, and the life everlasting. Amen.

THE SCRIPTURE LESSON *The minister, the people responding.*

Upon the first day of the week, very early in the morning, they came unto the sepulchre, bringing the spices which they had prepared. And they found the stone rolled away from the sepulchre.

Hallelujah!

And they departed quickly from the sepulchre with fear and great joy. And behold, Jesus met them, saying, All hail.

Hallelujah!

But Mary stood without at the sepulchre weeping. She saith, They have taken away my Lord, and I know not where they have laid him. And she saw Jesus standing, and knew not that it was Jesus, supposing him to be the gardener. Jesus saith unto her, Mary. She turned, and saith unto him, Master.

Hallelujah!

And, behold, two of them went that same day to Emmaus. And while they communed together, Jesus himself drew near, and went with them.

Hallelujah!

When the doors were shut where the disciples were, came Jesus and stood in the midst, and saith unto them, Peace be unto you. And when he had so said, he showed unto them his hands and his side.

Hallelujah!

Simon Peter saith unto them, I go a fishing. They say unto him, We also go with thee. And that night they caught nothing. But when the morning was now come, Jesus stood on the shore. Therefore that disciple whom Jesus loved saith unto Peter, It is the Lord.

Hallelujah!

I was in the Spirit on the Lord's day, and heard behind me a great voice, and I turned to see the voice that spake with me. And being turned, I saw one like unto the Son of man, clothed with a garment down to the foot, and girt about the breasts with a golden girdle. And his hairs were as white as snow; and his eyes were as a flame of fire; and his feet like unto fine brass, and his voice as the sound of many waters. And when I saw him, I fell at his feet as dead. And he laid his right hand upon me, saying, Fear not; I am the first and the last; I am he that liveth and was dead; and, behold, I am alive for evermore, and have the keys of hell and of death.

Hallelujah! Hallelujah! Hallelujah!

ANTHEM

SILENT MEDITATION

PASTORAL PRAYER

CHORAL RESPONSE

> Through love to light! O wonderful the way
> That leads from darkness to the perfect day;
> From darkness and from sorrow of the night
>> To morning that comes singing o'er the sea!
>> Through love to light! Through light, O God, to thee,
> Who art the Love of love, th' eternal Light of light.
>> Amen.

OFFERTORY *The dedication of gifts and tithes.*

DOXOLOGY *The people standing.*

HYMN OF PREPARATION

THE EASTER DAY SERMON

AN INVITATION TO CHRISTIAN DISCIPLESHIP

HYMN *The people standing.*

SILENT PRAYER

BENEDICTION

POSTLUDE

holy comfort; through the merits of Christ Jesus our
Saviour, who liveth and reigneth with thee in the unity
of the same Spirit, one God, world without end. Amen.

An Order of Worship for Whitsunday

*Let the service of worship begin at the time appointed. Let the people
kneel or bow in silent prayer upon entering the sanctuary.*

PRELUDE *The people in devout meditation.*

PROCESSIONAL HYMN *The people standing. If there be no processional, let the first hymn follow the Call to Worship.*

CALL TO WORSHIP

Minister: Behold, the tabernacle of God is with men, and
he will dwell with them, and they shall be his people.

People: **And he that sitteth upon the throne saith,
Behold, I make all things new.**

Minister: At the name of Jesus every knee shall bow, and
every tongue confess

People: **That Jesus Christ is Lord, to the glory of God
the Father. Amen.**

INVOCATION *The minister.*

Let us pray.

Almighty and most merciful God, grant, we beseech thee,
that by the indwelling of thy Holy Spirit we may be enlightened and strengthened for thy service; through Jesus
Christ our Lord, who liveth and reigneth with thee in the
unity of the same Spirit ever, one God, world without end.
Amen.

COLLECT FOR PENTECOST *Here let the people unite with the
minister in prayer.*

**O God, who as at this time didst teach the hearts of
thy faithful people by sending to them the light of thy
Holy Spirit; grant us by the same Spirit to have a right
judgment in all things, and evermore to rejoice in his**

83

holy comfort; through the merits of Christ Jesus our Saviour, who liveth and reigneth with thee in the unity of the same Spirit, one God, world without end. Amen.

PRAYER OF CONFESSION

Spirit of the Lord, Spirit of wisdom and understanding, Spirit of counsel and might; forgive the narrowness which causes us to regard only ourselves and our concerns. Lead us out of the bondage of fear into the glorious liberty of the sons of God, that by thy witness with our spirit we may know ourselves to be children of God and joint heirs with Christ. Amen.

SILENT MEDITATION

WORDS OF ASSURANCE *The minister.*

The Spirit of the Lord hath filled the whole earth: Hallelujah! The love of God is shed abroad in our hearts by the Holy Spirit, whereby we cry Abba, Father. Let the righteous be glad; let them rejoice before God: yea, let them exceedingly rejoice. Hallelujah!

WORDS OF FORGIVENESS *The minister.*

With a voice of singing declare ye, tell this, utter it even to the end of the earth: Hallelujah! The LORD hath redeemed his servants. Hallelujah!

THE LORD'S PRAYER

Our Father who art in heaven, hallowed be thy name; thy kingdom come; thy will be done on earth as it is in heaven. Give us this day our daily bread. And forgive us our trespasses, as we forgive those who trespass against us. And lead us not into temptation, but deliver us from evil. For thine is the kingdom, and the power, and the glory, forever. Amen.

ANTHEM

VENI, CREATOR SPIRITUS *Which may be sung or said responsively, the minister and the people uniting in the final couplet.*

Come, Holy Ghost, our souls inspire,
And lighten with celestial fire.

**Thou the anointing Spirit art,
Who dost thy sevenfold gifts impart.**

Thy blessed unction from above,
Is comfort, life, and fire of love.

**Enable with perpetual light
The dullness of our blinded sight.**

Anoint and cheer our soilèd face
With the abundance of thy grace.

**Keep far our foes; give peace at home;
Where thou art guide, no ill can come.**

Teach us to know the Father, Son,
And thee, of both, to be but One;

**That through the ages all along,
This may be our endless song:**

*Praise to thy eternal merit,
Father, Son, and Holy Spirit. Amen.*

THE LESSONS *From the Old and New Testament Scriptures.*

PASTORAL PRAYER

OFFERTORY *The dedication of gifts and tithes. An offertory sentence may be said or sung.*

HYMN

THE SERMON *Which may be followed by prayer.*

AN INVITATION TO CHRISTIAN DISCIPLESHIP

HYMN or DOXOLOGY *The people standing.*

SILENT PRAYER

BENEDICTION

POSTLUDE

An Order of Worship for Kingdomtide

Let the service of worship begin at the time appointed. Let the people kneel or bow in silent prayer upon entering the sanctuary.

PRELUDE *The people in devout meditation.*

HYMN *The people standing.*

CALL TO WORSHIP

Minister: Let thy mercy, O Lord, be upon us,

People: **According as we hope in thee.**

Minister: Show us thy mercy, O Lord.

People: **And grant us thy salvation.**

Minister: I will hear what God the Lord will speak.

People: **For he will speak peace unto his people, and to his saints. Amen.**

PRAYER OF CONFESSION *Here let the people unite with the minister in prayer.*

Most merciful Father, we have done little to forward thy Kingdom in this world, to foster the brotherhood of man, and to establish love as the law of life. We have allowed self to blind us, pains to embitter us. We have forgotten that whatsoever is done to one of the least of thy children is done unto thee. Pardon our shortcomings; forgive our neglect; give us a pure heart intent on pleasing thee. Help us in all our seeking to seek first thy Kingdom and thy righteousness. And make us to come, as came thy Son Jesus Christ, not to be ministered unto, but to minister. All which we ask through Jesus Christ our Lord. Amen.

PRAYER FOR GRACE *The minister.*

O God, by whom the meek are guided in judgment, and light riseth up in darkness for the godly; grant us, in all doubts and uncertainties, the grace to ask what thou wouldest have us to do; that the spirit of wisdom may save us from all false choices, and that in thy light we may see light, and in thy straight path may not stumble; through Jesus Christ our Lord. **Amen.**

THE LORD'S PRAYER

Our Father who art in heaven, hallowed be thy name; thy kingdom come; thy will be done on earth as it is in heaven. Give us this day our daily bread. And forgive us our trespasses, as we forgive those who trespass against us. And lead us not into temptation, but deliver us from evil. For thine is the kingdom, and the power, and the glory, forever. Amen.

ANTHEM

RESPONSIVE READING *Here let the people stand and remain standing during the singing of the* Gloria Patri.

O Lord God, to whom vengeance belongeth; O God, to whom vengeance belongeth, show thyself.

Lift up thyself, thou judge of the earth: render a reward to the proud.

Lord, how long shall the wicked, how long shall the wicked triumph?

How long shall they utter and speak hard things? and all the workers of iniquity boast themselves?

They break in pieces thy people, O Lord, and afflict thine heritage.

They slay the widow and the stranger, and murder the fatherless.

Yet they say, The Lord shall not see; neither shall the God of Jacob regard it.

Understand, ye brutish among the people: and ye fools, when will ye be wise?

He that planted the ear, shall he not hear? he that formed the eye, shall he not see?

He that chastiseth the heathen, shall he not correct? he that teacheth man knowledge, shall not he know?

The LORD knoweth the thoughts of man, that they are vanity.

But the LORD is my defense; and my God is the rock of my refuge.

GLORIA PATRI

THE LESSONS *From the Old and New Testament Scriptures.*

LITANY *The minister, the people responding.*

Let us pray.

O Lord, open thou our eyes, that we may see ourselves as thou seest us; in thy mercy show us that evil is in us, and cleanse us by thy mighty power. **Amen.**

From irresolute purpose, from unchastened desires, and from a weak and wavering will,

Good Lord, deliver us.

From slackness and indolence, from indifference to the treasures of knowledge, and a refusal to use the gifts with which thou hast endowed us,

Good Lord, deliver us.

From low ideals of life, and from thoughtless disregard of the influence of our conduct,

Good Lord, deliver us.

From pride and vanity and boasting, from self-assertion and self-seeking, and blindness to the common weal,

Good Lord, deliver us.

From dislike of criticism and love of popularity, and from unreadiness to do our duty at whatever cost,

Good Lord, deliver us.

From hastiness of speech and sullenness of temper, from readiness to think the worst of others, and from all unseemly and unworthy conversation,

Good Lord, deliver us.

Here let the minister and the people unite in saying:

Heavenly Father, blot out, we beseech thee, our past transgressions; forgive us all our negligences and ignorances; and lift us up to new energy of mind and devotion of heart, that we may have strength to persevere even to the end, through success and failure, through good report and evil report. Save us in all time of our tribulation, in all of our wealth. Amen.

OFFERTORY *The dedication of gifts and tithes.*

INTERCESSION *Here let the people unite with the minister in prayer.*

O God, whose Kingdom is an everlasting Kingdom, and whose dominion endureth from generation to generation; dethrone our pride, and shatter our complacency. Open our eyes to see the vanity of this world's riches and renown; make us to understand that there is no wealth but life, that living men are thy glory, and our life the vision of thee. Keep us from being terrorized by wealth and influence, beguiled by pleas of custom and expediency, or distracted by the glamor of prosperity. Keep us securely in thy way of righteousness and truth; through Jesus Christ our Lord. Amen.

HYMN

THE SERMON

PRAYER *The minister.*

Teach us, gracious God, to serve thee as thou deservest, to give and not to count the cost, to fight and not to heed the wounds, to toil and not to seek for rest, to labor and not to ask for any reward, save that of knowing that we do thy will; through Jesus Christ our Lord. **Amen.**

AN INVITATION TO CHRISTIAN DISCIPLESHIP

HYMN *The people standing.*

SILENT PRAYER

BENEDICTION

POSTLUDE

An Order of Worship for Christian Unity

PRELUDE

QUIET MOMENTS *Let the people kneel or bow in silent prayer upon entering the sanctuary and devoutly meditate on the following words.*

SCRIPTURE SENTENCES

Come, and let us return unto the LORD; and we shall live in his sight. His going forth is prepared as the morning; and he shall come unto us as the rain, as the latter and former rain unto the earth.

Behold, the tabernacle of God is with men, and he will dwell with them, and they shall be his people, and God himself shall be with them, and be their God.

Let us search and try our ways, and turn again to the LORD. Let us lift up our heart with our hands unto God in the heavens.

There is one God and Father of all, who is above all, and through all, and in you all.

Prepare ye the way of the LORD, make straight in the desert a highway for our God.

MEDITATION

"We are all united . . . in the use of the Holy Scriptures. We are further united in common prayer, which may be expressed in the spoken word, through silence, or by employment of the sacred treasures of Christian literature, art, and music. In this worship we all stand before God in adoration of His majesty, bringing to Him our own needs and the needs of our fellows. We wait for His grace in the forgiveness of our sins and for the restoration of our spirits

90

through renewed communion with Him, and we dedicate ourselves to His service and the service of all mankind."

*—Report of the Second World
Conference on Faith and Order*

PRAYER

Gracious Father, we humbly beseech thee for thy universal Church. Fill it with all truth, and in all truth with all peace. Where it is corrupt, purify it; where it is in error, direct it; where it is superstitious, rectify it; where anything is amiss, reform it; where it is right, strengthen and confirm it; where it is in want, furnish it; where it is divided and rent asunder, heal the breaches thereof, O thou Holy One of Israel; through Jesus Christ our Lord. Amen.

HYMN *The people standing.*

CALL TO WORSHIP

Minister: Praise waiteth for thee, O God, in Zion: and unto thee shall the vow be performed.

People: **O thou that hearest prayer, unto thee shall all flesh come.**

Minister: Blessed is the man whom thou choosest, and causest to approach unto thee, that he may dwell in thy courts.

People: **We shall be satisfied with the goodness of thy house, even of thy holy temple. Amen.**

Here let the people kneel or be seated and bow in prayer.

INVOCATION *The minister.*

Let us pray.

O God, our heavenly Father, we are all thy children, and we seek thy blessing. In thy presence may our thoughts be lifted to the wide horizon of thy Kingdom and the all-embracing purposes of thy love. Unite our spirits in worship and fellowship. In this hour may we renew our dedication of life, through faith and obedience, to the tasks of thy

Church, and thus fulfill the prayer of our Lord that they all may be one. **Amen.**

COLLECT *Here let the people unite with the minister in prayer.*

O God, whose will it is that all thy children should be one in Christ, we beseech thee to bless thy Church with growing influence and power. We pray that her ministers may be faithful, her members loyal, her witness to the truth a shining light, her proclamation of saving grace a joyous mission, that in the face of the unfinished task of the world's redemption we may hear again the supreme summons to discipleship and to service; through Jesus Christ our Lord. Amen.

ANTHEM

ACT OF PENITENCE *The minister, the people responding. Let all kneel or bow.*

Let us pray.

From the sin which is in us, leading us to prefer our will to thine,

Good Lord, deliver us.

From the prejudice and blindness, in our souls, in our nation, and in our religious fellowship,

Good Lord, deliver us.

From unreadiness to hear thy call, and from slothfulness in our obedience,

Good Lord, deliver us.

From racial pride and national arrogance, whereby we mar the harmony of life in thy great family,

Good Lord, deliver us.

From easy contentment with what is familiar, and from hesitation in making adventure for thy Kingdom,

Good Lord, deliver us.

From failure to recognize thy Holy Spirit dispensing to others gifts differing from those which we have received,

Good Lord, deliver us.

From love of all that hinders us from conformity to thy holy will,

Good Lord, deliver us.

Here let the minister and the people unite in saying:

Almighty God, in whom is calmness, peace, and concord; heal thou the divisions which separate thy children from one another, and enable them to keep the unity of the spirit in the bond of peace. While there are diversities of knowledge and faith, and we cannot all be of the same mind, may we be made one in brotherly love, and in devotion to thy holy will. Deliver us from all blindness and prejudice, from all clamor and evil speaking, that, by the charity of our temper and thought and life, we may show forth the power and beauty of the religion we profess, to the glory of thy holy name; through Jesus Christ our Lord. Amen.

GLORIA PATRI

THE SCRIPTURE LESSON

CALL TO PRAYER

Minister: The Lord be with you.

People: **And with thy spirit.**

Minister: Let us pray.

Here let the people kneel or be seated and bow in prayer.

Minister: O Lord, show thy mercy upon us.

People: **And grant us thy salvation.**

Minister: O God, make clean our hearts within us.

People: **And take not thy Holy Spirit from us.**

INTERCESSORY PRAYER *The minister, the people responding.*

Let us pray for a new spirit in the Church:

By this shall all men know that we are his disciples, if we have love one for another.

God our Shepherd, give to the Church a new vision and a new love, new wisdom and fresh understanding, the revival of her brightness and the renewal of her unity, that the eternal message of thy Son, undefiled by the traditions of men, may be hailed as the good news of the new age; through him who maketh all things new, Jesus Christ our Lord.

Let us pray for a new spirit in the state:
God shall wipe away all tears from their eyes; for the former things are passed away.

God our Ruler, give to every state the dawning spirit of human brotherhood, a new respect for man and for woman, new loyalty in service and charity, new happiness in work and justice in reward, that our homes may be restored in thee, our cities rebuilt, and all the world may reflect the radiance of that new Jerusalem whose river is the water of life, and whose light is the Lamb that was slain and now liveth for evermore.

Let us pray for a new spirit in the world:
Unto the Father of our Lord Jesus Christ, of whom the whole family in heaven and earth is named.

God our Father, give to the nations of the world a new heart of comradeship, the old man of ignorance and cruelty being done away, and the new man put on, renewed in knowledge, to strengthen and to serve the brethren; that every people may bring its tribute of excellence to the common treasury, without fear, and without the lust of domination, and all the world may go forward in the new and living way which he hath consecrated for us, who now liveth and reigneth, with thee and the Spirit of truth, one God, world without end. Amen.

THE LORD'S PRAYER

OFFERTORY *The dedication of gifts and tithes. An offertory sentence may be said or sung.*

HYMN

THE SERMON *Which may be followed by prayer.*

HYMN *The people standing.*

SILENT PRAYER

BENEDICTION

POSTLUDE

An Order of Worship for a Service of Commemoration

For Any Who Have Died During the Year

Especially for Use at an Annual Conference

PRELUDE

QUIET MOMENTS *Let the people kneel or bow in silent prayer upon entering the sanctuary and devoutly meditate on the following words.*

SCRIPTURE SENTENCES

Jesus said, Thou art Peter, and upon this rock I will build my church; and the gates of hell shall not prevail against it.

Christ also loved the church, and gave himself for it; that he might present it to himself a glorious church, not having spot, or wrinkle, or any such thing; but that it should be holy and without blemish.

The God of our Lord Jesus Christ hath put all things under his feet, and gave him to be the head over all things to the church, which is his body, the fullness of him that filleth all in all.

And he gave some to be apostles; and some, prophets; and some, evangelists; and some, pastors and teachers; for the perfecting of the saints, for the work of the ministry, for the edifying of the body of Christ.

And the Spirit and the bride say, Come. And let him that heareth say, Come. And let him that is athirst, come. And whosoever will, let him take the water of life freely.

MEDITATION

We need to call to remembrance the great and good, through whom the Lord hath wrought great glory. We need to be reminded of the noble army of good ministers of Jesus Christ

96

who have been the interpreters of faith and have given to us the heritage of freedom and truth. We need to be appreciative of the good example of the men and women who have truly loved and served God in creating the fabric of the Church that is ours today.

PRAYER

O God, who makest thine angels spirits and thy ministers a flame of fire; vouchsafe, we beseech thee, to stir up and confirm the sacred grace in all stewards of thy mysteries, that as ministering spirits they may gather out of thy kingdom all things that offend, and may kindle in the hearts of all that fire which thou didst send thy Son to cast upon the earth; through Jesus Christ our Lord. Amen.

PROCESSIONAL HYMN *The people standing. If there be no processional, let the first hymn follow the Call to Worship.*

CALL TO WORSHIP

Minister: O give thanks unto the Lord; for he is good; for his mercy endureth forever.

People: **Because thy lovingkindness is better than life, my lips shall praise thee.**

Minister: O magnify the Lord with me, and let us exalt his name together.

People: **It is of the Lord's mercies that we are not consumed, because his compassions fail not. Amen.**

Here let the people be seated.

INVOCATION *The minister.*

Let us pray.

Almighty and everliving God, whose nature it is to purify and to bless; in every age our fathers have experienced thy mercies and borne witness of thy power to save. To us also may the might of thy Spirit be given and the excellence of thy glory be made manifest, that, following in the steps of thy faithful servants, and finding our blessedness in the doing of thy will, we may cast our burden on thee and joyfully minister to the needs of our generation, until the work be finished which thou hast given us to do; through Jesus Christ our Lord. **Amen**

COLLECT *Here let the people unite with the minister in prayer.*

O heavenly Father, thy word is a lamp unto our feet, and a light unto our path; we humbly beseech thee that thou wouldest be pleased to open and enlighten our minds, through Jesus Christ, who is the true light of the world, that we may understand thy word in its plainness and purity, and frame accordingly the whole course of our lives; through the same Jesus Christ our Lord. Amen.

ANTHEM

A CANTICLE OF THE WORD *Here let the people stand and remain standing until after the Affirmation of Faith.*

How lovely are thy messengers, O Lord of hosts! My soul hath a desire and a longing for thy word.

Thou sendest forth thy prophets in every age, and thy truth runneth swiftly to the ends of the earth.

The pure in heart have seen thee, O God: the lowly have found thee near at hand.

These tell of thy lovingkindness: from the rising of the sun to the going down of the same they keep not silence;

Publishing peace upon the mountains, and bringing good tidings of great joy,

That thou art blessed forever, and in thy will is our peace.

Thou art the everlasting fountain of life, and they that drink thereof shall thirst no more;

Light of our seeing and soul of our souls, within all spirits and beyond all worlds,

Who sustainest the heavens with the might of thy power, and gladdenest the eyes of all living with the beauty of thy holiness,

That the children of men may behold thy glory, and see thy wonders in the great deeps.

GLORIA PATRI

AFFIRMATION OF FAITH *Here let the people, following the exhortation of the minister, unite with him in the creed.*

Where the Spirit of the Lord is, there is the one true Church, apostolic and universal, whose holy faith let us now reverently and sincerely declare.

I believe in God the Father Almighty, Maker of heaven and earth; and in Jesus Christ his only Son our Lord; who was conceived by the Holy Spirit, born of the Virgin Mary, suffered under Pontius Pilate, was crucified, dead, and buried; the third day he rose from the dead; he ascended into heaven, and sitteth at the right hand of God the Father Almighty; from thence he shall come to judge the quick and the dead. I believe in the Holy Spirit, the holy catholic Church, the communion of saints, the forgiveness of sins, the resurrection of the body, and the life everlasting. Amen.

THE LESSON *Ecclesiasticus 44:1-15.*

Let us now praise famous men, and our fathers that begat us;

In whom the Lord showed forth his glory, his mighty power in the days of old;

Men who bore dominion in the earth, and men famous for their might,

Giving counsel by their wisdom, and speaking with prophetic power;

Statesmen who were as princes of the people, and leaders trusted for their insight;

Sure were the words of their instruction, and their sayings as wise proverbs;

Such as sought our pleasant music, and fashioned songs in skillful rhymes;

Men of resource and furnished with strength, dwelling peaceably in their habitations.

All these were honored in their generation, and had glory in their day.

There be some of them that have left a name behind them, and their praises still continue.

And some there be that have no memorial, who are forgotten as though they had not been.

Nevertheless they were men of mercy, and their righteous deeds have not been in vain.

For they left a good inheritance to their seed, and their children are their testament.

Their seed shall remain forever, and their glory shall not be blotted out.

Their bodies were buried in peace, but their name liveth to all generations.

The assembly shall recount their wisdom, and the congregation shall tell of their praise.

LITANY OF APPRECIATION *The minister, the people responding.*

Let us pray.

Almighty and everlasting God, before whom stand the spirits of the living and the dead, Light of lights, Fountain of wisdom and goodness, who livest in all pure and humble and gracious souls;

For all who have witnessed a good confession for thy glory and the welfare of the world, patriarchs, prophets, and apostles, the wise of every land and nation, all teachers and preachers of thy truth,

We praise thee, O God, and bless thy name.

For the martyrs of our holy faith, the faithful witnesses to Christ of whom the world was not worthy, and for all who have resisted falsehood and wrong unto suffering or death,

We praise thee, O God, and bless thy name.

For all who have labored and suffered for freedom, good government, just laws, and the sanctity of the home, and for all who have given their lives for their country,

We praise thee, O God, and bless thy name.

For all who have sought to bless men by their service and life, and to lighten the dark places of the earth,

We praise thee, O God, and bless thy name.

For those who have been tender and true and brave in all times and places, for those who have been devoted ministers and faithful shepherds of souls in thy holy Church, and for all who have been one with thee in the communion of Christ's Spirit and in the strength of his love,

We praise thee, O God, and bless thy name.

Here let the minister and the people unite in saying:

O Almighty God, who in thy mercy hast redeemed the world by the love of thy dear Son; we give thee hearty thanks for thy servants who are in the ministry of thy Church; endue them richly with the gifts of the Holy Spirit, and grant that in all their words and deeds they may seek thy glory and the increase of thy kingdom; through Jesus Christ our Lord. Amen.

RECORD OF REMEMBRANCE *Here the names of those memorialized may be read.*

SILENT MEDITATION

PASTORAL PRAYER

THE LORD'S PRAYER

HYMN OF COMMEMORATION *The people standing.*

THE SERMON *Which may be followed by prayer.*

AN INVITATION TO CHRISTIAN DISCIPLESHIP

HYMN *The people standing.*

SILENT PRAYER

BENEDICTION

POSTLUDE

An Order of Dedication of Seed, Soil, and Sowers

Let the service of worship begin at time appointed. Let the people kneel or bow in silent prayer upon entering the sanctuary.

PRELUDE *The people in devout meditation.*

HYMN *The people standing.*

CALL TO WORSHIP *The minister, the people responding.*

Dearly beloved, as we learn from the Scriptures, in the beginning God created the heaven and the earth, and caused the sun to shine, the rain to fall, the plants to grow, and the earth to give forth her increase. Then God said, Let us make man in our image, and let him have dominion over everything upon the earth.

It is meet, right, and our bounden duty to recognize God's ownership and his providence in the fruition of the earth and the return of the seasons. He is the giver of life in the seed, in the soil, and in the sowers.

We are therefore now assembled for the purpose of dedicating the seed that shall be planted, the soil that shall be cultivated, and the sowers that labor to the service of God and for the good of mankind.

The earth is the LORD's, and the fullness thereof; the world, and they that dwell therein.

For he hath founded it upon the seas, and established it upon the floods.

Who shall ascend into the hill of the LORD? or who shall stand in his holy place?

He that hath clean hands, and a pure heart; who hath not lifted up his soul unto vanity, nor sworn deceitfully.

He shall receive the blessing from the LORD, and righteousness from the God of his salvation.

102

This is the generation of them that seek him, that seek thy face.

Lift up your heads, O ye gates; and be ye lift up, ye everlasting doors.

And the King of glory shall come in.

Who is this King of glory?

The LORD strong and mighty, the LORD mighty in battle.

Lift up your heads, O ye gates; even lift them up, ye everlasting doors.

And the King of glory shall come in.

Who is this King of glory?

The LORD of hosts, he is the King of glory.

GLORIA PATRI

THE SCRIPTURE LESSON *Luke 8:5-15.*

PASTORAL PRAYER *Followed by the Lord's Prayer.*

OFFERTORY *The dedication of gifts and tithes. An offertory sentence may be said or sung.*

ANTHEM

HYMN

THE SERMON

THE DEDICATION OF SEED, SOIL, AND SOWERS
The minister shall say:

Life is a unity and is a result of the co-operative activity of the trinity of God, man, and nature. Without the gift of vital life, man and nature would not be able to produce food and complete processes whereby man is sustained. Without man, God would not bring forth from nature that which glorifies himself and brings companionship unto him. Without nature, God and man would not have the structural basis for growth of human personality. This trinity is ever dependent one upon the other, and this dependence is here today realized again and recognized for the humility of man and to the glory of God. Let us now consider our responsibilities.

Then a person appointed to present seed shall say:

This seed is symbolic of the various types of seed that shall be planted in this community. When sown it shall bring forth fruit, food, and fiber, so that little children may eat and become strong, so that men and women shall be nurtured and nourished, so that the wheels of industry may turn, and so that life may be maintained among both man and beast. This seed is holy, for it contains life, and all seed shall be counted as holy in the sight of God. It shall be planted in a spirit of reverence, and that which comes of it shall be cultivated and harvested in a true spirit of recognition and thankfulness, we being fully mindful of its high origin and destiny.

Then a person appointed to present soil of the earth shall say:

This soil is symbolic of the earth of this community, in which seed shall be planted in hope, and from which the harvest shall be anticipated with joy. This soil, this earth, is the result of the creative activity of God. It was created by God for man and beast. It contains the minerals, salts, and fertilizers necessary to nourish the seed and bring forth sturdy plants capable of producing food for both man and beast. This soil will be watered by the rains of God. It will be warmed by the sunshine of God. It will be as a home to the seed, so that the seed and plants may develop and bring forth an abundant harvest. This soil is holy earth and shall be cultivated and cared for as a gift of God.

ACT OF DEDICATION *Then shall the minister receive the seed and the soil of the earth, lay them upon the altar, and place the open Bible upon them. The people shall stand and join the minister in saying:*

And the Lord God formed man of the dust of the ground, and breathed into his nostrils the breath of life; and man became a living soul. And out of the ground made the Lord God to grow every tree that is pleasant to the sight, and good for food; the tree of life also in the midst of the garden, and the tree of knowledge of good and evil.

Thus saith God the LORD, he that created the heavens, and stretched them out; he that spread forth the earth, and that which cometh out of it; he that giveth breath unto the people upon it, and spirit to them that walk therein; I the LORD have called thee in righteousness, and will hold thine hand, and will keep thee, and give thee for a covenant of the people, and for a light.

In the beginning was the Word, and the Word was with God, and the Word was God. The same was in the beginning with God. All things were made by him; and without him was not anything made that was made. In him was life; and the life was the light of men.

I am come that they might have life, and that they might have it more abundantly.

PRAYER OF DEDICATION *The minister. Here let the people kneel or be seated and bow in prayer.*

Let us pray.

Almighty God, creator of life and sustainer of seed and soil, thou who hast by thy mighty arm brought forth this world and given it unto us for a heritage and a home, thou who hast given unto us life through thy Son Jesus Christ, thou who hast granted unto us the high and holy task of propagating thy faith and serving thee in this day and generation; unto thee we come in this act of dedication and blessing. We recognize that thou art the giver of life. We recognize that thou art the sender of rain, sunshine, and fertility. Without thee we should not be able to maintain life nor creature existence. To thee we come in this hour seeking to dedicate all the seed that shall be sown in this community this year. We bless it in thy name. We pray that it may fall in good ground, and that it may be cultivated and bring forth harvest for a hungry world. Multiply it by thy creative power, and let it bring forth manyfold. We recognize in this act our dependence upon thee for the life hid within the seed and the soil. As they join in partnership to bring forth fruit, may we join in partnership with thee to preserve the soil and cultivate the fruit of the seed to thy glory and our good. We dedicate and bless this seed in thy name. We dedicate and bless this soil in thy name. We dedicate and bless the sowers of this seed and cultivators of this soil in thy name. Grant unto them strength, wisdom, and power, that they may do that which is right in thy sight. This we ask in the name of him who was the sower of good seed in the soil of the life of mankind, even Jesus Christ our Lord. **Amen.**

ACT OF COMMITMENT *The people.*

We are the sowers of the seed and the tillers of the soil. We recognize the holiness of the seed and the sacredness of the soil. We acknowledge our responsibility to plant this seed with reverence and to cultivate this soil with care. We will not waste the seed in wanton scattering. We will not destroy the soil by allowing erosion to wash it off nor weeds to sap its vitality. We will husband our resources of seed and soil and guard them with our lives. We recognize the sacred task that is ours; we recognize the high calling that is ours; we recognize the purpose for which we plant the seed and till the soil: that man and beast may be fed, and that life may be maintained for the glory of God and the good of mankind. We commit ourselves to these tasks, and to the privilige of working together as children in the family of God in the high and holy duty of growing food for the distant members of the community of the family. We dedicate ourselves, our lives, and our sacred honor to the discharging of these duties, knowing that life is of God and that God will never fail those who go forth in his name to do his will.

Here let the minister and the people unite in saying:

O God, our seed and our soil in this act we have committed unto the security of thy providence. While the earth turns, we will be about our tasks, confident of thy power to quicken, grow, and make fruitful that which shall ultimately be used for the good of mankind and to the glory of thy name; through Jesus Christ our Lord. Amen.

HYMN *The people standing.*

SILENT PRAYER

BENEDICTION

Now unto him that is able to keep you from falling, and to present you faultless before the presence of his glory with exceeding joy, to the only wise God our Saviour, be glory and majesty, dominion and power, both now and evermore. **Amen.**

POSTLUDE

An Order of Thanksgiving for Harvest, Land, and Liberty

Let the service of worship begin at the time appointed. Let the people kneel or bow in silent prayer upon entering the sanctuary.

PRELUDE *The people in devout meditation.*

HYMN *The people standing.*

CALL TO WORSHIP *The minister, the people responding.*

We learn from Scriptures that holy men of old took the first fruits of the harvest into the temple and presented them unto Almighty God in humble thanksgiving for his blessings and mercies. By this act of devotion they declared allegiance unto him and expressed gratitude for harvests and for liberty. Our nation's founding fathers, in similar manner, gathered to give thanks unto Almighty God for deliverance from famine and for freedom of worship.

Therefore it is just, right, and our joyful duty that we should recognize God's gracious providence in granting unto us this harvest from our labors on lands of his creation.

We are therefore now assembled for the purpose of giving thanks unto Almighty God for this harvest, for the land on which it was grown, for the liberty of worship which is ours, and for the nation in which we live.

O come, let us sing unto the LORD: let us make a joyful noise to the rock of our salvation.

Let us come before his presence with thanksgiving, and make a joyful noise unto him with psalms.

For the LORD is a great God, and a great King above all gods.

In his hand are the deep places of the earth: the strength of the hills is his also.

The sea is his, and he made it: and his hands formed the dry land.

O come, let us worship and bow down: let us kneel before the LORD **our maker.**

Make a joyful noise unto the LORD, all ye lands.

Serve the LORD **with gladness: come before his presence with singing.**

Know ye that the LORD he is God: it is he that hath made us, and not we ourselves; we are his people, and the sheep of his pasture.

Enter into his gates with thanksgiving, and into his courts with praise: be thankful unto him, and bless his name.

For the LORD is good; his mercy is everlasting; and his truth endureth to all generations.

Praise ye the LORD. **O give thanks unto the** LORD; **for he is good: for his mercy endureth forever.**

GLORIA PATRI

THE SCRIPTURE LESSON *Mark 4:26-32.*

PASTORAL PRAYER *Followed by the Lord's Prayer.*

OFFERTORY *The dedication of gifts and tithes. An offertory sentence may be said or sung.*

ANTHEM

HYMN

THE SERMON

THE THANKSGIVING FOR HARVEST, LAND, AND LIBERTY
The minister shall say:

In the gracious providence of God this world came into being. God is the source of all life: the land was created by his might; fertility was developed in the soil by his wisdom;

the sun was caused to shine by his power; and the rain was given to parched lands by his mercies. Man was created and placed in dominion over all things upon the earth. Man has at all times and in all places recognized his dependence upon God for food, for faith, for fellowship, and for freedom. Man the creature is in eternal debt to God the creator. Mortal man becomes immortal spirit through the life of God within him, and man's highest privilege and greatest pleasure is to work for the good of mankind and to the glory of God. This nation, under God, has been granted life that the free spirit of man might find a home and the will of God find expression in the life of a people. We are here today as a result of God's blessings and mercies. Let us consider God's goodness and give thanks for his providence.

Then a person appointed to present fruits of the harvest shall say:

These fruits of the harvest are symbols of the gifts of God in response to the labors of man. Whether it be the glint of the gold in the grain, the white of the cotton boll, the tawny tan of the pumpkin, the brown of the shock of corn, or the russet of the leaves in the woods, each reflects the handiwork of God. In the spring we plowed the fields with hope and planted the seed in expectation. In the summer we cultivated our crops by faith. This autumn we reaped our harvest in joy. We have not been disappointed in the abundance of the yield, an evidence of the providence of God. In the sowing and the reaping we have known the grace of God. To him who is the author of life we give thanks. And in humble recognition of his providence we present these fruits of the harvest as a symbol of our dependence and gratitude. We pray that the harvest from our fields may be used for the benefit of man and the growth of God's kingdom.

Then a person appointed to present soil of the earth shall say:

This soil is a symbol of the earth from which this harvest was gathered; it is a symbol of the land in which we live, and our presence here is evidence of our liberty. Without the radiant energies of the sun given to earth there would be no growing crops, no fruitful harvest. Without the fertility of the soil, God's gift of life, there would be no increase from planting seed or labor of man. Without land man is homeless, and without man the land is desolation. There is an eternal partnership of God, man, and land. To the meaning of this partnership we have been faithful this year and are grateful for the mercies of God. When man is faithful to land he has a country, and his nation is secure. Our liberty of life is dependent upon our nation, and our nation is dependent upon our land. These are dependent upon the love of God made manifest in the life of man. We present this soil as a symbol of our love of the land, our love of our nation, and our love of liberty.

ACT OF DEDICATION *Then shall the minister receive the fruits of the harvest and the soil of the earth, lay them upon the altar, and place the open Bible upon them. The people shall stand and join the minister in saying:*

In the beginning God created the heaven and the earth. And God said, Let us make man in our image, after our likeness: and let them have dominion over all the earth. And the Lord God took the man, and put him into the garden of Eden to dress it and to keep it. Thou shalt keep the commandments of the Lord thy God, to walk in his ways, and to fear him. Thou shalt love the Lord thy God with all thy strength, and with all thy mind; and thy neighbor as thyself.

PRAYER OF DEDICATION *The minister. Here let the people kneel or be seated and bow in prayer.*

Let us pray.

Almighty God, creator of the universe and sustainer of the laws of seed and soil; unto thee we come with hearts full of thanksgiving because of the abundant spiritual and material blessings thou hast given us. Thou hast given us the soil; thou hast given us seed with life; thou hast given us wisdom to seek scientific knowledge with which to cultivate; thou hast crowned our labors with an abundant harvest of food and fiber. Thou hast given unto us bountifully for ourselves, for our neighbors, and for those dependent upon us. For all of these things we humbly thank thee. Thou hast given to us providential blessings of freedom, grace, and mercy which we this day enjoy. We recognize thy goodness unto us and again renew our allegiance unto thee and proclaim our dependence upon thee. Guide thou us, we pray, in this our thanksgiving for harvest, for land, and for liberty; and lead this nation to acknowledge its dependence upon thee for food, for faith, and for freedom. This we ask in the name of him who was the sower of good seed in the soil of the life of mankind, even Jesus Christ our Lord. **Amen.**

ACT OF THANKSGIVING *The people.*

We are the harvesters of the fields and the gatherers of the grain. We are those who live on land and labor for liberty. We are thankful for the privilege of toil. Our ability to produce food and fiber for man and beast gives us a sense of achievement and adds meaning to life. We are thankful for the land on which we live. We love its slopes and its hills. The mountains speak of God, and the valleys tell of his virtues. The green of the grass is a reminder of the eternal strength of God. The freshness of dawn breathes a promise of life. The barrenness of winter is but a silent rest after a year of labor, an interlude in the continued symphony of life. This land is ours. We have learned to preserve its treasures and restore its vitality with returned humus and retained rain. We have not allowed our land to be lost through erosion or weakened through misuse. We are thankful for the harvest of this year, which we planted in hope and cultivated in faith. We are thankful for the nation of which we are a humble part. We are proud of its historic past. We rejoice in its glorious present. And we pray for its righteous future. We count our liberty a thing to be highly prized and are thankful to God for the experience of freedom. In recognition of his goodness and our dependence upon him we now renew our allegiance to him in this order of gratitude and thanksgiving.

Here let the minister and the people unite in saying:

Therefore with angels and archangels, and with all the company of heaven, we laud and magnify thy glorious name, evermore praising thee, and saying: Holy, holy, holy, Lord God of hosts, heaven and earth are full of thy glory. Glory be to thee, O Lord most high! Amen.

HYMN *The people standing.*

SILENT PRAYER

BENEDICTION

The peace of God, which passeth all understanding, keep your hearts and minds in the knowledge and love of God, and of his Son Jesus Christ our Lord; and the blessing of God Almighty, the Father, the Son, and the Holy Spirit, be among you, and remain with you always. Amen.

POSTLUDE

An Order of Worship for Thanksgiving Day

Let the service of worship begin at the time appointed. Let the people kneel or bow in silent prayer upon entering the sanctuary.

PRELUDE *The people in devout meditation.*

PROCESSIONAL HYMN *The people standing. If there be no processional, let the first hymn follow the Call to Worship.*

CALL TO WORSHIP

Minister: God be merciful unto us, and bless us,

People: **And cause his face to shine upon us.**

Minister: Let us worship the Lord in the beauty of holiness.

People: **Let us worship him in spirit and in truth. Amen.**

Here let the people kneel or be seated and bow in prayer.

INVOCATION *The minister.*

Let us pray.

Most gracious God, by whose appointment the seasons come and go, and who makest the fruits of the earth to minister to the needs of men; we offer thee our thanksgivings that thou hast brought us through the circuit of another year, and that according to thy promise seedtime and harvest have not failed. At the remembrance of thy bounty we offer unto thee the sacrifices of our thanksgiving, and pray that thou wilt feed our souls with the Bread of Life; through Jesus Christ our Lord. **Amen.**

PRAYER OF THANKSGIVING *Here let the people unite with the minister in prayer.*

O God, we praise thee, we give thanks unto thee for thy bountiful providence, for all the blessings and all

114

the hopes of life. Above all we praise and adore thee for thine unspeakable gift in thine only Son our Lord and Saviour Jesus Christ. Let the memory of thy goodness, we beseech thee, fill our hearts with joy and thankfulness to thee; through Jesus Christ our Lord. Amen.

THE LORD'S PRAYER

Our Father who art in heaven, hallowed be thy name; thy kingdom come; thy will be done on earth as it is in heaven. Give us this day our daily bread. And forgive us our trespasses, as we forgive those who trespass against us. And lead us not into temptation, but deliver us from evil. For thine is the kingdom, and the power, and the glory, forever. Amen.

ACT OF PRAISE *Here let the people stand and, after the singing of each stanza by the choir, unite in singing the response.*

> For the beauty of the earth,
>> For the glory of the skies,
> For the love which from our birth
>> Over and around us lies:
>
> **Lord of all, to thee we raise**
> **This our hymn of grateful praise.**
>
> For the beauty of each hour,
>> Of the day and of the night,
> Hill and vale, and tree and flower,
>> Sun and moon, and stars of light:
>
> **Lord of all, to thee we raise**
> **This our hymn of grateful praise.**
>
> For the joy of ear and eye;
>> For the heart and mind's delight;
> For the mystic harmony
>> Linking sense to sound and sight:
>
> **Lord of all, to thee we raise**
> **This our hymn of grateful praise.**

For the joy of human love,
  Brother, sister, parent, child,
Friends on earth, and friends above;
  For all gentle thoughts and mild:
Lord of all, to thee we raise
This our hymn of grateful praise.

For thy Church, that evermore
  Lifteth holy hands above,
Offering up on every shore
  Her pure sacrifice of love:
Lord of all, to thee we raise
This our hymn of grateful praise.

For thyself, best Gift Divine!
  To our race so freely given;
For that great, great love of thine,
  Peace on earth, and joy in heaven:
Lord of all, to thee we raise
This our hymn of grateful praise. Amen.

Here let the people be seated.

LITANY OF THANKSGIVING AND INTERCESSION *The minister, the people responding.*

Let us pray.

We thank thee, O God, for thy blessings.

For all thy blessings in creation, for the beauty of earth and sea and sky, for thy manifold works, and the wisdom with which thou hast made them all,

We thank thee, O God.

For the happiness of our earthly life, for peaceful homes and healthful days, for our powers of mind and body, for faithful friends, for the joy of loving and being loved,

We thank thee, O God.

For the revelation of thy love and for newness of life in our Saviour, for the blessings brought to us by thy holy Church, and for our fellowship with thee in Christ,

We thank thee, O God.

That it may please thee to bless with wisdom and courage thy servant the President of the United States, and all who bear with him the responsibility of the nation, and to give thy guidance and blessing to all the councils of the people,

We humbly beseech thee, our Father.

That it may please thee to strengthen and encourage all those who by reason of temptation, hardness of circumstances, or personal loss find it difficult to be thankful and to praise thy holy name,

We humbly beseech thee, our Father.

That it may please thee to inspire all who are seeking to improve the conditions of our industrial life, and to give courage and devotion to all who do the work of every day, and to restore ordered prosperity and peace to our world,

We humbly beseech thee, our Father.

That it may please thee to solace all who have lost those whom they most loved, to uphold all who are sick and suffering, to protect such as have lost the kindly light of reason, and to supply the needs of the blind, the deaf, and the dumb,

We humbly beseech thee, our Father. Amen.

ASCRIPTION OF PRAISE *The minister, the people standing.*

May the Lord Jesus Christ, who is the splendor of the eternal light, remove from our hearts all darkness. Unto thee, O God, do we give thanks; unto thee do we give thanks for thy great mercy toward us: for our creation, preservation, and redemption; for the pardon of sin; for the manifold gifts of thy love; and for the promise of eternal life in Jesus Christ our Saviour.

RESPONSE *The people.*

Therefore with angels and archangels, and with all the company of heaven, we laud and magnify thy glorious name, evermore praising thee, and saying: Holy, holy, holy, Lord God of hosts, heaven and earth are full of thy glory. Glory be to thee, O Lord most high! Amen.

THE RESPONSIVE READING

GLORIA PATRI

THE SCRIPTURE LESSON

PASTORAL PRAYER *The people seated and bowed, or kneeling.*

ANTHEM OF PRAISE

THANKSGIVING OFFERING

RESPONSE *The people standing.*

Praise God, from whom all blessings flow;
Praise him, all creatures here below;
Praise him above, ye heavenly host:
Praise Father, Son, and Holy Ghost. Amen.

HYMN OF PREPARATION

THE THANKSGIVING SERMON

AN INVITATION TO CHRISTIAN DISCIPLESHIP

HYMN *The people standing.*

SILENT PRAYER

BENEDICTION

POSTLUDE

An Order of Morning Worship for a Family or Other Small Group

To be said responsively, one person acting as leader.

The earth is the Lord's, and the fullness thereof: the world, and they that dwell therein.

Glory be to the Father, and to the Son, and to the Holy Ghost.

As it was in the beginning, is now, and ever shall be, world without end. Amen.

Praise ye the Lord.

The Lord's name be praised.

Then shall be said or sung the following ancient morning hymn:

> Now that the daylight fills the sky,
> We make our prayer to God on high,
> That he in all we do or say,
> Would keep us free from harm this day;
>
> Would guard our hearts and thoughts from shame,
> Our tongues from strife, our lips from blame,
> From evil sights defend our eyes,
> And turn them from all vanities;
>
> Would keep our inmost conscience pure,
> Our souls from folly would secure,
> The passion and the pride of sense
> Restrain by prayer and abstinence.
>
> So we, when this new day is gone,
> And night once more is drawing on,
> With conscience by the world unstained,
> May praise his name for victory gained.

119

All praise to God the Father be,
All praise, eternal Son, to thee,
Whom with the Spirit we adore,
For ever and for evermore. Amen.

Then shall the leader say:
Let us pray.

All shall unite with him in the Lord's Prayer, after which shall be said:
Unto thee, O Lord, have I cried.
And in the morning shall my prayer come before thee.
Let my mouth be filled with thy praise;
That I may sing of thy glory and of thy greatness all the day long.
Hide thy face from my sins.
And blot out all mine iniquities.
Create in me a clean heart, O God.
And renew a right spirit within me.
O Lord, let thy mercy light upon us,
As our trust is in thee.

O Lord, our heavenly Father, almighty and everlasting God, who hast safely brought us to the beginning of this day; defend us in the same with thy mighty power; and grant that this day we fall into no sin, neither run into any kind of danger; but that all our doings, being ordered by thy governance, may be righteous in thy sight; through Jesus Christ our Lord. **Amen.**

The Lord be with you.
And with thy spirit.
Let us bless the Lord.
Thanks be to God.

All shall then join in the benediction:
The Lord bless us, and keep us: the Lord make his face shine upon us, and be gracious unto us: the Lord lift up his countenance upon us, and give us peace. Amen.

An Order of Evening Worship for a Family or Other Small Group

To be said responsively, one person acting as leader.

Jesus spake unto them, saying, I am the light of the world: he that followeth me shall not walk in darkness, but shall have the light of life. Do thou, O Lord, have mercy upon us.

Thanks be to God.

Our help is in the name of the Lord;

Who made heaven and earth.

Glory be to the Father, and to the Son, and to the Holy Ghost.

As it was in the beginning, is now, and ever shall be, world without end. Amen.

Praise ye the Lord.

The Lord's name be praised.

Then shall be said or sung the following ancient evening hymn:

> Before the ending of the day,
> Creator of the world, we pray
> That with thy wonted favor thou
> Would'st be our guard and keeper now.
>
> From all ill dreams defend our eyes,
> From nightly fears and fantasies;
> Tread under foot our ghostly foe
> That no pollution we may know.
>
> O Father, that we ask be done,
> Through Jesus Christ thine only Son,
> Who, with the Holy Ghost and thee,
> Doth live and reign eternally. Amen.

Then shall the leader say:

Let us pray.

All shall unite with him in the Lord's Prayer, after which shall be said:

Blessed art thou, O Lord God of our Fathers;

And worthy to be praised and glorious forever.

Let us bless the Father, the Son, and the Holy Spirit.

Let us praise and exalt him above all forever.

Blessed art thou, O Lord, in the firmament of heaven;

And worthy to be praised, and glorious and exalted above all forever.

The almighty and merciful Lord bless us and guard us.

Amen.

O Lord, let thy mercy light upon us,

As our trust is in thee.

Lighten our darkness, we beseech thee, O Lord; and by thy great mercy defend us from all perils and dangers of this night; for the love of thine only Son, our Saviour Jesus Christ. **Amen.**

O Lord, support us all the day long of this troublous life, until the shadows lengthen, and the evening comes, and the busy world is hushed, and the fever of life is over, and our work is done. Then of thy mercy grant us a safe lodging, and a holy rest, and peace at the last; through Jesus Christ our Lord. **Amen.**

The Lord be with you.

And with thy spirit.

Let us bless the Lord.

Thanks be to God.

All shall then join in the benediction:

The almighty and merciful Lord, the Father, the Son, and the Holy Spirit, bless and preserve us. Amen.

Aids for General Use

PRAYERS FOR USE UPON ENTERING CHURCH

For Purity of Heart

Almighty God, unto whom all hearts are open, all desires known, and from whom no secrets are hid; cleanse the thoughts of our hearts by the inspiration of thy Holy Spirit, that we may perfectly love thee, and worthily magnify thy holy name; through Christ our Lord. Amen.

For Grace and Guidance

O Lord, our heavenly Father, who hast safely brought us to the beginning of this day; defend us with thy mighty power; and grant that this day we fall into no sin, neither run into any kind of danger, but that all our doings may be ordered by thy governance, to do always that which is righteous in thy sight; through Jesus Christ our Lord. Amen.

For God's Continued Help

Direct us, O Lord, in all our doings, with thy most gracious favor, and further us with thy continual help, that in all our works, begun, continued, and ended in thee, we may glorify thy holy name, and finally, by thy mercy, obtain everlasting life; through Jesus Christ our Lord. Amen.

Preparation for Worship

O God our Father, may the meditations of our hearts, in this hour, be acceptable in thy sight; may we strive for a new understanding of thy word and will; may we here resolve upon a more complete obedience to thy commands, a richer ministry to thy people and purpose. Through thy Spirit lift us up into a greater steadfastness, a finer courage, a fuller loyalty, a devotion worthy of those who name themselves after thee; through Jesus Christ our Lord. Amen.

A Prayer of St. Chrysostom

Almighty God, who hast given us grace, at this time, with one accord to make our common supplications unto thee, and dost promise that, when two or three are gathered together in thy name, thou wilt grant their requests; fulfill now, O Lord, the desires and petitions of thy servants, as may be most expedient for them, granting us in this world knowledge of thy truth, and in the world to come life everlasting. Amen.

The Lord's Prayer

Our Father who art in heaven, hallowed be thy name; thy kingdom come; thy will be done on earth as it is in heaven. Give us this day our daily bread. And forgive us our trespasses, as we forgive those who trespass against us. And lead us not into temptation, but deliver us from evil. For thine is the kingdom, and the power, and the glory, forever. Amen.

INVOCATIONS

Almighty God, from whom every good prayer cometh, and who pourest out on all who desire it the spirit of grace and supplication; deliver us, when we draw nigh to thee, from coldness of heart and wanderings of mind, that with steadfast thoughts, and kindled affections, we may worship thee in spirit and in truth; through Jesus Christ our Lord. Amen.

Almighty God, purify our hearts from every vain and sinful thought; prepare our souls to worship thee this day acceptably, with reverence and godly fear. Set our affection on things above, and give us grace to receive thy word into good and honest hearts, so that we may rise to newness of life; through Jesus Christ our Lord. Amen.

O God our Father, who hast bidden the light to shine out of darkness, who hast again wakened us to praise thy goodness and ask for thy grace; accept now the sacrifice of our worship and thanksgiving. Make us to be children of the light and of the day, and heirs of thy everlasting inheritance. Remember, O God, thy whole Church, all our brethren by land or sea who stand in need of thy grace. Pour out the riches of thy mercy, so that we, being redeemed, and steadfast in faith, may ever praise thy wonderful and holy name; through Jesus Christ our Lord. Amen.

Almighty God, who hast given a day of rest to thy people, and, through thy Spirit in the Church, hast consecrated the first day of the week to be a perpetual memorial of thy Son's resurrection; grant that we may so use thy gift that, refreshed and strengthened in soul and body, we may serve thee faithfully all the days of our life; through the same Jesus Christ our Lord. Amen.

Grant, O Lord, that all who worship within this place may present their bodies a living sacrifice, holy, acceptable unto thee; and that they may themselves be temples of the Holy Spirit wherein thou wilt dwell for evermore. Amen.

Regard, O Lord, the supplication of thy servants, and grant that thy word, which shall be read and preached in this place, may have such acceptance that it may never be spoken in vain. Grant also that the people may have grace to hear and receive what shall be delivered out of thy most holy word as the means of their salvation, that in all their words and deeds they may seek thy glory and the increase of thy kingdom; through Jesus Christ our Lord. Amen.

O God, to whom belong adoration and praise; prepare us, through the active presence of thy Spirit, to come before thee worthily and to ask of thee rightly; enlighten our understanding; purify our every desire; quicken our wills unto instant obedience to thy word; strengthen every right purpose; direct this hour of worship to the magnifying of thy name, and to the enduring good of us thy children and servants; through Jesus Christ our Lord. Amen.

Almighty God, author of eternal light; illumine our hearts by the light of thy grace, that our lips may praise thee, that our lives may bless thee, that our worship may glorify thee; through Jesus Christ our Lord. Amen.

For Evening

Almighty God, our heavenly Father; receive us in this evening hour as we offer ourselves anew to thee in body, soul, and spirit. Let not thy holy day pass except it leave its benediction with us. Give to us the still and quiet heart. Speak to us thy truth, that we may glorify thee; through Jesus Christ our Lord. Amen.

Praised be thou, O Lord our God, Ruler of the world, by whose law the shadows of evening fall and the gates of morn are opened. In wisdom thou hast established the changes of times and seasons, and ordered the ways of the stars in their heavenly courses. Creator of heaven and earth, O living God, rule thou over us forever. Praised be thou, O Lord, for the day and its work and for the night and its rest. Amen.

PRAYERS OF CONFESSION

Have mercy upon us, O God, according to thy lovingkindness; according to the multitude of thy tender mercies blot out our transgressions. Wash us thoroughly from our iniquities, and cleanse us from our sins. For we acknowledge our transgressions, and our sin is ever before us. Create in us clean hearts, O God, and renew a right spirit within us; through Jesus Christ our Lord. Amen.

Almighty and most merciful Father, we have erred and strayed from thy ways like lost sheep. We have followed too much the devices and desires of our own hearts. We have offended against thy holy laws. We have left undone those things which we ought to have done, and we have done those things which we ought not to have done. But thou, O Lord, have mercy upon us. Spare thou those, O God, who confess their faults. Restore thou those who are penitent, according to thy promises declared unto mankind in Christ Jesus our Lord. And grant, O most merciful Father, for his sake, that we may hereafter live a godly, righteous, and sober life; to the glory of thy holy name. Amen.

O holy and merciful God, we confess that we have not always taken upon ourselves with joy the yoke of obedience, nor been willing to seek and to do thy perfect will. We have not loved thee with all our heart and mind and soul and strength, neither have we loved our neighbors as ourselves. Thou hast called to us in the need of our fellows, and we have passed unheeding on our way. In the pride of our hearts, and our unwillingness to repent, we have turned away from the cross of Christ, and have grieved thy Holy Spirit. Amen.

O God, our heavenly Father, we have sinned against thee and are not worthy to be called thy children. We have forsaken thy way, and walked in the light of our own eyes. We have not loved thee with our whole heart. We have not loved our neighbor as ourselves. We have not had in us the mind of Christ. We have grieved thy Holy Spirit. We have been conformed to this world which passeth away. We have not endured as seeing him who is invisible. Forgive us, we beseech thee, most merciful Father, and renew us again in the strength of thy grace; through Jesus Christ our Lord. Amen.

Almighty and most merciful God, who knowest the thoughts of our hearts, we confess that we have sinned against thee and done evil in thy sight. Forgive us, O Lord, we beseech thee, and cleanse us from the defilement of our sin. Give us grace and power, and put away all hurtful things, that, being delivered from evil, we may persevere in the way of thy righteousness all the days of our life; through Jesus Christ our Lord. Amen.

Our heavenly Father, who by thy love hast made us, and through thy love hast kept us, and in thy love wouldest make us perfect; we humbly confess that we have not loved thee with all our heart and soul and mind and strength, and that we have not loved one another as Christ hath loved us. Thy life is within our souls, but our selfishness hath hindered thee. We have not lived by faith. We have resisted thy Spirit. We have neglected thine inspirations. Forgive what we have been; help us to amend what we are; and in thy Spirit direct what we shall be; that thou mayest come into the full glory of thy creation, in us and in all men; through Jesus Christ our Lord. Amen.

Almighty God, Father of our Lord Jesus Christ, Maker of all things, Judge of all men; we acknowledge and bewail our manifold sins and wickedness, which we from time to time most grievously have committed, by thought, word, and deed, against thy divine majesty. We do earnestly repent, and are heartily sorry for these our misdoings; the remembrance of them is grievous unto us. Have mercy upon us, have mercy upon us, most merciful Father; for thy Son our Lord Jesus Christ's sake, forgive us all that is past; and grant that we may ever hereafter serve and please thee in newness of life, to the honor and glory of thy name; through Jesus Christ our Lord. Amen.

Almighty and eternal God, who searchest the hearts of men; we acknowledge and confess that we have sinned against thee in thought, word, and deed; that we have not loved thee with all our heart and soul, with all our mind and strength; and that we have not loved our neighbors as ourselves. Forgive us our transgressions, and help us to amend our ways, and of thine eternal goodness direct what we shall be, so that we may henceforth walk in the way of thy commandments, and do those things which are worthy in thy sight; through Jesus Christ our Lord. Amen.

O Thou who art of purer eyes than to behold evil, if thou shouldest mark iniquities, who should stand? Enter not into judgment with thy servants, for in thy sight shall no man living be justified; for thou knowest our foolishness, and our sins are not hid from thee. But thou, O Lord, art full of compassion and gracious, slow to anger and plenteous in mercy; there is forgiveness with thee, that thou mayest be obeyed. Cleanse us from secret faults; keep back thy servants also from presumptuous sins; deliver us from all our transgressions; draw nigh unto our souls and redeem them, and purge away our sins; through Jesus Christ our Lord. Amen.

Almighty and merciful God, the fountain of all goodness, who knowest the thoughts of our hearts; we confess that we have sinned against thee, and done evil in thy sight. Cleanse us from sin; give us grace and power to put away all hurtful things; that, being delivered from the bondage of sin, we may bring forth fruits worthy of repentance, and, following in the footsteps of thy blessed Son, obtain thy mercy, and enter into thy promised joy. Amen.

Most merciful Father, we have done little to forward thy Kingdom in this world, to foster the brotherhood of man, and to establish love as the law of life. We have allowed self to blind us, pains to embitter us. We have forgotten that whatsoever is done to one of the least of thy children is done unto thee. Pardon our shortcomings; forgive our neglect; give us a pure heart intent on pleasing thee. Help us in all our seeking to seek first thy kingdom and thy righteousness. And make us to come, as came thy Son Jesus Christ, not to be ministered unto, but to minister. All which we ask through Jesus Christ our Lord. Amen.

WORDS OF ASSURANCE

Hear what comfortable words our Saviour Christ saith unto all that truly turn to him: Come unto me, all ye that labor and are heavy laden, and I will give you rest.

Hear also the words from St. John's Gospel: God so loved the world, that he gave his only begotten Son, that whosoever believeth in him should not perish, but have everlasting life.

Hear also these words of Scripture: The LORD is gracious, and full of compassion; slow to anger, and of great mercy.

The sacrifices of God are a broken spirit: a broken and a contrite heart, O God, thou wilt not despise.

As the heaven is high above the earth, so great is his mercy toward them that fear him.

As far as the east is from the west, so far hath he removed our transgressions from us.

Like as a father pitieth his children, so the LORD pitieth them that fear him.

If we confess our sins, he is faithful and just to forgive us our sins, and to cleanse us from all unrighteousness.

This is a faithful saying, and worthy of all acceptation, that Christ Jesus came into the world to save sinners.

There is therefore now no condemnation to them who are in Christ Jesus, who walk not after the flesh, but after the Spirit.

This is the message which we have heard of him, and declare unto you, that God is light, and in him is no darkness at all. If we walk in the light, as he is in the light, we have fellowship one with another, and the blood of Jesus Christ his Son cleanseth us from all sin.

The LORD is my light and my salvation; whom shall I fear? the LORD is the strength of my life; of whom shall I be afraid?

In the time of trouble he shall hide me in his pavilion: in the secret of his tabernacle shall he hide me.

Wait on the LORD: be of good courage, and he shall strengthen thine heart: wait, I say, on the LORD.

The LORD is nigh unto them that are of a broken heart; and saveth such as be of a contrite spirit.

The LORD redeemeth the soul of his servants: and none of them that trust in him shall be desolate.

Trust in the LORD; wait patiently for him; and he shall give thee the desires of thine heart.

Ask, and it shall be given you; seek, and ye shall find; knock, and it shall be opened unto you: for everyone that asketh receiveth; and he that seeketh findeth; and to him that knocketh it shall be opened.

Jesus said: Him that cometh to me I will in no wise cast out.

My God shall supply all your need according to his riches in glory by Christ Jesus.

PRAYERS FOR PARDON AND
WORDS OF FORGIVENESS

May the almighty and merciful God grant us pardon, forgiveness, and remission of our sins; through Jesus Christ our Lord. Amen.

May Almighty God have mercy upon us, forgive us our sins, and bring us to everlasting life. Amen.

May the almighty and merciful Lord grant us remission of all our sins, true repentance, amendment of life, and the grace and consolation of his Holy Spirit. Amen.

O Lord, we beseech thee, mercifully hear our prayers, and spare all those who confess their sins unto thee, that they whose consciences by sin are accused, by thy merciful pardon may be absolved; through Christ our Lord. Amen.

May Almighty God, who caused light to shine out of darkness, shine in our hearts, cleansing us from all our sins, and restoring us to the light of the knowledge of his glory in the face of Jesus Christ our Lord. Amen.

May God, whose mercy droppeth as the gentle rain from heaven, forgive your sins, strengthen you in all goodness, and bring you to everlasting life; through Jesus Christ our Lord. Amen.

O God, forgive those who repent of their sins, that returning from the path of error to the way of righteousness they may retain in fullness what thy grace hath given, and may enjoy forever what thy mercy hath restored; through Jesus Christ our Lord. Amen.

Who is like unto God, that pardoneth iniquity and passeth by the transgression of his heritage? He retaineth not his anger forever, because he delighteth in mercy. He will turn again and have compassion upon us; he will tread our iniquities under foot, and cast all our sins into the depths of the sea. Amen.

O Lord, we beseech thee, forgive thy people their offenses, that through thy bountiful goodness we may be delivered from the bonds of those sins which by our frailty we have committed. Grant this, O heavenly Father, for Jesus Christ's sake, our blessed Lord and Saviour. Amen.

Grant, we beseech thee, Almighty God, that we who are burdened with the consciousness of our guilt may by thy mercy be forgiven, that being cleansed from sin we may be clothed in thy righteousness, and worthily rejoice in the joy of thy saints; through Jesus Christ our Lord. Amen.

Almighty God, our heavenly Father, who of thy great mercy hast promised forgiveness of sins to all them that with hearty repentance and true faith turn unto thee; have mercy upon us; pardon and deliver us from all our sins; confirm and strengthen us in all goodness; and bring us to everlasting life; through Jesus Christ our Lord. Amen.

O Lord God, there is none like unto thee, in the heavens or upon the earth; yet hast thou promised to hear the cry of those who call upon thee; wherefore have respect unto the supplications of thy servants, and hearken unto the prayer that they make before thee; and, howsoever they may have sinned, yet hear thou in heaven thy dwelling place; and when thou hearest, Lord, forgive. Amen.

Almighty God, the Father of our Lord Jesus Christ, who desirest not the death of a sinner, but rather that he may turn from his wickedness and live; thou dost pardon and absolve all them that truly repent and unfeignedly believe thy holy gospel. Wherefore we beseech thee to grant us true repentance, and thy Holy Spirit, that those things may please thee which we do at this present, and that the rest of our living hereafter may be pure and holy, so that at the last we may come to eternal joy; through Jesus Christ our Lord. Amen.

GENERAL PRAYERS

For All Conditions of Men

O God, the Creator and Preserver of all mankind; we humbly beseech thee for all sorts and conditions of men, that thou wouldest be pleased to make thy ways known unto them, thy saving health unto all nations. More especially we pray for thy holy Church universal, that it may be so guided and governed by thy good Spirit, that all who profess and call themselves Christians may be led into the way of truth, and hold the faith in unity of spirit, in the bond of peace, and in righteousness of life. Finally, we commend to thy fatherly goodness all those who are in any way afflicted or distressed in mind, body, or estate, that it may please thee to comfort and relieve them according to their several necessities, giving them patience under their suffering, and a happy issue out of all their afflictions. And this we ask for Jesus Christ's sake. Amen.

General Intercession

O God, at whose word man goeth forth unto his work and to his labor until the evening; be merciful to all whose duties are difficult or burdensome, and comfort them concerning their toil. Shield from bodily accident and harm the workmen at their work. Protect the efforts of sober and honest industry, and suffer not the hire of the laborers to be kept back. Incline the hearts of employers and of those whom they employ to mutual forbearance, fairness, and good will. Give the spirit of grace and of a sound mind to all in places of authority. Bless all those who labor in works of mercy and schools of good learning. Care for all aged persons, and all little children, the sick and the afflicted, and those who travel by land, by sea, or by air. Remember all who by reason of weakness are overtasked, or because of poverty are forgotten. Let the sorrowful sighing of the prisoners come before thee, and according to the greatness of thy power preserve thou those that draw nigh unto death. Give ear unto our prayer, O merciful and gracious Father, for the love of thy dear Son, our Saviour Jesus Christ. Amen.

General Thanksgiving

Almighty God, Father of all mercies, we thine unworthy servants do give thee most humble and hearty thanks for all thy goodness and lovingkindness to us, and to all men. We bless thee for our creation, preservation, and all the blessings of this life; but above all for thine inestimable love in the redemption of the world by our Lord Jesus Christ, for the means of grace, and for the hope of glory. And we beseech thee, give us that due sense of all thy mercies, that our hearts may be unfeignedly thankful, and that we may show forth thy praise, not only with our lips, but in our lives, by giving up ourselves to thy service, and by walking before thee in holiness and righteousness all our days; through Jesus Christ our Lord, to whom, with thee and the Holy Spirit, be all honor and glory, world without end. Amen.

For the Church

O God, we pray for thy Church, which is set today amid the perplexities of a changing order, face to face with a great new task. We remember with love the nurture she gave to our spiritual life in its infancy, the tasks she set for our growing strength, the influence of the devoted hearts she gathers, the steadfast power for good she has exerted. When we compare her with all human institutions, we rejoice, for there is none like her. But when we judge her by the mind of her Master, we bow in contrition. Oh, baptize her afresh in the life-giving spirit of Jesus! Put upon her lips the ancient gospel of her Lord. Fill her with the prophets' scorn of tyranny, and with a Christlike tenderness for the heavy-laden and downtrodden. Bid her cease from seeking her own life, lest she lose it. Make her valiant to give up her life to humanity, that, like her crucified Lord, she may mount the path of the cross to a higher glory. Amen.

For the Unity of the Church

Almighty and most merciful God, our heavenly Father; we confess that we have grievously sinned against thee in thought, in word, and in deed. We have come short of thy glory; we have broken the unity of thy holy Church; and we have turned every one of us aside from the way of life. Yet do thou, O most merciful Father, hear us when we call upon thee with penitent hearts. Pardon our sins, and grant us thy peace. Confirm us in all goodness, that we may serve thee with a quiet mind; and bring us to the life everlasting; through Jesus Christ our Lord. Amen.

For Missions

O Thou who art the light and the life of the world, have compassion, we pray thee, upon those who are sitting in darkness and in the shadow of death; and, as thou didst at the first, by the preaching of thine apostles, cause the light of thy gospel to shine throughout the world, be pleased to make thy ways known upon earth, thy saving health unto all nations. Bless thy servants who have gone into hard fields and unto distant lands to proclaim the message of salvation. Endue them with thy Holy Spirit, enrich them with thy heavenly grace, prosper them in all their labors, and give them souls as their reward. And, O thou Lord of the harvest, we pray thee to send forth more laborers into thy harvest. May they both sow the seed and reap the fruit of their labors! And give us grace to do our part in the great field of this world in sowing and in reaping; through the grace of Jesus Christ. Amen.

For Evangelism

Increase, O God, the faith and the zeal of all thy people, that they may more earnestly desire, and more diligently seek, the salvation of their fellow men, through the message of thy love in Jesus Christ our Lord. Send forth a mighty call unto thy servants who labor in the gospel, granting unto them a heart of love, sincerity of speech, and the power of the Holy Spirit, that they may be able to persuade men to forsake sin and return unto thee. And so bless and favor the work of thine evangelists, that multitudes may be brought from the kingdom of evil into the Kingdom of thy dear Son, our Saviour Jesus Christ. Amen.

For Social Service

O Lord, our heavenly Father, who by thy blessed Son hast taught us that thou art love; we beseech thee graciously to bless all those who, following his steps, give themselves to the service of their fellow men. Grant unto them clear vision to perceive those things which in our social order are amiss; give them true judgment, courage, and perseverance to help those that suffer wrong, and endue them with unfailing love to minister to the poor, the suffering, and the friendless. Make us sensible of our union one with another as thy children, that we may strive wisely to order all things among us according to thy will; for the sake of him who laid down his own life for us, thy Son our Saviour Jesus Christ. Amen.

For the President and Others in Authority

O God, who art the hope of all the ends of the earth; remember us in love, and guide us by thine infinite wisdom. Most heartily we beseech thee to grant thy blessing upon thy servants, the President of the United States, the Governor of this state, and all others in authority. Imbue them with the spirit of wisdom, goodness, and truth; and so rule their hearts, and bless their endeavors, that law and order, justice and peace, may everywhere prevail, to the honor of thy holy name; through Jesus Christ our Lord. Amen.

For the Country

Almighty God, who in the former time didst lead our fathers forth into a wealthy place; give thy grace, we humbly beseech thee, to us their children, that we may always approve ourselves a people mindful of thy favor, and glad to do thy will. Bless our land with honorable industry, sound learning, and pure religion. Defend our liberties; preserve our unity. Save us from violence, discord, and confusion, from pride and arrogance, and from every evil way. Fashion into one happy people the multitudes brought hither out of many kindreds and tongues. Endue with the spirit of wisdom those whom we entrust in thy name with the authority of governance, to the end that there be peace at home, and that we keep a place among the nations of the earth. In the time of prosperity fill our hearts with thankfulness, and in the day of trouble suffer not our trust in thee to fail; all of which we ask for Jesus Christ's sake. Amen.

Grant us peace, thy most precious gift, O thou eternal source of peace. Bless our country, that it may ever be a stronghold of peace, and the advocate of peace in the councils of nations. May contentment reign within its borders, health and happiness within its homes. Strengthen the bonds of friendship and fellowship between all the inhabitants of our land. Plant virtue in every soul; and may the love of thy name hallow every home and every heart. Praised be thou, O Lord, giver of peace. Amen.

AFFIRMATIONS OF FAITH

Introduction to an Affirmation of Faith

Where the Spirit of the Lord is, there is the one true Church, apostolic and universal, whose holy faith let us now reverently and sincerely declare.

The Apostles' Creed

I believe in God the Father Almighty, Maker of heaven and earth; and in Jesus Christ his only Son our Lord; who was conceived by the Holy Spirit, born of the Virgin Mary, suffered under Pontius Pilate, was crucified, dead, and buried; the third day he rose from the dead; he ascended into heaven, and sitteth at the right hand of God the Father Almighty; from thence he shall come to judge the quick and the dead. I believe in the Holy Spirit, the holy catholic Church, the communion of saints, the forgiveness of sins, the resurrection of the body, and the life everlasting. Amen.

or

I believe in God the Father Almighty, Maker of heaven and earth; and in Jesus Christ his only Son our Lord; who was conceived by the Holy Ghost, born of the Virgin Mary, suffered under Pontius Pilate, was crucified, dead, and buried; the third day he rose again from the dead; he ascended into heaven, and sitteth at the right hand of God the Father Almighty; from thence he shall come to judge the quick and the dead. I believe in the Holy Ghost, the holy catholic Church, the communion of saints, the forgiveness of sins, the resurrection of the body, and the life everlasting. Amen.

The Nicene Creed

I believe in one God the Father Almighty, Maker of heaven and earth, and of all things visible and invisible:

And in one Lord Jesus Christ, the only-begotten Son of God, begotten of his Father before all worlds, God of God, Light of Light, very God of very God, begotten, not made, being of one substance with the Father, by whom all things were made; who for us men and for our salvation came down from heaven, and was incarnate by the Holy Ghost of the Virgin Mary, and was made man, and was crucified also for us under Pontius Pilate; he suffered and was buried, and the third day he rose again according to the Scriptures, and ascended into heaven, and sitteth on the right hand of the Father; and he shall come again with glory, to judge both the quick and the dead, whose kingdom shall have no end.

And I believe in the Holy Ghost, the Lord and Giver of life, who proceedeth from the Father and the Son, who with the Father and the Son together is worshiped and glorified, who spake by the prophets. And I believe one catholic and apostolic Church. I acknowledge one baptism for the remission of sins. And I look for the resurrection of the dead, and the life of the world to come. Amen.

A Modern Affirmation

We believe in God the Father, infinite in wisdom, power, and love, whose mercy is over all his works, and whose will is ever directed to his children's good.

We believe in Jesus Christ, Son of God and Son of man, the gift of the Father's unfailing grace, the ground of our hope, and the promise of our deliverance from sin and death.

We believe in the Holy Spirit as the divine presence in our lives, whereby we are kept in perpetual remembrance of the truth of Christ, and find strength and help in time of need.

We believe that this faith should manifest itself in the service of love as set forth in the example of our blessed Lord, to the end that the Kingdom of God may come upon the earth. Amen.

The Korean Creed

We believe in the one God, Maker and Ruler of all things, Father of all men, the source of all goodness and beauty, all truth and love.

We believe in Jesus Christ, God manifest in the flesh, our teacher, example, and redeemer, the Saviour of the world.

We believe in the Holy Spirit, God present with us for guidance, for comfort, and for strength.

We believe in the forgiveness of sins, in the life of love and prayer, and in grace equal to every need.

We believe in the Word of God contained in the Old and New Testaments as the sufficient rule both of faith and of practice.

We believe in the Church as the fellowship for worship and for service of all who are united to the living Lord.

We believe in the Kingdom of God as the divine rule in human society, and in the brotherhood of man under the fatherhood of God.

We believe in the final triumph of righteousness, and in the life everlasting. Amen.

A Creed in the Words of St. John

We believe that God is Spirit, and they that worship him must worship him in spirit and in truth.

We believe that God is Light, and that if we walk in the light, as he is in the light, we have fellowship one with another.

We believe that God is Love, and that everyone that loveth is born of God and knoweth God.

We believe that Jesus Christ is the Son of God, and that God hath given to us eternal life, and this life is in his Son.

We believe that he is the Resurrection and the Life, and that whosoever believeth on him, though he were dead, yet shall he live.

We believe that we are children of God, and that he hath given us of his Spirit.

We believe that if we confess our sins, he is faithful and just to forgive us our sins, and to cleanse us from all uncleanness.

We believe that the world passeth away and the lust thereof, but he that doeth the will of God abideth forever. Amen.

OFFERTORY SENTENCES AND PRAYERS

All things come of thee, O Lord, and of thine own have we given thee. Amen.

> We give thee but thine own,
>   Whate'er the gift may be;
> All that we have is thine alone,
>   A trust, O Lord, from thee. Amen.

Bless thou the gifts our hands have brought;
  Bless thou the work our hearts have planned;
Ours is the faith, the will, the thought;
  The rest, O God, is in thy hand. Amen.

All things are thine; no gift have we,
Lord of all gifts, to offer thee;
And hence with grateful hearts today,
Thine own before thy feet we lay. Amen.

Praise God, from whom all blessings flow;
Praise him, all creatures here below;
Praise him above, ye heavenly host:
Praise Father, Son, and Holy Ghost. Amen.

Accept, O Lord, these offerings thy people make unto thee, and grant that the cause to which they are devoted may prosper under thy guidance, to the glory of thy name; through Jesus Christ our Lord. Amen.

Accept these offerings, we beseech thee, O Lord, and mercifully direct and enable us by thy Holy Spirit, that all things which we do in thy name may be truly wrought in thee; through Jesus Christ our Lord. Amen.

Heavenly Father, giver of all good things, who hast taught us that it is more blessed to give than to receive; we dedicate these our offerings to the service of thy Church, humbly beseeching thee that all our gifts and energies may be consecrated to the extension of thy Kingdom on earth; through Jesus Christ our Lord. Amen.

O God, most merciful and gracious, of whose bounty we have all received; accept this offering of thy people. Remember in thy love those who have brought it, and those for whom it is given, and so follow it with thy blessing that it may promote peace and good will among men, and advance the Kingdom of our Lord and Saviour Jesus Christ. Amen.

Thine, O LORD, is the greatness, and the power, and the glory, and the victory, and the majesty: for all that is in the heaven and in the earth is thine; thine is the kingdom, O LORD, and thou art exalted as head above all. Amen.

RESPONSES

Opening Sentences

The LORD is in his holy temple: let all the earth keep silence before him. Amen.

Father of lights, in whom there is no shadow,
Giver of every good and perfect gift,
With one accord we seek thy holy presence,
Gladly our hearts to thee in praise we lift. Amen.

Jesus, stand among us
In thy risen power;
Let this time of worship
Be a hallowed hour.

Breathe the Holy Spirit
Into every heart;
Bid the fears and sorrows
From each soul depart.

Thus with quickened footsteps
We pursue our way,
Watching for the dawning
Of eternal day. Amen.

Let all mortal flesh keep silence,
And with fear and trembling stand;
Ponder nothing earthly minded,
For with blessing in his hand,
Christ our God to earth descendeth,
Our full homage to demand. Amen.

O worship the LORD in the beauty of holiness: serve him with gladness, all the earth. Amen.

Responses After Prayer

Hear our prayer, O Lord; incline thine ear to us, and grant us thy peace. Amen.

Let the words of my mouth, and the meditation of my heart, be acceptable in thy sight, O LORD, my strength, and my redeemer. Amen.

Almighty Father, hear our prayer, and bless all souls that wait before thee. Amen.

Saviour, hear us, we pray:
Keep us safe through this day;
Keep our lives free from sin
And our hearts pure within.

Jesus, Lord, hear our prayer;
May we rest in thy care.

Be our Guardian and Guide;
May we walk by thy side
Till the evening shades fall
Over us—over all.

Through love to light! O wonderful the way
That leads from darkness to the perfect day;
From darkness and from sorrow of the night
　To morning that comes singing o'er the sea!
　Through love to light! Through light, O God, to thee
Who art the Love of love, th' eternal Light of light. Amen.

　　Hear thou in love, O Lord, our cry,
　　In heaven, thy dwelling place on high. Amen.

Responses After Scripture

Hosanna in the highest!

God be merciful unto us, and bless us; and cause his face to shine upon us; that thy way may be known upon earth, thy saving health among all nations. Amen.

Thy testimonies are very sure: holiness becometh thine house, O LORD, forever. Amen.

O Lord, open thou our eyes, that we may behold wondrous things out of thy law. Amen.

VERSICLES

VERSICLES are commonly used to introduce certain acts of worship.

To Introduce an Anthem
　Minister: O Lord, open thou our lips.
　People: **And our mouth shall show forth thy praise.**
　Minister: Praise ye the Lord.
　People: **The Lord's name be praised.**

To Introduce a Prayer, Intercession, or Litany
　Minister: The Lord be with you.
　People: **And with thy spirit.**

Minister: Let us pray.

Here let the people kneel or be seated and bow in prayer.

Minister: O Lord, show thy mercy upon us.
People: **And grant us thy salvation.**
Minister: O God, make clean our hearts within us.
People: **And take not thy Holy Spirit from us.**

To Introduce a Prayer, Intercession, or Litany

Minister: The Lord be with you.
People: **And with thy spirit.**
Minister: Let us pray.

Here let the people kneel or be seated and bow in prayer.

Minister: O Lord, show thy mercy upon us.
People: **And grant us thy salvation.**
Minister: O Lord, save the nation.
People: **And mercifully hear us when we call upon thee.**
Minister: Endue thy ministers with righteousness.
People: **And make thy chosen people joyful.**
Minister: O Lord, save thy people.
People: **And bless thine inheritance.**
Minister: Give peace in our time, O Lord;
People: **Because there is none other that fighteth for us, but only thou, O God.**
Minister: O God, make clean our hearts within us.
People: **And take not thy Holy Spirit from us.**

To Introduce a Responsive Reading

Minister: O magnify the Lord with me.
People: **And let us exalt his name together.**

Here let the people stand.

Minister: Let the people praise thee, O God.

People: **Yea, let all the people praise thee.**

To Introduce a Prayer

Minister: Glory to God in the highest.

People: **On earth peace, good will toward men.**

Minister: May God order our days and our times in his peace.

People: **May God grant us his peace and eternal life.**

Kyrie Eleison

Minister: Lord, have mercy upon us.

People: **Christ, have mercy upon us.**

Minister: Lord, have mercy upon us.

SALUTATIONS

In the name of the Father, and of the Son, and of the Holy Spirit. Amen.

Peace be to this house, in the name of the Father, and of the Son, and of the Holy Spirit. Amen.

The God of hope fill you with all joy and peace in believing, that ye may abound in hope, through the power of the Holy Spirit. Amen.

Grace be unto you, and peace, from God the Father, and from our Lord Jesus Christ. Amen.

Peace be to this house, and to all that dwell in it. Amen.

ASCRIPTIONS

Thine, O LORD, is the greatness, and the power, and the glory, and the victory, and the majesty: for all that is in the heaven and in the earth is thine; thine is the kingdom, O LORD, and thou art exalted as head above all. Amen.

Now unto him who is able to do exceeding abundantly above all that we ask or think, according to the power that worketh in us, unto him be glory in the Church by Christ Jesus throughout all ages, world without end. Amen.

Now unto the King eternal, immortal, invisible, the only wise God, be honor and glory for ever and ever. Amen.

Now unto the God of all grace, who hath called us unto his eternal glory by Christ Jesus, be glory and dominion for ever and ever. Amen.

Unto him that loved us, and washed us from our sins in his own blood, and hath made us kings and priests unto God and his Father; to him be glory and dominion for ever and ever. Amen.

Blessing, and honor, and glory, and power, be unto him that sitteth upon the throne, and unto the Lamb for ever and ever. Amen.

Now unto him that is able to keep you from falling, and to present you faultless before the presence of his glory with exceeding joy, to the only wise God our Saviour, be glory and majesty, dominion and power, both now and evermore. Amen.

BENEDICTIONS

The grace of the Lord Jesus Christ, and the love of God, and the communion of the Holy Spirit, be with you all. Amen.

The peace of God, which passeth all understanding, keep your hearts and minds in the knowledge and love of God, and of his Son Jesus Christ our Lord; and the blessing of God Almighty, the Father, the Son, and the Holy Spirit, be among you, and remain with you always. Amen.

And now may the blessing of God Almighty, Father, Son, and Holy Spirit, be among you and abide with you, now and evermore. Amen.

The Lord bless you, and keep you: the Lord make his face shine upon you, and be gracious unto you: the Lord lift up his countenance upon you, and give you peace. Amen.

Now the God of peace, that brought again from the dead our Lord Jesus, that great Shepherd of the sheep, through the blood of the everlasting covenant, make you perfect in every good work to do his will, working in you that which is well-pleasing in his sight, through Jesus Christ; to whom be glory for ever and ever. Amen.

Unto God's gracious mercy and protection we commit you; and the blessing of God Almighty, the Father, the Son, and the Holy Spirit, be upon you, and remain with you always. Amen.

PRAYERS FOR USE UPON LEAVING CHURCH

Let the words of our mouths, and the meditations of our hearts be acceptable in thy sight, O Lord, our strength, and our redeemer. Amen.

May that which hath been performed by our humble ministrations be fulfilled by thy effectual power; through Jesus Christ our Lord. Amen.

O most gracious and merciful God, grant that what hath

been done by our devotion and service may be confirmed by thy benediction; through our Lord Jesus Christ. Amen.

Dismiss us now, O Lord, with thy blessing, and accompany us ever with thy grace, that we may henceforth live in peace, love, and holiness; through Jesus Christ our Lord. Amen.

O Lord God, Father Almighty, bless and sanctify this sacrifice of praise which has been offered unto thee to the honor and glory of thy name; through Jesus Christ our Lord. Amen.

Grant, O Lord, that what hath been said with our lips we may believe in our hearts, and that what we believe in our hearts we may practice in our lives; through Jesus Christ our Lord. Amen.

Almighty God, our heavenly Father, grant that the aspirations of mind and heart that have come to us this hour be transformed into a Christlike way of living through the effectual power of the Holy Spirit. Amen.

A Prayer of St. Chrysostom

Almighty God, who hast given us grace, at this time, with one accord to make our common supplications unto thee, and dost promise that, when two or three are gathered together in thy name, thou wilt grant their requests; fulfill now, O Lord, the desires and petitions of thy servants, as may be most expedient for them, granting us in this world knowledge of thy truth, and in the world to come life everlasting. Amen.

The Christian Year[1]

Scripture Sentences, Calls to Worship, and Prayers

ADVENT

Season of Expectancy—Always 4 Sundays

Lift up your heads, O ye gates; and be ye lift up, ye everlasting doors; and the King of glory shall come in.

Prepare ye the way of the LORD, make straight in the desert a highway for our God.

The glory of the LORD shall be revealed, and all flesh shall see it together: for the mouth of the LORD hath spoken it.

For God, who commanded the light to shine out of darkness, hath shined in our hearts, to give the light of the knowledge of the glory of God in the face of Jesus Christ.

And it shall be said in that day, Lo, this is our God; we have waited for him, and he will save us; this is the LORD; we have waited for him, we will be glad and rejoice in his salvation.

Sing and rejoice, O daughter of Zion: for lo, I come, and I will dwell in the midst of thee, saith the LORD. And many nations shall be joined to the LORD in that day, and shall be my people: and I will dwell in the midst of thee, and thou shalt know that the LORD of hosts hath sent me unto thee.

Now it is high time to awake out of sleep: for now is our salvation nearer than when we believed. The night is far spent, the day is at hand: let us therefore cast off the works of darkness, and let us put on the armor of light.

[1] For a calendar of the Christian Year see pages 209-12.

CALLS TO WORSHIP

Minister: Praise be to God

People: **Blessed be the Lord God; for he hath visited and redeemed his people.**

Minister: Blessed is he that cometh in the name of the Lord.

People: **Blessed be the name of the Lord. Amen.**

Minister: How beautiful upon the mountains are the feet of him that bringeth good tidings,

People: **That publisheth peace; that bringeth good tidings of good,**

Minister: That publisheth salvation;

People: **That saith unto Zion, Thy God reigneth!**

Minister: The Lord is in his holy temple.

People: **Let all the earth keep silence before him.**

Minister: Be still, and know that I am God.

People: **I will be exalted among the nations, I will be exalted in the earth. Amen.**

Minister: Sing unto the Lord a new song, and his praise from the end of the earth.

People: **Show us thy mercy, O Lord, and grant us thy salvation.**

Minister: The Lord is nigh unto all them that call upon him in truth.

People: **O Lord, thou art our help and our deliverer: we bow down and worship thee. Amen.**

PRAYERS AND COLLECTS

Almighty God, who in thy providence hast made all ages a preparation for the kingdom of thy Son; we beseech thee to make ready our hearts for the brightness of thy glory and the fullness of thy blessing in Jesus Christ our Lord. Amen.

O Thou who art the source of all existence and the light of all seeing; we remember with joy and awe that the world is thy creation, and that life is thy gift. Uplift our thoughts from the littleness of our own works to the greatness, the majesty, and the wonder of thine, and teach us so to behold thy glory that we may grow into thy likeness; through Jesus Christ our Lord. Amen.

O God, who in the days of old didst make thyself known to prophets and poets, and in the fullness of time didst reveal thyself in thy Son Jesus Christ; help us so to meditate upon the revelation of thyself which thou hast given, that thy constant love may become known to us, and we may feel thy presence always with us; through the same Jesus Christ our Lord. Amen.

O God, who hast taught us that the night is far spent and the day is at hand; grant that we may ever be found watching for the coming of thy Son; save us from undue love of the world, that we may wait with patient hope for the day of the Lord, and so abide in him that, when he shall appear, we may not be ashamed; through Jesus Christ our Lord. Amen.

O God, who hast set before us the great hope that thy Kingdom shall come on earth, and hast taught us to pray for its coming; make us ever ready to thank thee for the signs of its dawning, and to pray and work for that perfect day when thy will shall be done on earth as it is in heaven; through Jesus Christ our Lord. Amen.

Most merciful God, who so loved the world as to give thine only-begotten Son, that whosoever believeth in him should not perish, but have everlasting life; grant unto us, we humbly pray thee, the precious gift of faith, whereby we may know that the Son of God is come, and may have power to overcome the world and gain a blessed immortality; through Jesus Christ our Lord. Amen.

O God, who hast made of one blood all nations of men for to dwell on the face of the earth, and didst send thy blessed Son Jesus Christ to preach peace to them that are afar off and to them that are nigh; grant that all the peoples of the world may feel after thee and find thee; and hasten, O Lord, the fulfillment of thy promise to pour out thy Spirit upon all flesh; through Jesus Christ our Lord. Amen.

Bible Sunday

O Lord God, heavenly Father, we beseech thee so to rule and guide us by thy Holy Spirit, that we may hear and receive thy holy word with our whole heart, in order that through thy word we also may be sanctified, and may learn to place all our trust and hope in Jesus Christ thy Son, and following him may be led safely through all evil, until through thy grace we come to everlasting life; through the same Jesus Christ thy Son our Lord. Amen.

Blessed Lord, who hast caused all holy Scriptures to be written for our learning; grant that we may in such wise hear them, read, mark, learn, and inwardly digest them, that by patience, and comfort of thy holy Word, we may embrace and ever hold fast the blessed hope of everlasting life, which thou hast given us in our Saviour Jesus Christ. Amen.

CHRISTMASTIDE

Season of the Nativity—Usually 2 Sundays

SCRIPTURE SENTENCES

The grace of God that bringeth salvation hath appeared to all men.

God so loved the world, that he gave his only-begotten Son, that whosoever believeth in him should not perish, but have everlasting life.

Thanks be unto God for his unspeakable gift.

Behold, I bring you good tidings of great joy, which shall be to all people. For unto you is born this day in the city of David a Saviour, which is Christ the Lord.

Glory to God in the highest, and on earth peace, good will toward men.

In the beginning was the Word, and the Word was with God, and the Word was God. And the Word was made flesh, and dwelt among us, full of grace and truth.

CALLS TO WORSHIP

Minister: Behold, I bring you good tidings of great joy, which shall be to all people. For unto you is born a Saviour, which is Christ the Lord.

People: **This child is set for the fall and rising again of many.**

Minister: Let us with wise men, lowly shepherds, and all the heavenly host, worship the holy Babe.

People: **O come, let us adore him, Christ the Lord. Amen.**

Minister: The Lord hath made known his salvation.

People: **His righteousness hath he openly showed in the sight of the nations.**

Minister: Light shall shine out of darkness; he hath shined in our hearts.

People: **We have the light of the knowledge of the glory of God in the face of Jesus Christ. Amen.**

PRAYERS AND COLLECTS

O God our Father, who hast brought us again to the glad season when we commemorate the birth of thy Son Jesus Christ our Lord; grant that his Spirit may be born anew in our hearts this day and that we may joyfully welcome him to reign over us. Open our ears that we may hear again the angelic chorus of old; open our lips that we too may sing with uplifted hearts, Glory to God in the highest, and on earth peace, good will toward men. Amen.

O Father, who hast declared thy love to men by the birth of the holy Child at Bethlehem; help us to welcome him with gladness and to make room for him in our common days, so that we may live at peace with one another and in good will with all thy family; through Jesus Christ our Lord. Amen.

Eternal Father, who by the birth of thy beloved Son Jesus Christ didst give thyself to mankind; grant that, being born in our hearts, he may save us from all our sins, and restore within us the image and likeness of our Creator, to whom be everlasting praise and glory, world without end. Amen.

O Lord God, whose chosen dwelling is the heart of the lowly; we give thee thanks that thou didst reveal thyself in the holy Child Jesus, and that all childhood has been sanctified in him. We beseech thee to make us humble in faith and love, that we may know the joy of the gospel that is hidden from the wise and prudent and revealed unto babes. And this we ask in his name, who, wearing our mortal flesh, grew in wisdom and in favor with God and man. Amen.

O God, who hast given us grace at this time to celebrate the birth of our Saviour Jesus Christ; we laud and magnify thy glorious name for the countless blessings which he hath brought unto us, and we beseech thee to grant that we may ever set forth thy praise in joyful obedience to thy will; through the same Jesus Christ our Lord. Amen.

O Lord our God, most merciful and mighty; fill our hearts with joy and our tongues with praise as this day we keep the festival of our Saviour's birth. Let the Holy Spirit come upon us as we approach the mystery of his appearing in the flesh of a little child. Stir up in our hearts the precious gift of faith, that he may be born anew in us, and that his presence may shed abroad in our hearts the light of heavenly joy and peace. Grant this, O God, we beseech thee, for the love of Christ thy Son, our only Saviour. Amen.

The Closing Year: Watch Night

SCRIPTURE SENTENCES

LORD, thou hast been our dwelling place in all generations. Even from everlasting to everlasting, thou art God.

The heavens shall perish, but thou shalt endure: yea, all of them shall wax old like a garment; as a vesture shalt thou change them, and they shall be changed: but thou art the same, and thy years shall have no end.

Beloved, be not ignorant of this one thing, that one day is with the Lord as a thousand years, and a thousand years as one day.

God will be our guide even unto death.

Let the beauty of the LORD our God be upon us: and establish thou the work of our hands upon us; yea, the work of our hands establish thou it.

CALL TO WORSHIP

Minister: The Lord hath been mindful of us: and he will bestow his mercy upon us.

People: **He will bless them that fear the Lord, both small and great.**

Minister: Oh that men would praise the LORD for his goodness,

People: And for his wonderful works to the children of men! Amen.

PRAYERS AND COLLECTS

O Almighty God, our refuge and strength; keep us, we beseech thee, under thy watchful providence during the coming year. Protect our country, guard our homes, and sanctify our lives. So guide our hearts, we pray thee, that we may use and not abuse the liberty wherewith thy Son Jesus Christ hath made us free. In times of prosperity kindle in us a spirit of grateful service; and in adversity endue us with courage, faith, and sympathy for others. May truth, purity, and charity dwell among us this year and from generation to generation. Hasten, Lord, we pray thee, the coming of thy kingdom on this earth; through Jesus Christ our Lord. Amen.

Almighty God, who hast been the dwelling place of thy people in all generations, and who in thy mercy hast brought us to the close of another year; we praise thee for all the way by which thou hast led us, and we humbly beseech thee to continue to us thy lovingkindness. Help us to cast our weakness on thy strength, that amid all the changes of time we may rest ourselves on thy unchanging love; through Jesus Christ our Lord. Amen.

Father, as the old year ends and the new year begins, forgive us for the failures of the vanished days, and bless us in whatever we have truly striven for in days that do not die. Keep us from vain regrets, and let us face forward in the light of the best that we have learned. Purge our hearts both of shallow self-confidence and of cowardly fears, so that we may know that without thee we can do nothing, but that in thee all things are possible; through Jesus Christ our Lord. Amen.

The Opening Year

He that sat upon the throne said, Behold, I make all things new.

Be strong and of a good courage.

Behold, I have set before thee an open door, and no man can shut it.

So teach us to number our days, that we may apply our hearts unto wisdom.

Cast away from you all your transgressions, whereby ye have transgressed; and make you a new heart and a new spirit.

I will be with thee: I will not fail thee, nor forsake thee.

Minister: O sing unto the Lord a new song: sing unto the Lord, all the earth.

People: **Sing unto the Lord, bless his name; show forth his salvation from day to day.**

Minister: Declare his glory among the nations, his wonders among all people.

People: **Honor and majesty are before him; strength and beauty are in his sanctuary. Amen.**

Minister: He that sat upon the throne said, Behold, I make all things new.

People: **Our help is in the name of the Lord, who made heaven and earth.**

Minister: Days should speak, and multitude of years should teach wisdom.

People: **The counsel of the Lord standeth forever, the thoughts of his heart to all generations. Amen.**

PRAYERS AND COLLECTS

O thou eternal Father, who art ever the same; grant us so to pass through the coming year with faithful hearts that we may be able in all things to please thee; through Jesus Christ our Lord. Amen.

O Almighty God, who alone art without variableness or shadow of turning, and hast safely brought us through the changes of time to the beginning of another year; we beseech thee to pardon the sins we have committed in the year which is past, and to give us grace that we may spend the remainder of our days to thy honor and glory; through Jesus Christ our Lord. Amen.

Eternal God, who makest all things new, and abidest forever the same; grant us to begin this year in thy faith, and to continue it in thy favor; that, being guided in all our doings and guarded all our days, we may spend our lives in thy service, and finally by thy grace attain the glory of everlasting life; through Jesus Christ our Lord. Amen.

EPIPHANY

Season of the Evangel—From 4 to 9 Sundays

SCRIPTURE SENTENCES

Nations shall come to thy light, and kings to the brightness of thy rising. They shall bring gold and incense; and they shall show forth the praises of the LORD.

The LORD hath made known his salvation; his righteousness hath he openly showed in the sight of the nations.

We have also a more sure word of prophecy; whereunto ye do well that ye take heed, as unto a light that shineth in a dark place, until the day dawn, and the day star arise in your hearts.

Arise, shine; for thy light is come, and the glory of the LORD is risen upon thee. Nations shall come to thy light, and kings to the brightness of thy rising.

And they shall come from the east, and from the west, and from the north and from the south, and shall sit down in the kingdom of God.

Other sheep I have, which are not of this fold: them also I must bring, and they shall hear my voice; and there shall be one fold, and one shepherd.

Then saith he unto his disciples, The harvest truly is plenteous, but the laborers are few; pray ye therefore the Lord of the harvest, that he will send forth laborers into his harvest.

CALLS TO WORSHIP

Minister: O magnify the Lord with me, and let us exalt his name together.

People: **With him is the fountain of life; in his light shall we see light.**

Minister: Light is sown for the righteous, and gladness for the upright in heart.

People: **From the rising of the sun unto the going down of the same the Lord's name is to be praised. Amen.**

Minister: It is good that a man should both hope and quietly wait for the salvation of the Lord.

People: **The secret of the Lord is with them that fear him; and he will show them his covenant.**

Minister: God is our refuge and strength, a very present help in trouble.

People: **We will lift up our voices in praise unto God, our strength and our redeemer. Amen.**

Minister: Blessed be the name of God, for ever and ever: for wisdom and might are his.

People: **He giveth wisdom unto the wise, and knowledge to them that know understanding.**

Minister: Seek ye the Lord while he may be found, call ye upon him while he is near.

People: **For great is the Lord, and greatly to be praised. Amen.**

Minister: The Lord is nigh unto all them that call upon him.

People: **He will fulfill the desire of them that fear him.**

Minister: The Lord hath made known his salvation.

People: **Our help is in the name of the Lord. Amen.**

Minister: Praise waiteth for thee, O God, and unto thee shall a vow be performed.

People: **I was glad when they said unto me, Let us go into the house of the Lord.**

Minister: Enter into his gates with thanksgiving, and into his courts with praise.

People: **For the Lord is good; his mercy is everlasting; and his truth endureth to all generations. Amen.**

Minister: The law of the Lord is perfect, converting the soul.

People: **The testimony of the Lord is sure, making wise the simple.**

Minister: The statutes of the Lord are right, rejoicing the heart.

People: **The commandment of the Lord is pure, enlightening the eyes. Amen.**

Minister: O Lord, open thou our eyes,

People: **That we may see the beauty of goodness.**

Minister: O Lord, open thou our ears,

People: **That we may hear the appeal of truth.**

Minister: O Lord, open thou our lips.

People: **And our mouth shall show forth thy praise. Amen.**

Minister: God is light, and in him is no darkness at all.

People: **Send out thy light and thy truth; let them lead me.**

Minister: Sing unto the Lord, all the earth; show forth his salvation from day to day.

People: **Declare his glory among the nations, his marvelous works among all peoples. Amen.**

Minister: How shall we be able to magnify the Lord? for he is great above all his works.

People: **The Lord is very great, and marvelous is his power.**

Minister: When ye glorify the Lord, put forth all your strength, and be not weary.

People: **For the Lord hath made all things; and to the godly hath he given wisdom. Amen.**

PRAYERS AND COLLECTS

O Thou who art the true sun of the world, ever rising, and never going down, who by thy most wholesome appearing and light dost nourish and make joyful all things in heaven and in earth; we beseech thee mercifully to shine into our hearts, that the night and darkness of sin and the mists of error on every side may be driven away, and that all our life long we may walk without stumbling as children of the light and the day. Amen.

Everlasting Father, the radiance of faithful souls, who didst bring the nations to thy light and kings to the brightness of thy rising; fill, we beseech thee, the world with thy glory, and show thyself unto all the nations; through him who is the true light and the bright and morning star, Jesus Christ thy Son our Lord. Amen.

O God, whose blessed Son came not to do his own will but thine alone; open our hearts to every call from thee, and over all worldly fears let thy plans for us prevail, that in full surrender to thy purpose we may find our reward as the ministers of thy grace and the messengers of thy love; through Jesus Christ our Lord. Amen.

O our God, we believe in thee, we hope in thee, and we love thee because thou hast created us, redeemed us, and dost sanctify us. Increase our faith, strengthen our hope, and deepen our love, that, giving ourselves up wholly to thy will, we may serve thee faithfully all the rest of our life. And we pray that finally we may be found worthy through thy grace to inherit life eternal; through Jesus Christ our Lord. Amen.

Teach us, gracious God, to serve thee as thou deservest, to give and not to count the cost, to fight and not to heed the wounds, to toil and not to seek for rest, to labor and not to ask for any reward, save that of knowing that we do thy will; through Jesus Christ our Lord. Amen.

Almighty God, from whom every good prayer cometh, and who pourest out on all who desire it the spirit of grace and supplication; deliver us, when we draw nigh to thee, from coldness of heart and wanderings of mind; that with steadfast thoughts, and kindled affections, we may worship thee in spirit and in truth; through Jesus Christ our Lord. Amen.

O Thou who didst command thine apostles to go into all the world, and to preach the gospel to every creature; let thy name be great among the nations from the rising up of the sun unto the going down of the same. Amen.

O Lord, who hast taught us that all our doings without charity are nothing worth; send thy Holy Spirit, and pour into our hearts that most excellent gift of charity, the very bond of peace and of all virtues, without which whosoever liveth is counted dead before thee. Grant this for thine only Son Jesus Christ's sake. Amen.

O Almighty God, who hast built thy Church upon the foundation of the apostles and prophets, Jesus Christ himself being the head cornerstone; grant us so to be joined together in unity of spirit by their doctrine, that we may be made a holy temple acceptable unto thee; through the same Jesus Christ our Lord. Amen.

We beseech thee, O God, to pour thy holy light into our souls, that we may ever be devoted to thee, by whose unsearchable wisdom we were created, and by whose loving providence we are governed; through Jesus Christ our Lord. Amen.

O God our Father, give to the Church a new vision and a new charity, new wisdom and fresh understanding, the revival of her brightness and the renewal of her unity; that the eternal message of thy Son, undefiled by the traditions of men, may be hailed as the good news of the new age; through him who maketh all things new, Jesus Christ our Lord. Amen.

O God our heavenly Father, who didst manifest thy love by sending thine only-begotten Son into the world that all might live through him; pour thy Spirit upon thy Church, that it may fulfill his command to preach the gospel to every creature; send forth, we beseech thee, laborers into thy harvest; defend them in all dangers and temptations; give them grace to bear faithful witness unto thee; endue them with zeal and love, that they may turn many to righteousness; through the same thy Son Jesus Christ our Lord. Amen.

O God, who willest that all men should be saved and come to the knowledge of the truth; prosper, we pray thee, our brethren who labor in distant lands [especially those for whom our prayers are desired]. Protect them in all perils by land and sea; support them in loneliness and in the hour of trial; give them grace to bear faithful witness unto thee; and endue them with burning zeal and love, that they may turn many to righteousness, and finally obtain a crown of glory; through Jesus Christ our Lord. Amen.

Missionary Day

Almighty God our heavenly Father, who through thy Son Jesus Christ hast given commandment unto thy people to go into all the world and preach the gospel to every creature; grant us a ready will to obey thy word; and as we have entered into the labors of other men, help us to serve thee, that others may enter into our labors, and that we with them, and they with us, may attain unto everlasting life; through the same Jesus Christ thy Son our Lord. Amen.

Race Relations Day

Almighty and everliving God, who hast made of one blood all nations of men for to dwell on all the face of the earth, and hast taught us by thy holy prophets that thou art our Father and all men our brethren; move upon the heart of thy Church, we beseech thee, that it may obey thy high command to proclaim the gospel of Jesus to every race and nation, until all peoples shall hear the wonders of thy love for the children of men; through Jesus Christ our Lord. Amen.

Lord of the nations, who in Christ hast broken down the wall of partition between Jew and Gentile, bond and free; unite the people of different races in bonds of true brotherhood, that East and West, North and South, made one in thee, may together labor for the bringing in of thy kingdom of righteousness and peace; through Jesus Christ our Lord. Amen.

Day of Prayer for Students

O thou only wise God, in whom are all the treasures of wisdom and knowledge; we beseech thee to illuminate all universities, colleges, and schools with the light that cometh from above, that those who teach may be taught of thee, and those who learn may be led by thy Spirit, and by the increase of knowledge thy truth may be confirmed, and thy glory manifested; through Jesus Christ the living Word. Amen.

O God, who didst reveal thy Son Jesus Christ to wise men of old; grant us to welcome the revelation of wisdom and science through which in our own day thou dost make thy works known among men. Reveal thyself again to men of learning, that through their work the world may come to know thee anew, and may offer new gifts and treasures to the glory of thy name, who art evermore revealed in thy Son Jesus Christ our Lord. Amen.

Brotherhood Day

O God, we pray for thy Church, which is set today amid the perplexities of a changing order, and face to face with a great new task. Baptize her afresh in the life-giving spirit of Jesus. Put upon her lips the ancient gospel of her Lord. Fill her with the prophets' scorn of tyranny, and with a Christlike tenderness for the heavy-laden and downtrodden. Bid her cease from seeking her own life, lest she lose it. Make her valiant to mount by the path of the cross to a higher glory; through Christ the Lord. Amen.

LENT AND HOLY WEEK

Season of Penitence and Renewal—Always 6 Sundays

SCRIPTURE SENTENCES

Come ye, and let us walk in the light of the Lord. He will teach us of his ways, and we will walk in his paths.

Draw nigh to God, and he will draw nigh to you. Humble yourselves in the sight of the Lord, and he shall lift you up.

Rend your heart and not your garments, and turn unto the Lord your God: for he is gracious and merciful, slow to anger, and of great kindness.

In returning and rest shall ye be saved; in quietness and in confidence shall be your strength.

Watch and pray, that ye enter not into temptation: the spirit indeed is willing, but the flesh is weak.

Beloved, let us cleanse ourselves from all filthiness of the flesh and spirit, perfecting holiness in the fear of God.

Let thy mind be upon the ordinances of the Lord, and meditate continually in his commandments: he shall establish thine heart, and give thee wisdom at thine own desire.

How great is the lovingkindness of the Lord our God, and his compassion unto such as turn unto him in holiness!

For thus saith the high and lofty One that inhabiteth eternity, whose name is Holy; I dwell in the high and holy place, with him also that is of a contrite and humble spirit, to revive the spirit of the humble, and to revive the heart of the contrite ones.

CALLS TO WORSHIP

Minister: Let us search and try our ways, and turn again to the Lord.

People: **God shall bless us; and all the ends of the earth shall fear him.**

Minister: Seek ye the Lord while he may be found, call ye upon him while he is near: let the wicked forsake his way and the unrighteous man his thoughts: and let him return unto the Lord.

People: **The sacrifices of God are a broken spirit: a broken and a contrite heart he will not despise. Amen.**

Minister: O magnify the Lord with me, and let us exalt his name together.

People: **Blessed be the Lord God, who only doeth wondrous things. Blessed be his glorious name forever; and let the whole earth be filled with his glory.**

Minister: Come and let us return unto the Lord; and we shall live in his sight.

People: **Behold, the tabernacle of God is with men, and he will dwell with them, and they shall be his people, and God himself shall be with them, and be their God. Amen.**

Minister: The Lord is merciful and gracious, slow to anger, and plenteous in mercy.

People: **He hath not dealt with us after our sins; nor rewarded us according to our iniquities.**

Minister: What shall we render unto the Lord for all his benefits toward us?

People: **We will take the cup of salvation, and call upon the name of the Lord. Amen.**

Minister: Draw nigh to God, and he will draw nigh to you.

People: **The Lord is nigh unto all them that call upon him, to all that call upon him in truth.**

Minister: Let not mercy and truth forsake thee; write them upon the table of thine heart.

People: **God is light, and in him is no darkness at all. If we walk in the light, we have fellowship one with another. Amen.**

Minister: O magnify the Lord with me, and let us exalt his name together.

People: **Our help is in the name of the Lord, who made heaven and earth.**

Minister: Let us lift up our hearts with our voices unto God our Father.

People: **We lift them up unto God, our strength and our redeemer. Amen.**

PRAYERS AND COLLECTS

Almighty and everlasting God, who hatest nothing that thou hast made, and dost forgive the sins of all those who are penitent; create and make in us new and contrite hearts, that we, truly lamenting our sins and acknowledging our wickedness, may obtain of thee, the God of all mercy, perfect remission and forgiveness; through Jesus Christ our Lord. Amen.

O God, who by thy Word dost marvelously work out the reconciliation of mankind; grant, we beseech thee, that following the example of our blessed Lord, and walking in such a way as thou dost choose, we may be subjected to thee with all our hearts, and united to each other in holy love; through Jesus Christ our Lord. Amen.

O God our Father, who hast led us apart from the busy world into the quiet of thy house; grant us grace to worship thee in spirit and in truth, to the comfort of our souls and the upbuilding of every good purpose and holy desire. Enable us to do more perfectly the work to which thou hast called us, that we may not fear the coming of night, when we shall resign into thy hands the tasks which thou hast committed to us. So may we worship thee not with our lips only at this hour, but in word and deed all the days of our lives; through Jesus Christ our Lord. Amen.

Almighty God, who through thy Son dost continually prompt us to conform our wills to thine; grant that we may love the thing which thou desirest for us, and find thy commandments in the purified wishes of our hearts; through Jesus Christ our Lord. Amen.

Grant us, O Lord, in all our ways of life thy help, in all our perplexities of thought thy counsel, in all our dangers of temptations thy protection, and in all our sorrows of heart thy peace; through Jesus Christ our Lord. Amen.

Almighty God, who seest that we have no power of ourselves to help ourselves; keep us, both outwardly in our bodies and inwardly in our souls, that we may be defended from all adversities which may happen to the body, and from all evil thoughts which may hurt the soul; through Jesus Christ our Lord. Amen.

Stewardship Sunday

Almighty God, grant us thy gift of loyalty. For our homes give us love and obedience; for our country, sacrifice and service; for our church, reverence and devotion; and in everything make us true to thee; through thy Son our Saviour Jesus Christ our Lord. Amen.

O God, who in thine infinite love didst send thy Son to bring light to all that are in darkness; fill us with thine own love for men; and, since thou hast entrusted to us both the knowledge of thy truth and the gifts of thy bounty, help us to use them as good stewards, giving liberally, praying instantly, and working diligently, that we may be sharers in bringing all men to thy light and hastening the coming of thy kingdom. Amen.

Passion Sunday

Almighty God, help us when we are tempted that we sin not. Strengthen us, we pray thee, with the power of thy Holy Spirit. Let us never forget that thou art with us, and that both our souls and bodies are thine. Fill us with the love of thee, that we may have strength to persevere in the work which thou hast given to us; through Jesus Christ our Lord. Amen.

O God, to whom alone is known the meaning of the mystery of suffering; we beseech thee in behalf of the many who are afflicted in mind and body. May they have faith to claim the healing of the Great Physician. May those about them continue in that prayer of faith which will save the sick; through Jesus Christ our Lord. Amen.

Palm Sunday

SCRIPTURE SENTENCES

The voice of rejoicing and salvation is in the tabernacles of the righteous.

Blessed is he that cometh in the name of the Lord.

God hath highly exalted him, and given him a name which is above every name.

Behold my servant, whom I uphold; mine elect, in whom my soul delighteth; I have put my spirit upon him.

The kingdoms of this world are become the kingdoms of our Lord, and of his Christ.

CALLS TO WORSHIP

Minister: I was glad when they said unto me, Let us go into the house of the Lord.

People: **Enter into his gates with thanksgiving, and into his courts with praise.**

Minister: Rejoice greatly, O daughter of Zion; shout, O daughter of Jerusalem: behold, thy King cometh unto thee.

People: **He shall have dominion from sea to sea, and from the river unto the ends of the earth. Amen.**

Minister: Rejoice greatly, O daughter of Zion; behold, thy King cometh unto thee.

People: **In his days shall the righteous flourish; and abundance of peace so long as the moon endureth.**

Minister: He shall have dominion also from sea to sea, and from the river unto the ends of the earth.

People: **Blessed be the King that cometh in the name of the Lord; peace in heaven, and glory in the highest. Amen.**

Minister: And the disciples began to rejoice and praise God; saying, Hosanna!

People: **Hosanna to the son of David!**

Minister: Blessed be the King that cometh in the name of the Lord.

People: **Blessed be the kingdom of our father David, that cometh in the name of the Lord.**

Minister: Hosanna!

People: **Hosanna in the highest!**

PRAYERS AND COLLECTS

Our Father, as on this day we keep the special memory of our Redeemer's entry into Jerusalem, so grant, O Lord, that now and ever he may triumph in our hearts. Let the King of grace and glory enter in, and let us lay ourselves and all we are in full and joyful homage before him; through Jesus Christ our Lord. Amen.

O God, we praise thee for the Master, who rode in triumph into the city of his fathers. We thank thee that he came not as a conqueror to destroy, but as a Messiah to save, and that he appealed to human hearts with the glory of love. In the spirit of praise and worship we ask that every knee shall bow, and every tongue confess that Jesus Christ is Lord, to the glory of God the Father. Amen.

Come, O Christ, and reign among us, in love and joy and peace; extend thine empire over human hearts; let the burning vision of thy beauty shine out before the eyes of the world; hasten the consummation of thy kingdom in which love shall be the only king. Amen.

O King of men, Master of our lives, entering into thy glory by the cross, to whom all authority is given, both in heaven and on earth; we acknowledge thy sovereignty over every realm of life. Come, O Lord; enter into thy kingdom; subdue the world by the might of thy love. Amen.

Holy Week

SCRIPTURE SENTENCES

The Spirit itself beareth witness with our spirit, that we are the children of God: and if children, then heirs; heirs of God, and joint heirs with Christ; if so be that we suffer with him, that we may be also glorified together.

Let us run with patience the race that is set before us, looking unto Jesus the author and finisher of our faith; who for the joy that was set before him endured the cross, despising the shame, and is set down at the right hand of the throne of God.

Is it nothing to you, all ye that pass by? behold, and see if there be any sorrow like unto my sorrow.

If any man will come after me, let him deny himself, and take up his cross, and follow me. For whosoever will save his life shall lose it; but whosoever shall lose his life for my sake and the gospel's, the same shall save it.

CALL TO WORSHIP

Minister: Christ his own self bore our sin in his own body on the tree,

People: **That we, being dead to sins, should live unto righteousness. Amen.**

PRAYERS

Monday in Holy Week

Grant, we beseech thee, Almighty God, that we who in so many occasions of adversity, by reason of our frailty, are found wanting, may yet, through the passion and intercession of thine only-begotten Son, be continually refreshed; who liveth and reigneth with thee, in the unity of the Holy Spirit, world without end. Amen.

Tuesday in Holy Week

Almighty, everlasting God, grant us so perfectly to follow the passion of our Lord, that we may obtain the help and pardon of his all-sufficient grace; through him who liveth and reigneth with thee, in the unity of the Holy Spirit, world without end. Amen.

Wednesday in Holy Week

Assist us mercifully with thy help, O Lord God of our salvation, that we may enter with joy upon the meditation of those mighty acts through which thou hast given unto us life and immortality; through Jesus Christ our Lord. Amen.

Thursday in Holy Week, or Maundy Thursday

O God, who by the example of thy Son our Saviour Jesus Christ hast taught us the greatness of true humility, and dost call us to watch with him in his passion; give us grace to serve one another in all lowliness, and to enter into the fellowship of his sufferings; in his name and for his sake. Amen.

Good Friday

Almighty God, we beseech thee graciously to behold this thy family, for which our Lord Jesus Christ was content to be betrayed and given into the hands of wicked men, and to suffer death upon the cross; who now liveth and reigneth with thee and the Holy Spirit, ever one God, world without end. Amen.

Holy Saturday, or Easter Even

Grant us, O Lord, that as we are baptized into the death of thy blessed Son our Saviour Jesus Christ, so by continual mortifying of our corrupt affections we may be buried with him, and that through the grave and gate of death we may pass to our joyful resurrection; for his merits who died, and was buried, and rose again for us, thy Son Jesus Christ our Lord. Amen.

EASTERTIDE

Season of Resurrection—Always 7 Sundays

Easter Day

SCRIPTURE SENTENCES

Christ is risen! Hallelujah!

Now is Christ risen from the dead, and become the first-fruits of them that slept.

Break forth into joy, sing together, ye waste places of Jerusalem: for the LORD hath comforted his people.

CALLS TO WORSHIP

Minister: Sing unto the Lord; for he hath done excellent things!

People: **Sing, O heavens; and be joyful, O earth; for the Lord hath comforted his people.**

Minister: Thanks be to God, who giveth us the victory.

People: **Hallelujah: for the Lord God omnipotent reigneth. The kingdoms of this world are become the kingdoms of our Lord, and of his Christ; and he shall reign for ever and ever. King of kings, and Lord of lords. Hallelujah! Amen.**

Minister: Lift up your hearts.

People: **We lift them up unto the Lord.**

Minister: He is risen.

People: **He is risen indeed.**

Minister: Blessed be the God and Father of our Lord Jesus Christ, who according to his abundant mercy hath begotten us again unto a lively hope by the resurrection of Jesus Christ from the dead.

People: **We have an inheritance incorruptible, and undefiled, and that fadeth not away. Amen.**

PRAYERS AND COLLECTS

O God, who for our redemption didst give thine only-begotten Son to the death of the cross, and by his glorious resurrection hast delivered us from the power of our enemy; grant us so to die daily to sin that we may evermore live with him in the joy of his resurrection; through Jesus Christ our Lord. Amen.

O God, our Father in heaven, we consecrate ourselves anew to thee this Easter Day. Grant us loyalty to thy Church, and gladness in thy service. Fill us with the spirit of reverence and humility that we are permitted to sing thy praises. Keep us in the blessed remembrance that we are thy children and in thy presence, and make us faithful in our duty, and worthier of thy love; through Jesus Christ our Lord. Amen.

Almighty God, who through thine only-begotten Son hast overcome death, and opened unto us the gate of everlasting life; grant us, we beseech thee, that we who celebrate our Lord's resurrection may by the renewing of thy Spirit arise from the death of sin to the life of righteousness; through the same Jesus Christ our Lord. Amen.

Almighty and everlasting God, who didst turn the despair of the disciples into triumph by the resurrection of Christ; give us faith to believe that every good which hath seemed to be overcome by evil, and every love which hath seemed to be buried in darkness and in death, shall rise again to life immortal; through the same Jesus Christ, who liveth with thee for evermore. Amen.

Six Sundays After Easter Day

SCRIPTURE SENTENCES

Sing, O heavens; and be joyful, O earth; and break forth into singing, O mountains: for the LORD hath comforted his people.

The ransomed of the LORD shall return with songs and everlasting joy upon their heads; they shall obtain joy and gladness, and sorrow and sighing shall flee away.

Lay hold upon the hope set before us: which hope we have as an anchor of the soul, both sure and steadfast, and which entereth into that within the veil; whither the forerunner is for us entered, even Jesus.

There is a natural body, and there is a spiritual body. As we have borne the image of the earthy, we shall also bear the image of the heavenly.

Praise ye the LORD. Praise ye the LORD from the heavens: praise him in the heights. His glory is above the earth and heaven.

If ye then be risen with Christ, seek those things which are above, where Christ sitteth on the right hand of God.

Trust in the LORD at all times; ye people, pour out your heart before him.

Set your affection on things above, not on things on the earth.

Where the Spirit of the Lord is, there is liberty.

Seeing then that we have a great high priest, that is passed into the heavens, Jesus the Son of God, let us hold fast our profession.

It is a good thing to give thanks unto the LORD, and to sing praises unto thy name, O most high; to show forth thy loving-kindness in the morning, and thy faithfulness every night.

CALLS TO WORSHIP

Minister: There is one God and Father of all, who is above all, and through all, and in you all.

People: **For as many as are led by the Spirit of God, they are the sons of God.**

Minister: Come, walk in the way of the Lord with songs of gladness and joy.

People: **The Lord is nigh unto all them that call upon him, to all that call upon him in truth. Amen.**

Minister: O magnify the Lord with me, and let us exalt his name together.

People: **Sing praises to God; sing praises unto the Lord.**

Minister: According to thy name, O God, so is thy praise unto the ends of the earth.

People: **For this God is our God for ever and ever: he will be our guide. Amen.**

Minister: Honor and majesty are before the Lord: strength and beauty are in his sanctuary.

People: **Let us search and try our ways, and turn again to the Lord. Let us lift up our heart with our hands unto God in the heavens.**

Minister: Give unto the Lord the glory due unto his name: bring an offering, and come into his courts.

People: **Blessed be the Lord God; for he hath visited and redeemed his people, and hath raised up an horn of salvation for us. Amen.**

Minister: Lift up your hearts.

People: **We lift them up unto the Lord.**

Minister: Let us worship and give thanks unto him.

People: **He is the way, the truth, and the life; both now and for evermore. Amen.**

Minister: I was glad when they said unto me, Let us go into the house of the Lord.

People: **I will hear what God the Lord will speak: for he will speak peace unto his people.**

Minister: Peace, peace to him that is far off, and to him that is near, saith the Lord.

People: **Blessed are the peacemakers: for they shall be called the children of God. Amen.**

Minister: Seeing that we have a great high priest, that is passed into the heavens, Jesus the Son of God,

People: **We come boldly unto the throne of grace, that we may obtain mercy, and find grace to help in time of need.**

Minister: Give unto the Lord glory and strength.

People: **Blessing, and honor, and glory, and power, be unto him that sitteth upon the throne, and unto the Lamb for ever and ever. Amen.**

PRAYERS AND COLLECTS

O God, who art the source of all true joy; grant us a vision of our risen Lord, that we may know the peace which passeth understanding, which the world can neither give nor take away, and that pure joy which shall make radiant all our duty and our toil; through the same Jesus Christ our Lord. Amen.

O Thou who hast ordered this wondrous world, who knowest all things in earth and heaven; so fill our hearts with trust in thee that by night and by day, at all times and in all seasons, we may without fear commit all that we have and hope to be to thy never-failing love, for this life and the life to come; through Jesus Christ our Lord. Amen.

O God, who through the resurrection of Jesus Christ hast freed us from the power of darkness and brought us into the kingdom of thy love; grant, we beseech thee, that, as by his death he has recalled us into life, so by his abiding presence he may bring us to the joys eternal; through him who for our sakes died and rose again, and is ever with us in power, the same Jesus Christ our Lord. Amen.

O God our Father, renew our spirits and draw our hearts to thyself, that our work may not be to us a burden, but a delight; and give us such love to thee as may sweeten all our obedience. Help us that we may serve thee with the cheerfulness and gladness of children, delighting ourselves in thee and rejoicing in all that is to the honor of thy name; through Jesus Christ our Lord. Amen.

Lord of life and love, help us to worship thee in the holiness of beauty, that some beauty of holiness may appear in us. Quiet our souls in thy presence with the stillness of a wise trust. Lift us above dark moods and the shadow of sin, that we may find thy will for our lives; through Jesus Christ our Lord. Amen.

Most gracious God, to know and love whose will is righteousness; enlighten our souls with the brightness of thy presence, that we may both know thy will and be enabled to perform it; through Jesus Christ our Lord. Amen.

O God, who through the grace of thy Holy Spirit dost pour the gift of love into the hearts of thy faithful people; grant us health, both of mind and body, that we may love thee with our whole strength and with glad hearts may perform those things which are pleasing unto thee; through Jesus Christ our Lord. Amen.

O Lord our God, who art always more ready to bestow thy good gifts upon us than we are to seek them, and art willing to give more than we desire or deserve; help us so to seek that we may truly find, so to ask that we may joyfully receive, so to knock that the door of thy mercy may be opened unto us; through Jesus Christ our Lord. Amen.

Almighty and everlasting God, who dost govern all things in heaven and earth; mercifully hear the supplications of thy people, and grant us thy peace all the days of our life; through Jesus Christ our Lord. Amen.

Festival of the Christian Home

O God our Father, we pray thee to regard with thy loving-kindness the homes of our country, that marriage may be held in due honor, and that husbands and wives may live faithfully together, in honor preferring one another. We pray that the members of every family may be rich in mutual understanding and forbearance, in courtesy and kindness, bearing one another's burdens, and so fulfilling the law of thy blessed Son Jesus Christ our Lord. Amen.

Church Loyalty Day

Almighty God, giver of every good and perfect gift; teach us to render unto thee all that we have and all that we are, that we may praise thee not with our lips only, but with our whole lives, turning the duties, the sorrows, and the joys of all our days into a living sacrifice unto thee; through Jesus Christ our Lord. Amen.

Memorial Day

Almighty and everlasting God, by whose mercy we come to this high hour in the story of the Church; regard us with thy favor, and further us with thy continual help, as with devoted minds we consecrate our fellowship of faith to thee and thy kingdom; through Jesus Christ our Lord. Amen.

Ascension Day

O God our Father, the Father of our ascended Lord and of all created spirits; even as our Lord Jesus Christ ascended into the heavens, so may we also in heart and mind ascend into the heavenly realm of thy Spirit, and with him continually dwell, who liveth and reigneth with thee and the Holy Spirit, one God, world without end. Amen.

WHITSUNTIDE

*Season of Expansion and Growth of the Church—
From 11 to 16 Sundays*

Whitsunday, or Pentecost

SCRIPTURE SENTENCES

It shall come to pass, that I will pour out my spirit upon all flesh; and your sons and your daughters shall prophesy, your old men shall dream dreams, your young men shall see visions: and also upon the servants and upon the handmaids will I pour out my spirit.

God hath not given us the spirit of fear; but of power, and of love, and of a sound mind.

The love of God is shed abroad in our hearts by the Holy Spirit which is given unto us.

Beloved, let us love one another: for love is of God; and everyone that loveth is born of God, and knoweth God.

CALLS TO WORSHIP

Minister: This is the day which the Lord hath made.

People: **We will rejoice and be glad in it.**

Minister: This is that which was spoken by the prophet Joel; I will pour out of my Spirit upon all flesh.

People: **And your sons and your daughters shall prophesy, and your young men shall see visions, and your old men shall dream dreams: and whosoever shall call on the name of the Lord shall be saved.**

Minister: This is the day of which Jesus declared: Ye shall receive power, after that the Holy Spirit is come upon you.

People: **And ye shall be witnesses unto me both in Jerusalem, and in all Judea, and in Samaria, and unto the uttermost part of the earth. Amen.**

Minister: Where the Spirit of the Lord is, there is liberty.

People: **There are diversities of gifts, but the same Spirit.**

Minister: As many as are led by the Spirit of God, they are the sons of God.

People: **The Spirit itself beareth witness with our spirit, that we are the children of God. Amen.**

PRAYERS AND COLLECTS

Grant, we beseech thee, merciful God, that thy Church, being gathered together in unity by thy Holy Spirit, may manifest thy power among all peoples, to the glory of thy name; through Jesus Christ our Lord, who liveth and reigneth with thee and the same Spirit, one God, world without end. Amen.

O gracious Father, we humbly beseech thee for thy holy Church universal that thou wouldest be pleased to fill it with all truth, in all peace. Where it is corrupt, purify it; where it is in error, direct it; where in anything it is amiss, reform it. Where it is right, establish it; where it is in want, provide for it; where it is divided, reunite it; for the sake of him who died and rose again and ever liveth to make intercession for us, Jesus Christ thy Son our Lord. Amen.

O God, who didst send the Holy Spirit to enkindle the zeal of Christ's followers waiting in Jerusalem for his promised gift; we beseech thee to pour the same inspiration on thy people here assembled, and on the Church of Christ throughout the world. Revive the power of the gospel in our hearts, that it may be to us a sacred trust for the blessing of mankind.

Enable thy Church to spread the good news of salvation, so that all nations may hear it in their own tongue, and welcome it into their own life. Protect, encourage, and bless all missionaries of the cross, and prosper their word and work, so that Jesus, being lifted up, may draw all men unto him, and the kingdoms of the world may become the kingdom of our Lord and of his Christ. Amen.

Almighty God our Father, send, we beseech thee, thy Holy Spirit into our hearts, that we may be directed and controlled according to thy will, led into all truth, defended from all sin, and enriched in all grace; through Jesus Christ our Lord. Amen.

Trinity Sunday

SCRIPTURE SENTENCES

Canst thou by searching find out God? canst thou find out the Almighty unto perfection?

No man hath seen God at any time. If we love one another, God dwelleth in us, and his love is perfected in us. God is love; and he that dwelleth in love dwelleth in God, and God in him.

Strive for the truth unto death, and the Lord shall fight for thee.

CALLS TO WORSHIP

Minister: Know ye that the Lord he is God: it is he that hath made us, and not we ourselves.

People: **We are his people, and the sheep of his pasture.**

Minister: Enter into his gates with thanksgiving, and into his courts with praise.

People: **We give thanks unto him, and bless his name: for the Lord is good. Amen.**

Minister: O worship the Lord in the beauty of holiness: fear before him, all the earth.

People: **Holy, holy, holy, is the Lord of hosts: the whole earth is full of his glory.**

Minister: Holy, holy, holy, Lord God Almighty, which was, and is, and is to come.

People: **O Lord God, great and mighty is thy name, and to thee we ascribe all honor and glory, Father, Son, and Holy Spirit. Amen.**

PRAYERS AND COLLECTS

Almighty God, whose glory the heavens are telling, whose power the earth and sea declare, and whose greatness is revealed in all feeling and thinking creatures everywhere; to thee belong glory, honor, dominion, and power, now and forever, world without end. Amen.

O eternal God, Father, Son, and Holy Spirit, grant that in the majesty of all creation we may behold thy power that upholds us, in the face of Jesus Christ thy love that seeks and saves us, and in new life within our souls thy Spirit kindling in us; that so even to our littleness thine infinite wonder may be revealed, O blessed Triune God. Amen.

O God, grant us thy children strength for the work thou hast given us to do; make us strong of body, strong of mind, strong of will, that we may be effective laborers in thy vineyard, valiant against the evil of the world, a power for good among our fellow men; through Jesus Christ our Lord. Amen.

O God, the strength of all those who put their trust in thee; mercifully accept our prayers; and because through the weakness of our mortal nature we can do no good thing without thee, grant us the help of thy grace, that in keeping thy commandments we may please thee, both in will and in deed; through Jesus Christ our Lord. Amen.

O Thou who art the light of the minds that know thee, the life of the souls that love thee, and the strength of the hearts that serve thee; help us so to know thee that we may truly love thee, so to love thee that we may fully serve thee, whom to serve is perfect freedom; through Jesus Christ our Lord. Amen.

Sundays After Pentecost and Trinity

SCRIPTURE SENTENCES

The hour cometh, and now is, when the true worshipers shall worship the Father in spirit and in truth: for the Father seeketh such to worship him. God is a Spirit: and they that worship him must worship him in spirit and in truth.

Hereby know we that we dwell in him, and he in us, because he hath given us of his Spirit.

The wind bloweth where it listeth, and thou hearest the sound thereof, but canst not tell whence it cometh, and whither it goeth: so is everyone that is born of the Spirit.

The love of God is shed abroad in our hearts by the Holy Spirit which is given unto us.

Then saith he unto his disciples, The harvest truly is plenteous, but the laborers are few; pray ye therefore the Lord of the harvest, that he will send forth laborers into his harvest.

And they shall come from the east, and from the west, and from the north, and from the south, and shall sit down in the kingdom of God.

It is of the LORD's mercies that we are not consumed, because his compassions fail not. They are new every morning; great is thy faithfulness. The LORD is my portion, saith my soul; therefore will I hope in him.

Whither shall I go from thy spirit? or whither shall I flee from thy presence? If I take the wings of the morning, and dwell in the uttermost parts of the sea; even there shall thy hand lead me, and thy right hand shall hold me.

Acquaint now thyself with God, and be at peace; thereby good shall come unto thee; the Almighty shall be thy defense. For then shalt thou have thy delight in the Almighty, and shalt lift up thy face.

It is the spirit that quickeneth; the flesh profiteth nothing: the words that I speak unto you, they are spirit, and they are life. The letter killeth, but the spirit giveth life.

Whatsoever a man soweth, that shall he also reap. For he that soweth to his flesh shall of the flesh reap corruption; but he that soweth to the Spirit shall of the Spirit reap life everlasting.

CALLS TO WORSHIP

Minister: Come and see the works of God: the works of the Lord are great.

People: **His work is honorable and glorious: and his righteousness endureth forever.**

Minister: Let us search and try our ways, and turn again to the Lord.

People: **We will lift up our heart unto God in the heavens. Amen.**

Minister: I will bless the Lord at all times: his praise shall continually be in my mouth.

People: **My soul shall make her boast in the Lord: the humble shall hear thereof, and be glad.**

Minister: O magnify the Lord with me, and let us exalt his name together.

People: **For with him is the fountain of life: in his light shall we see light. Amen.**

Minister: This is the day which the Lord hath made; let us rejoice and be glad in it.

People: **Surely this is none other but the house of God, and this is the gate of heaven.**

Minister: Enter into his gates with thanksgiving, and into his courts with praise.

People: **The hour cometh, and now is, when the true worshipers shall worship the Father in spirit and in truth. Amen.**

Minister: The Lord hath made known his salvation.

People: **His righteousness hath he openly showed in the sight of the nations.**

Minister: Let the people praise thee, O God.

People: **God shall bless us; and all the ends of the earth shall fear him. Amen.**

Minister: God is light, and in him is no darkness at all.

People: **If we walk in the light, we have fellowship one with another.**

Minister: O magnify the Lord with me, and let us exalt his name together;

People: **For with him is the fountain of life: in his light shall we see light. Amen.**

Minister: I will praise the Lord with my whole heart in the congregation.

People: **Rejoice in the Lord and give thanks at the remembrance of his holiness.**

Minister: I will extol thee, my God, O king; and I will bless thy name for ever and ever.

People: **Great is the Lord, and greatly to be praised; and his greatness is unsearchable. Amen.**

Minister: The Lord reigneth; let the earth rejoice.

People: **We will be glad and rejoice in thee: we will sing praise to thy name, O thou most High.**

Minister: Thine, O Lord, is the greatness, and the power, and the glory, and the victory.

People: **Because thy lovingkindness is better than life, our lips shall praise thee. Amen.**

Minister: It is a good thing to give thanks unto the Lord, and to sing praises unto thy name, O most High:

People: **To show forth thy lovingkindness in the morning, and thy faithfulness every night.**

Minister: O bless our God, ye people, and make the voice of his praise to be heard.

People: **Our lips shall greatly rejoice when we sing unto thee; and our souls, which thou hast redeemed. Amen.**

Minister: The Lord is nigh unto all them that call upon him, to all that call upon him in truth.

People: **We will call upon the Lord, who is worthy to be praised; so shall we be saved.**

Minister: O thou that hearest prayer, unto thee shall all flesh come.

People: **He shall have dominion also from sea to sea, and from the river unto the ends of the earth. Amen.**

Minister: The Lord is in his holy temple.

People: **Let all the earth keep silence before him.**

Minister: O come, let us worship and bow down.

People: **Let us worship him in spirit and in truth. Amen.**

Minister: Oh that men would praise the Lord for his goodness, and for his wonderful works to the children of men!

People: **The Lord is good to all: and his tender mercies are over all his works.**

Minister: Blessed be the Lord God, who only doeth wondrous things.

People: **Blessed be his glorious name forever: and let the whole earth be filled with his glory. Amen.**

Minister: Let such as love thy salvation say continually, The Lord be magnified.

People: **Our heart shall rejoice in him, because we have trusted in his holy name.**

Minister: Make a joyful noise unto the Lord, all the earth: rejoice, and sing praise.

People: **We praise thee, O God; we acknowledge thee to be the Lord. Amen.**

Student Day

Minister: One thing have I desired of the Lord, that will I seek after; that I may behold the beauty of the Lord, and inquire in his temple.

People: **Send out thy light and thy truth: let them lead me; let them bring me unto thy holy hill.**

Minister: Let us worship the Lord in the beauty of holiness.

People: **Let us worship him in spirit and in truth. Amen.**

Independence Day

Minister: The Lord thy God bringeth thee into a good land. Thou shalt bless the Lord thy God for the good land which he hath given thee.

People: **Our soul waiteth for the Lord: he is our help and our shield.**

Minister: Blessed is the nation whose God is the Lord; and the people whom he hath chosen for his own inheritance.

People: **Righteousness exalteth a nation: but sin is a reproach to any people. Amen.**

PRAYERS AND COLLECTS

Almighty God, author of eternal light; illumine our hearts by the light of thy grace, that our lips may praise thee, that our lives may bless thee, that our worship may glorify thee; through Jesus Christ our Lord. Amen.

O God, who hast taught us to keep all thy heavenly commandments by loving thee and our neighbor; grant us the spirit of peace and grace, that we may be both devoted to thee with our whole heart and united to each other with a pure will; through Jesus Christ our Lord. Amen.

Our heavenly Father, we thy humble children invoke thy blessing for this hour of worship. We adore thee, whose name is love, whose nature is compassion, whose presence is joy, whose word is truth, whose spirit is goodness, whose holiness is beauty, whose will is peace, whose service is perfect freedom, and in knowledge of whom standeth our eternal life. Unto thee be all honor and all glory; through Jesus Christ our Lord. Amen.

Almighty and everlasting God, in whom we live and move and have our being, who hast created us for thyself, so that our hearts are restless until they find rest in thee; grant unto us purity of heart and strength of purpose, so that no selfish passion may hinder us from knowing thy will, and no weakness from doing it. In thy light may we see life clearly, and in thy service find perfect freedom; through Jesus Christ our Lord. Amen.

O thou eternal God, speak to each of us the word that we need, and let thy word abide with us until it hath wrought in us thy holy will. Cleanse, quicken, and refresh our hearts; direct and increase our faith; and grant that we, by our worship at this time, may be enabled to see thee more clearly, to love thee more fully, and to serve thee more perfectly; through Jesus Christ our Lord. Amen.

Almighty God, whose mercy is over all thy works; we praise thee for the blessings which have been brought to mankind by thy holy Church throughout all the world. We bless thee for thy grace, for our fellowship in Christ with thee and with one another, for the teaching of the Scriptures and for the preaching of thy word. We thank thee for the example of thy people in all ages, for thy servants departed this life in thy faith and fear, and for the memory and example of all that has been true and good in their lives. And we humbly beseech thee that we may be numbered with them in thy fellowship of love and service here and hereafter; through Jesus Christ our Lord. Amen.

Most merciful Father, we beseech thee to send thy heavenly blessings upon this thy Church, that all its members may dwell together in unity and brotherly love. Keep far from us all self-will and discord. Endue thy ministers with righteousness, and enable them faithfully to fulfill their ministry, to bring again the outcasts, and to seek the lost. And grant to us so to receive their ministrations, and to use thy means of grace, that in all our words and deeds we may seek thy glory and the advancement of thy kingdom; through Jesus Christ our Lord. Amen.

O Lord our God, grant us grace to desire thee with our whole heart, that so desiring we may find thee, and so finding thee we may love thee, and so loving thee we may rejoice in thee forever; through Jesus Christ our Lord. Amen.

O God, in whom alone we find rest from our weariness and comfort for our sorrow, and from whom alone comes all true joy; keep our hearts, we beseech thee, ever fixed on thee through life and death, waiting patiently for that glorious day when we shall rejoice in the fullness of thy love for evermore; through Jesus Christ our Lord. Amen.

O God, who art the source of all true peace and joy; grant us so perfectly to do thy will that we may find both that inward peace which the world can neither give nor take away, and that pure joy which shall make radiant all our duty and our toil; through Jesus Christ our Lord. Amen.

O Lord our God, great, eternal, wonderful in glory, who keepest covenant and promise for those that love thee with their whole hearts, who art the life of all, the help of those who flee unto thee, the hope of those who cry unto thee; cleanse us from our sins, and from every thought displeasing to thy goodness, that with a pure heart and a clean mind, with perfect love and calm hope, we may venture confidently and fearlessly to pray unto thee; through Jesus Christ our Lord. Amen.

O God, who art a hiding-place from the wind and shelter from the storm; help us to turn from the tumult and clamor of the world to the calm of thy great assurance; through Jesus Christ our Lord. Amen.

Almighty and everlasting God, unite thy servants that they may seek thee with their whole heart, serve thee with submissive mind, humbly implore thy mercy, and perpetually rejoice in thy blessings; through Jesus Christ our Lord. Amen.

Almighty and everlasting God, who hast built thy Church upon the foundation of the apostles and prophets, Jesus Christ himself being the chief cornerstone; we pray thee to inspire the Church universal with the spirit of truth, unity, and concord; and grant that all who confess thy holy name may abide in the truth and live in unity and godly love; through Jesus Christ our Lord. Amen.

Lord, we beseech thee to keep thy household the Church in continual godliness, that through thy protection it may be free from all adversities, and devoutly given to serve thee in good works, to the glory of thy name; through Jesus Christ our Lord. Amen.

O Lord, we pray for the universal Church, for all sections of thy Church throughout the world, for their truth, unity, and stability, that love may abound and truth flourish in them all; through Jesus Christ our Lord. Amen.

Almighty God, Father of our Lord Jesus Christ; make us aware, in our communion with thee, of our fellowship with all faithful and devout souls in thy holy Church throughout all ages and in all the world. Especially may we realize our communion with all thy servants who have finished their course in faith and are with thee; grant us to serve thee in unbroken fellowship through the same Jesus Christ our Saviour, who is the author and finisher of our faith. Amen.

Student Day

Almighty God, our heavenly Father, who hast committed to thy holy Church the care and nurture of thy children; enlighten with thy wisdom those who teach and those who learn, that, rejoicing in the knowledge of thy truth, they may worship thee and serve thee all the days of their life; through Jesus Christ our Lord. Amen.

O God of truth, we pray thee for the people of our day, that there may be found from them teachers who love thee with understanding, who, being both reverent and enlightened, shall be able to show their learners an ever clearer vision of eternal truth. Thou who guidest the wisdom of the scholar, be thyself the shepherd of those who feed thy sheep, that their thoughts and words may come from thee; through Jesus Christ our Lord. Amen.

Nature Sunday

O God, who hast placed us as thy children in a world thou hast created for us; give us thankful hearts as we work and as we pray. We praise thee for the day of light and life, for the night which brings rest and sleep, and for the ordered course of nature, seedtime and harvest, which thou hast given us. We bless thee that thou hast given us the joy of children, the wisdom of old men. We thank thee for all holy and humble men of heart, for the love of God and man which shines forth in commonplace lives, and above all for the vision of thyself, in loneliness and in fellowship, in sacrament and in prayer; for these and all other benefits we praise and glorify thy name, now and for evermore. Amen.

God of all beauty, who dost make the sun to rise in splendor, and in glory set, and the stars to march in quiet radiance across the sky; open our eyes until we see thy beauty on the face of the earth, that we may more fully know thee and may love all beauty because it speaks to us of thee; through Jesus Christ our Lord. Amen.

O heavenly Father, who hast filled the world with beauty; open, we beseech thee, our eyes to behold thy gracious hand in all thy works, that rejoicing in thy whole creation we may learn to serve thee with gladness; for the sake of him by whom all things were made, thy Son Jesus Christ our Lord. Amen.

Independence Day

O Lord, God of our fathers, keep this day ever in the thought of thy people, and prepare our heart unto thee, to keep thy commandments, thy testimonies, and thy statutes, throughout all generations; through Jesus Christ our Lord. Amen.

KINGDOMTIDE

Season of the Kingdom of God on Earth—13 or 14 Sundays

SCRIPTURE SENTENCES

The kingdom of God is righteousness, and peace, and joy.

O sing unto the LORD a new song: sing unto the LORD, all the earth; for he cometh, for he cometh to judge the earth: he shall judge the world with righteousness, and the people with his truth.

Let judgment run down as waters, and righteousness as a mighty stream.

Choose you this day whom ye will serve; but as for me and my house, we will serve the LORD. The LORD our God will we serve, and his voice will we obey.

Thus saith the LORD, Let not the wise man glory in his wisdom, neither let the mighty man glory in his might, let not the rich man glory in his riches: but let him that glorieth glory in this, that he understandeth and knoweth me, that I am the LORD which exercise lovingkindness, judgment, and righteousness, in the earth: for in these things I delight, saith the LORD.

Blessed are they who do hunger and thirst after righteousness: for they shall be filled.

All souls are mine, saith the Lord GOD; as the soul of the father, so also the soul of the son is mine.

All thy works shall praise thee, O LORD; and thy saints shall bless thee. They shall speak of the glory of thy kingdom, and talk of thy power.

Seeing we also are compassed about with so great a cloud of witnesses, let us lay aside every weight, and the sin which doth so easily beset us, and let us run with patience the race that is set before us.

They that be wise shall shine as the brightness of the firmament; and they that turn many to righteousness as the stars for ever and ever.

The earth is the LORD'S, and the fullness thereof; the world, and they that dwell therein.

Oh that men would praise the LORD for his goodness, and for his wonderful works to the children of men!

Thou crownest the year with thy goodness. The pastures are clothed with flocks; the valleys also are covered over with corn; they shout for joy, they also sing.

I will cause the shower to come down in his season; there shall be showers of blessing. And the tree of the field shall yield her fruit, and the earth shall yield her increase, and they shall be safe in their land, and shall know that I am the Lord.

CALLS TO WORSHIP

Minister: Make a joyful noise unto the Lord, all ye lands. Serve the Lord with gladness; come before his presence with singing.

People: **Know ye that the Lord he is God: it is he that hath made us, and not we ourselves; we are his people, and the sheep of his pasture.**

Minister: Enter into his gates with thanksgiving, and into his courts with praise: be thankful unto him, and bless his name.

People: **For the Lord is good; his mercy is everlasting; and his truth endureth to all generations. Amen.**

Minister: Let us search and try our ways, and turn again to the Lord.

People: **Let us lift up our heart unto God.**

Minister: Wherewith shall I come before the Lord, and bow myself before the high God?

People: **He hath showed thee, O man, what is good; and what doth the Lord require of thee, but to do justly, and to love mercy, and to walk humbly with thy God? Amen.**

Minister: Behold, I stand at the door, and knock: if any man hear my voice, and open the door, I will come in.

People: **Come unto me, all ye that labor and are heavy laden, and I will give you rest.**

Minister: The hour cometh, and now is, when the true worshipers shall worship the Father in spirit and in truth.

People: **For the Father seeketh such to worship him. Amen.**

Minister: Blessed be the name of God for ever and ever: for wisdom and might are his.

People: **He giveth wisdom unto the wise, and knowledge to them that know understanding.**

Minister: Seek ye the Lord while he may be found, call ye upon him while he is near.

People: **For great is the Lord, and greatly to be praised. Amen.**

Minister: Trust ye in the Lord.

People: **The Lord God is everlasting strength.**

Minister: Worship the Lord in the beauty of holiness.

People: **Blessed be the Lord God, who turneth not our prayer away, nor his mercy from us. Amen.**

Minister: Trust in the Lord, and do good.

People: **The Lord will give strength unto his people.**

Minister: O taste and see that the Lord is good.

People: **God is our refuge and strength. Amen.**

Minister: Let us go into the house of the Lord; let us take counsel together.

People: **Let our feet stand within his gates, and heart and voice give thanks unto the Lord.**

Minister: Blessed be the temple hallowed by his name; pray for peace within its walls.

People: **Peace to young and old that enter here, peace to every soul abiding herein. Amen.**

Minister: O magnify the Lord with me, and let us exalt his name together.

People: **Our help is in the name of the Lord, who made heaven and earth.**

Minister: Let us search and try our ways, and turn again to the Lord.

People: **Let us lift up our hearts and sing praises unto our God. Amen.**

Minister: Come, and let us return unto the Lord: and we shall live in his sight.

People: **His going forth is prepared as the morning; and he shall come unto us as the rain.**

Minister: Let us search and try our ways, and turn again to the Lord. Let us lift up our heart with our hands unto God.

People: **The Lord is gracious, and full of compassion; slow to anger, and of great mercy. The Lord is good to all: and his tender mercies are over all his works. Amen.**

Minister: It is good that we should both hope and quietly wait for the salvation of the Lord.

People: **God is our refuge and strength, a very present help in trouble.**

Minister: Let us lift up our hearts with our voices unto God, our strength and redeemer.

People: **We will lift them up unto God, who is our strength and our salvation. Amen.**

Minister: O come, let us sing unto the Lord:

People: **Let us make a joyful noise to the rock of our salvation.**

Minister: Let us come before his presence with thanksgiving,

People: **And make a joyful noise unto him with psalms. Amen.**

Minister: O come, let us worship and bow down; let us kneel before the Lord our maker.

People: **O Lord, open thou our lips; and our mouth shall show forth thy praise.**

Minister: Seek ye the Lord while he may be found, call ye upon him while he is near.

People: **For great is the Lord, and greatly to be praised. Amen.**

Minister: I will praise thee, O Lord, with my whole heart; I will show forth all thy marvelous works.

People: **The Lord is King for ever and ever.**

Minister: I will be glad and rejoice in thee, I will sing praise to thy name, O thou most High.

People: **We will rejoice in thy salvation, and in the name of our God we will set up our banners. Amen.**

Thanksgiving Sunday

Minister: Oh that men would praise the Lord for his goodness, and for his wonderful works to the children of men!

People: **Blessed be his glorious name forever: and let the whole earth be filled with his glory.**

Minister: Lord, thou hast been favorable unto thy land: the earth is full of thy riches.

People: **Sing unto the Lord; for he hath done excellent things: this is known in all the earth. Amen.**

PRAYERS AND COLLECTS

O Thou who art the light of the world, the desire of all nations, and the shepherd of our souls; let thy light shine in the darkness, that all the ends of the earth may see the salvation of our God; by the lifting up of thy cross gather the peoples to thine obedience, so that there may be one flock, one shepherd, one holy kingdom of righteousness and peace, one God and Father of us all, above all, and through all, and in all. Amen.

Almighty God, stir the hearts of thy people, that by their prayers, their gifts, and their labors they may have part in the spreading of thy gospel over all the earth; and hasten the time when all the ends of the world shall remember and turn unto thee, and all kindreds of the nations shall worship thee; through Jesus Christ our Lord. Amen.

O God, who hast joined together divers nations in the confession of thy name; grant us both to will and to do what thou commandest, that thy people, being called to an eternal inheritance, may hold the same faith in their hearts, and show the same godliness in their lives; through Jesus Christ our Lord. Amen.

O Holy Spirit of God, abide with us; inspire all our thoughts; pervade our imaginations; suggest all our decisions; order all our doings. Be with us in our silence and in our speech, in our haste and in our leisure, in company and in solitude, in the freshness of the morning and in the weariness of the evening; and give us grace at all times humbly to rejoice in thy mysterious companionship; through Jesus Christ our Lord. Amen.

O Lord, open thou our lips and purify our hearts, that we may worthily magnify thy holy name; and help us to be reverent in thought, word, and act, and to worship thee now and always in the filial faith and spirit of Jesus Christ our Lord. Amen.

Our heavenly Father, we adore thee, whose name is love, whose nature is compassion, whose presence is joy, whose word is truth, whose spirit is goodness, whose holiness is beauty, whose will is peace, whose service is perfect freedom, and in knowledge of whom standeth our eternal life; through Jesus Christ our Lord. Amen.

O Lord our God, make thy people one. Whatever be our differences, may we ever realize that we are all one in Christ Jesus; and may the blessed bond of union between believers be increasingly strengthened; through the same Jesus Christ our Lord. Amen.

Almighty God, who hast created man in thine own image; grant us grace fearlessly to contend against evil, and to make no peace with oppression; and, that we may reverently use our freedom, help us to employ it in the maintenance of justice among men and nations, to the glory of thy holy name; through Jesus Christ our Lord. Amen.

Almighty God, who hast given unto thy Son Jesus Christ a kingdom, that all peoples, nations, and languages should serve him; make us loyal followers of our living Lord, that we may always hear his word, obey his commands, and live in his Spirit; and hasten the day when every knee shall bow and every tongue confess that he is the Lord; to thine eternal glory. Amen.

O heavenly Father, in whom we live and move and have our being; we humbly pray thee so to guide and govern us by thy Holy Spirit that in all the cares and occupations of our daily life we may remember that we are ever walking in thy sight; for thine own name's sake. Amen.

Great art thou, O Lord, and greatly to be praised; great is thy power, and thy wisdom is infinite. Thee would we praise without ceasing, for thou callest us to delight in thy praise. Thou hast made us for thyself, and restless is our heart until it finds rest in thee. Amen.

O God, who by thy Spirit in our hearts dost lead men to desire thy perfection, to seek for truth, and to rejoice in beauty; enlighten and inspire, we beseech thee, all thinkers, writers, artists, craftsmen, that in whatsoever is true and pure and lovely thy name may be hallowed and thy kingdom come on earth; through Jesus Christ our Lord. Amen.

O God, who art the author of truth, of beauty, and of goodness; inspire, we pray thee, all who enrich the lives of the people, all artists and poets, dramatists and musicians, that our common life may be made radiant with the beauty of him in whom thy fullness dwelt, even Jesus Christ our Lord. Amen.

Almighty God, our Father, grant, we beseech thee, a great outpouring of thy Holy Spirit upon thy people, so as to cause a deep and widespread revival of a living faith in Christ, working by love, and bringing forth the fruits of the Spirit, love of humanity, joy in sacrifice, and fraternity in righteousness; through Jesus Christ our Lord. Amen.

Almighty God, who of thy great mercy hast gathered us into thy Church; grant that we may so honor thee, both in spirit and in outward form, that thy name may be glorified, and we may be true members of thy living fellowship; through Jesus Christ our Lord. Amen.

O thou Holy One who inhabitest eternity, visit us with the inward vision of thy glory, that we may bow our hearts before thee, and obtain that grace which thou hast promised to the lowly; through Jesus Christ our Saviour. Amen.

O Lord, who, though thou wast rich, yet for our sake didst become poor, and hast promised in thy gospel that whatsoever is done unto the least of thy brethren thou wilt receive as done unto thee; give us grace, we humbly beseech thee, to be ever willing and ready to minister, as thou dost enable us, to the necessities of our fellow men; in thine own name we pray. Amen.

Almighty God, who in a world of change hast placed eternity in our hearts and hast given us power to discern good from evil; grant us sincerity that we may persistently seek the things that endure, refusing those which perish, and that, amid things vanishing and deceptive, we may see the truth steadily, follow the light faithfully, and grow ever richer in that love which is the life of men; through Jesus Christ our Lord. Amen.

Labor Sunday

O God our Father, renew our spirits and draw our hearts unto thyself, that our work may not be to us a burden but a delight; and give us such a mighty love for thee as may gladden all our obedience. Let us serve thee, not with the spirit of bondage as slaves, but with the cheerfulness and gladness of children, delighting ourselves in thee and rejoicing in thy work; through Jesus Christ our Lord. Amen.

Almighty God, our heavenly Father, who declarest thy glory and showest forth thy handiwork in the heavens and in the earth; deliver us, we beseech thee, in our several callings from the service of mammon, that we may do the work which thou givest us to do in truth, in beauty, and in righteousness, with singleness of heart as thy servants, and to the benefit of our fellow men; for the sake of him who came among us as one that serveth, thy Son Jesus Christ our Lord. Amen.

O God, the King of righteousness, lead us, we pray thee, in ways of justice and peace; inspire us to break down all tyranny and oppression, to gain for every man his due reward, and from every man his due service; that each may live for all and all may care for each; in Jesus Christ our Lord. Amen.

Opening of School

Almighty God, we beseech thee that knowledge may be increased among us, and all good learning flourish and abound. Bless all who teach and all who learn; and grant that in humility of heart they may ever look unto thee, who art the fountain of all wisdom; through Jesus Christ our Lord. Amen.

Church-School Rally Day

O thou Teacher of all who come to thee for light and guidance, give us the faithfulness of learners and the courage of believers in thee; give us boldness to examine, and faith to trust, all truth; give us patience and insight to master difficulty, and stability to hold fast to that which is good; through Jesus Christ our Lord. Amen.

International Temperance Sunday

Accept us, O God, we beseech thee, and draw us to thyself, that we who are already all thine own as thy creatures may henceforth be thine by self-control, obedience, and faith; even thine, O Lord, who livest and reignest for ever and ever. Amen.

Almighty God, our heavenly Father, may we ever be aware that thou hast created us in thine own image, that these bodies are the temple of thy Spirit and the instruments of thy service. May we never permit the desecration of those talents divinely given us or profane thy dwelling place within through indulgence or lust. Stay the powers of evil that feed on the weaknesses of humanity and degrade society. May thy Church be aroused by a militant zeal against all evil and endued with power to establish thy kingdom of righteousness; through Jesus Christ our Lord. Amen.

Eternal God, who hast taught us that our bodies are temples of thy Spirit; keep us, we most humbly beseech thee, temperate and holy in thought, word, and deed, that we, with all the pure in heart, may see thee and be made like unto thee; through Jesus Christ our Lord. Amen.

All Saints Day

Almighty God, who holdest in thy hand the souls of the righteous; we give thee thanks and praise for all the generations of the faithful who have served thee here in godliness and love, and who dwell forever in thy presence. We bless thee for all who have enriched the world with truth and beauty, who have labored in the service of their fellows, who have done great things for thee and for thy Church, and have handed on to us our gracious heritage. We bless thee for all near and dear to us, for our fathers and mothers, our brothers and sisters, for those who have helped and defended and loved and cherished us. Grant that all the good we have seen and known in them may continue to inspire and guide us, that we may always love them and hallow their memory, and that when we have fulfilled our time on earth we may have part with them in thy heavenly kingdom; through Jesus Christ our Lord. Amen.

O King eternal, immortal, invisible, who in the righteousness of thy saints hast given us an example of godly life, and in their blessedness a glorious pledge of the hope of our calling; we beseech thee that, being compassed about with so great a cloud of witnesses, we may run with patience the race that is set before us, and with them receive the crown of glory that fadeth not away; through Jesus Christ our Lord. Amen.

National or Civic Celebration

Almighty Lord, deepen the root of our national life in everlasting righteousness; and let not the crown of our life be as a fading flower. Make us equal to our high trusts, reverent in our use of freedom, just in the exercise of power, generous in the protection of weakness; through Jesus Christ our Lord. Amen.

World Peace Sunday

Almighty God, from whom all thoughts of truth and peace proceed; kindle, we pray thee, in the hearts of all men the true love of peace, and guide with thy pure and peaceable wisdom those who take counsel for the nations of the earth, that in tranquillity thy Kingdom may go forward, till the earth be filled with the knowledge of thy love; through Jesus Christ our Lord. Amen.

O God, who through thy prophets of old hast foretold a day when the armaments of war shall be beaten into the implements of peace; hasten, we beseech thee, the fulfillment of thy most sure promise. Still the tumult of the nations, and set at naught the peoples that delight in war, that we may be speedily delivered from our present confusion into the order and righteousness of thy kingdom; through Jesus Christ our Lord. Amen.

Thanksgiving Day, or Harvest-Home Festival

Almighty God and heavenly Father, we glorify thee that we are once more permitted to enjoy the fulfillment of thy gracious promise, that, while the earth remaineth, seedtime and harvest shall not fail. Blessed be thou, who hast given us the fruits of the earth in their season. Teach us to remember that it is not by bread alone that man doth live; but grant that we may feed on him who is the true bread which cometh down from heaven, even Jesus Christ our Lord and Saviour; to whom, with thee, O Father, and thee, O Holy Spirit, be honor and glory, for ever and ever. Amen.

O God, Father of mercies and author of all good, whose providence for thy children never faileth, and whose continual blessings are unnumbered; grant that with devotion and gratitude we may live in the fellowship of work and the brotherhood of thy family, enjoying thy bounty with rejoicing hearts; through Jesus Christ our Lord. Amen.

A CALENDAR AND LECTIONARY FOR THE CHRISTIAN YEAR

THE number of Sundays in Christmastide, Epiphany, Whitsuntide, and Kingdomtide varies. In the following table the maximum number of Sundays in each season is listed, and the Sundays which sometimes do not occur are indicated by an asterisk (*).

ADVENT

First Sunday in Advent (Sunday near- est November 30)	Isa. 35	John 4:34-38
Second Sunday in Advent	Isa. 40:25-31	Luke 20:9-18
Third Sunday in Advent	Gal. 6:1-10	John 3:11-21
Fourth Sunday in Advent	Isa. 52:7-10	Luke 4:16-22

CHRISTMASTIDE

Christmas Day (December 25)	Heb. 1:1-12	John 1:1-14
Sunday after Christmas	Gal. 4:1-7	Matt. 1:18-25
The New Year (January 1) or *Second Sunday after Christmas	Rev. 21:1-7	Luke 2:15-21

EPIPHANY

Epiphany (January 6)	II. Cor. 3:18– 4:6	Matt. 2:1-12

First Sunday after Epiphany	John 1:1-9	Matt. 5:1-12
Second Sunday after Epiphany	Rom. 10:8-15	Matt. 28:16-20
Third Sunday after Epiphany	John 3:1-11	Matt. 6:19-24
Fourth Sunday after Epiphany	I Cor. 14:8-12, 23-25	Matt. 6:1-8, 14-18
*Fifth Sunday after Epiphany	II Cor. 5:20–6:10	Luke 12:49-53
*Sixth Sunday after Epiphany	Acts 9:10-16	John 15:13-20
*Seventh Sunday after Epiphany	Rom. 8:12-25	John 5:17-21
*Eighth Sunday after Epiphany	Heb. 2:5-10	Luke 10:21-24
*Ninth Sunday after Epiphany	I Cor. 13	John 14:1-10

LENT

Ash Wednesday, or Day of Fasting and Prayer (forty-sixth day before Easter)	Mic. 6:6-8	Mark 12:28-34
First Sunday in Lent	Isa. 58:6-12	Matt. 4:1-11
Second Sunday in Lent	Rev. 19:5-10	Mark 11:15-18
Third Sunday in Lent	Rom. 12:1-5	Luke 14:16-24
Fourth Sunday in Lent	Acts 10:23-33	Luke 10:38-42
Fifth Sunday in Lent, or Passion Sunday	Heb. 9:11-15	Mark 10:32-45
Sixth Sunday in Lent, or Palm Sunday	Phil. 2:5-11	Mark 11:1-11
Holy Week:		
Monday	Rom. 5:1-8	Mark 14:1-16
Tuesday	Eph. 2:13-22	Mark 14:17-42
Wednesday	John 4:7-11	Mark 14:43-65
Maundy Thursday	I Cor. 11:23-29	Mark 14:66–15:15
Good Friday	Heb. 10:4-25	Mark 15:16-41
Easter Even	Heb. 13:20-21	Mark 15:42-47

EASTERTIDE

Easter Day (see table on page 212)	Col. 3:1-11	John 20:1-10
First Sunday after Easter	Rom. 6:2-11	Luke 24:13-35
Second Sunday after Easter	I Pet. 2:21-25	John 10:1-16
Third Sunday after Easter	Eph. 3:14-21	John 6:27-40
Fourth Sunday after Easter	Rev. 22:1-5	John 15:1-12
Fifth Sunday after Easter	I Cor. 12:12-15, 26, 27	John 17:11, 14-26
Ascension Day (Thursday, fortieth day of Eastertide)	Rev. 5	Luke 24:44-53
Sixth Sunday after Easter	Eph. 4:1-13	John 14:12-21

WHITSUNTIDE

Whitsunday, or Pentecost (seventh Sunday after Easter Day)	Gal. 5:13-26	John 16:5-16
Trinity Sunday (first Sunday after Pentecost)	Rev. 4	John 4:19-26
Second Sunday after Pentecost	Col. 1:9-20	Matt. 13:31-33, 44-49
Third Sunday after Pentecost	Eph. 3:1-13	Matt. 9:35–10:1
Fourth Sunday after Pentecost	Heb. 11:13-16	Mark 12:13-17
Fifth Sunday after Pentecost	Rev. 21:21-27	Matt. 5:43-48
Sixth Sunday after Pentecost	Zech. 8:3-5	Matt. 7:21-27
Seventh Sunday after Pentecost	Phil. 4:8-9	Luke 2:40-51
Eighth Sunday after Pentecost	Jas. 1:5, 17, 22-25	Matt. 6:26-30
Ninth Sunday after Pentecost	I Cor. 12:14-27	Luke 12:15, 22, 23, 29-34
Tenth Sunday after Pentecost	Joel 2:21-29	Mark 6:30-43
Eleventh Sunday after Pentecost	I Thess. 5:16-24	Mark 1:29-39
*Twelfth Sunday after Pentecost	Eph. 5:1-14	Matt. 5:13-16, 20
*Thirteenth Sunday after Pentecost	II Thess. 3:6-12	Matt. 25:14-30
*Fourteenth Sunday after Pentecost	Acts 4:32-35	Luke 12:13, 14, 16-21
*Fifteenth Sunday after Pentecost	Eph. 5:25-6:4	John 13:3-7, 12-17
*Sixteenth Sunday after Pentecost	Rom. 14:7-14	Luke 16:19-31

KINGDOMTIDE

First Sunday in Kingdomtide, or Festival of Christ the King (last Sunday in August)	I Pet. 5:5-11	Luke 15:3-10
Second Sunday in Kingdomtide	II Cor. 5:14-21	Luke 15:11-32
Third Sunday in Kingdomtide	Phil. 3:7-16	Mark 4:26-29
Fourth Sunday in Kingdomtide	Rom. 8:26-28	Luke 11:1-13
Fifth Sunday in Kingdomtide	Acts 8:26-39	John 6:47-58
Sixth Sunday in Kingdomtide	Phil. 4:4-7	John 14:23-31
Seventh Sunday in Kingdomtide	I Pet. 1:3-9	Luke 17:11-19
Eighth Sunday in Kingdomtide	II Cor. 3:2-11	John 5:39-47
Ninth Sunday in Kingdomtide	Heb. 4:14-16	Luke 22:24-34, 39-46
Tenth Sunday in Kingdomtide	Rom. 8:24, 25, 31-39	Matt. 4:12-17

All Saints Day (November 1)	Rev. 7:9-17	Matt. 11:25-30
Eleventh Sunday in Kingdomtide	Phil. 1:3-11	Matt. 18:21-35
Twelfth Sunday in Kingdomtide	Phil. 3:17-21	Matt. 22:15-22
Thirteenth Sunday in Kingdomtide	Eph. 5:15-21	Luke 10:23-37
*Fourteenth Sunday in Kingdomtide	Jer. 23:5-8	Matt. 9:9-13
Thanksgiving Day (set by civil proclamation, a Thursday in November)	II Cor. 9:6-11	Matt. 7:7-12

OTHER OBSERVANCES

Bible Sunday—second Sunday in Advent
Watch Night, or New Year's Eve—December 31
Missionary Day—second Sunday after Epiphany
Race Relations Day—second Sunday in February
Day of Prayer for Students—third Sunday in February
Brotherhood Day—Sunday nearest February 22 (Washington's Birthday)
Stewardship Sunday—fourth Sunday in Lent
Festival of the Christian Home (Mother's Day)—second Sunday in May
Church Loyalty Day—set by local church, usually just before or after
    Annual Conference
Memorial Day—set by state law, in most states May 30
Student Day—set by Board of Education, usually second Sunday in June
Nature Sunday—last Sunday in June
Independence Day—July 4
Labor Sunday—Sunday preceding Labor Day (first Monday in September)
Church-School Rally Day—set by Board of Education, usually mid-September or early October
International Temperance Sunday—last Sunday in October
World Peace Sunday—Sunday nearest November 11

DATES OF EASTER DAY

1945...April 1	1958...April 6	1971...April 11	1984...April 22
1946...April 21	1959..March 29	1972...April 2	1985...April 7
1947...April 6	1960..April 17	1973...April 22	1986..March 30
1948..March 28	1961...April 2	1974...April 14	1987...April 19
1949...April 17	1962...April 22	1975..March 30	1988...April 3
1950...April 9	1963...April 14	1976...April 18	1989..March 26
1951..March 25	1964..March 29	1977...April 10	1990...April 15
1952...April 13	1965...April 18	1978..March 26	1991..March 31
1953...April 5	1966...April 10	1979...April 15	1992...April 19
1954...April 18	1967..March 26	1980...April 6	1993...April 11
1955...April 10	1968...April 14	1981...April 19	1994...April 3
1956...April 1	1969...April 6	1982...April 11	1995...April 16
1957...April 21	1970..March 29	1983...April 3	1996...April 7

Special Acts of Worship

RESPONSES to be said by the people are printed in **bold-faced type.** Sentences to be said or sung by the minister and the people together are printed in *italic bold-faced type.*

A THANKSGIVING I

Let us pray.

Almighty God, we lift up our hearts in gratitude to thee, and for all thy lovingkindness we bless thy holy name.

For life and health, for love and friendship, and for the goodness and mercy that have followed us all the days of our life,

We praise thee, O God.

For the wonder and beauty of the world, and for all things true and honest, just and pure, lovely and of good report,

We praise thee, O God.

For the gift of Jesus Christ, thine only-begotten Son, for the grace and truth which came by him, and for his obedience unto death, even the death of the cross,

We praise thee, O God.

For his glorious resurrection and ascension to thy right hand, and for his kingdom and glory and everlasting dominion,

We praise thee, O God.

For the Holy Spirit, the Comforter, the Lord and Giver of life, for thy holy Church throughout the world, for thy word and sacraments and all the means of grace, and for the fellowship of the redeemed in heaven and on earth,

We praise thee, O God.

Glory, thanksgiving, and praise be unto thee, O Father Almighty, through Jesus Christ our Lord, who liveth and reigneth with thee and the Holy Spirit, one God, world without end. **Amen.**

213

A THANKSGIVING II

Let us pray.

O God our Father, merciful and gracious, hear the thanksgivings with which we come before thy throne, in the name of Jesus Christ thy Son.

For the wonder of thy beauty, manifest in the world, for thy wisdom inspiring the works of men, and for thy fatherly love shown forth to us in Christ Jesus,

Praise be to thee, O God.

For the happiness of our earthly life, for home and friends, and for the joy of loving and being loved,

Praise be to thee, O God.

For the power to love thee, for the right to pray to thee, and for thine answers to our prayers,

Praise be to thee, O God.

For thy love in stooping to our race throughout the ages, revealing the fullness of thy grace and truth, and for all prophets, saints, benefactors, and lovers of God and men, who have seen the vision of thy glory,

Praise be to thee, O God.

But above all for Jesus Christ thy Son, the Word Incarnate, who came to end the reign of sin and death, and to bring in the reign of righteousness and life,

Praise be to thee, O God. *Amen.*

AN INTERCESSION I

We pray, O blessed God, for thy holy and universal Church, that thou wouldest deepen her life, and increase and perfect her witness to thee in the world.

We pray for all nations, that to each may be given the blessings of Christian light and truth, a right mind, and just counsels. Grant peace on earth and good will among men, that all may employ thy good gifts of order and liberty to the welfare of mankind and to thy glory. Guide and strengthen the President and all others in authority, and continue thy favor to our beloved land.

Let thy blessing rest, O Lord, upon our common life, that our spirit be disciplined and earnest. Grant that our homes be holy, our work honorable, and our pleasures and enjoyments pure. Guard and save us from every selfish use of the liberty in which we stand. Bless our just and lawful undertakings, and grant that in time of prosperity we may not forget thee, nor in time of adversity think ourselves forgotten of thee.

Into thy hands, O Father, we commit the sick, the sorrowful, the lonely, the tempted, that they may know thy healing and sanctifying power, and obtain the victory of faith; through Jesus Christ thy Son. Amen.

AN INTERCESSION II

Father of all, who hast declared thy love to all men; hear us as we bring their needs to thee in prayer.

We pray for thy Church throughout the world. Enlighten her ministers with the knowledge and understanding of thy word. Send down the healthful dew of thy grace upon all her congregations. Deliver her from false doctrine. Manifest more and more her unity, and clothe her with the beauty of holiness and peace. [Especially we ask thy blessing upon . . . every good work carried on in this congregation.] Reveal and establish thy glory among the nations. Send the light of thy gospel to the dark places of the earth; call back to thy fold those who have wandered from thee. And bring in speedily the full victory of thine everlasting Kingdom.

Pour forth thy Spirit upon all flesh, that discord and strife may be brought to a perpetual end. Deliver men everywhere from all contempt for others not of their race or color, condition or creed. Quicken by thy gospel the sense of brotherhood among all peoples, and bring them to true unity of spirit, in the bond of peace.

Bless our country; give grace and guidance to our President and all in authority over us, that they may stand firm for truth and right, none making them afraid. Bless all sorts and conditions of the people, and hasten among us the upbuilding of the city of God, wherein righteousness, love, and peace shall reign.

Father of mercies, the rest of weary souls and the joy of them that sorrow; pity the helpless, succor the friendless and the oppressed, deliver the tempted, sustain the sick, and uphold the dying. Take our loved ones, here and everywhere, into thy care and keeping, and evermore shield and guide them; through Jesus Christ our Lord. Amen.

AN INTERCESSION III

Remember, O Lord, thy Church upon earth; deepen her influence and extend her power for good, till the kingdoms of this world become the kingdom of our Lord and of his Christ.

We pray for our beloved land: for our leaders and governors, and for all who have part in public service. Make them pure in motive, wise in counsel, and strong in action, doing right in the fear of thy holy name.

Father in heaven, look down in mercy upon our distraught and fevered world; forgive the mistaken ambitions, the selfish passions, and the presumptuous claims of men; remove all suspicion and bitterness from among the nations, and bring them to peace and concord by the redeeming love of Christ.

Have mercy, O Lord, upon those who are passing through sore trial: the poor, the sick, the anxious, the oppressed, those who are in danger from the fury of the elements or from the violence of men. Inspire in us and in our fellow men the will to help our suffering brethren. Heal, protect, and strengthen them according to their need. Comfort those in sorrow with the comfort which is in Christ Jesus our Lord.

We pray for our own dear ones, wheresoever they are, that, surrounded by thy love, they may be kept in health and joy, and abide in safety and peace; through Jesus Christ our Lord. Amen.

AN INTERCESSION AT EVENTIDE

Almighty and everlasting God, who by thy Son Jesus Christ hast revealed thy glory among all nations; preserve the works of thy mercy, that thy Church throughout the world may persevere with steadfast faith in the confession of thy name.

Have mercy, we beseech thee, on all our brethren this night: on our President and all those in authority or command, that they may be strengthened with counsel; on those toiling in lonely places or at bitter tasks, that they may have courage to endure; on the sinful, that they may repent; on the sick, that they may obtain rest in sleep; on the mourners, that they may be comforted; on the dying, that they may find repose.

Into thy hands, O Lord, we commend our spirits.

Into thy hands, O Lord, we commend all who are near and dear to us.

Into thy hands, O Lord, we commend this church and congregation, with all thy people.

Thou hast promised, saying: I will never leave thee; I will help thee; I will redeem thee; I will keep thee always, even unto the end of the world.

The eternal God is our refuge, and underneath are the everlasting arms. Amen.

A SUPPLICATION

Let us pray.

Be pleased, O Lord, to hear our humble supplication, and to keep us in thy way.

From indolence and weakness of purpose, from indifference, carelessness, and insincerity,

O Lord, deliver us.

From despondency and lack of faith, from cowardice and self-conceit,

O Lord, deliver us.

From dishonesty, extravagance, and debt, and all injustice to others,

O Lord, deliver us.

From all temptation to put pleasure above duty, and from all frailty of the flesh,

O Lord, deliver us.

In all times of ignorance or perplexity, in all times of mistake or misunderstanding,

Help us, O Lord.

That we may love thee in our fellow men, and find thee in our work and prayers,

We beseech thee to hear us, O Lord.

O God, the protector of all that trust in thee, without whom nothing is strong, nothing is holy; increase and multiply upon us thy mercy, that, thou being our ruler and guide, we may so pass through things temporal that we finally lose not the things eternal; through Jesus Christ our Lord, to whom with the Father and the Holy Spirit, one God, be honor, glory, dominion, and praise for ever and ever. *Amen.*

AN ACT OF SELF-EXAMINATION

Jesus said: Seek ye first the kingdom of God, and his righteousness; and all these things shall be added unto you.

It is the will of God:

To gather together in one all things in Christ, both which are in heaven, and which are on earth.

That we should show forth the praises of him who hath called us out of darkness into his marvelous light.

That we should believe in him, and love him with all our heart, and with all our soul, and with all our mind, and with all our strength.

That we should worship him and put our whole trust in him all the days of our life.

Lord, have mercy upon us, and incline our hearts to do thy will.

Jesus said: Ye are the salt of the earth: but if the salt have lost its savor, wherewith shall it be salted? Ye are the light of the world.

It is the will of God:

That our light should so shine before men, that they may see our good works, and glorify our Father who is in heaven.

That speaking the truth in love, we should grow up into him in all things, which is the head of the body, even Christ.

That we should train our minds and be true in our thinking and just in all our judging.

That we should be honest, truthful, and upright in thought, word, and deed.

That we should be diligent and faithful in our several callings, doing our daily work in all simplicity and integrity, and laboring only for the things which are just and good.

Lord, have mercy upon us, and incline our hearts to do thy will.

Jesus said: Not everyone that saith unto me, Lord, Lord, shall enter into the kingdom of heaven; but he that doeth the will of my Father who is in heaven. Whosoever shall do the will of God, the same is my brother, and my sister.

It is the will of God:

That we should rule our spirits, bear with each other's infirmities, and as much as lieth in us, live peaceably with all men.

That we should live chiefly to minister to others' needs and not to seek only our own pleasure and gain.

That we should do what we can to take away the sin and sorrow of the world, and to overcome evil with good.

That we should not be anxious for the morrow; nor for our life, what we shall eat, or what we shall drink; nor yet for our body, what we shall put on.

Lord, have mercy upon us, and incline our hearts to do thy will.

Grant to us, Lord, we beseech thee, the spirit to think and do always such things as are right, that we, who cannot do anything that is good without thee, may by thee be enabled to live according to thy will; through Jesus Christ our Lord. Amen.

A RECOLLECTION OF JESUS

Let us remember Jesus:

Who, though he was rich, yet for our sakes became poor and dwelt among us.

Who was content to be subject to his parents, the child of a poor man's home.

Who lived for nearly thirty years the common life, earning his living with his own hands and declining no humble tasks.

Whom the common people heard gladly, for he understood their ways.

May this mind be in us which was in Jesus Christ.

Let us remember Jesus:

Who was mighty in deed, healing the sick and the disordered, using for others the powers he would not invoke for himself.

Who refused to force men's allegiance.

Who was Master and Lord to his disciples, yet was among them as their companion and as one who served.

Whose meat was to do the will of the Father who sent him.

May this mind be in us which was in Jesus Christ.

Let us remember Jesus:

Who loved men, yet retired from them to pray, rose a great while before day, watched through a night, stayed in the wilderness, went up into a mountain, sought a garden.

Who, when he would help a tempted disciple, prayed for him.

Who prayed for the forgiveness of those who rejected him, and for the perfecting of those who received him.

Who observed good customs, but defied conventions which did not serve the purposes of God.

Who hated sin because he knew the cost of pride and selfishness, of cruelty and impurity, to man, and still more to his Father in heaven.

May this mind be in us which was in Jesus Christ.

Let us remember Jesus:

Who believed in men to the last and never despaired of them.

Who through all disappointment never lost heart.

Who disregarded his own comfort and convenience, and thought first of others' needs, and though he suffered long, was always kind.

Who, when he was reviled, reviled not again, and when he suffered, threatened not.

Who humbled himself and carried obedience to the point of death, even death on the cross, wherefore God hath highly exalted him.

May this mind be in us which was in Jesus Christ.

O Christ, our only Saviour, so come to dwell in us that we may go forth with the light of thy hope in our eyes, and with thy faith and love in our hearts. Amen.

AN INTERCESSION FOR CHURCH, STATE, AND WORLD

Let us pray for a new spirit in the Church:

By this shall all men know that we are his disciples, if we have love one to another.

God our Shepherd, give to the Church a new vision and a new love, new wisdom and fresh understanding, the

revival of her brightness and the renewal of her unity, that the eternal message of thy Son, undefiled by the traditions of men, may be hailed as the good news of the new age; through him who maketh all things new, Jesus Christ our Lord.

Let us pray for a new spirit in the state:
Thou shalt wipe away all tears from their eyes: for the former things are passed away.

God our Ruler, give to every state the dawning spirit of human brotherhood, a new respect for man and for woman, new loyalty in service and charity, new happiness in work and justice in reward, that our homes may be restored in thee, our cities rebuilt, and all the world may reflect the radiance of that new Jerusalem whose river is the water of life, and whose light is the Lamb that was slain and now liveth for evermore.

Let us pray for a new spirit in the world:
Unto the Father of our Lord Jesus Christ, of whom the whole family in heaven and earth is named.

God our Father, give to the nations of the world a new heart of comradeship, the old man of ignorance and cruelty being done away, and the new man put on, renewed in knowledge, to strengthen and to serve the brethren; that every people may bring its tribute of excellence to the common treasury, without fear, and without the lust of domination, and all the world may go forward in the new and living way which he hath consecrated for us, who now liveth and reigneth, with thee and the Spirit of truth, one God, world without end. *Amen.*

THE TEN COMMANDMENTS WITH RESPONSES

God spake all these words, saying,

I am the LORD thy God. Thou shalt have no other gods before me.

Lord, have mercy upon us, and incline our hearts to keep this law.

Thou shalt not make unto thee any graven image, or any likeness of anything that is in heaven above, or that is in the earth beneath, or that is in the water under the earth: thou shalt not bow down thyself to them, nor serve them.

Lord, have mercy upon us, and incline our hearts to keep this law.

Thou shalt not take the name of the LORD thy God in vain.

Lord, have mercy upon us, and incline our hearts to keep this law.

Remember the sabbath day, to keep it holy. Six days shalt thou labor, and do all thy work: but the seventh day is the sabbath of the LORD thy God.

Lord, have mercy upon us, and incline our hearts to keep this law.

Honor thy father and thy mother.

Lord, have mercy upon us, and incline our hearts to keep this law.

Thou shalt not kill.

Lord, have mercy upon us, and incline our hearts to keep this law.

Thou shalt not commit adultery.

Lord, have mercy upon us, and incline our hearts to keep this law.

Thou shalt not steal.

Lord, have mercy upon us, and incline our hearts to keep this law.

Thou shalt not bear false witness.

Lord, have mercy upon us, and incline our hearts to keep this law.

Thou shalt not covet.

Lord, have mercy upon us, and write all these thy laws in our hearts, we beseech thee. *Amen.*

OUR LORD'S SUMMARY OF THE LAW WITH RESPONSES

Our Lord Jesus Christ said: The first of all the commandments is, Hear, O Israel; The Lord our God is one Lord: and thou shalt love the Lord thy God with all thy heart, and with all thy soul, and with all thy mind, and with all thy strength: this is the first commandment.

Lord, have mercy upon us, and incline our hearts to keep this law.

And the second is like, namely this, Thou shalt love thy neighbor as thyself.

Lord, have mercy upon us, and incline our hearts to keep this law.

A new commandment I give unto you, That ye love one another; as I have loved you, that ye also love one another.

Lord, have mercy upon us, and write all these thy laws in our hearts, we beseech thee. *Amen.*

THE BEATITUDES WITH RESPONSES

Hear the Beatitudes of our Lord Jesus Christ:

Blessed are the poor in spirit: for theirs is the kingdom of heaven.

Lord, be gracious unto us, and help us to obtain this blessing.

Blessed are they that mourn: for they shall be comforted.

Lord, be gracious unto us, and help us to obtain this blessing.

Blessed are the meek: for they shall inherit the earth.

Lord, be gracious unto us, and help us to obtain this blessing.

Blessed are they which do hunger and thirst after righteousness: for they shall be filled.

Lord, be gracious unto us, and help us to obtain this blessing.

Blessed are the merciful: for they shall obtain mercy.

Lord, be gracious unto us, and help us to obtain this blessing.

Blessed are the pure in heart: for they shall see God.

Lord, be gracious unto us, and help us to obtain this blessing.

Blessed are the peacemakers: for they shall be called the children of God.

Lord, be gracious unto us, and help us to obtain this blessing.

Blessed are they which are persecuted for righteousness' sake: for theirs is the kingdom of heaven.

Blessed are ye, when men shall revile you, and persecute you, and shall say all manner of evil against you falsely, for my sake.

Rejoice, and be exceeding glad: for great is your reward in heaven: for so persecuted they the prophets which were before you.

Grant unto us thy Holy Spirit, O God, and enable us to obtain all these blessings; through Jesus Christ our Lord. *Amen*.

A LITANY

Let us pray.

O Lord, open thou our eyes, that we may see ourselves as thou seest us; in thy mercy show us that evil that is in us, and cleanse us by thy mighty power. *Amen.*

From irresolute purpose, from unchastened desires, and from a weak and wavering will,

Good Lord, deliver us.

From slackness and indolence, from indifference to the treasures of knowledge, and a refusal to use the gifts with which thou hast endowed us,

Good Lord, deliver us.

From low ideals of life, and from thoughtless disregard of the influence of our conduct,

Good Lord, deliver us.

From pride and vanity and boasting, from self-assertion and self-seeking, and blindness to the common weal,

Good Lord, deliver us.

From dislike of criticism and love of popularity, and from unreadiness to do our duty at whatever cost,

Good Lord, deliver us.

From hastiness of speech and sullenness of temper, from readiness to think the worst of others, and from all unseemly and unworthy conversation,

Good Lord, deliver us.

Heavenly Father, blot out, we beseech thee, our past transgressions; forgive us all our negligences and ignorances; and lift us up to new energy of mind and devotion of heart, that we may have strength to persevere even to the end, through success and failure, through good report and evil report. Save us in all time of our tribulation, in all time of our wealth. Amen.

A LITANY OF THE DIVINE WILL

Jesus said: Whosoever shall do the will of God, the same is my brother and sister and mother.

O God, who hast created us all and called us to take our part in thy tremendous purpose,

Thy will be done on earth as it is in heaven.

O God, who hast shown us thy eternal will in the life of Christ our Lord,

Thy will be done on earth as it is in heaven.

O God, who art ever working in men's hearts by the operation of thy Spirit, to make us fellow workers with thy will,

Thy will be done on earth as it is in heaven.

O God, who willest that all men should be saved, and come to the knowledge of thy truth,

Thy will be done on earth as it is in heaven.

From all reliance on ourselves alone, from trying to limit the range of thy purposes, from doubts of thy mightiness in operation,

Save us and help us, we humbly beseech thee, O Lord.

From all unwillingness to learn thy will, from clinging to our own plans and desires, from all want of faith that hinders self-committal to thy guidance,

Save us and help us, we humbly beseech thee, O Lord.

From cowardice in following thy leading, from ever suffering our own ambitions to cloud the vision of thy will for us, from trying to serve thee and escape the cost,

Save us and help us, we humbly beseech thee, O Lord.

From weakness when we are faced with big decisions, from overconfidence in making them, from acting without trying to learn thy will,

Save us and help us, we humbly beseech thee, O Lord.

From shirking the responsibility of our place in the divine

order, from fearing new truth and new ways of thought and life,

Save us and help us, we humbly beseech thee, O Lord.

From seeking to set forward human progress, whether in the Church or in the world, by doing our own will instead of loyally asking to know thine,

Save us and help us, we humbly beseech thee, O Lord. *Amen.*

A LITANY OF THANKSGIVING

Let us pray.

Our Father, for the gift of thy Son to mankind,

Accept our thanks, we pray.

For the example of his life, and for his death upon the cross,

We give thee thanks, O Lord.

For the gospel of the Resurrection and the hope of new life which it brings,

We give thee thanks, O Lord.

For the gift of thy Holy Spirit,

We give thee thanks, O Lord.

For every impulse to follow the way of the cross,

We give thee thanks, O Lord.

Come into our lives and help us to triumph over all sin.

Help us so to know Christ and the power of his resurrection that we may walk with him in newness of life; through Jesus Christ, our risen Lord. *Amen.*

A LITANY OF COMMEMORATION

Let us pray.

Almighty and everlasting God, before whom stand the spirits of the living and the dead, Light of lights, Fountain of wisdom and goodness, who livest in all pure and humble and gracious souls;

For all who have witnessed a good confession for thy glory and the welfare of the world, patriarchs, prophets, and apostles, the wise of every land and nation, all teachers and preachers of thy truth,

We praise thee, O God, and bless thy name.

For the martyrs of our holy faith, the faithful witnesses to Christ of whom the world was not worthy, and for all who have resisted falsehood and wrong unto suffering or death,

We praise thee, O God, and bless thy name.

For all who have labored and suffered for freedom, good government, just laws, and the sanctity of the home, and for all who have given their lives for their country,

We praise thee, O God, and bless thy name.

For all who have sought to bless men by their service and life, and to lighten the dark places of the earth,

We praise thee, O God, and bless thy name.

For those who have been tender and true and brave in all times and places, and for all who have been one with thee in the communion of Christ's Spirit and in the strength of his love,

We praise thee, O God, and bless thy name.

For the dear friends and kindred ministering in the spiritual world, whose faces we see no more, but whose love is with us forever,

We praise thee, O God, and bless thy name.

For the teachers and companions of our childhood and youth, and the members of our household of faith who worship thee now in heaven,

We praise thee, O God, and bless thy name.

For the grace which was given to all these, and for the trust and hopes in which they lived and died,

We praise thee, O God, and bless thy name.

And that we may hold them in continual remembrance, that the sanctity of their wisdom and goodness may rest upon our earthly days, and that we may prepare ourselves to follow them in their upward way,

We beseech thee to hear us, O God.

That we may ever think of them as with thee, and be sure that where they are, there we may be also,

We beseech thee to hear us, O God.

That we may have a hope beyond this world for all thy children, even for wanderers who must be sought and brought home, that we may be comforted and sustained by the promise of a time when none shall be a stranger and an exile from thy kingdom and household,

We beseech thee to hear us, O God.

In the communion of the Holy Spirit, with the faithful and the saintly in heaven, with the redeemed in all ages, with our beloved who dwell in thy presence and peace, we, who still fight and suffer on earth, unite in ascribing

Thanksgiving, glory, honor, and power unto thee, O Lord our God. *Amen.*

A LITANY FOR A MEMORIAL DAY SERVICE

Let us pray.

O God the Father, almighty and everlasting, from whom we have come and unto whom we go,

Have mercy upon us.

O God the Son, Captain of the souls of men, who hast brought life and immortality to light,

Have mercy upon us.

O God the Holy Spirit, the Comforter, who dost take of the things of Christ and show them unto men.

Have mercy upon us.

Let us give thanks unto God.

For the land of our birth with all its chartered liberties, for all the wonder of our country's story,

We praise thee, O God.

For leaders in nation and state, and those who in days past and in these present times have labored for the commonwealth,

We praise thee, O God.

For those who in all times and places have been true and brave, and in the world's common ways have lived upright lives and ministered to their fellows,

We praise thee, O God.

For those who served their country in her hour of need, and especially those who gave even their lives,

We praise thee, O God.

O Almighty God and most merciful Father, whose nature and whose name is love; as we give thee thanks for the courage and the strength vouchsafed to these thy servants, we would remember before thee those who mourn them as their kindred. Look in mercy upon them; and as this day brings them memories of those whom they have lost, may it also bring them consolations from thee, quickening in them the sense of communion with the world unseen, and confirming their assurance of that great day when thou shalt restore to them their own in the very presence of our Lord and Saviour Jesus Christ. Amen.

A LITANY OF REMEMBRANCE

Let us pray.

O God, who art the Father of all; grant thy blessing upon us who are gathered here, and upon the multitudes of every name who are joined with us in one household of faith throughout the world.

We offer unto thee, O God, our thanksgiving, and come to pay our vows to the most High.

We remember the fathers from the beginning of the world, and all who have wrought righteousness, even down to the present day.

Grant unto us, O God, that we may have our part and lot with all thy saints.

We remember all whom we love and who love us, both those who have fallen asleep and those whose presence still blesses us. Thanks be to thee for their benediction upon our lives.

Establish thou the work of their hands, and keep us in one spirit with them.

We remember those in distress, who suffer in body, mind, or estate; those who are in prison and in bonds. As bound with them, and as sufferers with them, we bear them in our hearts and pray for their relief.

Teach us and lead us through all life's ways to an awareness of thy love and care.

We remember our enemies, if there be any who have injured us or cherish hatred against us. We pray thee to turn their hearts, and ours, that we may live peaceably with all men. If there be any whom we have wronged, move us to make amends and to seek forgiveness at their hands; and may we freely forgive all who have wronged us.

Grant us grace to surrender ourselves wholly to thee, that we may find that inward peace which the world can neither give nor take away.

We remember the whole family of man, and pray thee that the spirits of all flesh may taste of thy grace, and that all the ends of the earth may see the salvation of our God.

May the faith that makes faithful, and hope that endures, and the love that triumphs be with us always; through Jesus Christ our Lord. *Amen.*

A LITANY FOR CHRISTMAS I

Let us pray.

O Father of all, that we may be prepared for the coming of thy Son, the Babe of Bethlehem,

Help us to rid our hearts of selfishness, thoughtlessness, and vain pride.

As Mary, the mother, ever aware of thy presence, heard and received the promise that through her thy Son was to be born into the world,

So may we be ever aware of thee, alert and responsive to thy holy will.

As the messenger, John the Baptist, preached repentance to prepare the way of the Lord,

So may we live in preparation for the coming of thy kingdom.

As the ever-watchful shepherds saw thy glory in the skies,

May we too be mindful of thy glories.

As the wise men were guided by the star of peace,

So may the blessed Spirit always guide us and lead us into the ways of peace.

As the wise men in their journey toward the manger joyfully anticipated the manifestation of Jesus Christ,

So may we ever anticipate the manifestations of thy Son our Lord.

As they brought their gifts of gold, frankincense, and myrrh to the Christ Child,

So may we offer of ourselves and our substance.

May the message of the heavenly host, Peace on earth, good will toward men, ever find echo in our hearts, and be practiced in our lives.

We beseech thee to hear us, good Lord.

As thou didst humble thyself to be born a lowly babe in a manger, grant us true humility, that we may serve thee and thine in the lowly walks of life.

We beseech thee to hear us, good Lord.

Help us to realize that whatsoever we do unto one of the least of our brethren, we do unto thee, O Lord.

Open thou our eyes, that we may see thy way before us, and perceive the things we ought to do.

Open thou our ears, that we may hear thy voice urging us on to greater service.

Let us hear the cry of those who are in want, O Lord.

Touch our hearts, O Lord, that we may feel thy divine presence, that we may be strong and of good courage, that we may speak helpful words and do good deeds.

Help us, O Lord, to lose ourselves in service. *Amen.*

A LITANY FOR CHRISTMAS II

Glory to God in the highest.

And on earth peace, good will toward men.

O God, thou art our salvation; we will trust, and not be afraid. Thou art our strength and our song.

Therefore with joy shall we draw water out of the wells of salvation.

We thank thee for the birth of Jesus, that thy Spirit was upon him, that he was anointed to preach good tidings to the poor, to proclaim release to the captives, and recovering of sight to the blind, to set at liberty them that are bruised.

Help us to make our present time the acceptable year of the Lord.

O God, enable us, as we worship thee, to kindle with the joy of simple shepherds long ago at the thought of all that came to the world in the birth of the child Jesus.

Cast out our sin, and enter in; be born in us today.

Help us, O God, in the light of the shining star to realize the wastes and desolations of the world, to feel the weight of the world's sorrow and need, to be made aware of the power of evil, to see what spiritual loss is caused by man's hatred and sins.

Help us with the spirit of Jesus to build the old wastes and to raise up the former desolations.

Forgive us, O God, for our weariness of heart through great conflict and exertion. Suffer us not to become creatures and nations of selfishness, of narrow, foolish pride; marred with hardness of heart, and weakened by fear and suspicion.

Grant unto us that we being delivered out of the hand of our enemies may serve thee without fear.

Over the face of the ancient earth, weary and torn with strife, the passing generations have come and are gone, and have not seen the triumph of good will among men; yet we give thanks for the unceasing renewal of life born to new hopes and strong to achieve new victories of good.

For unto us a child is born, unto us a son is given: and the government shall be upon his shoulder.

In the light of the shining star that giveth happiness to little children and cheer to all, help us to renew our zeal for that good time when none shall be far off or forgotten, but shall live within the circle of the blessed life.

May the dayspring from on high visit us, to give light to them that sit in darkness, to guide our feet into the way of peace. *Amen.*

A LITANY FOR MISSIONS

Blessed be the Lord God for his tender mercy, whereby the dayspring from on high hath visited us,

To give light to them that sit in darkness and in the

shadow of death, to guide our feet into the way of peace.

Jesus said: They shall come from the east, and from the west, and from the north, and from the south, and shall sit down in the kingdom of God.

Thanks be to thee, O Christ, for thy holy gospel.

Other sheep I have, which are not of this fold: them also I must bring, and they shall hear my voice; and there shall be one fold, and one shepherd.

Thanks be to thee, O Christ, for thy holy promise.

Go ye therefore, and teach all nations, baptizing them in the name of the Father, and of the Son, and of the Holy Spirit: teaching them to observe all things whatsoever I have commanded you.

Thanks be to thee, O Christ, for thy holy word.

Ye shall receive power after that the Holy Spirit is come upon you: and ye shall be witnesses unto me both in Jerusalem, and in all Judea, and in Samaria, and unto the uttermost part of the earth.

Thanks be to thee, O Christ, for thy Holy Spirit.

We beseech thee to hear us, O Lord, that thou wouldest stir up the hearts of thy faithful people to greater obedience, and unite thy Church to face the world's great need. That thou wouldest send forth laborers into thy harvest,

Hear us, we beseech thee.

That those who have gone forth may be supported by thy presence, guided by thy counsel, and filled with thy power,

Hear us, we beseech thee.

Accept the devotion of our hearts, till we all come in the unity of the faith, and of the knowledge of thee, unto a perfect man, unto the measure of the stature of thy fullness. Amen.

THE EMMAUS LITANY: AN OFFICE FOR EASTERTIDE

Let us pray.

By the love with which thou didst draw near to thy disciples as they went to Emmaus and talked together of thy passion, draw near and join thyself to us, and give us a knowledge of thyself.

Hear us, blessed Jesus.

By the mercy with which at first their eyes were holden that they should not know thee, be merciful to those who are slow of heart to believe.

Hear us, blessed Jesus.

By the compassion with which, amid the joy of thy resurrection, thou didst seek them out who were sad, console the faint-hearted who have not yet learned to rejoice in thee.

Hear us, blessed Jesus.

By the patience with which, beginning at Moses, thou didst expound unto them in all the Scriptures the things concerning thyself, open thou our understanding and insight.

Hear us, blessed Jesus.

By the fire with which thou didst make their hearts to burn within them, as thou didst talk with them by the way, opening to them the Scriptures, inflame with devotion every heart that is not already burning with the love of thee, and consume with zeal those that thou hast kindled.

Hear us, blessed Jesus.

By the wisdom with which thou didst make as though thou wouldest have gone farther, thus inviting them to constrain thee to tarry with them, may no soul thou desirest to bless suffer thee to depart until it hath received from thee the blessing which thou art waiting to give.

Hear us, blessed Jesus.

By the loyalty with which thou didst go in and tarry with thy disciples when the day was far spent, fulfill in every soul that loveth thee that word of thine which saith, I will come in to him, and will sup with him, and he with me.

Hear us, blessed Jesus.

By the blessing wherewith thou didst manifest thyself to thy disciples in the breaking of bread, let every act of thine, whether of nature or of grace, be to us a sacrament, opening the eyes of our faith, that we may know thee.

Hear us, blessed Jesus.

By the power whereby thou didst vanish out of their sight, that their faith in the mystery of thy resurrection might be increased, strengthen and confirm this faith in us.

Hear us, blessed Jesus.

O blessed Jesus, who, when the doors were shut where the disciples were assembled, didst come and stand in the midst and say, Peace be unto you; may no fear ever place a barrier between our souls and thee, or hinder us from that peace which the world cannot give.

May the peace which thou gavest to thine apostles, sending them forth in thy Father's name as thou thyself wast sent, be also upon us, and remain with us always. Amen.

A LITANY OF PRAISE

Which may be sung as a hymn with responses as shown.

> For the beauty of the earth,
>   For the glory of the skies,
> For the love which from our birth
>   Over and around us lies:
>
> **Lord of all, to thee we raise**
> **This our prayer of grateful praise.**

For the beauty of each hour
 Of the day and of the night,
Hill and vale, and tree and flower,
 Sun and moon, and stars of light:
Lord of all, to thee we raise
This our prayer of grateful praise.

For the joy of ear and eye;
 For the heart and mind's delight;
For the mystic harmony
 Linking sense to sound and sight:
Lord of all, to thee we raise
This our prayer of grateful praise.

For the joy of human love,
 Brother, sister, parent, child,
Friends on earth, and friends above;
 For all gentle thoughts and mild:
Lord of all, to thee we raise
This our prayer of grateful praise.

For thy Church, that evermore
 Lifteth holy hands above,
Offering up on every shore
 Her pure sacrifice of love:
Lord of all, to thee we raise
This our prayer of grateful praise.

For thyself, best Gift Divine!
 To our race so freely given;
For that great, great love of thine,
 Peace on earth, and joy in heaven:
Lord of all, to thee we raise
This our prayer of grateful praise. *Amen.*

SANCTUS, WITH PREFACE

Therefore with angels and archangels, and with all the company of heaven, we laud and magnify thy glorious name, evermore praising thee, and saying:

Holy, holy, holy, Lord God of hosts, heaven and earth are full of thy glory. Glory be to thee, O Lord most high! *Amen.*

GLORIA IN EXCELSIS

Glory be to God on high.

And on earth peace, good will toward men.

We praise thee, we bless thee, we worship thee, we glorify thee.

We give thanks to thee for thy great glory, O Lord God, heavenly King, God the Father Almighty!

O Lord, the only-begotten Son Jesus Christ; O Lord God, Lamb of God, Son of the Father, that takest away the sins of the world, have mercy upon us.

Thou that takest away the sins of the world, have mercy upon us.

Thou that takest away the sins of the world, receive our prayer.

Thou that sittest at the right hand of God the Father, have mercy upon us.

For thou only art holy; thou only art the Lord.

Thou only, O Christ, with the Holy Ghost, art most high in the glory of God the Father. *Amen.*

TE DEUM LAUDAMUS

We praise thee, O God; we acknowledge thee to be the Lord.

All the earth doth worship thee, the Father everlasting.

To thee all angels cry aloud, the heavens and all the powers therein.

To thee cherubim and seraphim continually do cry, Holy, holy, holy, Lord God of Sabaoth;

Heaven and earth are full of the majesty of thy glory.

The glorious company of the apostles praise thee.

The goodly fellowship of the prophets praise thee.

The noble army of martyrs praise thee.

The holy Church throughout all the world doth acknowledge thee;

The Father of an infinite majesty;

Thine adorable, true, and only Son; also the Holy Ghost, the Comforter.

Thou art the King of glory, O Christ.

Thou art the everlasting Son of the Father.

When thou tookest upon thee to deliver man, thou didst humble thyself to be born of a virgin.

When thou hadst overcome the sharpness of death, thou didst open the kingdom of heaven to all believers.

Thou sittest at the right hand of God in the glory of the Father.

We believe that thou shalt come to be our judge.

We therefore pray thee, help thy servants whom thou hast redeemed with thy precious blood.

Make them to be numbered with thy saints in glory everlasting.

O Lord, save thy people and bless thine heritage.

Govern them and lift them up forever.

Day by day, we magnify thee.

And we worship thy name ever, world without end.

Vouchsafe, O Lord, to keep us this day without sin.

O Lord, have mercy upon us, have mercy upon us.

O Lord, let thy mercy be upon us as our trust is in thee.

O Lord, in thee have I trusted; let me never be confounded.

VENITE

O come, let us sing unto the Lord.

Let us heartily rejoice in the strength of our salvation.

Let us come before his presence with thanksgiving, and show ourselves glad in him with psalms.

For the Lord is a great God and a great King above all gods.

In his hand are all the corners of the earth; and the strength of the hills is his also.

The sea is his and he made it; and his hands prepared the dry land.

O come, let us worship and fall down, and kneel before the Lord our Maker.

For he is the Lord our God; and we are the people of his pasture, and the sheep of his hand.

O worship the Lord in the beauty of holiness; let the whole earth stand in awe of him.

For he cometh, for he cometh to judge the earth, and with righteousness to judge the world, and the people with his truth.

Glory be to the Father, and to the Son, and to the Holy Ghost; as it was in the beginning, is now, and ever shall be, world without end. Amen.

BENEDICTUS

Blessed be the Lord God of Israel; for he hath visited and redeemed his people,

And hath raised up a mighty salvation for us in the house of his servant David;

As he spake by the mouth of his holy prophets, which have been since the world began:

That we should be saved from our enemies, and from the hand of all that hate us;

To perform the mercy promised to our forefathers, and to remember his holy covenant;

To perform the oath which he sware to our forefather Abraham, that he would give us;

That we, being delivered out of the hand of our enemies, might serve him without fear,

In holiness and righteousness before him, all the days of our life.

And thou, child, shalt be called the prophet of the Highest, for thou shalt go before the face of the Lord, to prepare his ways;

To give knowledge of salvation unto his people for the remission of their sins,

Through the tender mercy of our God, whereby the dayspring from on high hath visited us,

To give light to them that sit in darkness, and in the shadow of death, and to guide our feet into the way of peace.

Glory be to the Father, and to the Son, and to the Holy Ghost; as it was in the beginning, is now, and ever shall be, world without end. Amen.

JUBILATE DEO

O be joyful in the LORD, all ye lands; serve the LORD with gladness, and come before his presence with a song.

Be ye sure that the LORD, he is God; it is he that hath

made us, and not we ourselves; we are his people, and the sheep of his pasture.

O go your way into his gates with thanksgiving, and into his courts with praise; be thankful unto him, and speak good of his name.

For the LORD is gracious; his mercy is everlasting; and his truth endureth from generation to generation.

Glory be to the Father, and to the Son, and to the Holy Ghost; as it was in the beginning, is now, and ever shall be, world without end. Amen.

MAGNIFICAT

My soul doth magnify the Lord, and my spirit hath rejoiced in God my Saviour.

For he hath regarded the lowliness of his handmaiden.

For behold, from henceforth all generations shall call me blessed.

For he that is mighty hath magnified me, and Holy is his Name.

And his mercy is on them that fear him throughout all generations.

He hath showed strength with his arm; he hath scattered the proud in the imagination of their hearts.

He hath put down the mighty from their seat, and hath exalted the humble and meek.

He hath filled the hungry with good things, and the rich he hath sent empty away.

He, remembering his mercy hath holpen his servant Israel,

As he promised to our forefathers, Abraham and his seed, forever.

Glory be to the Father, and to the Son, and to the Holy Ghost; as it was in the beginning, is now, and ever shall be, world without end. Amen.

BONUM EST

It is a good thing to give thanks unto the LORD, and to sing praises unto thy name, O most Highest;

To tell of thy lovingkindness early in the morning, and of thy truth in the night season;

Upon an instrument of ten strings and upon the lute; upon a loud instrument and upon the harp.

For thou, LORD, hast made me glad through thy works; and I will rejoice in giving praise for the operations of thy hands.

Glory be to the Father, and to the Son, and to the Holy Ghost; as it was in the beginning, is now, and ever shall be, world without end. Amen.

VENI, CREATOR SPIRITUS

Come, Holy Ghost, our souls inspire,
And lighten with celestial fire,
Thou the anointing Spirit art,
Who dost thy sevenfold gifts impart.

Thy blessed unction from above,
Is comfort, life, and fire of love.
Enable with perpetual light
The dullness of our blinded sight.

Anoint and cheer our soilèd face
With the abundance of thy grace.
Keep far our foes; give peace at home;
Where thou art guide, no ill can come.

Teach us to know the Father, Son,
And thee, of both, to be but One;
That through the ages all along,
This may be our endless song:

Praise to thy eternal merit,
Father, Son, and Holy Spirit. Amen.

DE PROFUNDIS

Out of the depths have I cried unto thee, O LORD.

Lord, hear my voice: let thine ears be attentive to the voice of my supplications.

If thou, LORD, shouldest mark iniquities, O Lord, who shall stand?

But there is forgiveness with thee, that thou mayest be feared.

I wait for the LORD, my soul doth wait, and in his word do I hope.

My soul waiteth for the Lord more than they that watch for the morning: I say, more than they that watch for the morning.

Let Israel hope in the LORD: for with the LORD there is mercy, and with him is plenteous redemption.

And he shall redeem Israel from all his iniquities.

Glory be to the Father, and to the Son, and to the Holy Ghost; as it was in the beginning, is now, and ever shall be, world without end. Amen.

NUNC DIMITTIS

Lord, now lettest thou thy servant depart in peace, according to thy word,

For mine eyes have seen thy salvation,

Which thou hast prepared before the face of all people;

To be a light to lighten the Gentiles and to be the glory of thy people, Israel.

Glory be to the Father, and to the Son, and to the Holy Ghost; as it was in the beginning, is now, and ever shall be, world without end. Amen.

A CANTICLE OF PRAISE

Blessed art thou, LORD God of our father Israel, forever and forever.

Thine, O LORD, is the greatness, and the power, and the glory, and the victory, and the majesty.

For all that is in the heaven and in the earth is thine.

Thine is the kingdom, O LORD; that thou art exalted above all.

Both riches and honor are thine, and thou rulest over all; in thine hand is power and might; it is thine to make great and to give strength to all.

Now therefore, our God, we thank thee, and praise thy glorious name.

Glory be to the Father, and to the Son, and to the Holy Ghost; as it was in the beginning, is now, and ever shall be, world without end. Amen.

A CANTICLE OF SALVATION

O LORD, I will praise thee; for thou hast been my comfort.

Behold, God is my salvation; I will trust, and not be afraid.

For the LORD is my strength and my song; and he is become my salvation.

Therefore with joy shall ye draw water out of the wells of salvation.

And in that day shall ye say, Praise the LORD, call upon his name,

Declare his doings among the people, make mention that his name is exalted.

Sing unto the LORD; for he hath done excellent things: let this be known in all the earth.

Cry aloud and shout, thou inhabitant of Zion: for great is the Holy One of Israel in the midst of thee.

Glory be to the Father, and to the Son, and to the Holy Ghost; as it was in the beginning, is now, and ever shall be, world without end. Amen.

A CANTICLE OF VICTORY

Holy, holy, holy, Lord God Almighty,

Which was, and which is, and which is to come.

Great and marvelous are thy works, Lord God Almighty.

Just and true are thy ways, thou King of saints.

Worthy art thou, O Lord, to receive glory and honor and power: for thou hast created all things, and because of thy will they came to be and were created.

Worthy is the Lamb that was slain to receive power, and riches, and wisdom, and strength, and honor, and glory, and blessing.

We give thee thanks, O Lord God Almighty, because thou hast taken unto thee thy great power, and hast reigned.

The kingdoms of this world are become the kingdom of our Lord, and of his Christ; and he shall reign for ever and ever.

Salvation to our God which sitteth on the throne, and unto the Lamb.

Hallelujah: for the Lord God the Almighty reigneth.

Glory be to the Father, and to the Son, and to the Holy Ghost; as it was in the beginning, is now, and ever shall be, world without end. Amen.

A CANTICLE OF REDEMPTION

It is of the Lord's mercies that we are not consumed, because his compassions fail not.

They are new every morning: great is thy faithfulness.

The Lord is my portion, saith my soul; therefore will I hope in him.

The Lord is good unto them that wait for him, to the soul that seeketh him.

It is good that a man should both hope and quietly wait for the salvation of the Lord.

It is good for a man that he bear the yoke in his youth. He sitteth alone and keepeth silence, because he hath borne it upon him.

He putteth his mouth in the dust; if so be there may be hope

He giveth his cheek to him that smiteth: he is filled with reproach.

For the Lord will not cast off forever: but though he cause grief, yet will he have compassion.

For he doth not afflict willingly nor grieve the children of men.

Let us search and try our ways, and turn again to the Lord. Let us lift up our hearts with our hands unto God in the heavens.

O Lord, thou hast pleaded the cause of my soul; thou hast redeemed my life.

Glory be to the Father, and to the Son, and to the Holy Ghost; as it was in the beginning, is now, and ever shall be, world without end. Amen.

THE CANTICLE OF THE THREE CHILDREN

Blessed art thou, Lord God of our fathers, and worthy to be praised and glorified forever.

Blessed is thy glorious and holy name, and worthy to be praised and exalted above all forever.

Blessed art thou in thy holy temple, and worthy to be praised and glorified forever.

Blessed art thou who beholdest the depths and dwellest above the cherubim, and worthy to be praised and exalted above all forever.

Blessed art thou on the throne of thy kingdom, and worthy to be praised and extolled forever.

Blessed art thou, O Lord, in the firmament of heaven, and worthy to be praised and glorified forever.

Glory be to the Father, and to the Son, and to the Holy Ghost; as it was in the beginning, is now, and ever shall be, world without end. Amen.

A CANTICLE OF MISSIONS

Have mercy upon us, O Lord, the God of all, and show us thy salvation.

Send thy fear upon the nations who have not known thy name,

That they may know that there is none beside thee, and that they also may tell forth all thy wonders.

Lift up thy hand over the strange nations, and let them see thy mighty power.

Even as thou hast been sanctified amongst us in their sight, so be thou magnified in them before our eyes.

And let them know thee as we also have known thee, that there is no God but only thou, O Lord.

Renew thy signs, and work great wonders: strengthen thine arm, and make glorious thy right hand.

Haste the time, and bring near the end, and let all declare thy mighty works.

Gather together all the tribes of Jacob, and take them for thine inheritance as in former days.

Have mercy upon thy people who are called by thy name, and upon Israel, whom thou didst make thy first-born.

Have compassion upon the holy city, even on Jerusalem, the city of thy rest.

Fill Zion with the sacred oracles, and thy temple with thy glory.

Give reward to them that wait upon thy word, and fulfill the prophecies that have been spoken in thy name,

That all upon the earth may know that thou art the Lord, the eternal God.

Glory be to the Father, and to the Son, and to the Holy Ghost; as it was in the beginning, is now, and ever shall be, world without end. Amen.

A CANTICLE OF THE CHURCH

Arise, shine; for thy light is come, and the glory of the Lord is risen upon thee.

For behold, darkness shall cover the earth, and gross darkness the people.

But the Lord shall arise upon thee, and his glory shall be seen upon thee.

And the nations shall come to thy light, and kings to the brightness of thy rising.

The abundance of the sea shall be turned unto thee; the wealth of the nations shall come unto thee.

Thy gates shall stand always open; they shall not be shut day nor night,

That men may bring unto thee the wealth of the nations, and their kings led with them.

For the nation and kingdom that will not serve thee shall perish; yea, it shall be utterly wasted.

Violence shall no more be heard in thy land, wasting nor destruction within thy borders.

But thou shalt call thy walls Salvation, and thy gates thou shalt call Praise.

The sun shall be no more thy light by day; neither for brightness shall the moon give light unto thee.

But the Lord shall be unto thee an everlasting light, and thy God thy glory.

Thy sun shall no more go down; neither shall thy moon withdraw itself.

For the Lord shall be thine everlasting light, and the days of thy mourning shall be ended.

Glory be to the Father, and to the Son, and to the Holy Ghost; as it was in the beginning, is now, and ever shall be, world without end. Amen.

A CANTICLE OF THANKSGIVING

Praise ye the Lord: for it is a good thing to sing praises unto our God; for it is pleasant, and praise is comely.

The Lord doth build up Jerusalem: he gathereth together the outcasts of Israel.

He healeth those that are broken in heart, and bindeth up their wounds.

He covereth the heavens with clouds, and prepareth rain for the earth; he maketh the grass to grow upon the mountains.

He giveth to the beast his food, and to the young ravens which cry.

Praise the Lord, O Jerusalem; praise thy God, O Zion.

For he hath strengthened the bars of thy gates; he hath blessed thy children within thee.

He maketh peace in thy borders, and filleth thee with the finest of the wheat.

Glory be to the Father, and to the Son, and to the Holy Ghost; as it was in the beginning, is now, and ever shall be, world without end. Amen.

THE PASCHAL CANTICLE

Christ our passover is sacrificed for us: therefore let us keep the feast,

Not with the old leaven, nor with the leaven of malice and wickedness; but with the unleavened bread of sincerity and truth.

Christ being raised from the dead dieth no more; death hath no more dominion over him.

For in that he died, he died unto sin once: but in that he liveth, he liveth unto God.

Likewise reckon ye also yourselves to be dead indeed unto sin, but alive unto God through Jesus Christ our Lord.

Christ is risen from the dead, and become the first-fruits of them that slept.

For since by man came death, by man came also the resurrection of the dead.

For as in Adam all die, even so in Christ shall all be made alive.

Glory be to the Father, and to the Son, and to the Holy Ghost; as it was in the beginning, is now, and ever shall be, world without end. Amen.

A CANTICLE OF THE DEPARTED

The souls of the righteous are in the hand of God, and no torment shall touch them.

In the eyes of the foolish they seemed to die: and their departure was accounted for their hurt,

And their going from us was taken to be their ruin: but they are in peace.

For though in the sight of men they be punished, yet is their hope full of immortality.

And having borne a little chastening, they shall receive great good: because God made trial of them, and found them worthy for himself.

As gold in the furnace he proved them, and as a whole burnt offering he accepted them.

They that trust in him shall understand truth; and the faithful shall abide with him in love:

Because grace and mercy are to his chosen, and he will graciously visit his holy ones.

For in the Lord is their reward, and the care of them is with the most High.

Therefore shall they receive a glorious kingdom, and a crown of beauty from the Lord's own hand.

Glory be to the Father, and to the Son, and to the Holy Ghost; as it was in the beginning, is now, and ever shall be, world without end. Amen.

A CANTICLE OF CONQUEST OVER DEATH

O Lord, thou art my God; I will exalt thee, I will praise thy name.

For thou hast done wonderful things; thy counsels of old are faithfulness and truth.

For thou hast been a stronghold to the poor, a strength to the needy in his distress,

A refuge from the storm, a shadow from the heat, when the blast of the terrible one is as a storm against the wall.

And he will destroy in this mountain the covering that is cast over the face of the peoples,

And the veil that is spread over all the nations.

He hath swallowed up death forever; and the Lord God will wipe away tears from off all faces.

The reproach of his people shall he take away from off the earth: for the Lord hath spoken it.

And it shall be said in that day, Lo, this is our God; we have waited for him, and he will save us.

This is the LORD; we have waited for him, we will be glad and rejoice in his salvation.

Thou wilt keep him in perfect peace, whose mind is stayed on thee: because he trusteth in thee.

Trust ye in the Lord forever: for in the LORD Jehovah is everlasting strength.

Glory be to the Father, and to the Son, and to the Holy Ghost; as it was in the beginning, is now, and ever shall be, world without end. Amen.

A CANTICLE OF COMMEMORATION

Let us now praise famous men, and our fathers that begat us;

In whom the Lord showed forth his glory, his mighty power in the days of old;

Men who bore dominion in the earth, and men famous for their might,

Giving counsel by their wisdom, and speaking with prophetic power;

Statesmen who were as princes of the people, and leaders trusted for their insight;

Sure were the words of their instruction, and their sayings as wise proverbs;

Such as sought out pleasant music, and fashioned songs in skillful rhymes;

Men of resource and furnished with strength, dwelling peaceably in their habitations.

All these were honored in their generation, and had glory in their day.

There be some of them that have left a name behind them, and their praises still continue.

And some there be that have no memorial, who are forgotten as though they had not been.

Nevertheless they were men of mercy, and their righteous deeds have not been in vain.

For they left a good inheritance to their seed, and their children are their testament.

Their seed shall remain forever, and their glory shall not be blotted out.

Their bodies were buried in peace, but their name liveth to all generations.

The assembly shall recount their wisdom, and the congregation shall tell out their praise.

Glory be to the Father, and to the Son, and to the Holy Ghost; as it was in the beginning, is now, and ever shall be, world without end. Amen.

A CANTICLE OF PENTECOST

The grace of the Holy Spirit be present with us and make our hearts his dwelling.

Merciful Spirit, illuminator of mankind, purge all fear and darkness from our mind.

Holy lover of thoughts that are wise, pour forth thine anointing on our understanding.

Thou purifier of all iniquities, Holy Spirit, cleanse our hearts from secret faults;

That the Father of all things may be beheld by us, whom the eyes of none save the pure in heart can see.

Thou didst inspire the prophets to chant aforetime their glorious heralding of Christ, and didst confirm the apostles to bear Christ's trophy throughout the world.

When by his word God made the heavens, the earth, and the sea, thou didst stretch out thy Godhead over the waters, and didst cherish them, O Spirit.

By thine inspiration thou grantest men to be spiritual; thou didst unite the world, divided both in tongue and faith, O Lord.

Best of teachers, thou recallest idolaters to the worship of God; wherefore by thy mercy, hear us who call upon thee, Holy Spirit.

Without thee all our prayers are vain and unworthy of the ears of God.

Thou, O Spirit, who by embracing the saints of all ages, dost teach them by the impulse of thy divinity,

By bestowing upon the apostles a gift immortal thou hast made this day forever glorious.

Glory be to the Father, and to the Son, and to the Holy Ghost; as it was in the beginning, is now, and ever shall be, world without end. Amen.

THE CANTICLE OF ST. FRANCIS OF ASSISI

O most high, almighty, good Lord God, to thee belong praise, glory, honor, and all blessing!

Praised be my Lord God with all his creatures, and especially our brother the sun, who bringeth us the day and who bringeth us the light; fair is he and shineth with a very great splendor: O Lord, he signifieth to us thee!

Praised be my Lord for our sister the moon, and for the stars, the which he hath set clear and lovely in heaven.

Praised be my Lord for our brother the wind, and for air and cloud, calms and all weather by the which thou upholdest life in all creatures.

Praised be my Lord for our sister water, who is very serviceable unto us and humble and precious and clean.

Praised be my Lord for our brother fire, through whom thou givest us light in the darkness; and he is bright and pleasant and very mighty and strong.

Praised be my Lord for our mother the earth, the which doth sustain us and keep us, and bringeth forth divers fruits and flowers of many colors, and grass.

Praised be my Lord for all those who pardon one another for his love's sake, and who endure weakness and tribulation; blessed are they who peaceably shall endure, for thou, O most Highest, shalt give them a crown.

Praised be my Lord for our sister, the death of the body, from which no man escapeth. Woe to him who dieth in mortal sin! Blessed are they who are found walking by thy most holy will, for the second death shall have no power to do them harm.

Praise ye and bless the Lord, and give thanks unto him and serve him with great humility. Amen.

Glory be to the Father, and to the Son, and to the Holy Ghost; as it was in the beginning, is now, and ever shall be, world without end. Amen.

A CANTICLE OF THE WORD

How lovely are thy messengers, O Lord of hosts! My soul hath a desire and a longing for thy word.

Thou sendest forth thy prophets in every age, and thy truth runneth swiftly to the ends of the earth.

The pure in heart have seen thee, O God: the lowly have found thee near at hand.

These tell of thy lovingkindness: from the rising of the sun to the going down of the same they keep not silence;

Publishing peace upon the mountains, and bringing good tidings of great joy,

That thou art blessed forever, and in thy will is our peace.

Thou art the everlasting fountain of life, and they that drink thereof shall thirst no more;

Light of our seeing and soul of our souls, within all spirits and beyond all worlds,

Who sustainest the heavens with the might of thy power, and gladdenest the eyes of all living with the beauty of thy holiness,

That the children of men may behold thy glory, and see thy wonders in the great deeps.

Glory be to the Father, and to the Son, and to the Holy Ghost; as it was in the beginning, is now, and ever shall be, world without end. Amen.

A CANTICLE OF THE SANCTUARY

I was glad when my companions said unto me: Come, it is our holy day;

Let us go into the house of the Lord; let us take sweet counsel together;

Let our feet stand within his gates, and heart and voice give thanks unto him.

Blessed be the temple hallowed by his name; pray for peace within its walls,

Peace to young and old that enter there, peace to every soul abiding therein.

For friends' and brethren's sake I will never cease to say: Peace be within thee!

What though for him who filleth heaven and earth there can be no dwelling made with hands;

What though his way is in the deep, and his knowledge too wonderful for us, and before him we are as children that cannot speak;

Yet, touched by the altar's living glow, we learn, as an infant, to lisp his name,

And try the wings that beat for his refuge, and flee as a bird to the mountain.

O Lord, when we cry unto thee from the deep, and wait for thee as they that wait for the morning,

Thou wilt have regard to our entreaty; the sigh of the lowly thou wilt not despise.

Not long, O Lord, shall we feel after thee in these courts below: not long wilt thou hearken to these faltering lips.

Our fathers thou hast called to thy higher praise, and gathered to their fathers must all the children be.

Let the dead and living praise thee, O God above, below: let all the generations praise thee.

Let angels in the height praise thee, who dwellest in the heavens.

Let thy Church on earth praise thee, the delight of whose wisdom is in the children of men.

O House of the Lord's praise, peace be to them that love thee!

Glory be to the Father, and to the Son, and to the Holy Ghost; as it was in the beginning, is now, and ever shall be, world without end. Amen.

A CANTICLE OF LIGHT

My heart shall indite a good matter: I will bless the Lord, who giveth me light:

I will say to the sorrowful, Be comforted; and to them that wait for the morning, Be glad of heart.

For the glory of the Lord is risen upon the earth; the day breaketh, and the shadows flee away.

Lo, the Master calleth his servants; be ready to meet him, O my soul;

Who forgiveth all thy sins, who healeth all thine infirmities,

Who openeth thy way into the kingdom of heaven, who maketh thee heir of eternal life.

O Lord our God, lift up the light of thy countenance upon us.

In thy light we shall see light; and thou wilt lead us to thy holy hill.

And dwell with us, and be our God; and the days of our lamentation shall be ended.

And all tribes shall be gathered together, and thy spirit poured out upon all flesh.

The old men shall dream dreams, and the young men shall see visions.

Then shall the earth clothe her in beautiful raiment, she shall shine as the daughter of the Great King.

The houses of mourning shall be full of light, and the rod of the oppressor shall be broken forever.

And men shall rejoice in the work of his hands, and the habitations of darkness shall be no more.

Be glad, O ye nations, and shout for joy: be strong and of a good courage, ye servants of the Lord.

For the living God is our helper: he that sitteth above the heavens shall bring it to pass.

Glory to him that hath his throne in the heavens, and his kingdom in the heart of his servants.

His kingdom is an everlasting kingdom, of his dominion there shall be no end.

Glory be to the Father, and to the Son, and to the Holy Ghost; as it was in the beginning, is now, and ever shall be, world without end. Amen.

A CANTICLE OF COMFORT

When my soul is in heaviness, and my heart is disquieted within me;

When darkness is round about my path, and all thy tempests go over my head;

Then will I betake me to the great congregation, to hear the psalm of thy redeemed and to cast my burden on the Lord.

Thou shalt cause me to hear of joy and gladness: the songs of the blessed shall visit me in the night.

They shall declare the might of thy spirit: they shall also make mention of thy peace,

Of love made perfect through suffering, and the rest that remaineth for the children of God.

As a cloud of witnesses they shall surround me; as ministering spirits they shall strengthen my soul.

They fought the good fight; they kept the faith: they came through great tribulation, enduring unto the end.

And now, O Lord, they rest in thy keeping: they shine as the stars forever and ever;

That the lost may be gathered in from all nations, and thy way made known to the uttermost parts of the earth;

To such as wander in the wilderness, and to them that are afar off upon the sea.

Thou callest us into the communion of thy beloved, the glorious fellowship of the children of light;

That we may walk in the joy of thy presence, who wilt greatly refresh us with the river of thy life.

Oh send out thy light and thy truth, let them lead me; let them bring me to thy holy hill, and to thy dwelling place.

Oh draw me from out the great waters: lead me to the rock that is higher than I.

Then shall my soul return unto her rest: I shall come to the haven where I would be.

Glory be to the Father, and to the Son, and to the Holy Ghost; as it was in the beginning, is now, and ever shall be, world without end. Amen.

The paragraphs preceding "Scriptures for Reading and Meditation" and "Daily Readings and Prayers for a Month" are intended not as comments or interpretations but as suggestions to invite attention and to stimulate meditation. Each passage is permitted to speak for itself, thus relating the religious experience of a former day to our own.

No attempt is made to imitate the language of the King James Version; on the contrary these paragraphs are phrased in the common speech of today in response to the church-wide demand that modern materials be incorporated and modern language be used.

Scriptures for Reading and Meditation

Psalm 1

To the devout Hebrews the Law was so precious that its study was the highest privilege and virtue. The writer of this psalm was one of these. He was speaking of that which stirred his soul, and for all those who seek, now as then, to learn and to obey God's law.

Blessed is the man that walketh not in the counsel of the
    ungodly,
Nor standeth in the way of sinners,
Nor sitteth in the seat of the scornful.
But his delight is in the law of the LORD;
And in his law doth he meditate day and night.
And he shall be like a tree planted by the rivers of water,
That bringeth forth his fruit in his season;
His leaf also shall not wither;
And whatsoever he doeth shall prosper.
The ungodly are not so:
But are like the chaff which the wind driveth away.
Therefore the ungodly shall not stand in the judgment,
Nor sinners in the congregation of the righteous.
For the LORD knoweth the way of the righteous:
But the way of the ungodly shall perish.

Psalm 8

From a starlit night, a poet, and God, came this psalm, suffused with the divine glory. God alone bestows any earthly supremacy which man may assume or attain.

O LORD our Lord,
How excellent is thy name in all the earth!
Who hast set thy glory above the heavens.
Out of the mouth of babes and sucklings hast thou ordained strength
Because of thine enemies,
That thou mightest still the enemy and the avenger.
When I consider thy heavens, the work of thy fingers,
The moon and the stars, which thou hast ordained;
What is man, that thou art mindful of him?
And the son of man, that thou visitest him?
For thou hast made him a little lower than the angels,
And hast crowned him with glory and honor.
Thou madest him to have dominion over the works of thy hands;
Thou hast put all things under his feet:
All sheep and oxen,
Yea, and the beasts of the field;
The fowl of the air, and the fish of the sea,
And whatsoever passeth through the paths of the seas.
O LORD our Lord,
How excellent is thy name in all the earth!

Psalm 15

What qualifies one to come into the divine presence? The behavior which springs spontaneously from inner standards of uprightness.

LORD, who shall abide in thy tabernacle?
Who shall dwell in thy holy hill?
He that walketh uprightly, and worketh righteousness,
And speaketh the truth in his heart.
He that backbiteth not with his tongue,
Nor doeth evil to his neighbor,
Nor taketh up a reproach against his neighbor.
In whose eyes a vile person is contemned;

But he honoreth them that fear the LORD.
He that sweareth to his own hurt, and changeth not.
He that putteth not out his money to usury,
Nor taketh reward against the innocent.
He that doeth these things shall never be moved.

Psalm 19, Part 1

Addison's paraphrase beginning, "The spacious firmament on high," is in *The Methodist Hymnal* and should be read as a reflection and an interpretation of this hymn of night and day.

The heavens declare the glory of God;
And the firmament showeth his handiwork.
Day unto day uttereth speech,
And night unto night showeth knowledge.
There is no speech nor language
Where their voice is not heard.
Their line is gone out through all the earth,
And their words to the end of the world.
In them hath he set a tabernacle for the sun,
Which is as a bridegroom coming out of his chamber,
And rejoiceth as a strong man to run a race.
His going forth is from the end of the heaven,
And his circuit unto the ends of it:
And there is nothing hid from the heat thereof.

Psalm 19, Part 2

This is a companion piece to Psalm 1, enumerating the beauties of the Law and closing with a simple prayer that the Lord will accept what the psalmist has said.

The law of the LORD is perfect, converting the soul:
The testimony of the LORD is sure, making wise the simple.
The statutes of the LORD are right, rejoicing the heart:
The commandment of the LORD is pure, enlightening the eyes.
The fear of the LORD is clean, enduring forever:
The judgments of the LORD are true and righteous altogether.
More to be desired are they than gold, yea, than much fine
gold:

Sweeter also than honey and the honeycomb.
Moreover by them is thy servant warned:
And in keeping of them there is great reward.
Who can understand his errors?
Cleanse thou me from secret faults.
Keep back thy servant also from presumptuous sins;
Let them not have dominion over me:
Then shall I be upright,
And I shall be innocent from the great transgression.
Let the words of my mouth, and the meditation of my heart,
Be acceptable in thy sight,
O LORD, my strength, and my redeemer.

Psalm 23

Looking back over the course of his life the psalmist realizes anew that, whether in God's out-of-doors, in the presence of enemies, or in the holy temple, God has been his guide and protector.

The LORD is my shepherd; I shall not want.
He maketh me to lie down in green pastures:
He leadeth me beside the still waters.
He restoreth my soul:
He leadeth me in the paths of righteousness for his name's sake.
Yea, though I walk through the valley of the shadow of death,
I will fear no evil: for thou art with me;
Thy rod and thy staff they comfort me.
Thou preparest a table before me in the presence of mine enemies:
Thou anointest my head with oil;
My cup runneth over.
Surely goodness and mercy shall follow me all the days of my life:
And I will dwell in the house of the LORD forever.

Psalm 24

This song of power, purity, and praise may have been sung as the ark was brought to the temple at the close of a religious procession.

The earth is the LORD'S, and the fullness thereof;
The world, and they that dwell therein.
For he hath founded it upon the seas,
And established it upon the floods.
Who shall ascend into the hill of the LORD?
Or who shall stand in his holy place?
He that hath clean hands, and a pure heart;
Who hath not lifted up his soul unto vanity,
Nor sworn deceitfully.
He shall receive the blessing from the LORD,
And righteousness from the God of his salvation.
This is the generation of them that seek him,
That seek thy face, O Jacob.

Lift up your heads, O ye gates;
And be ye lift up, ye everlasting doors;
And the King of glory shall come in.
Who is this King of glory?
The LORD strong and mighty,
The LORD mighty in battle.
Lift up your heads, O ye gates;
Even lift them up, ye everlasting doors;
And the King of glory shall come in.
Who is this King of glory?
The LORD of hosts,
He is the King of glory.

Psalm 34

Beginning with a joyful thanksgiving for deliverance, perhaps from sickness, the psalmist cannot stop with that, but must tell others, too, of the goodness of God.

I will bless the LORD at all times:
His praise shall continually be in my mouth.
My soul shall make her boast in the LORD:
The humble shall hear thereof, and be glad.
O magnify the LORD with me,
And let us exalt his name together.

I sought the LORD, and he heard me,
And delivered me from all my fears.
They looked unto him, and were lightened:
And their faces were not ashamed.
The poor man cried, and the LORD heard him,
And saved him out of all his troubles.
The angel of the LORD encampeth round about them that fear
  him,
And delivereth them.
O taste and see that the LORD is good:
Blessed is the man that trusteth in him.
O fear the LORD, ye his saints:
For there is no want to them that fear him.
The young lions do lack, and suffer hunger:
But they that seek the LORD shall not want any good thing.
Come, ye children, hearken unto me:
I will teach you the fear of the LORD.
What man is he that desireth life,
And loveth many days, that he may see good?
Keep thy tongue from evil,
And thy lips from speaking guile.
Depart from evil, and do good;
Seek peace, and pursue it.
The eyes of the LORD are upon the righteous,
And his ears are open unto their cry.
The face of the LORD is against them that do evil,
To cut off the remembrance of them from the earth.
The righteous cry, and the LORD heareth,
And delivereth them out of all their troubles.
The LORD is nigh unto them that are of a broken heart;
And saveth such as be of a contrite spirit.
Many are the afflictions of the righteous:
But the LORD delivereth him out of them all.
He keepeth all his bones:
Not one of them is broken.
Evil shall slay the wicked:

And they that hate the righteous shall be desolate.
The LORD redeemeth the soul of his servants:
And none of them that trust in him shall be desolate.

Psalms 42–43

There is no break between these two parts of a single psalm. One who has been carried away captive by "an ungodly nation" (43:1), pours into this tear-stained page his memories of the happy times when he joined in the temple processions, his laments over his present fate, and his confidence that God will someday see that he is released from his captivity and restored to his home.

As the hart panteth after the water brooks,
So panteth my soul after thee, O God.
My soul thirsteth for God, for the living God:
When shall I come and appear before God?
My tears have been my meat day and night,
While they continually say unto me, Where is thy God?
When I remember these things, I pour out my soul in me:
For I had gone with the multitude, I went with them to the
    house of God,
With the voice of joy and praise, with a multitude that kept
    holyday.
Why art thou cast down, O my soul?
And why art thou disquieted in me?
Hope thou in God: for I shall yet praise him
For the help of his countenance.

O my God, my soul is cast down within me:
Therefore will I remember thee from the land of Jordan,
And of the Hermonites, from the hill Mizar.
Deep calleth unto deep at the noise of thy waterspouts:
All thy waves and thy billows are gone over me.
Yet the LORD will command his lovingkindness in the day-
    time,
And in the night his song shall be with me,
And my prayer unto the God of my life.
I will say unto God my rock,
Why hast thou forgotten me?

Why go I mourning because of the oppression of the enemy?
As with a sword in my bones, mine enemies reproach me;
While they say daily unto me, Where is thy God?
Why art thou cast down, O my soul?
And why art thou disquieted within me?
Hope thou in God: for I shall yet praise him,
Who is the health of my countenance, and my God.

Judge me, O God, and plead my cause against an ungodly
    nation:
O deliver me from the deceitful and unjust man.
For thou art the God of my strength: why dost thou cast
    me off?
Why go I mourning because of the oppression of the enemy?
O send out thy light and thy truth: let them lead me;
Let them bring me unto thy holy hill,
And to thy tabernacles.
Then will I go unto the altar of God, unto God my exceeding
    joy:
Yea, upon the harp will I praise thee, O God my God.
Why art thou cast down, O my soul?
And why art thou disquieted within me?
Hope in God: for I shall yet praise him,
Who is the health of my countenance, and my God.

Psalm 46

One tries in vain to imagine how the first singing of this hymn stirred
the hearts of those who heard it. Even today one is thrilled by that
refrain which voices the faith of the ages.

God is our refuge and strength,
A very present help in trouble.
Therefore will not we fear, though the earth be removed,
And though the mountains be carried into the midst of the
    sea;
Though the waters thereof roar and be troubled,
Though the mountains shake with the swelling thereof.

There is a river, the streams whereof shall make glad the
 city of God,
The holy place of the tabernacles of the most High.
God is in the midst of her; she shall not be moved:
God shall help her, and that right early.
The heathen raged, the kingdoms were moved:
He uttered his voice, the earth melted.
The LORD of hosts is with us;
The God of Jacob is our refuge.

Come, behold the works of the LORD,
What desolations he hath made in the earth.
He maketh wars to cease unto the end of the earth;
He breaketh the bow, and cutteth the spear in sunder;
He burneth the chariot in the fire.
Be still, and know that I am God:
I will be exalted among the heathen, I will be exalted in the
 earth.
The LORD of hosts is with us;
The God of Jacob is our refuge.

Psalm 51

When one reads this psalm he almost feels himself an unwarranted
intruder into a soul's privacy. But ever since it was written it has spoken
for all who seek forgiveness and cleansing.

Have mercy upon me, O God, according to thy lovingkind-
 ness:
According unto the multitude of thy tender mercies blot out
 my transgressions.
Wash me throughly from mine iniquity,
And cleanse me from my sin.
For I acknowledge my transgressions:
And my sin is ever before me.
Against thee, thee only, have I sinned,
And done this evil in thy sight:
That thou mightest be justified when thou speakest,

And be clear when thou judgest.
Behold, I was shapen in iniquity;
And in sin did my mother conceive me.
Behold, thou desirest truth in the inward parts:
And in the hidden part thou shalt make me to know wisdom.
Purge me with hyssop, and I shall be clean:
Wash me, and I shall be whiter than snow.
Make me to hear joy and gladness;
That the bones which thou hast broken may rejoice.
Hide thy face from my sins,
And blot out all mine iniquities.
Create in me a clean heart, O God;
And renew a right spirit within me.
Cast me not away from thy presence;
And take not thy holy spirit from me.
Restore unto me the joy of thy salvation;
And uphold me with thy free spirit.
Then will I teach transgressors thy ways;
And sinners shall be converted unto thee.
Deliver me from bloodguiltiness, O God, thou God of my
    salvation:
And my tongue shall sing aloud of thy righteousness.
O Lord, open thou my lips;
And my mouth shall show forth thy praise.
For thou desirest not sacrifice; else would I give it:
Thou delightest not in burnt offering.
The sacrifices of God are a broken spirit:
A broken and a contrite heart, O God, thou wilt not despise.

Jeremiah 7:1-7

Does true religion consist in going to church and repeating pious
phrases, or must there be an inner principle that determines daily behavior? Jeremiah here contrasts the two ideas so clearly that his hearers
could hardly have misunderstood him.

The word that came to Jeremiah from the LORD, saying,
Stand in the gate of the LORD's house, and proclaim there this
word, and say, Hear the word of the LORD, all ye of Judah,

that enter in at these gates to worship the LORD. Thus saith the LORD of hosts, the God of Israel, Amend your ways and your doings, and I will cause you to dwell in this place. Trust ye not in lying words, saying, The temple of the LORD, The temple of the LORD, The temple of the LORD, are these. For if ye throughly amend your ways and your doings; if ye throughly execute judgment between a man and his neighbor; if ye oppress not the stranger, the fatherless, and the widow, and shed not innocent blood in this place, neither walk after other gods to your hurt: then will I cause you to dwell in this place, in the land that I gave to your fathers, for ever and ever.

Jeremiah 31:31-34

It seems almost incredible that, centuries before Jesus, the prophet Jeremiah could have looked for a time to come when men would think God's thoughts after him and do the divine will because it was their own. Perhaps it was this that Jesus had in mind when he spoke of "the new covenant."

Behold, the days come, saith the LORD, that I will make a new covenant with the house of Israel, and with the house of Judah: not according to the covenant that I made with their fathers in the day that I took them by the hand to bring them out of the land of Egypt; which my covenant they brake, although I was an husband unto them, saith the LORD: but this shall be the covenant that I will make with the house of Israel; After those days, saith the LORD, I will put my law in their inward parts, and write it in their hearts; and will be their God, and they shall be my people. And they shall teach no more every man his neighbor, and every man his brother, saying, Know the LORD: for they shall all know me, from the least of them unto the greatest of them, saith the LORD: for I will forgive their iniquity, and I will remember their sin no more.

Isaiah 40:1-11

The rapture with which such words as these would first be heard can be imagined only against the background of the despair of the exiles in Babylon, whose feelings are unforgettably described by the psalmist (Psalm 137), and to whom these words were first spoken.

Comfort ye, comfort ye my people, saith your God. Speak ye comfortably to Jerusalem, and cry unto her, that her warfare is accomplished, that her iniquity is pardoned: for she hath received of the LORD's hand double for all her sins.

The voice of him that crieth in the wilderness, Prepare ye the way of the LORD, make straight in the desert a highway for our God. Every valley shall be exalted, and every mountain and hill shall be made low: and the crooked shall be made straight, and the rough places plain: and the glory of the LORD shall be revealed, and all flesh shall see it together, for the mouth of the LORD hath spoken it.

The voice said, Cry. And he said, What shall I cry? All flesh is grass, and all the goodliness thereof is as the flower of the field: the grass withereth, the flower fadeth: because the spirit of the LORD bloweth upon it: surely the people is grass. The grass withereth, the flower fadeth: but the word of our God shall stand forever.

O Zion, that bringest good tidings, get thee up into the high mountain; O Jerusalem, that bringest good tidings, lift up thy voice with strength; lift it up, be not afraid; say unto the cities of Judah, Behold your God! Behold, the Lord GOD will come with strong hand, and his arm shall rule for him: behold, his reward is with him, and his work before him. He shall feed his flock like a shepherd: he shall gather the lambs with his arm, and carry them in his bosom, and shall gently lead those that are with young.

Isaiah 40:25-31

The God of Israel is as well able to care for his people in distant Babylon as he is to care for the stars in the distant skies. He can be relied on to find and to strengthen those who wait for him.

To whom then will ye liken me, or shall I be equal? saith the Holy One. Lift up your eyes on high, and behold who hath created these things, that bringeth out their host by number: he calleth them all by names by the greatness of his might, for that he is strong in power; not one faileth. Why sayest thou, O

Jacob, and speakest, O Israel, My way is hid from the LORD, and my judgment is passed over from my God?

Hast thou not known? hast thou not heard, that the everlasting God, the LORD, the Creator of the ends of the earth, fainteth not, neither is weary? there is no searching of his understanding. He giveth power to the faint; and to them that have no might he increaseth strength. Even the youths shall faint and be weary, and the young men shall utterly fall: but they that wait upon the LORD shall renew their strength; they shall mount up with wings as eagles; they shall run, and not be weary; and they shall walk, and not faint.

Isaiah 53

One imagines the prophet in profound perplexity, meditating on the tragic fate of someone whose bitter sufferings seemed wholly undeserved. Then he sees the suffering to have been on behalf of others, and dramatizes the whole moving story of his vision. No wonder that Christians long afterward used this as a picture of the Jesus they knew. But the prophet is concerned more with a principle than a person, and he offers a key to the meaning of a fate that many a courageous and exalted soul has met.

Who hath believed our report? and to whom is the arm of the LORD revealed? For he shall grow up before him as a tender plant, and as a root out of a dry ground: he hath no form nor comeliness; and when we shall see him, there is no beauty that we should desire him. He is despised and rejected of men; a man of sorrows, and acquainted with grief: and we hid as it were our faces from him; he was despised, and we esteemed him not.

Surely he hath borne our griefs, and carried our sorrows: yet we did esteem him stricken, smitten of God, and afflicted. But he was wounded for our transgressions, he was bruised for our iniquities: the chastisement of our peace was upon him; and with his stripes we are healed. All we like sheep have gone astray; we have turned every one to his own way; and the LORD hath laid on him the iniquity of us all.

He was oppressed, and he was afflicted, yet he opened not his mouth: he is brought as a lamb to the slaughter, and as a sheep before her shearers is dumb, so he openeth not his mouth. He was taken from prison and from judgment: and who shall declare his generation? for he was cut off out of the land of the living: for the transgression of my people was he stricken. And he made his grave with the wicked, and with the rich in his death; because he had done no violence, neither was any deceit in his mouth.

Yet it pleased the LORD to bruise him; he hath put him to grief; when thou shalt make his soul an offering for sin, he shall see his seed, he shall prolong his days, and the pleasure of the LORD shall prosper in his hand. He shall see of the travail of his soul, and shall be satisfied: by his knowledge shall my righteous servant justify many; for he shall bear their iniquities. Therefore will I divide him a portion with the great, and he shall divide the spoil with the strong; because he hath poured out his soul unto death: and he was numbered with the transgressors; and he bare the sin of many, and made intercession for the transgressors.

I Thessalonians 5:12-22

This brief catalogue of criticisms is applicable to many congregations today. It indicates Paul's own feelings when he realized more and more the pettiness and backwardness of his converts.

And we beseech you, brethren, to know them which labor among you, and are over you in the Lord, and admonish you; and to esteem them very highly in love for their work's sake. And be at peace among yourselves. Now we exhort you, brethren, warn them that are unruly, comfort the feebleminded, support the weak, be patient toward all men. See that none render evil for evil unto any man; but ever follow that which is good, both among yourselves, and to all men. Rejoice evermore. Pray without ceasing. In everything give thanks: for this is the will of God in Christ Jesus concerning you. Quench not the Spirit. Despise not prophesyings. Prove all things; hold fast that which is good. Abstain from all appearance of evil.

Philippians 2:1-11

Paul sets exacting standards for his converts when he pleads with them to act in their own situations on the same principles that Christ acted in his. The more clearly one thinks of Christ the more exacting these principles become.

If there be therefore any consolation in Christ, if any comfort of love, if any fellowship of the Spirit, if any bowels and mercies, fulfill ye my joy, that ye be like-minded, having the same love, being of one accord, of one mind. Let nothing be done through strife or vainglory; but in lowliness of mind let each esteem other better than themselves. Look not every man on his own things, but every man also on the things of others. Let this mind be in you, which was also in Christ Jesus: who, being in the form of God, thought it not robbery to be equal with God: but made himself of no reputation, and took upon him the form of a servant, and was made in the likeness of men: and being found in fashion as a man, he humbled himself, and became obedient unto death, even the death of the cross. Wherefore God also hath highly exalted him, and given him a name which is above every name: that at the name of Jesus every knee should bow, of things in heaven, and things in earth, and things under the earth; and that every tongue should confess that Jesus Christ is Lord, to the glory of God the Father.

Romans 12:1-8

It is not easy to realize that the converts to whom Paul wrote were hearing from him for the first time what it meant to be a Christian. They had no gospels to read and knew of Christ by word of mouth only. Paul is here showing them that the Christian life is based on inner thought and purpose.

I beseech you therefore, brethren, by the mercies of God, that ye present your bodies a living sacrifice, holy, acceptable unto God, which is your reasonable service. And be not conformed to this world: but be ye transformed by the renewing of your mind, that ye may prove what is that good, and acceptable, and perfect, will of God.

For I say, through the grace given unto me, to every man that is among you, not to think of himself more highly than he ought to think; but to think soberly, according as God hath dealt to every man the measure of faith. For as we have many members in one body, and all members have not the same office: so we, being many, are one body in Christ, and every one members one of another. Having then gifts differing according to the grace that is given to us, whether prophecy, let us prophesy according to the proportion of faith; or ministry, let us wait on our ministering: or he that teacheth, on teaching; or he that exhorteth, on exhortation: he that giveth, let him do it with simplicity; he that ruleth, with diligence; he that showeth mercy, with cheerfulness.

Mark 12:28-34

In recognizing the distinction between forms and motives this scribe was not far from the kingdom—the kingdom that is made up of those who not only talk of it but act according to its principles.

And one of the scribes came, and having heard them reasoning together, and perceiving that he had answered them well, asked him, Which is the first commandment of all? And Jesus answered him, The first of all the commandments is, Hear, O Israel; The Lord our God is one Lord: and thou shalt love the Lord thy God with all thy heart, and with all thy soul, and with all thy mind, and with all thy strength: this is the first commandment. And the second is like, namely this, Thou shalt love thy neighbor as thyself. There is none other commandment greater than these. And the scribe said unto him, Well, Master, thou hast said the truth: for there is one God; and there is none other but he: and to love him with all the heart, and with all the understanding, and with all the soul, and with all the strength, and to love his neighbor as himself, is more than all whole burnt offerings and sacrifices. And when Jesus saw that he answered discreetly, he said unto him, Thou art not far from the kingdom of God. And no man after that durst ask him any question.

John 1:1-5, 10-12, 14, 16, 18

The early Christians felt that all their hopes and ideals were fulfilled in Christ, and they did not hesitate to give Christian meanings to the best things they knew. The "Word," well known in the philosophy of the Greeks, found its fulfillment in the greater Christian "Word" of which the poet sings.

In the beginning was the Word, and the Word was with God, and the Word was God. The same was in the beginning with God. All things were made by him; and without him was not anything made that was made. In him was life; and the life was the light of men. And the light shineth in darkness; and the darkness comprehended it not.

He was in the world, and the world was made by him, and the world knew him not. He came unto his own, and his own received him not. But as many as received him, to them gave he power to become the sons of God.

And the Word was made flesh, and dwelt among us (and we beheld his glory, the glory as of the only-begotten of the Father), full of grace and truth. And of his fullness have all we received, and grace for grace.

No man hath seen God at any time; the only-begotten Son, which is in the bosom of the Father, he hath declared him.

Genesis 1:1–2:3, in part

The devout man who wrote this chapter might feel sadly mis-understood if he knew that it is usually read without the climax which, for him, marked its goal and purpose. For him the whole majestic procession of creation, as he understood it, moved toward the Sabbath as the day ordained of God from the creation of the world.

In the beginning God created the heaven and the earth. And the earth was without form, and void; and darkness was upon the face of the deep. And the Spirit of God moved upon the face of the waters. And God said, Let there be light: and there was light. And God saw the light, that it was good: and God divided the light from the darkness. And God called the light Day, and the darkness he called Night. And the evening and the morning were the first day. . . . And the evening and the morning were the second day. . . . And the evening and the morning were the third day. . . . And the evening and the morning were the fourth day. . . . And the evening and the morning were the fifth day. . . . And God said, Let us make man in our image, after our likeness: and let them have dominion over the fish of the sea, and over the fowl of the air, and over the cattle, and over all the earth, and over every creeping thing that creepeth upon the earth. So God created man in his own image, in the image of God created he him; male and female created he them. And God blessed them, and God said unto them, Be fruitful, and multiply, and replenish the earth, and subdue it. . . . And the evening and the morning were the sixth day. And on the seventh day God ended his work which he had made; and he rested on the seventh day from all his work which he had made. And God blessed the seventh day, and sanctified it; because that in it he had rested from all his work which God created and made.

II Samuel 18:24-33

Reading this chapter today, one forgets Absalom's revolt against his father and is aware only of the heartbroken David, whose "chamber over the gate" has become a tragic symbol of lonely sorrow ever since.

And David sat between the two gates: and the watchman went up to the roof over the gate unto the wall, and lifted up his eyes, and looked, and behold a man running alone. And the watchman cried and told the king. And the king said, If he be alone, there is tidings in his mouth. And he came apace, and drew near. And the watchman saw another man running: and the watchman called unto the porter, and said, Behold another man running alone. And the king said, He also bringeth tidings. And the watchman said, Me thinketh the running of the foremost is like the running of Ahimaaz the son of Zadok. And the king said, He is a good man, and cometh with good tidings.

And Ahimaaz called, and said unto the king, All is well. And he fell down to the earth upon his face before the king, and said, Blessed be the LORD thy God, which hath delivered up the men that lifted up their hand against my lord the king. And the king said, Is the young man Absalom safe? And Ahimaaz answered, When Joab sent the king's servant, and me thy servant, I saw a great tumult, but I knew not what it was. And the king said unto him, Turn aside, and stand here. And he turned aside, and stood still.

And, behold, Cushi came; and Cushi said, Tidings, my lord the king; for the LORD hath avenged thee this day of all them that rose up against thee. And the king said unto Cushi, Is the young man Absalom safe? And Cushi answered, The enemies of my lord the king, and all that rise against thee to do thee hurt, be as that young man is. And the king was much moved, and went up to the chamber over the gate, and wept; and as he went, thus he said, O my son Absalom, my son, my son Absalom! would God I had died for thee, O Absalom, my son, my son!

Psalm 121

Not from the hills, splendid as they are, but from their divine Maker come the help and protection in which the faithful can safely trust.

I will lift up mine eyes unto the hills;
From whence cometh my help?
My help cometh from the LORD,
Which made heaven and earth.

He will not suffer thy foot to be moved:
He that keepeth thee will not slumber.
Behold, he that keepeth Israel
Shall neither slumber nor sleep.
The LORD is thy keeper:
The LORD is thy shade upon thy right hand.
The sun shall not smite thee by day,
Nor the moon by night.
The LORD shall preserve thee from all evil:
He shall preserve thy soul.
The LORD shall preserve thy going out and thy coming in
From this time forth, and even for evermore.

Psalm 130

These words must have come from one who was profoundly penitent; he prays so simply and movingly to God for forgiveness that he has spoken for all, ever since, "who do truly and earnestly repent of their sins."

Out of the depths have I cried unto thee, O LORD.
Lord, hear my voice:
Let thine ears be attentive
To the voice of my supplications.
If thou, LORD, shouldest mark iniquities,
O Lord, who shall stand?
But there is forgiveness with thee,
That thou mayest be feared.
I wait for the LORD, my soul doth wait,
And in his word do I hope.
My soul waiteth for the Lord
More than they that watch for the morning:
I say, more than they that watch for the morning.
Let Israel hope in the LORD:
For with the LORD there is mercy,
And with him is plenteous redemption.
And he shall redeem Israel
From all his iniquities.

Psalm 139, in part

Who has not occasionally met saintly souls who seem to live constantly in the divine presence, where perfect love has cast out fear?

I sought the Lord, and afterward I knew
He moved my soul to seek him, seeking me;
It was not I that found, O Saviour true,
No, I was found of thee.

O LORD, thou hast searched me, and known me.
Thou knowest my downsitting and mine uprising,
Thou understandest my thought afar off.
Thou compassest my path and my lying down,

And art acquainted with all my ways.
For there is not a word in my tongue,
But, lo, O Lord, thou knowest it altogether.
Thou hast beset me behind and before,
And laid thine hand upon me.
Such knowledge is too wonderful for me;
It is high, I cannot attain unto it.
Whither shall I go from thy spirit?
Or whither shall I flee from thy presence?
If I ascend up into heaven, thou art there:
If I make my bed in hell, behold, thou art there.
If I take the wings of the morning,
And dwell in the uttermost parts of the sea;
Even there shall thy hand lead me,
And thy right hand shall hold me.
If I say, Surely the darkness shall cover me;
Even the night shall be light about me.
Yea, the darkness hideth not from thee;
But the night shineth as the day:
The darkness and the light are both alike to thee.
How precious also are thy thoughts unto me, O God!
How great is the sum of them!
If I should count them, they are more in number than the
    sand:
When I awake, I am still with thee.
Search me, O God, and know my heart:
Try me, and know my thoughts:
And see if there be any wicked way in me,
And lead me in the way everlasting.

Isaiah 1:10-17

Even today one can feel the burning intensity of these passionate
words in which the prophet Isaiah was fighting another battle in the
agelong conflict between organized religion and ethical conduct. Christians today do not offer burnt offerings and such sacrifices; but they bring
other kinds of offerings; they keep special days; they call assemblies,

have solemn meetings, and make many prayers in much the same way that the prophet condemns.

Hear the word of the LORD, ye rulers of Sodom; give ear unto the law of our God, ye people of Gomorrah. To what purpose is the multitude of your sacrifices unto me? saith the LORD: I am full of the burnt offerings of rams, and the fat of fed beasts; and I delight not in the blood of bullocks, or of lambs, or of he goats. When ye come to appear before me, who hath required this at your hand, to tread my courts? Bring no more vain oblations; incense is an abomination unto me; the new moons and sabbaths, the calling of assemblies, I cannot away with; it is iniquity, even the solemn meeting. Your new moons and your appointed feasts my soul hateth: they are a trouble unto me; I am weary to bear them. And when ye spread forth your hands, I will hide mine eyes from you: yea, when ye make many prayers, I will not hear: your hands are full of blood. Wash you, make you clean; put away the evil of your doings from before mine eyes; cease to do evil; learn to do well; seek judgment, relieve the oppressed, plead for the widow.

Isaiah 55:6-11

The real "Word of God," as the prophet thought of it, was far greater than anything that could be written. For him it meant the divine power at work, as when God said, Let there be light. God's word, for the prophet, was God's will in action. And it can still be found—if sought!

Seek ye the LORD while he may be found, call ye upon him while he is near. Let the wicked forsake his way, and the unrighteous man his thoughts: and let him return unto the LORD, and he will have mercy upon him; and to our God, for he will abundantly pardon. For my thoughts are not your thoughts, neither are your ways my ways, saith the LORD. For as the heavens are higher than the earth, so are my ways higher than your ways, and my thoughts than your thoughts. For as the rain cometh down, and the snow from heaven, and returneth not thither, but watereth the earth, and maketh it bring forth and bud, that it may give seed to the sower, and bread to the eater: so shall my word be that goeth forth out of my mouth: it shall not return unto me void, but it shall accomplish that which I please, and it shall prosper in the thing whereto I sent it.

Daily Readings and Prayers for a Month

A WEEK WITH THE GOSPEL OF LUKE

The First Day *(Suitable for Sunday)*

From the days of Jesus till now the observance of the Sabbath by
the orthodox Jew has been far more exacting than the observance of
Sunday by most Christians. Jesus' rejection of the common legalism of
his day is still a revolutionary idea in religion.

And it came to pass on the second sabbath after the first,
that he went through the cornfields; and his disciples plucked
the ears of corn, and did eat, rubbing them in their hands. And
certain of the Pharisees said unto them, Why do ye that which
is not lawful to do on the sabbath days? And Jesus answering
them said, Have ye not read so much as this, what David did,
when himself was an hungred, and they which were with him;
how he went into the house of God, and did take and eat the
showbread, and gave also to them that were with him; which it
is not lawful to eat but for the priests alone? And he said
unto them, That the Son of man is Lord also of the sabbath.

—Luke 6:1-5

O God, our guardian by night, our guide by day; thou hast
led us forth from darkness into the light of life, and it is thy
day. May it be a holy time, and passed in thy nearer presence,
and in the love of Jesus Christ our Lord. Amen.

Whereinsoever we have erred and strayed from thy ways,
whereinsoever we have come short, or done that which we
ought not to have done, graciously forgive us, we beseech thee.
Help us to turn from all evil to that which is holy and good.
Teach us to love what is right, and to do it forever; through
Jesus Christ our Lord. Amen.

Merciful Father, who willest not that thy children should
wander in darkness; pour the light of thy Spirit into our minds

and hearts, that we may discover what is thy holy will, and discern the true from the false, the evil from the good, that we may henceforth walk in all humility in the paths of heavenly wisdom and peace, to the glory of thy holy name; through Jesus Christ our Lord. Amen.

THE LORD'S PRAYER

The Second Day

The homely humor and common sense of Jesus are nowhere more in evidence than here. Of course no one ever had a beam of wood in his eye, nor expected thorny weeds to bear grapes, but in these broad strokes Jesus is simply sketching the absurdities to which men are carried by a sense of self-importance and desire for show.

And he spake a parable unto them, Can the blind lead the blind? shall they not both fall into the ditch? The disciple is not above his master: but everyone that is perfect shall be as his master.

And why beholdest thou the mote that is in thy brother's eye, but perceivest not the beam that is in thine own eye? Either how canst thou say to thy brother, Brother, let me pull out the mote that is in thine eye, when thou thyself beholdest not the beam that is in thine own eye Thou hypocrite, cast out first the beam out of thine own eye, and then shalt thou see clearly to pull out the mote that is in thy brother's eye.

For a good tree bringeth not forth corrupt fruit; neither doth a corrupt tree bring forth good fruit. For every tree is known by his own fruit. For of thorns men do not gather figs, nor of a bramble bush gather they grapes. A good man out of the good treasure of his heart bringeth forth that which is good; and an evil man out of the evil treasure of his heart bringeth forth that which is evil: for of the abundance of the heart his mouth speaketh.   —*Luke 6:39-45*

Almighty and all-merciful God, our Father in heaven; grant that we may desire and will, both now in our prayers, and at all times in our life, what is pleasing to thee. Give us grace that we may never have any wish which we cannot bring to thee, nor any purpose in which we cannot seek thy help. So may our spirits be ever at one with thee, and our prayers such as thou wilt hear and answer; according to thy lovingkindness declared unto us through Jesus Christ our Lord. Amen.

O heavenly Father, shed forth thy blessed Spirit richly on all the members of this household. Make each one of us an instrument in thy hands for good. Purify our hearts; strengthen our minds and bodies; fill us with mutual love. Let no pride, no self-conceit, no rivalry, no dispute, ever spring up among us. Make us earnest and true, wise and prudent, giving no just cause for offence; and may thy holy peace rest upon us this day and every day, sweetening our trials, cheering us in our work, and keeping us faithful to the end; through Jesus Christ our Lord. Amen.

THE LORD'S PRAYER

The Third Day

If one reads these words with any care, they inevitably raise the question as to how the seed which is "the word of God" fares in his own case: does it wither away and die, or does it grow and bear fruit?

And he spake by a parable: A sower went out to sow his seed: and as he sowed, some fell by the wayside; and it was trodden down, and the fowls of the air devoured it. And some fell upon a rock; and as soon as it was sprung up, it withered away, because it lacked moisture. And some fell among thorns, and the thorns sprang up with it, and choked it. And other fell on good ground, and sprang up, and bare fruit an hundredfold.

Now the parable is this: The seed is the word of God. Those by the wayside are they that hear; then cometh the devil, and taketh away the word out of their hearts, lest they should believe and be saved. They on the rock are they, which, when they hear, receive the word with joy; and these have no root, which for a while believe, and in time of temptation fall away. And that which fell among thorns are they, which, when they have heard, go forth, and are choked with cares and riches and pleasures of this life, and bring no fruit to perfection. But that on the good ground are they, which in an honest and good heart, having heard the word, keep it, and bring forth fruit with patience.   —*Luke 8:4-8, 11-15*

Most gracious Father, who willest us to give thanks for all things, to dread nothing but the loss of thee, and to cast all our cares on thee, who carest for us; preserve us from faithless fears and worldly anxieties, and grant that no clouds of this mortal life may hide from us the light of that love which is immortal, and from which nothing can separate us; through Jesus Christ our Lord. Amen.

O God, who hast taught us by Jesus Christ that except we become as little children we cannot enter into the kingdom of heaven; give us a childlike spirit, that we may seek to know thy truth and do thy will. May it please thee, of thy great mercy, ministering grace to us in the time of our temptation and our failing purpose, to enable us to strive against the spirit of pride, envy, and selfishness and to overcome all evil; through Jesus Christ our Lord. Amen.

THE LORD'S PRAYER

The Fourth Day

Jesus spoke the parable of the good Samaritan in answer to the question, "Who is my neighbor?" One would like to know what the Samaritan would have said had he been asked: "What did this man ever do for you? What do you get out of it?"

Jesus said, A certain man went down from Jerusalem to Jericho, and fell among thieves, which stripped him of his raiment, and wounded him, and departed, leaving him half dead. And by chance there came down a certain priest that way: and when he saw him, he passed by on the other side. And likewise a Levite, when he was at the place, came and looked on him, and passed by on the other side. But a certain Samaritan, as he journeyed, came where he was: and when he saw him, he had compassion on him, and went to him, and bound up his wounds, pouring in oil and wine, and set him on his own beast, and brought him to an inn, and took care of him. And on the morrow when he departed, he took out two pence, and gave them to the host, and said unto him, Take care of him; and whatsoever thou spendest more, when I come again, I will repay thee. Which now of these three, thinkest thou, was neighbor unto him that fell among the thieves? And he said, He that showed mercy on him. Then said Jesus unto him, Go, and do thou likewise.   —*Luke 10:30-37*

O thou most holy and ever-loving God, we thank thee once more for the quiet rest of the night that has gone by, for the new promise that has come with this fresh morning, and for the hope of this day. While we have slept, the world in which we live has swept on, and we have rested under the shadow of thy love. May we trust thee this day for all the needs of the body, the soul, and the spirit. Give us this day our daily bread. Amen.

O God from whom we have received life and all earthly blessings; vouchsafe to give unto us each day what we need. Give unto all of us strength to perform faithfully our appointed tasks; bless the work of our hands and of our minds. Grant that we may ever serve thee, in sickness and in health, in necessity and in abundance; sanctify our joys and our trials; and give us grace to seek first thy kingdom and its righteousness, in the sure and certain faith that all else shall be added unto us; through Jesus Christ thy Son our Lord and Saviour. Amen.

THE LORD'S PRAYER

The Fifth Day

It was not the custom of Jesus to make the application of his parables. The last sentence of this passage seems to voice a spontaneous response from one of his hearers: "What a fool I would be if, in getting treasure for myself, I am not rich toward God!"

And one of the company said unto him, Master, speak to my brother, that he divide the inheritance with me. And he said unto him, Man, who made me a judge or a divider over you?

And he said unto them, Take heed, and beware of covetousness: for a man's life consisteth not in the abundance of the things which he possesseth, And he spake a parable unto them, saying, The ground of a certain rich man brought forth plentifully: and he thought within himself, saying, What shall I do, because I have no room where to bestow my fruits? And he said, This will I do: I will pull down my barns, and build greater; and there will I bestow all my fruits and my goods. And I will say to my soul, Soul, thou hast much goods laid up for many years; take thine ease, eat, drink, and be merry. But God said unto him, Thou fool, this night thy soul shall be required of thee: then whose shall those things be, which thou hast provided?

So is he that layeth up treasure for himself, and is not rich toward God.   —*Luke 12:13-21*

Almighty God, we thank thee for rest and health, for work to do and strength to do it, and for all the surroundings of our life that make it desirable and enjoyable. Do thou raise our thoughts and purify our aspirations. Strengthen our wills, we beseech thee, on the side of what is right and good, and against what is wrong and evil; through Jesus Christ our Lord. Amen.

O blessed Jesus, who for thirty years didst dwell in thy humble home in Nazareth; be with thy servants in this our home; keep from it all pride and selfishness and impurity, that it may be a dwelling place meet for thy sacred presence. Grant us to grow in grace and in the knowledge and love of thee; guide us throughout our life on earth; comfort us in all troubles; strengthen us in all weakness; and bring us at last to thy home in heaven; where, with the Father and the Holy Spirit, thou livest and reignest, one God, world without end. Amen.

THE LORD'S PRAYER

The Sixth Day

Taken by themselves these words suggest a life quite impossible in the world as we know it; but in the world as Jesus pictured it, a world peopled by those who live according to the Golden Rule, such a life is not incredible at all.

And he said unto his disciples, Therefore I say unto you, Take no thought for your life, what ye shall eat; neither for the body, what ye shall put on. The life is more than meat, and the body is more than raiment. Consider the ravens; for they neither sow nor reap; which neither have storehouse nor barn; and God feedeth them: how much more are ye better than the fowls? And which of you with taking thought can add to his stature one cubit? If ye then be not able to do that thing which is least, why take ye thought for the rest? Consider the lilies how they grow: they toil not, they spin not; and yet I say unto you, That Solomon in all his glory was not arrayed like one of these. If then God so clothe the grass, which is today in the field, and tomorrow is cast into the oven; how much more will he clothe you, O ye of little faith? And seek not ye what ye shall eat, or what ye shall drink, neither be ye of doubtful mind. For all these things do the nations of the world seek after: and your Father knoweth that ye have need of these things. But rather seek ye the kingdom of God; and all these things shall be added unto you. —*Luke 12:22-31*

Eternal God, who delightest to hear the cry of the contrite heart; by thy Holy Spirit so teach us to pray that we may enter into living communion with thee and all our worship may be acceptable in thy sight. As we wait before the throne of the heavenly grace, unite our minds in one solemn act of adoration, that our desires may ascend like incense acceptable unto thee; through Jesus Christ our Lord. Amen.

O God, who by the example of thy dear Son hast warned us that we should work thy works while it is day, before the night cometh when no man can work; keep us from sloth and idleness, and from the misuse of those talents which thou hast committed to our trust. Enable us to perform our several duties with such care and diligence that our work may never be reproved in thy sight. And forasmuch as the needful business of this life is apt to steal away our hearts from thee, give us grace to remember that we have a Master in heaven, and to do everything in singleness of heart, as unto thee and not unto men; through Jesus Christ our Lord. Amen.

THE LORD'S PRAYER

The Seventh Day

Two men embody answers to the question, "Are you as good as you ought to be?" One of them, thinking in terms of himself, felt that he was good enough and said, "I have a perfect claim." The other, thinking in terms of God, knew God's mercy to be his only hope and said, "I can make no claim."

And he spake this parable unto certain which trusted in themselves that they were righteous, and despised others: Two men went up into the temple to pray; the one a Pharisee, and the other a publican. The Pharisee stood and prayed thus with himself, God, I thank thee, that I am not as other men are, extortioners, unjust, adulterers, or even as this publican. I fast twice in the week, I give tithes of all that I possess. And the publican, standing afar off, would not lift up so much as his eyes unto heaven, but smote upon his breast, saying, God be merciful to me a sinner. I tell you, this man went down to his house justified rather than the other: for everyone that exalteth himself shall be abased; and he that humbleth himself shall be exalted.   —Luke 18:9-14

Most holy and gracious God, who turnest the shadow of night into morning; satisfy us early with thy mercy, that we may rejoice and be glad all the day. Lift the light of thy countenance upon us; calm every troubled thought; and guide our feet into the way of peace. Perfect thy strength in our weakness, and help us to worship thee in the spirit of Jesus Christ our Lord. Amen.

Heavenly Father, when from time to time we enter thy temple to pray, help us to come to thee with such a sense of thy love for us, and of our own need of all that thou alone canst give, that our worship may be acceptable in thy sight; and grant that we ourselves may carry with us the spirit of devotion and humility which dwelleth with those who worship thee in spirit and in truth. Amen.

THE LORD'S PRAYER

A WEEK WITH THE PSALMISTS

The Eighth Day (Suitable for Sunday)

Many of the temple songs were really anthems of praise and thanksgiving. This is one of them, and it springs from the profound conviction that God is the source of justice and welfare for the world.

God be merciful unto us, and bless us;
And cause his face to shine upon us.
That thy way may be known upon earth,
Thy saving health among all nations.
Let the people praise thee, O God;
Let all the people praise thee.
O let the nations be glad and sing for joy:
For thou shalt judge the people righteously
And govern the nations upon earth.
Let the people praise thee, O God;
Let all the people praise thee.
Then shall the earth yield her increase;
And God, even our own God, shall bless us.
God shall bless us;
And all the ends of the earth shall fear him.   —Ps. 67

Almighty God, we praise thee for the mercies which thou hast bestowed upon us as a household, and we beseech thee to bless all the families of earth with a Father's blessing. Look mercifully upon the lonely, the weary, and the heavy-laden, and grant them rest unto their souls. Shed abroad the holy influence of the Lord's Day throughout our land, and keep our whole country, with those who are chosen to govern it, in the way of righteousness and peace. We commend to thy fatherly goodness all who are near and dear to us, wherever they may be today, praying thee to watch over them, to provide for them, and to bless them in body and soul; through Jesus Christ our Lord. Amen.

Now unto him who is able to do exceeding abundantly above all that we ask or think, according to the power that worketh in us, unto him be glory in the Church by Christ Jesus, throughout all ages, world without end. Amen.

THE LORD'S PRAYER

The Ninth Day

Here speaks one who, out of bitter spiritual experience, has learned that he can find happiness and peace in God alone. The prosperity of the wicked no longer upsets him. He has found more than the wicked can ever gain.

Truly God is good to Israel,
Even to such as are of a clean heart.
But as for me, my feet were almost gone;
My steps had well nigh slipped.
For I was envious at the foolish,
When I saw the prosperity of the wicked.
Nevertheless I am continually with thee:
Thou hast holden me by my right hand.
Thou shalt guide me with thy counsel,
And afterward receive me to glory.
Whom have I in heaven but thee?
And there is none upon earth that I desire beside thee.
My flesh and my heart faileth:
But God is the strength of my heart, and my portion forever.
For lo, they that are far from thee shall perish.
But it is good for me to draw near to God:
I have put my trust in the Lord God,
That I may declare all thy works.   —*Ps. 73, in part*

We beseech thee, O Lord, remember all for good; have mercy upon all, O God. Remember every soul who, being in any affliction or trouble, standeth in need of thy mercy and help, all who are in necessity or distress. Thou, O Lord, art the helper of the helpless, the hope of the hopeless. Be thou within us to strengthen us, without us to keep us, above us to protect us, beneath us to uphold us, before us to direct us, behind us to keep us from straying, round about us to defend us. Blessed be thou, O Lord our Father, for ever and ever. Amen.

Grant us, O Lord, to pass this day in gladness and peace, without stumbling and without stain, that, reaching the eventide victorious over all temptations, we may praise thee, the eternal God, who art blessed forever, world without end. Amen.

THE LORD'S PRAYER

The Tenth Day

There may not be many Christians today who feel toward their church as this devout poet felt toward the temple, but the ardor of his devotion is a reminder that true religion is nourished and sustained by the sincere souls to whom it is as real as it was to the writer of this psalm.

How amiable are thy tabernacles,
O Lord of hosts!
My soul longeth, yea, even fainteth for the courts of the
Lord:
My heart and my flesh crieth out for the living God.
Yea, the sparrow hath found an house,
And the swallow a nest for herself, where she may lay her
young,
Even thine altars, O Lord of hosts, my King and my God.
Blessed are they that dwell in thy house:
They will be still praising thee.
Blessed is the man whose strength is in thee;
In whose heart are the ways of them:
Who passing through the valley of Baca make it a well;
The rain also filleth the pools.
They go from strength to strength;
Every one of them in Zion appeareth before God.

O LORD God of hosts, hear my prayer:
Give ear, O God of Jacob.

Behold, O God our shield,
And look upon the face of thine anointed.
For a day in thy courts is better than a thousand.
I had rather be a doorkeeper in the house of my God,
Than to dwell in the tents of wickedness.
For the LORD God is a sun and shield:
The LORD will give grace and glory;
No good thing will he withhold from them that walk up-
rightly.
O LORD of hosts,
Blessed is the man that trusteth in thee.   —*Ps. 84*

O God, who art Truth and Spirit; help us in spirit and in
truth to worship thy great name, not acknowledging thee in one
place or at one time only, but in every place and at every time,
in all we do and in all we see, in our work and in our rest,
in our laughter and our tears, in loneliness and in fellowship,
in the eye of day and in the shadow of night, beneath the open
sky as in the house of prayer, in the heart of the little child
as in the wisdom of the man, in the fullness of health and
strength and happiness as in the valley of the shadow of death;
through which, O Father Almighty, do thou in thy mercy bear
us to never-ending life and light and love. Amen.

Strengthen our hearts, O Lord, to obey thy commandments;
may the dayspring from on high visit us and give light to us
who sit in darkness. Direct our steps this day that we may
adore thee for thy majesty, follow thee for thy truth, desire
thee for thy mercy, who art the blessed Lord God for evermore.
Amen.

THE LORD'S PRAYER

The Eleventh Day

No comment can reflect adequately the impression of grandeur one
gets from this psalm; it strikes a cosmic note. It is worth while to read

along with it the metrical version made by Isaac Watts beginning, "O God, our help in ages past."

Lord, thou hast been our dwelling place
In all generations.
Before the mountains were brought forth,
Or ever thou hadst formed the earth and the world,
Even from everlasting to everlasting, thou art God.
Thou turnest man to destruction;
And sayest, Return, ye children of men.
For a thousand years in thy sight
Are but as yesterday when it is past,
And as a watch in the night.
Thou carriest them away as with a flood; they are as a sleep:
In the morning they are like grass which groweth up.
In the morning it flourisheth, and groweth up;
In the evening it is cut down, and withereth.
For we are consumed by thine anger,
And by thy wrath are we troubled.
The days of our years are threescore years and ten;
And if by reason of strength they be fourscore years,
Yet is their strength labor and sorrow;
For it is soon cut off, and we fly away.
So teach us to number our days,
That we may apply our hearts unto wisdom.
O satisfy us early with thy mercy;
That we may rejoice and be glad all our days.
Make us glad according to the days wherein thou hast afflicted
    us,
And the years wherein we have seen evil.
Let thy work appear unto thy servants,
And thy glory unto their children.
And let the beauty of the Lord our God be upon us:
And establish thou the work of our hands upon us;
Yea, the work of our hands establish thou it.

—*Ps. 90, in part*

We offer unto thee, O Lord, our praises and thanksgivings for all thy mercies multiplied upon us, more than we can number and far greater than we can express. More especially do we praise thee for those spiritual blessings which thou hast revealed to us in the life of thy dear Son. Eye hath not seen, nor ear heard, neither have entered into the heart of man, the things which thou, O God, hast prepared for those that love thee. Give us grace to love thee more and more, till we come to thine everlasting kingdom; through Jesus Christ our Lord. Amen.

Let thy mercy, O LORD, be upon us, and the brightness of thy Spirit illumine our inward souls, that he may kindle our cold hearts, and light up our dark minds; who abideth evermore with thee in thy glory. Amen.

THE LORD'S PRAYER

The Twelfth Day

As long ago as when this psalm was written, men looked forward to a time when righteousness, justice, and joy should cover the earth because of the presence of God. No wonder that such glad hymns as this were written and sung.

O sing unto the LORD a new song;
For he hath done marvelous things:
His right hand, and his holy arm, hath gotten him the victory.
The LORD hath made known his salvation:
His righteousness hath he openly showed in the sight of the nations.
He hath remembered his mercy and his truth toward the house of Israel:
All the ends of the earth have seen the salvation of our God.
Make a joyful noise unto the LORD, all the earth:
Make a loud noise, and rejoice, and sing praise.
Sing unto the LORD with the harp;
With the harp, and the voice of a psalm.
With trumpets and sound of cornet

Make a joyful noise before the LORD, the King.
Let the sea roar, and the fullness thereof;
The world, and they that dwell therein.
Let the floods clap their hands:
Let the hills be joyful together
Before the LORD; for he cometh to judge the earth:
With righteousness shall he judge the world,
And the people with equity.   —*Ps. 98*

Almighty and everlasting God, strengthen by thy presence all who dwell in this house, and be thou present with us this day in all our duties; through Jesus Christ our Lord. Amen.

O Lord, lift up the light of thy countenance upon us; let thy peace rule in our hearts, and may it be our strength and our song in the house of our pilgrimage. We commit ourselves to thy care and keeping this day; let thy grace be mighty in us and sufficient for us, and let it work in us both to will and to do of thine own good pleasure, and grant us strength for all the duties of the day. Keep us from sin. Give us the rule over our own spirits, and keep us from speaking unadvisedly with our lips. May we live together in peace and holy love, and do thou command thy blessing upon us, even life for evermore. Prepare us for all the events of the day, for we know not what a day may bring forth. Give us grace to deny ourselves, to take up our cross daily, and to follow in the steps of our Master, Jesus Christ our Lord. Amen.

THE LORD'S PRAYER

The Thirteenth Day

This psalmist significantly omits any word that would suggest self-importance or special deserving on his own part, but turns attention wholly toward God and God's loving care.

Bless the LORD, O my soul:
And all that is within me, bless his holy name.
Bless the LORD, O my soul,
And forget not all his benefits.

Who forgiveth all thine iniquities;
Who healeth all thy diseases;
Who redeemeth thy life from destruction;
Who crowneth thee with lovingkindness and tender mercies;
Who satisfieth thy mouth with good things;
So that thy youth is renewed like the eagle's.
The LORD executeth righteousness
And judgment for all that are oppressed.
He made known his ways unto Moses,
His acts unto the children of Israel.
The LORD is merciful and gracious,
Slow to anger, and plenteous in mercy.
He will not always chide:
Neither will he keep his anger forever.
He hath not dealt with us after our sins;
Nor rewarded us according to our iniquities.
For as the heaven is high above the earth,
So great is his mercy toward them that fear him.
As far as the east is from the west,
So far hath he removed our transgressions from us.

—*Ps. 103, Part 1*

We give this day hearty thanks for the rest of the past night and for the gift of a new day, with its opportunities of pleasing thee. Grant that we may so pass its hours in the perfect freedom of thy service that at eventide we may again give thanks unto thee; through Jesus Christ our Lord. Amen.

We seek thee daily, our Father, and daily thou offerest thyself to be found. Whensoever we seek we find thee: in the house, in the fields, in the temple, in the highway. Whatsoever we do, whether we eat or drink, whether we work, meditate, or pray, thou art ever with us, we feel some measure of thy mercies and thy love. Oh continue thy lovingkindness toward us, that all the world may see that thy power, thy mercy, and thy love endure forever; through Jesus Christ thy Son our Lord. Amen.

THE LORD'S PRAYER

The Fourteenth Day

One is inclined to think that Jesus, in such a psalm as this, found a background for his thought of God as Father, an idea which, because of his use of it, has become central in Christian thought.

Like as a father pitieth his children,
So the Lord pitieth them that fear him.
For he knoweth our frame;
He remembereth that we are dust,
As for man, his days are as grass:
As a flower of the field, so he flourisheth.
For the wind passeth over it, and it is gone;
And the place thereof shall know it no more.
But the mercy of the Lord is from everlasting to everlasting
    upon them that fear him,
And his righteousness unto children's children;
To such as keep his covenant,
And those that remember his commandments to do them.
The Lord hath prepared his throne in the heavens;
And his kingdom ruleth over all.
Bless the Lord, ye his angels,
That excel in strength, that do his commandments,
Hearkening unto the voice of his word.
Bless ye the Lord, all ye his hosts;
Ye ministers of his, that do his pleasure.
Bless the Lord, all his works
In all places of his dominion:
Bless the Lord, O my soul.   *—Ps. 103, Part 2*

O God, the might of all them that put their trust in thee; grant that we may triumph over all that makes war upon our souls; through Jesus Christ our Lord. Amen.

O heavenly Father, we humbly beseech thee to give unto this household, and unto each member of it in particular, a desire and taste for the things that are high and spiritual, the love of holiness, and the longing for the life of heaven. Grant that whatsoever things are true, whatsoever things are honorable, whatsoever things are just, whatsoever things are pure, whatsoever things are lovely and of good report, if there be anything which is unselfish and generous, if there be anything which thou wilt accept and reward, we may think on these things, and by the help of thy Holy Spirit may order our lives and form our characters according to them; through Jesus Christ our Lord. Amen.

THE LORD'S PRAYER

A WEEK WITH THE SERMON ON THE MOUNT

The Fifteenth Day (Suitable for Sunday)

The familiarity of these words should not cause them to be taken primarily as texts to be learned or even as doctrines which Jesus proclaimed. They are rather reflections of the faith, the hope, and the courage of Jesus himself, springing immediately out of the religion which he himself believed and practiced.

And seeing the multitudes, he went up into a mountain: and when he was set, his disciples came unto him: and he opened his mouth, and taught them, saying:

Blessed are the poor in spirit: for theirs is the kingdom of heaven.

Blessed are they that mourn: for they shall be comforted.

Blessed are the meek: for they shall inherit the earth.

Blessed are they which do hunger and thirst after righteousness: for they shall be filled.

Blessed are the merciful: for they shall obtain mercy.

Blessed are the pure in heart: for they shall see God.

Blessed are the peacemakers: for they shall be called the children of God.

Blessed are they which are persecuted for righteousness' sake: for theirs is the kingdom of heaven.

Blessed are ye, when men shall revile you, and persecute you, and shall say all manner of evil against you falsely, for my sake. Rejoice, and be exceeding glad: for great is your reward in heaven: for so persecuted they the prophets which were before you.   *—Matt. 5:1-12*

Almighty God, from whom every good prayer cometh, and who pourest out on all who desire it the spirit of grace and supplication; deliver us, when we draw nigh to thee, from coldness of heart and wanderings of mind, that with steadfast thoughts, and kindled affections, we may worship thee in spirit and in truth; through Jesus Christ our Lord. Amen.

O Lord, our heavenly Father, at the beginning of another week we come to thee for help and light. Grant, we beseech thee, that we may hallow this day of rest to thy service, and find in thee all peace and strength. Quicken our devotion, that we may serve thee in spirit and in truth, and lay a good foundation for our coming work. Be with us in all the public services of thy day, that we may join in them with heart and soul, and receive the blessing which thou hast promised to all who sincerely pray to thee and faithfully hear thy word. This we ask for the sake of Jesus Christ our Lord. Amen.

THE LORD'S PRAYER

The Sixteenth Day

It is a testimony to the supreme place Jesus had in the thought of the first Christians that, with their Jewish background, they should have seen in him the fulfillment of both law and prophecy. His teaching was not, for them, a substitute for the integrity taught by his predecessors, but a further building upon the foundations they had laid.

Ye are the salt of the earth: but if the salt have lost his savor, wherewith shall it be salted? it is thenceforth good for nothing, but to be cast out, and to be trodden under foot of men. Ye are the light of the world. A city that is set on a hill cannot be hid. Neither do men light a candle, and put it under a bushel, but on a candlestick; and it giveth light unto all that are in the house. Let your light so shine before men, that they may see your good works, and glorify your Father which is in heaven. Think not that I am come to destroy the law, or the prophets:

I am not come to destroy, but to fulfill. For verily I say unto you, Till heaven and earth pass, one jot or one tittle shall in no wise pass from the law, till all be fulfilled. Whosoever therefore shall break one of these least commandments, and shall teach men so, he shall be called the least in the kingdom of heaven: but whosoever shall do and teach them, the same shall be called great in the kingdom of heaven. For I say unto you, That except your righteousness shall exceed the righteousness of the scribes and Pharisees, ye shall in no case enter into the kingdom of heaven.   —Matt. 5:13-20

O God, by whom the meek are guided in judgment, and light riseth up in darkness for the godly; grant us, in all doubts and uncertainties, the grace to ask what thou wouldest have us to do, that the Spirit of wisdom may save us from all false choices, and that in thy light we may see light, and in thy straight path may not stumble; through Jesus Christ our Lord. Amen.

O Thou in whose hand are the hearts of thy creatures, shed abroad thy peace upon the world. By the might of thy Holy Spirit quench the pride, and anger, and greediness which cause man to strive against man, and people against people. Lead all nations in the ways of mutual help and good will, and hasten the time when the earth shall confess thee indeed for its Saviour and King, and no evil deeds of man shall defile thy glorious creation; through Jesus Christ our Lord. Amen.

THE LORD'S PRAYER

The Seventeenth Day

A passage like this throws an interesting and convincing light on the character of Jesus himself. He felt that there were far more important things than legal decisions, cloaks, or retaliations. Not only did he not seek such satisfactions, but he harbored no spirit of revenge and was always ready to do or to give more than was asked.

Ye have heard that it hath been said, An eye for an eye, and a tooth for a tooth: but I say unto you, That ye resist not evil: but whosoever shall smite thee on thy right cheek, turn to him the other also. And if any man will sue thee at the law, and take away thy coat, let him have thy cloak also. And whosoever shall compel thee to go a mile, go with him twain. Give to him that asketh thee, and from him that would borrow of thee turn not thou away.

Ye have heard that it hath been said, Thou shalt love thy neighbor, and hate thine enemy. But I say unto you, Love your enemies, bless them that curse you, do good to them that hate you, and pray for them which despitefully use you, and persecute you; that ye may be the children of your Father which is in heaven: for he maketh his sun to rise on the evil and on the good, and sendeth rain on the just and on the unjust. For if ye love them which love you, what reward have ye? do not even the publicans the same? And if ye salute your brethren only, what do ye more than others? do not even the publicans so? Be ye therefore perfect, even as your Father which is in heaven is perfect.   —*Matt. 5:38-48*

Father in heaven, whether it be thy will to give or to withhold the thing that we ask, grant that our prayers may always draw our hearts nearer to thee; for Jesus' sake. Amen.

O God, who knowest all things, and from whom nothing is hid; thou hast seen fit to limit our knowledge, and to set before us the slow learning of thy works and ways. Grant us grace to accept the mystery of life with a humble heart, to adore thine unsearchable majesty with a reverent mind, and to grow in wisdom daily, as more and more the order and beauty of thy universe are made clear to us by true science. Thus may the reason which thou hast given confirm the faith without which we cannot please thee; until at last we know even as we are known in Jesus Christ thy Son our Lord. Amen.

THE LORD'S PRAYER

The Eighteenth Day

Only one whose trust in God was profound and secure could pray in such a manner as this; and, although this "Lord's Prayer" is given to the disciples as a guide and suggestion rather than a formula to be recited, it springs from the spirit of Jesus himself and his own prayers.

And when thou prayest, thou shalt not be as the hypocrites are: for they love to pray standing in the synagogues and in the corners of the streets, that they may be seen of men. Verily I say unto you, They have their reward. But thou, when thou prayest, enter into thy closet, and when thou hast shut thy door, pray to thy Father which is in secret; and thy Father which seeth in secret shall reward thee openly. But when ye pray, use not vain repetitions, as the heathen do: for they think that they shall be heard for their much speaking. Be not ye therefore like unto them: for your Father knoweth what things ye have need of, before ye ask him. After this manner therefore pray ye: Our Father which art in heaven, hallowed be thy name. Thy kingdom come. Thy will be done in earth, as it is in heaven. Give us this day our daily bread. And forgive us our debts, as we forgive our debtors. And lead us not into temptation, but deliver us from evil: for thine is the kingdom, and the power, and the glory, forever. Amen. For if ye forgive men their trespasses, your heavenly Father will also forgive you. but if ye forgive not men their trespasses, neither will your Father forgive your trespasses.   —*Matt. 6:5-15*

O Lord, whose favor is life, and in whose presence there is fullness of peace and joy; grant unto us, we beseech thee, such an abiding sense of the reality and glory of those things which thou hast prepared for them that love thee as may serve to raise us above the vanity of this present world, both in its pleasures and in its necessary trials and pains, so that under thy guidance and help all things here shall work together for our everlasting salvation; through Jesus Christ our Lord. Amen.

Almighty God, give us grace to contend always for what is true and right, and to be ready if need be to suffer for it. Give us not over to fearfulness of soul, but lift us into that love which casteth out fear, so that we may glorify and enjoy thee now and forever; through Jesus Christ our Lord.

THE LORD'S PRAYER

The Nineteenth Day

Although these words are in the form of instructions for others, they are more significant when recognized as reflections of the spirit and character of Jesus himself. His heart was in the true treasures of which he spoke; he served but one Master; and his followers are those who share these fidelities.

When ye fast, be not, as the hypocrites, of a sad countenance: for they disfigure their faces, that they may appear unto men to fast. Verily I say unto you, They have their reward. But thou, when thou fastest, anoint thine head, and wash thy face; that thou appear not unto men to fast, but unto thy Father which is in secret: and thy Father, which seeth in secret, shall reward thee openly.

Lay not up for yourselves treasures upon earth, where moth and rust doth corrupt, and where thieves break through and steal: but lay up for yourselves treasures in heaven, where neither moth nor rust doth corrupt, and where thieves do not break through nor steal: for where your treasure is, there will your heart be also. The light of the body is the eye: if therefore thine eye be single, thy whole body shall be full of light: but if thine eye be evil, thy whole body shall be full of darkness. If therefore the light that is in thee be darkness, how great is that darkness! No man can serve two masters: for either he will hate the one, and love the other; or else he will hold to the one, and despise the other. Ye cannot serve God and mammon.   —*Matt. 6:16-24*

O God, who hast taught us to keep all thy heavenly commandments by loving thee and our neighbor; grant us the spirit of peace and grace, that we may be both devoted to thee with our whole heart, and united to each other with a pure will; through Jesus Christ our Lord. Amen.

O God our Father, of whom the whole family in heaven and on earth is named; bestow upon our household, at the beginning of this day, that grace which shall keep us in the fellowship of the Christian way: and grant unto each one of us that heavenly guidance and control, in all our labors, pleasures, and trials, which shall maintain our hearts in peace with one another and with thee. Graciously help and prosper us in the doing of our various duties, with a willing and a cheerful mind; and defend us all, by thine almighty power, both from inward evil and from outward harm, so that, when the day is ended, it may not leave us in sorrow, strife, or shame, but in true unity and thankful rest; through thy merciful favor and thy forgiving love in Christ Jesus our Lord. Amen.

THE LORD'S PRAYER

The Twentieth Day

The Golden Rule might better be called a Golden Principle, as it deals with motives for one's acts rather than with rules for particular cases. The emphasis on motive is clear in the words about prayer that lead up to the rule itself.

Ask, and it shall be given you; seek, and ye shall find; knock, and it shall be opened unto you: for everyone that asketh receiveth; and he that seeketh findeth; and to him that knocketh it shall be opened. Or what man is there of you, whom if his son ask bread, will he give him a stone? Or if he ask a fish, will he give him a serpent? If ye then, being evil, know how to give good gifts unto your children, how much more shall your Father which is in heaven give good things to them that ask him? Therefore all things whatsoever ye would that men should do to you, do ye even so to them: for this is the law and the prophets.   —*Matt. 7:7-12*

Almighty God, who seest that we have no power of ourselves to help ourselves; keep us both outwardly in our bodies and inwardly in our souls, that we may be defended from all adversities which may happen to the body, and from all evil thoughts which may assault and hurt the soul; through Jesus Christ our Lord. Amen.

Lift upon us the light of thy countenance, O God, that we may rejoice and be glad in thee; and send into our souls the purifying gift of thy pardon, that our sins may be utterly removed from us, and we may go forth with a clean spirit, a joyful courage, and strength sufficient for our needs, to meet whatever thou hast appointed for us during this day. And grant, O most merciful Lord, that we may neither forget the precepts and the promises of thy holy word, nor depart in thought, or word, or deed from the obedient faith of thy true children in Jesus Christ. Amen.

THE LORD'S PRAYER

The Twenty-first Day

As one considers what "these sayings" of Jesus tell him to *do,* he discovers that many of them tell him what to *be,* and that the right *doing* springs naturally from the right *being.* This is the way it was with Jesus, and it produces what might be called the well-founded life.

Enter ye in at the strait gate: for wide is the gate, and broad is the way, that leadeth to destruction, and many there be which go in thereat: because strait is the gate, and narrow is the way, which leadeth unto life, and few there be that find it. Not everyone that saith unto me, Lord, Lord, shall enter into the kingdom of heaven; but he that doeth the will of my Father which is in heaven. Many will say to me in that day, Lord, Lord, have we not prophesied in thy name? and in thy name have cast out devils? and in thy name done many wonderful works? And then will I profess unto them, I never knew you: depart from me, ye that work iniquity.

Therefore whosoever heareth these sayings of mine, and doeth them, I will liken him unto a wise man, which built his house upon a rock: and the rain descended, and the floods came, and the winds blew, and beat upon that house; and it fell not: for it was founded upon a rock. And everyone that heareth these sayings of mine and doeth them not, shall be likened unto a foolish man, which built his house upon the sand: and the rain descended, and the floods came, and the winds blew, and beat upon that house; and it fell: and great was the fall of it.

—Matt. 7:13-14, 21-27

Confirm, O Lord, we pray thee, the hearts of thy children, and strengthen them with the power of thy grace, that they may be both devout in prayer to thee and sincere in love for each other; through Jesus Christ our Lord. Amen.

O Thou who art the true sun of the world, evermore rising, and never going down, who by thy most wholesome appearing and light dost nourish and make joyful all things, as well that are in heaven, as also that are on earth; we beseech thee mercifully and favorably to shine into our hearts, that the night and darkness of sin and the mists of error on every side being driven away, thou brightly shining within our hearts, we may all our life long go without any stumbling or offense, and may walk as in the daytime, being pure and clean from the works of darkness, and abounding in all good works which thou hast prepared for us to walk in. Amen.

THE LORD'S PRAYER

A WEEK WITH THE PROPHETS AND APOSTLES

The Twenty-second Day (Suitable for Sunday)

This vision or dream was so vivid and so profound, and Isaiah was so obedient to it, that it really serves as a spiritual summary of his whole career, reflecting both his devotion and his experience.

In the year that king Uzziah died I saw also the Lord sitting upon a throne, high and lifted up, and his train filled the temple. Above it stood the seraphim: each one had six wings; with twain he covered his face, and with twain he covered his feet, and with twain he did fly. And one cried unto another, and said, Holy, holy, holy, is the LORD of hosts: the whole earth is full of his glory. And the posts of the door moved at the voice of him that cried, and the house was filled with smoke. Then said I, Woe is me! for I am undone; because I am a man of unclean lips, and I dwell in the midst of a people of unclean lips: for mine eyes have seen the King, the LORD of hosts. Then flew one of the seraphim unto me, having a live coal in his hand, which he had taken with the tongs from off the altar: and he laid it upon my mouth, and said, Lo, this hath touched thy lips; and thine iniquity is taken away, and thy sin is purged. Also I heard the voice of the Lord, saying, Whom shall I send, and who will go for us? Then said I, Here am I; send me. —*Isa. 6:1-8*

As the hart panteth after the water brooks, O God, our souls do thirst after thee, that we may see thy power and thy glory as we have seen them in the sanctuary, and be satisfied with the goodness of thy house. Lead us and guide us unto thy holy hill, and bring us together with sweet converse to the place of prayer, to hear thy word of truth in the spirit, to offer the sacrifices of joy with thy people, and to make melody in our hearts with the songs of Zion. Prepare us, we beseech thee, for a true entrance into the secret of thy tabernacle, and bless thy churches everywhere this day with the clear shining of thy presence, that the Holy Spirit may descend on many hearts, and multitudes may be brought from the kingdom of Satan into the kingdom of thy dear Son Jesus Christ. Amen.

Almighty and everlasting God, who hast revealed thy glory by Christ among all nations; preserve the works of thy mercy, that thy Church, which is spread throughout the world, may persevere with steadfast faith in the confession of thy name; through Jesus Christ our Lord. Amen.

THE LORD'S PRAYER

The Twenty-third Day

There can be no doubt that if wisdom and equity controlled the world today this ideal of peace and happiness, dreamed of so long ago, would be near fulfillment.

And there shall come forth a rod out of the stem of Jesse, and a Branch shall grow out of his roots: and the spirit of the LORD shall rest upon him, the spirit of wisdom and understanding, the spirit of counsel and might, the spirit of knowledge and of the fear of the LORD; and shall make him of quick understanding in the fear of the LORD: and he shall not judge after the sight of his eyes, neither reprove after the hearing of his ears: but with righteousness shall he judge tbe poor, and reprove with equity for the meek of the earth: and he shall smite the earth with the rod of his mouth, and with the breath of his lips shall he slay the wicked. And righteousness shall be the girdle of his loins, and faithfulness the girdle of his reins.

The wolf also shall dwell with the lamb, and the leopard shall lie down with the kid; and the calf and the young lion and the fatling together; and a little child shall lead them. And the cow and the bear shall feed; their young ones shall lie down together; and the lion shall eat straw like the ox. And the suckling child shall play on the hole of the asp, and the weaned child shall put his hand on the cockatrice's den. They shall not hurt nor destroy in all my holy mountain: for the earth shall be full of the knowledge of the LORD, as the waters cover the sea.   —*Isa. 11:1-9*

O God, who hast made of one blood all the nations of the earth; mercifully hear our supplications, and remove from the world forever the dreadful menace of war. Guide the rulers with thy counsel, and restrain the passions of the people, so that bloodshed may be averted and peace be preserved. By the pouring out of thy Spirit upon all flesh, quicken the sense of our common brotherhood; bind the nations into a new bond of fellowship; and hasten the time when the kingdoms of this world shall become the kingdom **of our** Lord and Saviour Jesus Christ. Amen.

O God our Father, give to the nations of the world a true heart of comradeship, that every people may contribute its excellence to the service of all, and the whole world may go forward in the new and living way revealed by Jesus Christ; who now liveth and reigneth with thee and the Spirit of Truth, one God, world without end. Amen.

THE LORD'S PRAYER

The Twenty-fourth Day

Out of real deserts and real afflictions came these words of hope and faith that speak now, as they have from the day they were first spoken, a promise of comfort and restoration to all who are in trouble and sorrow.

The wilderness and the solitary place shall be glad for them; and the desert shall rejoice, and blossom as the rose. They shall see the glory of the LORD, and the excellency of our God. Strengthen ye the weak hands, and confirm the feeble knees. Say to them that are of a fearful heart, Be strong, fear not: behold, your God will come with vengeance, even God with a recompense; he will come and save you.

Then the eyes of the blind shall be opened, and the ears of the deaf shall be unstopped. Then shall the lame man leap as an hart, and the tongue of the dumb sing: for in the wilderness shall waters break out, and streams in the desert. And an highway shall be there, and a way, and it shall be called The way of holiness; the unclean shall not pass over it; but it shall be for those: the wayfaring men, though fools, shall not err therein. No lion shall be there, nor any ravenous beast shall go up thereon, it shall not be found there: but the redeemed shall walk there: and the ransomed of the LORD shall return, and come to Zion with songs and everlasting joy upon their heads: they shall obtain joy and gladness, and sorrow and sighing shall flee away.   —*Isa. 35:1-6, 8-10*

O Thou who art beyond our sight, above our thought, infinite, eternal, and unsearchable; thy wisdom shines in all thy works; thy glory is shown in thy goodness to men; and thy grace and truth are revealed in Christ. Therefore we adore thee, our Father and our God, for ever and ever. Amen.

Most heartily do we thank thee, O Lord, for thy mercies of every kind, and thy loving care over all thy creatures. We bless thee for the many tokens of thy love, especially for the saving knowledge of thy dear Son our Saviour, and for the living presence of thy Spirit, our Comforter. We thank thee for friendship and duty, for good hopes and precious memories, for the joys that cheer us, and for the trials that teach us to trust in thee. O heavenly Father, make us wise unto a right use of thy benefits, and so direct us that in word and deed we may show gratitude to thee; in Jesus Christ our Lord. Amen.

THE LORD'S PRAYER

The Twenty-fifth Day

The Jews in Babylon, who had been taken there as captives from Jerusalem, must have found this letter hardly credible; but today one can see that it marks one of the steps in the long process of learning that God is everywhere immediately accessible.

Now these are the words of the letter that Jeremiah the prophet sent from Jerusalem unto the residue of the elders which were carried away captives, saying, Thus saith the LORD of hosts, the God of Israel, unto all that are carried away captives, whom I have caused to be carried away from Jerusalem unto Babylon; Build ye houses, and dwell in them; and plant gardens, and eat the fruit of them; take ye wives, and beget sons and daughters; and take wives for your sons, and give your daughters to husbands, that they may bear sons and daughters; that ye may be increased there, and not diminished. And seek the peace of the city whither I have caused you to be carried away captives, and pray unto the LORD for it: for in the peace thereof shall ye have peace. For I know the thoughts that I think toward you, saith the LORD, thoughts of peace, and not of evil, to give you an expected end. Then shall ye call upon me, and ye shall go and pray unto me, and I will hearken unto you. And ye shall seek me, and find me, when ye shall search for me with all your heart.   —*Jer. 29:1, 4-7, 11-13*

Almighty God, we thank thee for thy manifold mercies to us and to mankind. For the gift of life in body and in spirit, we thank thee; for health and strength, for our senses and a sound mind, we thank thee; for house and home, for food and raiment, for love and friendship, we thank thee; for a place in our country, and in the human brotherhood, and in the great

Kingdom of Christ, we thank thee. Lord, help us to value all thy mercies more and more, and so to use them that we may live to thy glory, and do good to our fellow men, and thus enter fully into the joy of Jesus our Lord. Amen.

Hear thy children, heavenly Father, as we make our supplication for our daily needs. Guard us and our dear ones amid the perils and dangers of this troubled world. Give us strength in our labors, wisdom in our perplexities, courage in our trials, patience in our sorrows, and a pure heart in all our joys. As thou knowest what we lack, supply all our need according to the riches of thy love; and bless us every one for Christ's sake. Amen.

THE LORD'S PRAYER

The Twenty-sixth Day

In this brief dialogue the prophet first rebukes the people. Then the penitent people, as one man, ask, "Wherewith shall I come . . .?" and to this question the prophet replies in words that strikingly anticipate the words of Jesus about the two supreme commandments.

Hear ye now what the LORD saith; Arise, contend thou before the mountains, and let the hills hear thy voice. Hear ye, O mountains, the LORD's controversy, and ye strong foundations of the earth: for the LORD hath a controversy with his people, and he will plead with Israel. O my people, what have I done unto thee? and wherein have I wearied thee? testify against me. For I brought thee up out of the land of Egypt, and redeemed thee out of the house of servants. O my people, remember now; that ye may know the righteousness of the LORD.

Wherewith shall I come before the LORD, and bow myself before the high God? shall I come before him with burnt offerings, with calves of a year old? Will the LORD be pleased with thousands of rams, or with ten thousands of rivers of oil? shall I give my firstborn for my transgression, the fruit of my body for the sin of my soul? He hath showed thee, O man,

what is good; and what doth the LORD require of thee, but to do justly, and to love mercy, and to walk humbly with thy God?
—*Mic. 6:1-8*

Lord God eternal; holy, just, and merciful; we adore thee for the wonders of the heavens and the earth, for thy saving love revealed in Jesus Christ, and thy living presence made known by the Holy Spirit. By day and night, with voice and heart, praise and adoration shall be given unto thee, O Lord, from generation unto generation, for ever and ever. Amen.

Heavenly Father, who art ever ready to give good things to them that ask thee; hear the supplications of thy children and supply all our needs, in body and in soul, according to thy knowledge and the fullness of thy love. Strengthen us to keep thy commandments; deliver us from our infirmities; and uphold us with thy free Spirit. Enable us for those duties which thou hast laid upon us, that, our work being well done, we may enjoy the fruit of our labor, in a good conscience and a contented mind. And so direct us in all our ways that we may have the light of thy word upon our path, and the fellowship of thy Spirit in our hearts, and may ever continue among the faithful followers of thy Son Jesus Christ. Amen.

THE LORD'S PRAYER

The Twenty-seventh Day

There is here an example of the way the reports about Jesus were circulated. They would be told in various ways depending on the occasion as well as on the reporter. Here, for instance, the earthly career of Jesus is described as that of a divinely directed good man. How natural!

Then Peter said, Of a truth I perceive that God is no respecter of persons: but in every nation he that feareth him, and worketh righteousness, is accepted with him. The word which God sent unto the children of Israel, preaching peace by Jesus Christ (he is Lord of all): that word, I say, ye know, which was published throughout all Judaea, and began from

Galilee, after the baptism which John preached; how God anointed Jesus of Nazareth with the Holy Ghost and with power: who went about doing good, and healing all that were oppressed of the devil; for God was with him. And we are witnesses of all things which he did both in the land of the Jews, and in Jerusalem; whom they slew and hanged on a tree: him God raised up the third day, and showed him openly; not to all the people, but unto witnesses chosen before of God, even to us, who did eat and drink with him after he rose from the dead. And he commanded us to preach unto the people, and to testify that it is he which was ordained of God to be the Judge of quick and dead. To him give all the prophets witness, that through his name whosoever believeth in him shall receive remission of sins.   —*Acts 10:34-43*

Almighty God, who by the birth of thy Holy One into the world didst give thy true light to dawn upon our darkness; grant that, as thou hast given us to believe in the mystery of his incarnation and hast made us partakers of the divine nature, so we may ever abide with him in this world and in the glory of his kingdom; through the same Jesus Christ our Lord. Amen.

Grant, O Lord, that this day which thou hast given unto us in mercy may be returned unto thee in service. As thou hast guarded us during the helpless hours of sleep, so do thou guide us during the appointed hours of labor; that all our tasks may be gladly and faithfully performed, as in thy sight; that our burdens may not be too heavy for us, because thine aid and comfort are with us continually; and that in nothing we may displease thee, or injure one another. But if in anything we fail or come short, through ignorance or weakness, O God, let thy fatherly wisdom correct us, and thine infinite mercy forgive us, and thy divine love amend our fault; through Jesus Christ our Saviour. Amen.

THE LORD'S PRAYER

The Twenty-eighth Day

The account of Paul's good-by leaves much to the imagination. One cannot read these words without sympathy for the great apostle as well as for his friends who heard him. It seems strange that no gospel writer picked up these "words of the Lord Jesus."

And from Miletus he sent to Ephesus, and called the elders of the church. And when they were come to him, he said unto them, Ye know, from the first day that I came into Asia, after what manner I have been with you at all seasons, serving the Lord with all humility of mind, and with many tears, and temptations, which befell me by the lying in wait of the Jews: and how I kept back nothing that was profitable unto you, but have showed you, and have taught you publicly, and from house to house, testifying both to the Jews, and also to the Greeks, repentance toward God, and faith toward our Lord Jesus Christ. And now, behold, I go bound in the spirit unto Jerusalem, not knowing the things that shall befall me there: save that the Holy Ghost witnesseth in every city, saying that bonds and afflictions abide me. But none of these things move me, neither count I my life dear unto myself, so that I might finish my course with joy, and the ministry, which I have received of the Lord Jesus, to testify the gospel of the grace of God. And now, behold, I know that ye all, among whom I have gone preaching the kingdom of God, shall see my face no more. And now I commend you to God, and to the word of his grace, which is able to build you up, and to give you an inheritance among all them which are sanctified. I have coveted no man's silver, or gold, or apparel. Yea, ye yourselves know, that these hands have ministered unto my necessities, and to them that were with me. I have showed you all things, how that so laboring ye ought to support the weak, and to remember the words of the Lord Jesus, how he said, It is more blessed to give than to receive. And when he had thus spoken, he kneeled down, and prayed with them all.   —*Acts 20:17-25, 32-36*

We praise thee, O God, with the morning light, and in the brightness of a new day we bless thy holy name. For all thou hast bestowed upon us with the gift of life, making us in thine own image, and granting us to share as children in thy knowledge and thy love, in thy work and thy joy, we thank thee, heavenly Father. For all good things in the world, for food and raiment, for home and friendship, for useful tasks and pure pleasures, we thank thee, heavenly Father. For all spiritual blessings, for thy holy word, for the Christian fellowship, for the good example and blessed memory of thy saints, for the secret influence of thy Spirit, we thank thee, heavenly Father. And above all we bless thee for the redeeming life and death of thy dear Son, our Saviour Jesus Christ. Amen.

O God, who hast commanded us to be perfect, as thou our Father in heaven art perfect; put into our hearts, we pray thee, a continual desire to obey thy holy will. Teach us day by day what thou wouldest have us do, and give us grace and power to fulfill the same. May we never from love of ease decline the path which thou pointest out, nor for fear of shame turn away from it. Amen.

THE LORD'S PRAYER

The Twenty-ninth Day (Suitable for Sunday)

Paul's determination to preach the gospel had kept him on the go in spite of everything, and now he wanted to go to Rome. He got there, but it was as a prisoner to be tried for his life. Yet he chose to go that way rather than not at all.

I thank my God through Jesus Christ for you all, that your faith is spoken of throughout the whole world. For God is my witness, whom I serve with my spirit in the gospel of his Son, that without ceasing I make mention of you always in my prayers; making request, if by any means now at length I might have a prosperous journey by the will of God to come unto you. For I long to see you, that I may impart unto you some spiritual gift, to the end ye may be established; that is, that I may be comforted together with you by the mutual faith both of you and me. I am debtor both to the Greeks, and to the Barbarians; both to the wise, and to the unwise. So, as much as in me is, I am ready to preach the gospel to you that are at Rome also. For I am not ashamed of the gospel of Christ: for it is the power of God unto salvation to everyone that believeth; to the Jew first, and also to the Greek. For therein is the righteousness of God revealed from faith to faith: as it is written, The just shall live by faith. —*Rom. 1:8-12, 14-17*

Into thy hands, O Lord, we commend our spirits, souls, and bodies, for thou hast created and redeemed them, O Lord God Almighty. Guide us and all whom we love this day with thine eye, and kindle thy light in our hearts, that, thy godly knowledge increasing in us more and more, we may always be found to walk and live after thy will and pleasure; through Jesus Christ our Lord. Amen.

O Lord, our heavenly Father, at the beginning of another week we come to thee for help and light. Grant, we beseech thee, that we may hallow this day of rest to thy service, and find in thee all peace and strength. Quicken our devotion that we may serve thee in spirit and in truth, and lay a good foundation for our coming work. Be with us in all the public services of thy day, that we may join in them with heart and soul, and receive the blessing which thou hast promised to all who sincerely pray to thee and faithfully hear thy word. This we ask for the sake of Jesus Christ our Lord. Amen.

THE LORD'S PRAYER

The Thirtieth Day

Not only Paul, but unnumbered Christians since his day have found the love of Christ triumphant over "these things" of which Paul speaks and through which Paul himself had passed. Paul affirms triumphantly that God's love is invincible.

What shall we then say to these things? If God be for us, who can be against us? He that spared not his own Son, but delivered him up for us all, how shall he not with him also freely give us all things? Who shall separate us from the love of Christ? shall tribulation, or distress, or persecution, or famine, or nakedness, or peril, or sword? Nay, in all these things we are more than conquerors through him that loved us. For I am persuaded, that neither death, nor life, nor angels, nor principalities, nor powers, nor things present, nor things to come, nor height, nor depth, nor any other creature, shall be able to separate us from the love of God, which is in Jesus Christ our Lord.   —*Rom. 8:31-32, 35, 37-39*

Preserve, O Lord, and deepen our trust in thee; increase our confidence in thy love, wisdom, and justice, that so we may not live without God in the world. Direct our thoughts and words aright this day; may integrity and uprightness preserve us and be expressed in everything that we do; through Jesus Christ our Lord. Amen.

Give us grace, O our God, to listen to thy call, to obey thy voice, and to follow thy guiding. Thou leadest us to pleasures that never fade, to riches which no moth nor rust can corrupt or destroy. Unsearchable riches are in thy hand; oh give us grace to know thy value of them and to covet them! Thou leadest us to fountains of living water; suffer us not to wander or turn aside till we attain unto the pleasures which are at thy right hand for evermore. Establish, settle, strengthen us, that our goodness may not be like the early dew, which passeth away; but make us steadfast, immovable, always abounding in the work of the Lord, forasmuch as we know that our labor is not in vain in the Lord. Grant this, we beseech thee, for thy dear Son Jesus Christ's sake. Amen.

THE LORD'S PRAYER

The Thirty-first Day

This matchless hymn of Christian love is an expression of our faith at the height of its beauty and power.

Though I speak with the tongues of men and of angels, and have not love, I am become as sounding brass, or a tinkling cymbal. And though I have the gift of prophecy, and understand all mysteries, and all knowledge; and though I have all faith, so that I could remove mountains, but have not love, I am nothing. And though I bestow all my goods to feed the poor, and though I give my body to be burned, and have not love, it profiteth me nothing. Love suffereth long, and is kind; love envieth not; love vaunteth not itself, is not puffed up, doth not behave itself unseemly, seeketh not her own, is not easily provoked, thinketh no evil; rejoiceth not in iniquity, but rejoiceth in the truth; beareth all things, believeth all things, hopeth all things, endureth all things. Love never faileth: but whether there be prophecies, they shall fail; whether there be tongues, they shall cease; whether there be knowledge, it shall vanish away. For we know in part, and we prophesy in part. But when that which is perfect is come, then that which is in part shall be done away. When I was a child, I spake as a child, I understood as a child, I thought as a child: but when I became a man, I put away childish things. For now we see through a glass, darkly; but then face to face: now I know in part; but then shall I know even as also I am known. And now abideth faith, hope, love, these three; but the greatest of these is love.

—I Cor. 13

O God, the God of all goodness and of all grace, who art worthy of a greater love than we can either give or understand; fill our hearts, we beseech thee, with such love toward thee that nothing may seem too hard for us to do or suffer in obedience to thy will; and grant that thus loving thee we may become daily more like unto thee, and finally obtain the crown of life which thou hast promised to those who love thee; through Jesus Christ our Lord. Amen.

THE LORD'S PRAYER

Family Prayers

Morning

O God, the King eternal, who dividest the day from the darkness, and turnest the shadow of death into the morning; drive far off from us all wrong desires, incline our hearts to keep thy law, and guide our feet into the way of peace, that having done thy will with cheerfulness while it was day, we may, when the night cometh, rejoice to give thee thanks; through Jesus Christ our Lord. Amen.

O Lord of all good life, we pray thee to purify our lives. Help us each day to know more of thee, and by the power of thy Spirit use us to show forth thyself to others. Make us humble, brave, and loving; make us ready for adventure. We do not ask that thou wilt keep us safe, but keep us ever loyal to the example of our Lord and Saviour Jesus Christ. Amen.

Evening

O Lord our God, who alone makest us to dwell in safety; refresh with quiet sleep this night those who are wearied with the labors of the day, and mercifully protect from harm all who put their trust in thee, that, lying down in peace to take our rest, we may fear no evil, but confidently give ourselves into thy holy keeping; through Jesus Christ our Lord. Amen.

Heavenly Father, who slumberest not nor sleepest; we commend to thy gracious care and keeping ourselves and all who belong to us. We thank thee for the light of the day now closing, and for the restful night. Lift from our minds the burdens of waking hours; visit our bodies with refreshing sleep; through the darkness keep us safe and undefiled. And wake us to meet tomorrow's duties in strength of body and vigor of mind, with peace in our souls and courage in our hearts; through Jesus Christ our Lord. Amen.

O God, with whom there is no darkness, but the night shineth as the day; keep and defend us and all thy children in soul and body during the coming night. Make us to rest in the peace of a good conscience, in the faith of thy providence, in the comfort of thy love, and in the hope of a better life; through Jesus Christ our Lord. Amen.

For Home and Kindred

O God, our heavenly Father, look in favor, we beseech thee, upon the homes of thy people. Defend them against all evil, and supply all their needs according to the riches of thy grace. Make them sanctuaries of purity and peace, love and joy. Bless all dear to us wherever they are, and grant that they and we may follow thee at every step of our daily life, that, though our paths may lead us far from one another, we may all abide within the safe shelter of thy love; through Jesus Christ our Lord. Amen.

For Children

O heavenly Father, who long ago didst watch thy Son on earth grow in stature and in wisdom and in perfect love of thee; teach, by the wondrous story of Jesus and his Church, the children whom thou watchest now, that they may grow into his likeness, loving thee, obedient to thy will, and happy in thy house; through the same Jesus Christ our Lord. Amen.

For One Leaving Home

O God, who art in every place beholding the evil and the good; take into thine own keeping our dear one about to start upon *his* journey. Give *him* courage, prudence, self-control. Grant *him* a right judgment in all things. Raise up for *him* friends, if it be thy will, and deliver *him* from the snares and sorrows of loneliness by the power and joy of thy presence. Grant that in every place *he* may find the house of God and the gate of heaven. Safeguard *him* with the ministry of thy never-failing providence, now and always; through Jesus Christ our Lord. Amen.

Dedication to God's Service

O Lord, give thy blessing, we pray thee, to our daily work, that we may do it in faith and heartily, as to the Lord and not unto men. All our powers of body and mind are thine, and we would fain devote them to thy service. Sanctify them, and the work in which they are engaged; let us not be slothful, but fervent in spirit; and do thou, O Lord, so bless our efforts that they may bring forth in us the fruits of true wisdom. Teach us to seek after truth, and enable us to gain it; but grant that we may ever speak the truth in love, that while we know earthly things we may know thee, and be known by thee, through and in thy Son Jesus Christ. Give us this day thy Holy Spirit, that we may be thine in body and spirit in all our work and all our pleasures; through Jesus Christ thy Son our Lord. Amen.

For Holiness

We bow our knees unto thee, Father, of whom the whole family in heaven and earth is named, that thou wouldest grant us, according to the riches of thy glory, to be strengthened with might by thy Spirit in the inner man; that Christ may dwell in our hearts by faith; that we, being rooted and grounded in love, may be able to comprehend with all saints, what is the breadth, and length, and depth, and height; and to know the love of Christ, which passeth knowledge, that we might be filled with all the fullness of God. Amen.

Dedication

Since it is of thy mercy, O gracious Father, that another day is added to our lives, we here dedicate both our souls and our bodies to thee and thy service, in a sober, righteous, and godly life; in which resolution do thou, O merciful God, confirm and strengthen us, that, as we grow in age, we may grow in grace, and in the knowledge of our Lord and Saviour Jesus Christ. Amen.

For Those in Distant Places

O Lord our God, who art in every place, and from whom no space or distance can ever part us; take into thy holy keeping those from whom we are now separated, and grant that both they and we, by drawing near to thee, may be drawn nearer to one another, in Jesus Christ our Lord. Amen.

For All Occasions

O God, the protector of all that trust in thee, without whom nothing is strong, nothing is holy; increase and multiply upon us thy mercy, that, thou being our ruler and guide, we may so pass through things temporal that we finally lose not the things eternal. Grant this, O heavenly Father, for the sake of Jesus Christ our Lord. Amen.

Bless, O God, all the members of this our family and household, especially those who are absent from us. Preserve them waking; guard them, in their going out and their coming in, free from sin and safe from danger; and when they sleep may they rest in peace; through Jesus Christ our Lord. Amen.

A Treasury of Prayers

For the Absent

O God, our heavenly Father, we pray for *N.*, to whom our hearts go out in absence. Let these our loving thoughts come up before thee as prayers and supplications; defend our beloved from danger and harm; enrich *him* with thy blessing; and grant that we may soon meet together in joy; through Christ Jesus our Lord. Amen.

O God, merciful and gracious, who art everywhere present; we beseech thee to have in thy keeping the absent members of our family. Let thy blessing be upon them day and night; keep them; through Jesus Christ our Lord. Amen.

For Birthdays

Watch over thy child, O Lord, as *his* days increase; bless and guide *him* wherever *he* may be. Strengthen *him* when *he* standeth; comfort *him* when discouraged or sorrowful; and in *his* heart may thy peace which passeth understanding abide all the days of *his* life; through Jesus Christ our Lord. Amen.

Eternal Father, the giver of life, who as on this day didst cause thy servant, *N.*, to be born into this world; we thank thee, O Lord, for all thy mercies vouchsafed to *him* from that time unto this present, humbly beseeching thee to continue thy gracious favor and protection unto *his* life's end. Assist *him* in every time of trial; shield *him* in danger; relieve and comfort *him* in trouble; succor *him* in temptation; defend *him* from the assaults of the enemy, that *his* days here may pass away in peace, and when *he* dies *he* may attain unto the everlasting rest that remaineth for thy people; through Jesus Christ our Lord. Amen.

We beseech thee, Lord, open thy heavens; from thence may thy gifts descend to *him*. Put forth thine own hand from heaven and touch *his* head. May *he* feel the touch of thy hand, and receive the joy of the Holy Spirit, that *he* may remain blessed for evermore. Amen.

For Blessings

Bless all who worship thee, from the rising of the sun unto the going down of the same. Of thy goodness give us; with thy love inspire us; by thy spirit guide us; by thy power protect us; in thy mercy receive us, now and always. Amen.

O holy Lord God, carry onward in us the gifts of thy grace, and mercifully bestow by thy Spirit what human frailty cannot attain; through Jesus Christ our Lord. Amen.

For the Blind

O God, who hast sent thy Son to be the true light; grant that they who cannot see the things of this world may be the more enlightened and comforted by his inward guidance. Cheer them in their blindness with the sense of thy presence, that, beholding thee with increasing love, they may be conformed to thy likeness, until they see thee as thou art, and awake to the full revelation of thy glory; through the same Jesus Christ our Lord. Amen.

For Children

O Lord Jesus Christ, we beseech thee, by the eagerness and obedience of thy childhood, and by thy reverence and love for little children, do thou guard the children of our land; do thou preserve them, strengthen them, and remove all that may hinder them from being brought up in thy faith and love; who livest and reignest, one God, world without end. Amen.

Before the child can talk, parents may pray at his bedside. Thus, by example, the child comes to know that prayer is part of life in his family. Parents may find this prayer useful:

O God, bless our home, our family, friends, and neighbors, and give us thankful hearts for all thy mercies. Amen.

When able to talk, the child will want to join his parents in prayer. He may use the following, or his parents may help him to express in his own words his thankfulness, his love, and his desires:

Thank you, God, for . . .

Dear Father in heaven, bless all our . . .

> Lord Jesus Christ, be with me today,
> And help me in all I think, do, and say. Amen

Almighty and everlasting God, we make our humble supplications unto thee for our children. Let thy fatherly hand, we beseech thee, ever be over them. Let thy Holy Spirit ever be with them, and so lead them in the knowledge and obedience of thy Word, that they may have life and that abundantly; through our Lord Jesus Christ. Amen.

Almighty God and heavenly Father, we thank thee for the children which thou hast given us; give us also grace to train them in thy faith, fear, and love, that as they advance in years they may grow in grace, and may hereafter be found in the number of thine elect children; through Jesus Christ our Lord. Amen.

O Lord Jesus Christ, who didst take little children into thine arms and bless them; bless, we beseech thee, all little children dear to us. Take them into the arms of thine everlasting mercy, keep them from all evil, and bring them into the company of those who ever behold the face of thy Father which is in heaven; through the glory of thy holy name. Amen.

Almighty God, giver of all good things; mercifully behold this thy child now going forth in thy name to school; so replenish *him* with the truth of thy doctrine and adorn *him* with innocency of life that both by word and good example *he* may faithfully serve thee to the glory of thy name and the edification of thy Church; through Jesus Christ our Lord. Amen.

For Christian Graces

O Lord, long-suffering and abundant in goodness and truth; make us long-suffering and patient, cordial and sympathizing, kind and good. Teach us to hold and speak the truth in love, and to show mercy; through Jesus Christ our Lord. Amen.

For Christlikeness

Grant, O Father, that as we move in the world of men, they may take knowledge of us that we have been with thy Son Jesus Christ. Amen.

O God, who hast given unto us thy Son to be an example and a help to our weakness in following the path that leadeth unto life; grant us so to be his disciples that we may walk in his footsteps. Amen.

On Joining the Church

Strengthen, O Lord, by thy Holy Spirit, thy servant [child] who is now about to take the vows of membership in the Church. Grant that *he* may confess thee boldly before men and may grow in the grace and knowledge of our Lord and Saviour Jesus Christ and be found worthy to be numbered among thy people; through the same Jesus Christ our Lord. Amen.

Commendations

Let thy fatherly hand, we beseech thee, ever be over us; let thy Holy Spirit ever be with us, and so lead us in the knowledge and obedience of thy Word; through Jesus Christ our Lord. Amen.

Into thy hands, O God, we commit ourselves this day. May we remember that thine eye is upon us, that thou seest all we do, and knowest all we think, and carest for all our joys and our sorrows. Look in tender love upon each one of us, and keep us; through Jesus Christ our Lord. Amen.

Confession

I know, O Lord, and do with all humility acknowledge myself an object altogether unworthy of thy love; but sure I am thou art an object altogether worthy of mine. I am not good enough to serve thee, but thou hast a right to the best service I can pay. Do thou then impart to me some of that excellence, and that shall supply my own want of worth. Help me to cease from sin according to thy will, that I may be capable of doing thee service according to my duty. Amen.

O Lord, we acknowledge our failures and defects; we humbly confess our errors and our sins; we beseech thee to pardon and forgive us, to deliver us from the burden of transgression, and to release us from the power of sin; through Jesus Christ our Lord. Amen.

O Lord our God, give unto us thy servants the spirit of true repentance, and take away from us all that separates us from thee. Assist us by thy Holy Spirit to show true sorrow for our sins, and to form a sincere resolution to amend our lives according to thy holy word. Have mercy on us, and succor us with thy grace; make in us new and contrite hearts, and pardon all our offences; for the sake of our Redeemer Jesus Christ. Amen.

O Almighty God, give us grace to approach thee at this time with penitent and believing hearts. We confess that we have sinned against thee and are not worthy to be called thy children; yet do thou in mercy keep us as thy children. Give us true repentance, and forgive us all our sins; through Jesus Christ our Lord. Amen.

For Courage

O Jesus Christ, the Lord of all good life, who hast called us to help build the city of God; do thou enrich and purify our lives and deepen in us our discipleship. Help us daily to know more of thee, and through us by the power of thy Spirit show forth thyself to other men. Make us humble, brave, and loving; make us ready for adventure. We do not ask that thou wilt keep us safe, but that thou wilt keep us loyal; who for us didst face death unafraid, and dost live and reign with the Father and the Holy Spirit, God for ever and ever. Amen.

O God, quicken in us the spirit of courage. We will go forth with hopeful minds to the duties and conditions of this day, confident that with thy help we can fashion something good out of whatever material the day will provide; through Jesus Christ our Lord. Amen.

Almighty and merciful God, to whom the light and the darkness are both alike, and without whom nothing befalls thy children; strengthen us to meet all the experiences of life with a steadfast and undaunted heart; help us to go on our way bravely whether it be rough or smooth and, when the mists hide thy face, to continue patiently till they are dispersed by the sun of thy unchanging love; through Jesus Christ our Lord. Amen.

For Doctors and Nurses

O Lord, the great healer and good physician of both body and soul; bless all, whether doctors or nurses, whom thou hast called to minister to the sick and suffering in our hospitals with skill and power, that they may exercise their art for the well-being of thy servants, and to thy glory, who livest and reignest with the Father and the Holy Spirit, world without end. Amen.

O Lord Jesus Christ, to whom all the sick were brought that they might be healed, and who didst send none of them away without thy blessing; look in pity upon all who come to thee for healing of heart and soul; send them not away without thy blessing, but now and evermore grant them thy healing grace. Amen.

For Those in Doubt

Almighty and everliving God, who hast given us the faith of Christ for a light to our feet amid the darkness of this world; have pity upon all who, by doubting or denying it, are gone astray from the path of safety; bring home the truth to their hearts, and grant them to receive it; through the same Jesus Christ our Lord and Saviour. Amen.

For Our Enemies

Lord Jesus Christ, who hast commanded us not to return evil for evil, but to pray for those who hate us; enable us by thy blessed example and thy loving Spirit to pray sincerely for our enemies. When we have offended, forgive us and help us to find a way of reconciliation. Let not anger burn between us, but deliver them and us from the power of hatred, that we may be as ready to grant forgiveness as to ask it, and the peace of God may rule in all our hearts, both now and evermore. Amen.

Evening and Night

Almighty God, Father of our spirits; grant us at close of day the peace which the world cannot give. May no disturbing thoughts or cares destroy the quiet of this evening hour. May we find rest in thee and thus receive strength, gain new hope, and feel the influence of things unseen. Amen.

Send thy peace into our hearts, O Lord, at this evening hour. Confident of thy protection for this night, may we be content with thy mercies of this day. And now, forgiving others, even as thou dost forgive us, may we have comfort and healthful rest within the shelter of this home; through Jesus Christ our Lord. Amen.

The day is past, O Lord, and we offer to thee our evening sacrifice, humbly beseeching thee that whatever in us is darkened by the night of sin may be illumined by the brightness of thy light, and that while our eyes are closed in sleep, our souls may be awake to thee, so that, at the close of night, we may welcome with thy praises the return of day. Amen.

O Lord, support us all the day long of this troublous life, until the shadows lengthen, and the evening comes, and the busy world is hushed, and the fever of life is over, and our work is done. Then of thy mercy grant us a safe lodging, and a holy rest, and peace at the last; through Jesus Christ our Lord. Amen.

O Lord, who hast pity for all our weakness; put from us worry and all misgiving. May we, now that night has come, commit ourselves, our tasks, and all we love into thy keeping; through Jesus Christ our Saviour. Amen.

I will lay me down in peace and take my rest: for thou, Lord, only, makest us to dwell in safety.

Thou, O Christ, art in the midst of us, and we are called by thy name; leave us not, O Lord our God.

Save us, O Lord, while waking, guard us while sleeping, that awake we may watch with Christ, and asleep we may rest in peace. Amen.

We thank thee, O Lord, for teaching us how to pray simply and sincerely to thee, and for hearing us when we so call upon thee. We thank thee for saving us from our sins and sorrows, and for directing all our ways this day. Lead us ever onward to thyself; through Jesus Christ our Lord. Amen.

For Faithfulness

O Almighty God and heavenly Father, who by thy divine providence hast appointed for each one of us our work in life, and hast commanded that we should not be slothful in business, but fervent in spirit, serving thee; help us always to remember that our work is thy appointment, and to do it heartily as unto thee. Preserve us from slothfulness, that we may finish the work that thou hast given us to do; through Jesus Christ our Lord. Amen.

For Family and Household

Shed the bright rays of thy light, O Father, upon this family and household, that every member, confident of thy guidance, may fulfill his daily duty with a gallant heart. Be close to us in time of stress and strain. May our courage and our hope never fail; may we be valiant in all peril; through Jesus Christ our Lord. Amen.

We beseech thee, Lord, to behold us with favor, folk of many families and nations, gathered together in the peace of this roof, weak men and women subsisting under the covert of thy patience. Be patient still; suffer us yet a while longer—with our broken purposes of good, with our idle endeavors against evil, suffer us a while longer to endure and (if it may be) help us to do better. Bless to us our extraordinary mercies; if the day come when these must be taken, brace us to play the man under affliction. Be with our friends, be with ourselves. Go with each of us to rest; if any awake, temper to them the dark hours of watching; and when the day returns, return to us, our sun and comforter, and call us up with morning faces and with morning hearts, eager to labor, eager to be happy, if happiness shall be our portion, and if the day be marked for sorrow, strong to endure it. Amen.

Almighty God, we beseech thee to look upon this household. Grant that every member of it may be taught and guided of thee. Bless the relations and friends of each of us. Thou knowest their several necessities. Prosper, we beseech thee, every effort at home and abroad to advance thy Kingdom; through Jesus Christ our Lord. Amen.

Visit, we beseech thee, most gracious Father, this family and household with thy protection. Let thy blessing descend and rest on all who belong to it. Guide us here, and hereafter bring us to thy glory; through Jesus Christ our Lord. Amen.

O heavenly Father, shed forth thy blessed Spirit richly on all the members of this household. Make each one of us an instrument in thy hands for good. Purify our hearts; strengthen our minds and bodies; fill us with mutual love. Let no pride, no self-conceit, no rivalry, no dispute, spring up among us. Make us earnest and true, giving no just cause for offence; and may thy holy peace rest upon us this day and every day, cheering us in our work, and keeping us faithful; through Jesus Christ our Lord. Amen.

May thy Holy Spirit continually descend and rest upon all in this house and upon all who are in any way connected with it. Send down thy blessing upon our handiwork, and keep each of us this day in body and soul; for the sake of Jesus Christ our Lord. Amen.

Bless, O God, all the members of this our family and household, especially those who are absent from us. Preserve them waking; guard them in their going out and their coming in, free from sin and safe from danger; through Jesus Christ our Lord. Amen.

O Almighty God, we thank thee for all thy blessings and all thy mercies which thou in thy love hast bestowed upon us. Do thou continue thy care for us. Help us to live as thy obedient and dutiful children. Let us never forget who thou art, and whose we are; and grant to every member of this house strength and courage for the battle of life; for the sake of Jesus Christ our Lord. Amen.

O Lord, we ask thee to bless and keep Father and Mother, and our brothers and sisters. Watch over them every day and night. Help us to try to help them, and grant that we may all love and serve thee more and more, that at last we may come to live with thee in heaven; through Jesus Christ. Amen.

Fears and Anxieties

Almighty and everlasting God, thou lover of peace and concord, who hast called us in Christ to love and unity; we pray thee so rule our hearts by thy Holy Spirit that we, being delivered by the true fear of God from all fear of man, may evermore serve thee in righteousness, mercy, humility, and gentleness toward each other; through thy dear Son Jesus Christ our Lord. Amen.

Grant calmness and control of thought to those who are facing uncertainty and anxiety; let their heart stand fast, believing in the Lord. Be thou all things to all men, knowing each one and his petition, each house and its need; for the sake of Jesus Christ. Amen.

For Forgiveness of Others

O holy and ever-blessed Lord, teach us, we beseech thee, to love one another, to exercise forbearance and forgiveness toward our enemies, to recompense no man evil for evil, but to be merciful even as thou, our Father in heaven, art merciful, that so we may continually follow after thee in all our doings, and be more and more conformed to thine image. Amen.

To Know and Find God's Will and Work

Thou hast showed us, O Lord, what is good; enable us, we beseech thee, to perform what thou dost require, even to do justly, to love mercy, and to walk humbly with our God. Amen.

O Lord, give us the grace of thy Spirit, early to seek out and evermore earnestly to follow the work which thou hast appointed for us to do. Amen.

Give ear, O Lord, unto our prayer; and attend to the voice of our supplications. Teach us thy way, O Lord; we will walk in thy truth: unite our hearts to fear thy name. We will praise thee, O Lord our God, with all our heart; and we will glorify thy name for evermore; for great is thy mercy toward us. Amen.

For Guidance

Enlighten our understandings with knowledge of right, and govern our wills by thy laws, that no deceit may mislead us, no temptation corrupt us, that we may always endeavor to do good and hinder evil. Amid all the hopes and fears of this world, take not thy Holy Spirit from us; for the sake of Jesus Christ our Lord. Amen.

O God, forasmuch as our strength is in thee, mercifully grant that thy Holy Spirit may in all things direct and rule our hearts; through Jesus Christ our Lord. Amen.

Grant us, O Lord, to know that which is worth knowing, to love that which is worth loving, to praise that which pleaseth thee most, to esteem that highly which to thee is precious. Give us the right judgment to discern between things visible and spiritual, and above all to seek after the good pleasure of thy will; through Jesus Christ thy Son. Amen.

For a High Calling

Our Father, who hast set a restlessness in our hearts, and made us all seekers after that which we can never fully find; forbid us to be satisfied with what we make of life. Draw us from base content, and set our eyes on far-off goals. Keep us at tasks too hard for us, that we may be driven to thee for strength. Deliver us from fretfulness and self-pity; make us sure of the goal we cannot see, and of the hidden good in the world. Open our eyes to simple beauty all around us, and our hearts to the loveliness men hide from us because we do not try enough to understand them. Save us from ourselves, and show us a vision of a world made new. May thy Spirit of peace and illumination so enlighten our minds that all life shall glow with new meaning and new purpose; through Jesus Christ our Lord. Amen.

Intercession

We most earnestly beseech thee to bless all thy people. Send into our hearts peace. Give life unto us, and let no deadly sin prevail against us, or any of thy people. Deliver all who are in trouble, for thou art our God, who settest the captives free, who givest hope to the hopeless and help to the helpless, who liftest up the fallen, and who art the haven of the shipwrecked. Preserve us in our pilgrimage from hurt and defeat; through Jesus Christ our Lord. Amen.

For Joy

Master of men, who hast given us a work to do; give us strength to do it with gladness and singleness of heart; and when it is done grant us a place in thy Kingdom; through Jesus Christ our Lord. Amen.

O Lord, renew our spirits and draw our hearts unto thyself, that our work may not be to us a burden, but a delight; and give us such a mighty love to thee as may sweeten all our obedience. Let us not serve thee with the spirit of bondage as slaves, but with the cheerfulness and gladness of children, delighting ourselves in thee, and rejoicing in thy work; for the sake of Jesus Christ. Amen.

For the Kingdom of God

Almighty God, we pray thee for the coming of thy Kingdom of righteousness and peace. In the midst of a changing social order may faith in thee and obedience to the teachings of thy dear Son prevail, to build a new life of love in which the ills of this present time may disappear and the glad day of brotherhood and mutual service may dawn. Strengthen all the agencies of thy Church which are laboring for the happiness and welfare of all people, that they may find in thee their salvation and their peace; through Jesus Christ our Lord. Amen.

Labor and Study

Almighty God, our heavenly Father, without whose help labor is useless, without whose light search is vain; invigorate my studies, and direct my inquiries, that I may, by due diligence and right discernment, establish myself and others in thy holy faith

Take not, O Lord, thy Holy Spirit from me; let not evil thoughts have dominion in my mind. Let me not linger in ignorance, but enlighten and support me, for the sake of Jesus Christ our Lord. Amen.

O God, who hast ordained that whatever is to be desired should be sought by labor, and who by thy blessing bringest honest labor to good effect; look with mercy upon my studies and endeavors. Grant me, O Lord, to design only what is lawful and right; and afford me calmness of mind and steadiness of purpose, that I may so do thy will in this short life as to obtain happiness in the world to come; through Jesus Christ our Lord. Amen.

O Lord Jesus Christ, who art the eternal Wisdom of the Father, we beseech thee to assist us with thy heavenly grace, that we may be blessed in our work this day, and above all things may attain the knowledge of thee, whom to know is life eternal; and that, according to thy most holy example, we may ever be found going about amongst our fellow men, doing good, healing the sick, and preaching the gospel of the Kingdom of Heaven; through Jesus Christ our Lord. Amen.

O blessed Lord, who by the example of thy work at Nazareth hast sanctified our daily toil, and by thy teaching hast revealed the sympathy of God in our common task; grant that in the midst of our work we may find rest and peace in thy presence and may take joy in all that ministers to thy service, who art ever our refuge, our strength, and our exceeding great reward. Amen.

For One Leaving Home

O God, who art the strength and the protector of thy people; we humbly place in thy hands the member of this family who is today about to leave us and enter a new sphere of life and work.

Keep and preserve *him,* O Lord, as it seemeth best to thy divine wisdom and love, in all health and safety, both of body and soul; through Jesus Christ our Lord. Amen.

We humbly commend unto thy fatherly care, O Lord, thy servant about to leave this house and family, beseeching thee that thy grace and mercy may never fail *him.* Succor *him* in temptation, preserve *him* in danger, assist *him* in every good work, and further *him* continually in the right way; and grant unto us all, O God our Saviour, that by thy merciful aid we may one day meet again in thy eternal Kingdom; through Jesus Christ our Lord. Amen.

For Light and Truth

O Lord, who seest that all hearts are empty except thou fill them, and all desires balked except they crave after thee; give us light and grace to seek and find thee, that we may be thine and thou mayest be ours forever. Amen.

Almighty God, we invoke thee, the fountain of everlasting light, and entreat thee to send forth thy truth unto our hearts, and to pour upon us the glory of thy brightness; through Christ our Lord. Amen.

O Lord our God, manifest thyself unto us, feeling after thee and seeking thee. Scatter our darkness, thou source of light and wisdom. Stretch forth thy hand to help us and preserve us this day; through Jesus Christ our Lord. Amen.

Bestow thy light upon us, O Lord, that, being rid of the darkness of our hearts, we may attain unto the true light; through Jesus Christ, who is the light of the world. Amen.

For Love of God

O God, who through the grace of thy Holy Spirit, dost pour the gift of love into the hearts of thy faithful people; grant unto us health of both mind and body, that we may love thee with our whole strength and may perform those things which are pleasing unto thee this day; through Christ our Lord. Amen.

Bless me, O God, with the love of thee and of my neighbor. Give me peace of conscience, the command of my affections; and for the rest, thy will be done! O King of peace, keep us in love and charity. Amen.

Grant, most gracious God, that we may love and seek thee always and everywhere, above all things and for thy sake, in the life present, and may at length find thee and forever hold thee fast in the life to come. Grant this for the sake of Jesus Christ our Lord. Amen.

O God, the sure defense of all who trust in thee; we beseech thee, give us contented and trustful hearts, that, casting all our care on thee, and bearing all our trials cheerfully, we may be united to thee in thy love in this world, and finally, by thy mercy, obtain that eternal reward which thou hast prepared for all who trust in thee; through Jesus Christ our Lord. Amen.

For Ministers

Remember all them that do the Lord's work in the ministry. Give them, we beseech thee, O father, great gifts and great holiness, that wisely and charitably, diligently and zealously, prudently and acceptably, they may be guides to the blind, comforters to the sad and weary; that they may strengthen the weak and confirm the strong; that in all their actions and ministrations they may advance the good of souls and the honor of our Lord Jesus Christ. Amen.

Almighty and everlasting God, look mercifully upon thy servants everywhere who visit the poor and the suffering, the needy and the distressed, in their homes; that, guarded by thy protection and kept by thy power, they may carry on their work for thee with joy and patience; through Jesus Christ our Lord. Amen.

For Missions and Missionaries

O God, who by thy Son Jesus Christ hast commanded us to go into all the world and preach the gospel to every creature; make us faithful and obedient to do thy holy will. Give us compassion for all who are unaware of thee in all the world. Send forth, we beseech thee, laborers into thy harvest. Protect and guide them wherever they go. Give them patience, love, and a right judgment in all things; and give them fruit for their labors; through Jesus Christ our Lord. Amen.

Most merciful Father, we beseech thee to send thy heavenly blessing upon thy servants the missionaries and teachers of thy Church, that they may be clothed with righteousness, and that thy Word spoken by their mouth may have such success that it may never be spoken in vain; through Jesus Christ our Lord. Amen.

O Lord Jesus Christ, to whom all the sick were brought that they might be healed, and who didst send none of them away without thy blessing; look in pity upon all who come to thee for healing of heart and soul; send them not away without thy blessing, but now and evermore grant them thy healing grace. Amen.

Father, we remember before thee all our brethren who have need of thee today. Grant thy blessing upon all missionary efforts for the extension of thy Kingdom. We pray especially for our country, that its rulers may be faithful to the Christian ideal, that truth may be more and more firmly established among us, and that that which is false or base may be removed from the hearts of our people. May our country be great in righteousness, wisdom, and peace; may its strength be used honorably for the good of mankind in succoring the oppressed, defending the right, and extending thy Kingdom; through Jesus Christ our Lord. Amen.

For the Misjudged

O Lord, strengthen and support, we entreat thee, all persons unjustly accused or underrated. Comfort them by the ever-present thought that thou knowest the whole truth, and wilt, in thine own good time, make their righteousness as clear as the light. Give them grace to pray for such as do them wrong, and hear and bless them when they pray; for the sake of Jesus Christ our Lord and Saviour. Amen.

Morning

O God our Father, as we begin this day, bestow upon our household that grace which shall keep us in the fellowship of the Christian way; and grant unto each one of us that guidance and control which shall maintain our hearts in peace with one another and with thee. Help and prosper us in the doing of our various duties; and defend us from inward evil and from outward harm so that when the day is ended it may not leave us in sorrow, strife, or shame, but in true unity and thankful rest, through Jesus Christ our Lord. Amen.

Grant, O Lord, that this day which thou hast given unto us in mercy may be one of service unto thee. As thou hast guarded us during the hours of sleep, so do thou guide us during the hours of labor. May all our tasks be performed as in thy sight. May our burdens be not too heavy for us. May we not injure one another or otherwise displease thee. But if we fail in any-thing, let thy wisdom correct us, thy mercy forgive us, thy love amend our fault; through Jesus Christ our Lord. Amen.

Our Father, may we walk as thy children today. May the sense of our relationship to thee fill us with a saving self-respect. May our lives be as glorious as our relationship. May we walk as children of God; through Jesus Christ our Lord. Amen.

For Others

We call to mind, O God, before thy throne of grace, all those whom thou hast given to be near and dear to us, and all for whom we are especially bound to pray, beseeching thee to remember them all for good, and to fulfill, as may be expedient for them, all their desires and wants. We commend to thee any who may have wronged us, praying thee to forgive them and us all our sins; through Jesus Christ our Lord. Amen.

O God of love, who art in all places and times; pour thy comfort upon every lonely heart. Have pity upon those who are bereft of human love, and on those to whom it has never come. Be unto them a strong consolation and fullness of joy; for the sake of Jesus Christ thy Son our Lord. Amen.

O Almighty God, kill in us all the seeds of envy and ill will; and help us, by cultivating within ourselves the love of our neighbor, to improve in the love of thee. Thou hast placed us in various kindreds, friendships, and relations. Help us to improve till all partial affection be lost in that entire universal one, and thou, O God, shall be all in all. Amen.

Be pleased, O Lord, to remember our friends, all that have prayed for us, and that have done us good. Do thou good to them and return all their kindness double into their bosom, rewarding them with blessings, sanctifying them with thy graces, and bringing them to glory; through Jesus Christ our Lord. Amen.

Parents' Thanksgiving

We thank thee, O God our Father, for this our child. Help us as true disciples to set *him* a good example in all we think or say or do; keep *him* well in body and mind; and grant that *he* may grow in grace and in the knowledge and love of thy Son our Saviour Jesus Christ. Amen.

Praise

Great art thou, O Lord, and greatly to be praised; great is thy power and thy wisdom is infinite. Thee would we praise without ceasing. Thou callest us to delight in thy praise, for thou hast made us for thyself, and our hearts find no rest until we rest in thee; to whom with the Father and the Holy Ghost all glory, praise, and honor be ascribed both now and evermore. Amen.

"Teach Us to Pray"

O God our Father, thou hast promised to hear thy children when they pray to thee. Help us now to pray; teach us what to ask for; help us to mean what we say, to love thee more, and to love the people from whom we pray; through Jesus Christ our Lord. Amen.

For Purity of Heart

O Lord, open our eyes that we may have a clear and uninterrupted sight of all the wonderful things which thou hast done for us. Let us not live as if we were strangers to thy commandments. Infuse into our hearts such an awe and fear to displease thee that nothing may seduce us from our obedience to thee. Grant this, O heavenly Father, for the sake of Christ Jesus our Saviour. Amen.

For Rest

Watch thou, dear Lord, with those who wake, or watch, or weep tonight; and give thine angels charge over those who sleep. Tend thy sick ones, O Lord Christ. Rest thy weary ones. Bless thy dying ones. Soothe thy suffering ones. Pity thine afflicted ones. Shield thy joyous ones. This we ask for thy love's sake. Amen.

Be present, O merciful God, and protect us through the silent hours of this night, so that we who are wearied by the work and the changes of this fleeting world may rest upon thy eternal changelessness; through Jesus Christ our Lord. Amen.

For Salvation

O Saviour of the world, who by thy cross and precious blood hast redeemed us; save us and help us, we humbly beseech thee, O Lord. Amen.

For Service

Send us, O God, as thy messengers to hearts without a home, to lives without love, to the crowds without a guide. Send us to the children whom none have blessed, to the famished whom none have visited, to the fallen whom none have lifted, to the bereaved whom none have comforted. Kindle thy flame on the altars of our hearts, that others may be warmed thereby; cause thy light to shine in our souls, that others may see the way; keep our sympathies and insight ready, our wills keen, our hands quick to help our brothers in their need; through Jesus Christ our Lord. Amen.

For the Sorrowing or Distressed

Almighty God, Father of mercies and giver of all comfort; deal graciously, we pray thee, with all those who mourn, that, casting every care on thee, they may know the consolation of thy love; through Jesus Christ our Lord. Amen.

Almighty God, who hast taught us that those who mourn shall be comforted; grant that in all our grief we may turn to thee; and, because our need is beyond the help of men, grant us the peace of thy consolation and the joy of thy love; through Jesus Christ our Lord. Amen.

Have compassion, we pray thee, upon all those whose hearts are touched with sorrow, whose spirits are troubled or cast down within them. O Lord, remember those to whom the burdens of this life bring dimness and darkness of soul, and have

mercy upon all who suffer in body or mind from whatever cause.
Let thy mercy rest upon them according as they hope in thee;
for the sake of Jesus Christ, who is the burden-bearer and the
Redeemer. Amen.

Almighty and everlasting God, the comfort of the sad, the
strength of sufferers; let the prayers of those that cry out in
any tribulation come unto thee, that all may rejoice to find
that thy mercy is present with them in their afflictions; through
Jesus Christ our Lord. Amen.

O LORD of hosts, God of Israel, that dwellest between the
cherubim; thou art the God, even thou alone, of all the kingdoms
of the earth; thou hast made heaven and earth. Incline thine ear,
O LORD, and hear; open thine eyes, O LORD, and see. Save us
from the hand of our enemies, that all the kingdoms of the
earth may know that thou art the LORD, even thou only. Amen.

Most merciful God, the helper of all men; so strengthen us
by thy power that our sorrow may be turned into joy, and
we may continually glorify thy holy name; through Jesus Christ
our Lord. Amen.

For Strength

Grant, we beseech thee, Almighty God, unto us who know
that we are weak, and who trust in thee because we know that
thou art strong, the gladsome help of thy lovingkindness. Amen.

O Lord our God, under the shadow of thy wings let us hope.
Thou wilt support us, both when young, and even to old age.
When our strength is of thee, it is strength; but when our own,
it is weakness. We return unto thee, O Lord, that from their
weariness our souls may rise toward thee, leaning on the
things which thou hast created, and passing on to thyself, who
hast wonderfully made them; for with thee is refreshment and
true strength. Amen.

O God, most merciful Father, thou speakest through thine only-begotten Son, our Lord Jesus Christ, saying: Ask, and it shall be given unto you. Give us now thy Holy Spirit, that our hearts may be strengthened for the work of this week; through Jesus Christ. Amen.

Give us now, O merciful Father, thy Holy Spirit, that we may be strengthened for the work of this day; through Jesus Christ thy Son our Lord. Amen.

For the Suffering and the Perplexed

O Thou who art love, and who seest all the suffering, injustice, and misery in the world; have pity, we implore thee, on the work of thy hands. Look mercifully upon the poor, the oppressed, and all who are heavy laden or in sorrow. Fill our hearts with deep compassion for those who suffer, and hasten the coming of thy Kingdom of justice and truth; for the sake of Jesus Christ our Lord. Amen.

O almighty and merciful Father, who art the help of the helpless, and the lifter-up of the fallen; look down with thy mercy on all who are oppressed in mind, body, or estate; comfort and relieve them, according to their several necessities; give them patience under their sufferings, and a happy issue out of all their affliction. Amen.

In Temptation

Preserve us this day from temptations. Suffer us not to fall into idle habits; and, if diligent in business, suffer not our hearts to be engrossed that we fail to serve thee; and grant that thy presence may be with us, giving us strength and confidence; through Jesus Christ our Lord. Amen.

O most Holy Spirit, give thy strength unto all who are tried by any special temptation. Help them to stand fast in thee, that they may be able to bear it; for the sake of Jesus Christ our Lord and Saviour. Amen.

Thanksgivings

We give thee thanks, O Lord our God, for all thy goodness. Thou hast shielded, rescued, helped, and guided us all the days of our lives, and brought us unto this hour. Grant in thy goodness that we may spend this day without sin, in joy and reverence of thee. Drive away from us all envy, all fear. Bestow upon us what is good and meet. And lead us not into temptation, but deliver us from evil. Amen.

Almighty and most merciful God, we give thanks to thee for the light of another day, for the work we have to do, and for the strength to do it. Guide us, we pray thee, by thy truth; uphold us by thy power; and purify us by the continual indwelling of thy Spirit. Grant that by every opportunity we have we may grow in wisdom, and, knowing the things that belong to our peace, obtain strength to persevere; through Jesus Christ our Lord. Amen.

We give thee thanks, O heavenly Father, who hast preserved us through the night. We pray thee to keep us through this day, and to bring us in safety to the evening hours; through Jesus Christ our Lord. Amen.

Thanks be to thee, O Lord Jesus Christ, for all the benefits which thou hast given us, for all the pains and insults which thou hast borne for us. O most merciful Redeemer, Friend, and Brother, may we know thee more clearly, love thee more dearly, and follow thee more nearly; for thine own sake. Amen.

Today and Its Needs

O God, give me strength to live this day. Let me not turn coward before its difficulties or prove recreant to its duties. Let me not lose faith in my fellow men. Keep me sweet and sound of heart, in spite of ingratitude, treachery, or meanness. Preserve me from minding little stings or giving them. Help me to keep clean, and to live honestly and fearlessly. Grant me this day some new vision of thy truth; inspire me with the spirit of joy and gladness; and make me the cup of strength to suffering souls; in the name of the strong Deliverer, our only Lord and Saviour Jesus Christ. Amen.

O God, of whose gifts come sunshine, and friendship, and the glory of a summer's day, who in the common things of daily life givest to us thy very self, making of bread and wine the sacrament of thy sustaining presence; strengthen and refresh us, that we may seek thee eagerly, find thee surely, and serve thee faithfully; through Jesus Christ our Lord. Amen.

We thank thee, O God, for the revelation of thyself in the common ways of life. Help us to be ever watchful for new knowledge of thee, so that in the temporal we may discern that which is eternal; through Jesus Christ our Lord. Amen.

The day returns and brings us the petty round of irritating concerns and duties. Help us to play the man; help us to perform them with laughter and kind faces; let cheerfulness abound with industry. Give us to go blithely on our business all this day; bring us to our resting beds weary and content and undishonored; and grant us in the end the gift of sleep. Amen.

Almighty God, we bless and praise thee that we have wakened to the light of another day. Teach us the meaning of our days. Our days are thine; let them be spent for thee. Our days are few; let them be spent with care. There are dark days behind us; forgive their sinfulness. There may be dark days before us; strengthen us for their trials. Lord, we go to our daily work; help us to take pleasure therein. Show us clearly what our duty is; help us to be faithful in doing it, that all we do be well done. Give us strength and patience; let our courage never fail; through Jesus Christ our Lord. Amen.

Enlighten our understandings with knowledge of right, and govern our wills by thy laws, that no deceit may mislead us, no temptation corrupt us, that we may always endeavor to do good and hinder evil. Amid all the hopes and fears of this world, take not thy Holy Spirit from us; for the sake of Jesus Christ our Lord. Amen.

For Travelers

O eternal Lord God, who rulest both sea and land; protect thy servant on the deep. Guard *him* from danger, from the violence of enemies, from every evil; and conduct *him* in safety to *his* journey's end; through Jesus Christ our Lord. Amen.

O Lord Jesus Christ, who on the sea didst teach thy disciples many heavenly things, and even in the storm didst come close to them, saying, It is I, be not afraid; we pray thee to show the voice of thy truth and the power of thy presence to thy children on the deep, and be thou the guide and guardian of all that sail the seas; who livest and reignest with the Father and the Holy Spirit, one God, world without end. Amen.

Preserve, O Lord, from all dangers those who are traveling, whether by land, sea, or air. Prosper them with all necessary things, and grant them ever steadfastly to abide in the way of thy commandments, and attain the end of their faith, even the salvation of their souls, in the home which thou hast provided for thy children; through Jesus Christ our Lord. Amen.

O Lord, be merciful to all travelers, and grant them a safe return, that they, beholding thy mercy, and praising thee for thy goodness here, may the more be quickened with a desire for the full enjoyment of their privileges as fellow citizens with the saints in thy heavenly household; through Jesus Christ. Amen.

For Unity

O merciful God, bless thy Church throughout all the world, and all those who love thee in sincerity, although they follow not with us in all things. Heal all strife, divisions, and discord, and make us all thine in willing devotion as we are all thine by redemption and grace; through Jesus Christ our Lord. Amen.

For a Wedding

O God, bless thy servants who are about to be joined together this day in holy matrimony; keep them, we beseech thee, under the protection of thy good providence, and make them to have a perpetual fear and love of thy holy name. Look, O Lord, mercifully upon them from heaven and bless them, that they, obeying thy will and always being in safety under thy protection, may abide in thy love unto their lives' end; through Jesus Christ our Lord. Amen.

O Thou who by thy presence in Cana of Galilee didst sanctify the holy estate of matrimony, send thy blessing upon thy servants who have this day entered upon this holy estate, and so fill them with all spiritual benediction and grace, that, living together in perfect love and holy peace in this world, in the world to come they may obtain life everlasting; through Jesus Christ our Lord. Amen.

For Workers

O blessed Saviour, who wast pleased thyself to be reckoned among the craftsmen; bless all who labor with their hands, that their work may be done for thy honor and rewarded with thy approval; for thine own name's sake. Amen.

O Lord, let us not live to be useless; for Christ's sake. Amen.

Have mercy, O Lord, upon all those who labor in the cultivation of the earth, and grant that by the power of thy grace their own souls may be made fruitful unto all good works; through Jesus Christ our Lord. Amen.

SPECIAL DAYS AND TOPICS

Armistice or Memorial Day

O God our heavenly Father, we bless thee again for the remembrance of this day, when by thy providence, and by the might of thine arm, thou madest wars to cease; accept our praise and thanksgivings.

As on this day we remember before thee all those who fought and died that we might live, accept our gratitude, and make us, we humbly beseech thee, more worthy of their sacrifice even unto death, and help us to follow more closely in the steps of thy blessed Son, that at last we with them may stand in thy presence; where all praise, thanksgiving, honor, and might be ascribed, world without end. Amen.

We bless thy holy name, O God, for all thy servants who, having finished their course, do now rest from their labors. Give us grace, we beseech thee, to follow the example of their steadfastness and faithfulness, to thy honor and glory; through Christ Jesus our Lord. Amen.

In remembrance of those who made the great sacrifice, O God, make us better men and women, and give peace in our time; through Jesus Christ thy Son our Saviour. Amen.

O God, the strength of those who suffer, and the repose of them that triumph; we rejoice in the communion of saints. We remember all who have faithfully lived, all who have passed on into heaven (especially those most dear to us). May we have the assurance of their continual fellowship in thee, and realize that, though converse be no longer possible according to the flesh, there is no separation in the realm of love. Lift us into that light and love where the Church on earth is one with the Church in heaven; through Jesus Christ our Lord. Amen.

O God of all mercy and comfort, accept the heartfelt praises and thanksgivings of those whose dear ones, after having fought a good fight, returned to them in safety. In the greatness of their joy may they ever be mindful of those whose lives are shadowed with abiding sorrow; for the sake of Christ Jesus our Saviour. Amen.

Christmas

Send, O God, into the darkness of this troubled world the light of thy Son. Let the star of thy hope touch the minds of all men with the bright beams of mercy and truth; and so direct our steps that we may ever walk in the way revealed to us, as the shepherds of Bethlehem walked with joy to the manger where he dwelt who now and ever reigns in our hearts, Jesus Christ our Lord. Amen.

Easter

Thou brightness of God's glory and express image of his person, whom death could not conquer nor the tomb imprison; as thou hast shared our mortal frailty in the flesh, help us to share thine immortal triumph in the spirit. Let no shadow of the grave affright us and no fear of darkness turn our hearts from thee. Reveal thyself to us this day as the first and the last, the Living One, our Saviour and Lord. Amen.

Christ is risen from the dead, and become the firstfruits of them that slept. For as in Adam all die, even so in Christ shall all be made alive. Glory be to thee, O God most high. Amen.

O gracious Lord, who as at this time didst raise thy Son Jesus Christ with power from the grave; raise us up, we beseech thee, from the death of sin to the life of righteousness. Revive our faith, and make us followers of him who hath taken away the sin of the world, who by his death hath destroyed death, and by his rising to life again hath restored to us everlasting life. Hear us, O merciful Father, we pray thee, for the sake of our risen Saviour, to whom, with thee and the Holy Ghost, be all honor and glory, world without end. Amen.

Gracious Lord, we remember that thou didst accompany thy two disciples as they journeyed to Emmaus. We too have a journey; we have a weary pilgrimage to perform. Do thou go with us, O Lord; be our fellow traveler; guide us, uphold us, strengthen us, make our hearts to burn within us, and evermore manifest thyself to our souls in gracious and in heavenly power; for thine own name's sake we ask it. Amen.

Good Friday

Forbid, O God, that we should forget, amid our earthly comforts, the pains and mortal anguish that our Lord Jesus endured for our salvation. Grant us this day a true vision of all that he suffered: his betrayal, his lonely agony, his false trial, his mocking and scourging, the torture of the cross; that, remembering his sufferings and death, we may give ourselves wholly to thee; through the same Jesus Christ, our only Lord and Saviour. Amen.

Lent

O Lord our God, teach us temperance and self-control, that we may live unto the spirit and be mindful of all that Jesus endured and sacrificed for our sakes, and how he was made perfect through sufferings; and help us so to keep the fast that thou hast chosen, that we may loose the bands of wickedness, undo the heavy burdens, and let the oppressed go free; through the grace of Christ Jesus, our crucified and risen Saviour. Amen.

New Year's Day

Thine, O Lord, are the times we measure off by days and years; for though the years pass, yet are we ever with thee, embosomed in thy beauty, love, and power. May the dawning year be new indeed, with new visions of truth, a new wonder of thy love, and a new service to our fellow man. May our home be better ordered, our work better done, and our faith more firmly fixed in thee, that life may show us its worth and wonder, in Jesus Christ our Lord. Amen.

Palm Sunday

O God, who by the passion of thy blessed Son hast made the instrument of shameful death to be unto us the means of life and peace; grant us so to glory in the cross of Christ that we may gladly suffer shame and loss; for the sake of the same thy Son our Lord. Amen.

Thanksgiving Day

O Lord our God, we cried unto thee in trouble, and thou heardest us; we put our trust in thee, and were not confounded. Thou hast turned our heaviness into joy, and girded us with gladness; therefore will we praise thee with all our heart, and give thanks unto thy holy name forever. Hear us and accept us; for the sake of Jesus Christ our Lord. Amen.

We give thee humble thanks, most merciful Father, that thou dost graciously hear the prayers of thy servants who call upon thee, and hast done for us great things whereof we rejoice. We desire to thank thee, O most loving Father, for all thy goodness vouchsafed unto us; through Jesus Christ our Lord. Amen.

Whitsunday

O God, who as at this time didst send down thy Holy Spirit from above upon thine apostles, and dost evermore send him to renew thine image in our souls; mercifully grant that by the working of his grace we may be saved from sin and may glorify thee; through the merits and mediation of thy Son our Saviour Jesus Christ, who liveth and reigneth with thee in the unity of the same Spirit, one God, world without end. Amen.

Breathe into our souls, O heavenly Father, the love of whatsoever is true and beautiful and good. May we fear to be unfaithful and have no other fear. Help us to remember that we are thy children, and belong to thee. In thy service may we live. and in thy favor may we die; through Jesus Christ our Lord. Amen.

For the Armed Forces

O Almighty God, protect our sailors and the fleet in which they serve from the dangers of the sea and the violence of the enemy. Strengthen them to meet the strain of waiting and their great responsibility for the welfare of the nation. Make them alert in watching and fearless in their warfare; through Jesus Christ our Lord. Amen.

Grant that the men of our armed forces may be brave in battle, high-hearted in hardships, dauntless in defeat, gentle in victory. Remember those who have trained themselves in peace to help their country in war; and give them skill and courage, endurance and self-control, in the work now set them. We ask it in the name and for the sake of Christ Jesus our Lord. Amen.

O Lord God, our Father, our Saviour, our Might; we commend to thy keeping all those who are venturing their lives on our behalf, that whether by life or by death they may win for the whole world the fruits of their sacrifice, and a holy peace; through Jesus Christ our Lord. Amen.

Look in thy mercy, we beseech thee, O Lord, on those who are called to tasks of special peril in the air or beneath the sea. Even there also shall thy hand lead them, and thy right hand shall hold them. Help them to do their duty with prudence and with fearlessness, confident that in life or in death the eternal God is their refuge, and underneath are the everlasting arms. Grant this for Jesus Christ's sake, thy Son our Lord. Amen.

O Thou who bringest the winds out of thy treasures, let thy guiding and protecting hand be about our airmen; and help those who love them to feel that underneath are the everlasting arms; through Jesus Christ. Amen.

For Our Country and Its Leaders

We humbly thank thee, Almighty God, for the many blessings which thou hast given to our country, and add this, O Lord, to thy other mercies, that we may be enabled to use them better to thy service. Oh take from among us all contempt of thy word and commandments. Break down all the barriers of selfishness and ignorance which keep men from thee. Convince the impenitent of the misery of sin, and comfort the broken-hearted with the assurance of thy love; through Jesus Christ our Lord. Amen.

Be gracious unto us, O Lord, and bless us. Stretch forth the right hand of thy protection to guard our country, that we, being devoted to thy service, may ever be defended by thy power; through Jesus Christ our Lord. Amen.

Grant and continue unto us legislators and rulers who themselves have been taught the wisdom of the Kingdom of Christ. Endow all members of Congress with a right understanding, a pure purpose, and sound speech. Enable them to rise above all self-seeking and party zeal into the larger sentiments of public good and human brotherhood. Cleanse our public life of every evil; subdue in our nation all that which is evil. Give us self-restraint, that we may do thy will on earth as it is done in heaven; even through Jesus Christ our Lord. Amen.

O God most high, the only Ruler, grant, we beseech thee, to all who rule over us the inspiration of thy Holy Spirit, that as they labor faithfully for our country, they may also advance thy Kingdom upon earth; through Jesus Christ our Lord. Amen.

O God, Almighty Father, King of kings and Lord of all our rulers; grant that the hearts and minds of all who go out as leaders before us, the statesmen, the judges, the men of learning, and the men of wealth, may be so filled with the love of thy laws, and of that which is righteous and life-giving, that they may serve as a wholesome salt unto the earth, and be worthy stewards of thy good and perfect gifts; through Jesus Christ our Lord. Amen.

Guide, O Lord, we pray thee, the mayors and other officers of our cities, with all those who share in the ordering of our community life. Give strength, honor, and charity to all our fellow citizens, that they may do their work, seeking not the good of any party or faction but of all our citizens. Sustain them by a vision of freedom and a peaceful and happy citizenry; through Jesus Christ our Lord. Amen.

For the Family of Nations

Almighty God, our heavenly Father, guide, we beseech thee, the nations of the world into the way of justice and truth, and establish among them that peace which is the fruit of righteousness, that they may become the Kingdom of our Lord and Saviour Jesus Christ. Amen.

O Thou in whose hand are the hearts of thy creatures, shed abroad thy peace upon the world. By the might of thy Holy Spirit quench the pride, and anger, and greediness which cause man to strive against man, and people against people. Lead all nations in the ways of mutual help and good will, and hasten the time when the earth shall confess thee indeed for its Saviour and King; through Jesus Christ our Lord. Amen.

O Lord, be merciful to us and bless us. As thou hast made our nation mighty in this world, so make it a source of wisdom and truth, of order and sanctity, to all who come under its influence. Let thy light pass from clime to clime and enlighten us all. Let thy truth be our truth. Unite us all as thy children in thy common blessing. Let the knowledge of thy righteousness and thy love unfeigned reign in all our hearts; through Jesus Christ our Lord. Amen.

In Time of War or National Anxiety

O Lord God of infinite mercy, reckon not against thy people their many iniquities. Look in mercy on those in peril, conflict, sickness, and death; comfort the prisoners, relieve the sufferings of the wounded, and in thy mercy be near to the dying. Of thy great goodness restore peace among the nations; through Jesus Christ our Lord. Amen.

O Lord God Almighty who from thy throne dost behold all the dwellers upon earth; look down with pity upon those on whom have fallen the miseries of war. Have compassion on the wounded and dying; comfort the broken-hearted; assuage the madness of the nations; make war to cease; give peace in our time, O Lord. We ask it in the name of him who is the Prince of Peace, even thy Son Jesus Christ our Lord. Amen.

Have mercy, O Lord, upon the wounded and the suffering, whether of our own people or of the enemy. Let thy grace be their comfort, although natural friends be far away. Raise them to health, if it be good, but chiefly give them such faith and patience that they may glorify thee upon the earth; through Jesus Christ our Lord. Amen.

Take from us, O God, all pride and vanity, all boasting and forwardness, and give us the true courage that shows itself by gentleness, the true wisdom that shows itself by simplicity, and the true power that shows itself by righteousness; through Jesus Christ our Lord. Amen.

Send thy blessing, O heavenly Father, on this our beloved land. Increase in our own and in every nation the spirit of truth and justice, peace and godly love. Turn the hearts of all men unto thee, and so hasten the blessed time when the kingdoms of the world shall become the Kingdom of our Lord Jesus Christ; in whose name we offer these petitions, even the same Christ Jesus thy Son our Lord. Amen.

Father of all men and God of peace, hear our prayers, we beseech thee, and grant that at this time those in authority may so faithfully conduct all negotiations between this country and _____ that peace may be maintained. Grant that all concerned may have a single eye to thy glory, and that while no injustice may be left unredressed they may honestly labor for peace as thy sons, from whom every family in heaven and on earth is named; through Jesus Christ our Lord. Amen.

O heavenly Father, we confess before thee with shame and sorrow that we have lived too much without thee in the world, that we have depended for our success and for our prosperity upon ourselves as a nation. Call us to repentance. May we humble ourselves now under thy mighty hand. And may it please thee to make this and every trial work for our everlasting good, so that we may be established in righteousness, strengthened and settled; through Jesus Christ our Lord. Amen.

Look graciously, and speedily have compassion upon thy people in thy abundant mercy, for the sake of thy name, O eternal God. Pity, compassionate, and save the sheep of thy pasture; suffer not wrath to prevail against us, for our eyes are directed toward thee. Save us, then, for the sake of thy name. Have mercy upon us. Regard and answer us in time of trouble, for unto thee belongeth salvation, in thee is our hope, O God of forgiveness. O pardon us, thou good and forgiving God, for thou, omnipotent King, art most gracious and compassionate. Hear us, we humbly beseech thee, for the glory of thy great name. Amen.

For World Peace and Concord

O Almighty God, we turn to thee in the time of trouble. Direct the course of our world; lead the nations into likemindedness and fellowship; prosper all counsels which make for the establishment and maintenance of rightful and abiding peace; through Jesus Christ our Lord. Amen.

O Lord Jesus Christ, who biddest thy Church to bring all men to thyself; make clear to each one of us his part in the task. Fire our minds with a vision of a more perfect society here on earth in which justice and right, peace and brotherhood, shall reign according to thy will; and help us, each one, O Lord, to do our part, that thy will may be done on earth as it is in heaven. Amen.

Almighty God, from whom all thoughts of truth and peace proceed; kindle, we pray thee, in the hearts of all men the true love of peace, and guide with thy pure and peaceable wisdom those who take counsel for the nations of the earth, that in tranquillity thy Kingdom may grow, till the earth is filled with the knowledge of thy love; through Jesus Christ our Lord. Amen.

Graces

To be said in unison:

Morning: Gracious Giver of all good,
             Thee we thank for rest and food;
             Grant that all we do or say,
             In thy service be this day. Amen.

Noon: Father, for this noonday meal
             We would speak the praise we feel.
             Health and strength we have in thee;
             Help us, Lord, to faithful be. Amen.

Evening: Tireless Guardian of our way,
             Thou hast kept us well this day;
             While we thank thee, we request
             Care continued, pardon, rest. Amen.

We thank thee, our heavenly Father, for thy care over us, and pray that thou wilt bless this food to our use. Amen.

O God, our Father, who giveth food for the body and truth for the mind; so enlighten and nourish us that we may grow wise and strong to do thy will. Amen.

Our heavenly Father, we thank thee that—
        Back of the loaf is the snowy flour,
        And back of the flour the mill,
        And back of the mill is the wheat and the shower
        And the sun and the Father's will. Amen.

For these and all his blessings God's holy name be praised; through Jesus Christ our Lord. Amen.

Bless, O Lord, this food to our use, and us in thy service; through Jesus Christ our Lord. Amen.

Thanks be to thee, O Lord, for these and all the blessings so generously provided. We thank thee in the name of Christ. Amen.

Almighty Giver of good, we thank thee for thy lovingkindness to us. Thou openest thy hand, and we are fed. Be at this table, we pray thee, and bless our gathering together; through Jesus Christ our Lord. Amen.

Our Father, we bless thee for this food and for all the expressions of thy goodness to us. Give us grace to do thy will; through Jesus Christ our Lord. Amen.

Let thy peace and blessing descend upon us as we take of thy bounty. Fill our hearts with love and praise unto him who doeth all things well. Amen.

Lord, make us truly grateful for the blessings of this day, and keep us thine evermore. Amen.

Heavenly Father great and good,
We thank thee for this daily food.
Bless us even as we pray;
Guide and keep us through this day. Amen.

O Lord, all creatures wait upon thee that they may receive their good. Thou openest thy hand and they are filled with good. Help us to remember always that we are dependent on thee and with thankfulness partake of the food before us; through Jesus Christ our Lord. Amen.

Sanctify, O Lord, we beseech thee, this food to our use, and us to thy service, and make us truly thankful for all these mercies; through Jesus Christ our Lord. Amen.

THE WESLEY GRACES

Grace Before Meat

> Be present at our table, Lord;
> Be here and everywhere adored.
> These creatures bless, and grant that we
> May feast in Paradise with thee. Amen.

Alternative Form

> Be present at our table, Lord;
> Be here and everywhere adored.
> Thy mercies bless, and grant that we
> May feast in fellowship with thee. Amen.

Grace After Meat

> We thank thee, Lord, for this our food,
> But more because of Jesus' blood.
> Let manna to our souls be given,
> The Bread of Life, sent down from heaven. Amen.

With gratitude we acknowledge these gifts and all the benefits of thy grace. Help us to live for thy glory; through Jesus Christ our Lord. Amen.

We bless thee, O God, for this food which betokens thy continued care over us; we acknowledge this gift, and thy love which prompts it, and pray for fidelity to use our strength in doing thy good pleasure; through Jesus Christ our Lord. Amen.

Accept, O Father, our humble thanks for this our daily food; and as it adds strength to our mortal bodies, may it give us power to render better service to thee; through Jesus Christ our Lord. Amen.

Transform this food into life, O God, and transform that life into useful service of thee; through Jesus Christ our Lord. Amen.

For this our daily bread, and for every good gift which cometh down from thee, we bless thy holy name; through Jesus Christ our Lord. Amen.

This food, which thou hast already blessed in the giving, do thou further bless in our partaking, that it may redound to thy glory; through Jesus Christ our Lord. Amen.

Almighty God, and gracious Father of men, who openest thy hand and fillest the earth with good, and hast provided thy children sufficient to satisfy all our need; teach us to render back to thee thy due thanksgiving, not only in words, but also in the manner of our living; through Jesus Christ our Lord. Amen.

Lord, thou hast not need of our thanks, but we have daily need to remind ourselves of our obligation unto thee. For all thy mercies make us ever truly grateful. Amen.

> Praise to God, immortal praise,
> For the love that crowns our days;
> Bounteous source of every joy!
> Let thy praise our tongues employ;
> All to thee, our God, we owe,
> Source whence all our blessing flow. Amen.

An Order for the Administration of the Sacrament of the Lord's Supper or Holy Communion I

THE following is a complete order of public worship and is intended to replace the regular order of morning worship when the Sacrament of the Lord's Supper is administered. The responses may be sung if desired. See numbers 565-88 in *The Methodist Hymnal*.

The Lord's Table should have upon it a fair linen cloth.

Let the pure, unfermented juice of the grape be used.

It is our custom to receive the Sacrament of the Lord's Supper kneeling, but if persons so desire, they may receive the elements while seated or standing.

Upon entering the church let the communicants bow in prayer and in the spirit of prayer and meditation approach the blessed Sacrament.

The people shall stand and join in singing the hymn, "Holy, holy, holy, Lord God Almighty," or other suitable hymn, and remain standing until after the singing of the Gloria Patri.

God is a Spirit. They that worship him must worship him in spirit and in truth.

Glory be to God on high.

God is Light. If we walk in the light, as he is in the light, we have fellowship one with another; and truly our fellowship is with the Father, and with his Son Jesus Christ.

Glory be to God on high.

God is Power. They that wait upon the Lord shall renew their strength; they shall mount up with wings as eagles; they shall run, and not be weary; and they shall walk, and not faint.

Glory be to God on high.

God is Love. Behold, what manner of love the Father hath bestowed upon us, that we should be called the sons of God.

Hereby perceive we the love of God, because he laid down his life for us.

Glory be to God on high.

Then the Gloria Patri *shall be said or sung:*

Glory be to the Father, and to the Son, and to the Holy Ghost; as it was in the beginning, is now, and ever shall be, world without end. Amen.

Then shall the minister say:

Let us pray.

Almighty God, unto whom all hearts are open, all desires known, and from whom no secrets are hid; cleanse the thoughts of our hearts by the inspiration of thy Holy Spirit, that we may perfectly love thee, and worthily magnify thy holy name; through Jesus Christ our Lord. Amen.

Our Father who art in heaven, hallowed be thy name; thy kingdom come; thy will be done on earth as it is in heaven. Give us this day our daily bread. And forgive us our trespasses, as we forgive those who trespass against us. And lead us not into temptation, but deliver us from evil. For thine is the kingdom, and the power, and the glory, forever. Amen.

Then may the minister read the Ten Commandments, and the people, still in the attitude of prayer, shall in response ask God's mercy for their transgressions in times past and grace to keep the law in time to come.

God spake these words, and said: I am the LORD thy God: Thou shalt have no other gods before me.

Thou shalt not make unto thee any graven image, or any likeness of any thing that is in heaven above, or that is in the earth beneath, or that is in the water under the earth: thou shalt not bow down thyself to them, nor serve them: for I the LORD thy God am a jealous God, visiting the iniquity of the fathers upon the children unto the third and fourth generation of them that hate me; and showing mercy unto thousands of them that love me, and keep my commandments.

Lord, have mercy upon us, and write all these thy laws in our hearts, we beseech thee.

Thou shalt not take the name of the LORD thy God in vain; for the LORD will not hold him guiltless that taketh his name in vain.

Remember the Sabbath day, to keep it holy. Six days shalt thou labor, and do all thy work: but the seventh day is the Sabbath of the LORD thy God: in it thou shalt not do any work, thou, nor thy son, nor thy daughter, thy manservant, nor thy maidservant, nor thy cattle, nor thy stranger that is within thy gates: for in six days the LORD made heaven and earth, the sea, and all that in them is, and rested the seventh day: wherefore the LORD blessed the Sabbath day, and hallowed it.

Lord, have mercy upon us, and write all these thy laws in our hearts, we beseech thee.

Honor thy father and thy mother: that thy days may be long upon the land which the LORD thy God giveth thee.

Thou shalt not kill.

Thou shalt not commit adultery.

Thou shalt not steal.

Thou shalt not bear false witness against thy neighbor.

Thou shalt not covet thy neighbor's house, thou shalt not covet thy neighbor's wife, nor his manservant, nor his maidservant, nor his ox, nor his ass, nor anything that is thy neighbor's.

Lord, have mercy upon us, and write all these thy laws in our hearts, we beseech thee.

In place of or in addition to the Ten Commandments the minister may read the summary of the divine law in the words of Jesus, and the people, in the attitude of prayer, shall ask God's mercy and gracious aid.

Hear what our Lord Jesus Christ saith:

Thou shalt love the Lord thy God with all thy heart, and with all thy soul, and with all thy mind. This is the first and great commandment. And the second is like unto it, Thou shalt love thy neighbor as thyself.

Lord, have mercy upon us, and write all these thy laws in our hearts, we beseech thee.

Then may the minister read the Beatitudes of the Lord Jesus, and the people, still in the attitude of prayer, shall humbly ask God that they may be fulfilled in their hearts. Or here Isaiah 53:1-10 may be used as a responsive scripture.

Hear the Beatitudes of our Lord Jesus Christ:

Blessed are the poor in spirit: for theirs is the kingdom of heaven.

Lord, be gracious unto us, and help us to obtain this blessing.

Blessed are they that mourn: for they shall be comforted.

Lord, be gracious unto us, and help us to obtain this blessing.

Blessed are the meek: for they shall inherit the earth.

Lord, be gracious unto us, and help us to obtain this blessing.

Blessed are they which do hunger and thirst after righteousness: for they shall be filled.

Lord, be gracious unto us, and help us to obtain this blessing.

Blessed are the merciful: for they shall obtain mercy.

Lord, be gracious unto us, and help us to obtain this blessing.

Blessed are the pure in heart: for they shall see God.

Lord, be gracious unto us, and help us to obtain this blessing.

Blessed are the peacemakers: for they shall be called the children of God.

Lord, be gracious unto us, and help us to obtain this blessing.

Blessed are they which are persecuted for righteousness' sake: for theirs is the kingdom of heaven.

Blessed are ye, when men shall revile you, and persecute you, and shall say all manner of evil against you falsely, for my sake.

Rejoice, and be exceeding glad: for great is your reward in heaven: for so persecuted they the prophets which were before you.

Grant unto us thy Holy Spirit, O God, and enable us to obtain all these blessings; through Jesus Christ our Lord. Amen.

If desired, the following form may be used:

Hear the Beatitudes of our Lord Jesus Christ:

Blessed are the poor in spirit: for theirs is the kingdom of heaven.

Blessed are they that mourn: for they shall be comforted.

Blessed are the meek: for they shall inherit the earth.

Lord, be gracious unto us, and help us to obtain these blessings.

Blessed are they which do hunger and thirst after righteousness: for they shall be filled.

Blessed are the merciful: for they shall obtain mercy.

Blessed are the pure in heart: for they shall see God.

Blessed are the peacemakers: for they shall be called the children of God.

Lord, be gracious unto us, and help us to obtain these blessings.

Blessed are they which are persecuted for righteousness' sake: for theirs is the kingdom of heaven.

Blessed are ye, when men shall revile you, and persecute you, and shall say all manner of evil against you falsely, for my sake.

Rejoice, and be exceeding glad: for great is your reward in heaven: for so persecuted they the prophets which were before you.

Grant unto us thy Holy Spirit, O God, and enable us to

obtain all these blessings; through Jesus Christ our Lord. Amen.

The responsive scripture, Isaiah 53:1-10:

Who hath believed our report? and to whom is the arm of the LORD revealed?

For he shall grow up before him as a tender plant, and as a root out of a dry ground: he hath no form nor comeliness; and when we shall see him, there is no beauty that we should desire him.

He is despised and rejected of men; a man of sorrows, and acquainted with grief: and we hid as it were our faces from him; he was despised, and we esteemed him not.

Surely he hath borne our griefs, and carried our sorrows: yet we did esteem him stricken, smitten of God, and afflicted.

But he was wounded for our transgressions, he was bruised for our iniquities: the chastisement of our peace was upon him; and with his stripes we are healed.

All we like sheep have gone astray; we have turned every one to his own way; and the LORD hath laid on him the iniquity of us all.

He was oppressed, and he was afflicted, yet he opened not his mouth: he is brought as a lamb to the slaughter, and as a sheep before his shearers is dumb, so he openeth not his mouth.

He was taken from prison and from judgment: and who shall declare his generation? for he was cut off out of the land of the living: for the transgression of my people was he stricken.

And he made his grave with the wicked, and with the rich in his death; because he had done no violence, neither was any deceit in his mouth.

Yet it pleased the LORD to bruise him; he hath put him to grief: when thou shalt make his soul an offering for

sin, he shall see his seed, he shall prolong his days, and the pleasure of the LORD shall prosper in his hand.

Then may the minister read the Epistle, to be followed by the Gospel.

Here may the minister and people repeat the Apostles' Creed or some other of the authorized affirmations of faith, the people standing.

Then may follow the sermon or communion meditation and a suitable hymn (see hymns 408-15). During the singing of this hymn the minister shall remove the linen cloth that covers the elements.

After the hymn has been sung, the minister, standing by the Lord's Table, shall announce the offering for the needy, using one or more of the following groups of sentences.

I

Remember the words of the Lord Jesus, how he said, It is more blessed to give than to receive.

Let your light so shine before men, that they may see your good works, and glorify your Father which is in heaven.

Not everyone that saith upon me, Lord, Lord, shall enter into the kingdom of heaven; but he that doeth the will of my Father which is in heaven.

And the King shall answer and say unto them, Verily I say unto you, Inasmuch as ye have done it unto one of the least of these my brethren, ye have done it unto me.

Therefore all things whatsoever ye would that men should do to you, do ye even so to them: for this is the law and the prophets.

II

They shall not appear before the LORD empty: every man shall give as he is able, according to the blessing of the LORD thy God which he hath given thee.

Blessed is he that considereth the poor: the LORD will deliver him in time of trouble.

Thou shalt open thine hand wide unto thy brother, to thy poor, and to thy needy, in thy land.

Be merciful after thy power. If thou hast much, give plenteously: if thou hast little, do thy diligence gladly to give of that little: for so gatherest thou thyself a good reward in the day of necessity.

He that hath pity upon the poor lendeth unto the LORD; and that which he hath given will he pay him again.

III

To do good and to communicate forget not: for with such sacrifices God is well pleased.

As we have therefore opportunity, let us do good unto all men, especially unto them who are of the household of faith.

He which soweth sparingly shall reap also sparingly; and he which soweth bountifully shall reap also bountifully. Every man according as he purposeth in his heart, so let him give; not grudgingly, or of necessity: for God loveth a cheerful giver.

Whoso hath this world's good, and seeth his brother have need, and shutteth up his compassion from him, how dwelleth the love of God in him?

God is not unrighteous to forget your work and labor of love, which ye have showed toward his name, in that ye have ministered to the saints, and do minister.

IV

Offer unto God thanksgiving; and pay thy vows unto the most High.

Lay not up for yourselves treasures upon earth, where moth and rust doth corrupt, and where thieves break through and steal: but lay up for yourselves treasures in heaven, where neither moth nor rust doth corrupt, and where thieves do not break through nor steal: for where your treasure is, there will your heart be also.

Zacchaeus stood, and said unto the Lord; Behold, Lord, the half of my goods I give to the poor; and if I have taken anything from any man by false accusation, I restore him fourfold.

Charge them that are rich in this world, that they be rich in good works, ready to distribute, willing to communicate; laying up in store for themselves a good foundation against the time to come, that they may lay hold on eternal life.

Godliness with contentment is great gain. For we brought nothing into this world, and it is certain we can carry nothing out.

As the minister receives the offering, the people shall stand, and the following may be said or sung:

All things come of thee, O Lord, and of thine own have we given thee.

Then may the minister say:

Thine, O Lord, is the greatness, and the power, and the glory, and the victory, and the majesty: for all that is in the heaven and in the earth is thine; thine is the kingdom, O Lord, and thou art exalted as head above all.

The people shall remain standing while the minister reads the invitation.

Ye that do truly and earnestly repent of your sins, and are in love and charity with your neighbors, and intend to lead a new life, following the commandments of God, and walking from henceforth in his holy ways; draw near with faith, and take this holy Sacrament to your comfort; and devoutly kneeling make your humble confession to Almighty God.

Then shall this general confession be made by the minister and those who are minded to receive the Holy Communion, the minister kneeling, facing the Lord's Table, and all the people in the attitude of prayer.

Almighty God, Father of our Lord Jesus Christ, Maker of all things, Judge of all men; we acknowledge and bewail our manifold sins and wickedness, which we from time to time most grievously have committed, by thought, word, and deed, against thy divine majesty. We do earnestly repent, and are heartily sorry for these our misdoings; the remembrance of them is grievous unto us. Have mercy upon us, have mercy upon us, most merciful Father; for thy Son our Lord Jesus Christ's sake, forgive us all that is past; and grant that we may ever hereafter serve and please thee in newness of life, to the honor and glory of thy name; through Jesus Christ our Lord. Amen.

Then shall the minister offer this prayer:

Almighty God, our heavenly Father, who of thy great mercy hast promised forgiveness of sins to all them that with hearty repentance and true faith turn unto thee; have mercy upon us; pardon and deliver us from all our sins; confirm and strengthen us in all goodness; and bring us to everlasting life; through Jesus Christ our Lord. **Amen.**

Then shall the minister say:

Hear what the Scripture saith to those of a humble and contrite heart:

If any man sin, we have an advocate with the Father, Jesus Christ the righteous: and he is the propitiation for our sins: and not for ours only, but also for the sins of the whole world.

This is a faithful saying, and worthy of all acceptation, that Christ Jesus came into the world to save sinners.

God so loved the world, that he gave his only-begotten Son, that whosoever believeth in him should not perish, but have everlasting life.

Come unto me, all ye that labor and are heavy laden, and I will give you rest.

After which the minister and people may say:

Lift up your hearts.

We lift them up unto the Lord.

Let us give thanks unto the Lord.

It is meet and right so to do.

Then the minister, still kneeling and facing the Lord's Table, shall say:

It is very meet, right, and our bounden duty that we should at all times and in all places give thanks unto thee, O Lord, holy Father, almighty, everlasting God.

Then shall be said or sung:

Therefore with angels and archangels, and with all the company of heaven, we laud and magnify thy glorious name, evermore praising thee, and saying: Holy, holy,

holy, Lord God of hosts, heaven and earth are full of thy glory. Glory be to thee, O Lord most high! Amen.

Then shall the minister offer the prayer of consecration:

Almighty God, our heavenly Father, who of thy tender mercy didst give thine only Son Jesus Christ to suffer death upon the cross for our redemption; who made there, by the one offering of himself, a full, perfect, and sufficient sacrifice for the sins of the whole world; and did institute, and in his holy gospel command us to continue, this memorial of his precious death: hear us, O merciful Father, we most humbly beseech thee, and grant that we, receiving this bread and wine, according to thy Son our Saviour Jesus Christ's holy institution, in remembrance of his death and passion, may also be partakers of the divine nature through him, who in the same night that he was betrayed took bread;[1] and when he had given thanks, he brake it, and gave it to his disciples, saying, Take, eat; this is my body, which is given for you; do this in remembrance of me. Likewise after supper he took the cup;[2] and when he had given thanks, he gave it to them, saying, Drink ye all of this; for this is my blood of the new covenant which is shed for you, and for many, for the remission of sins; do this, as oft as ye shall drink it, in remembrance of me. **Amen.**

Then shall the minister, kneeling before the Lord's Table, unite with the people in this prayer:

We do not presume to come to this thy table, O merciful Lord, trusting in our own righteousness, but in thy manifold and great mercies. We are not worthy so much as to gather up the crumbs under thy table. But thou art the same Lord, whose mercy is unfailing. Grant us therefore, gracious Lord, so to partake of these memorials of thy Son Jesus Christ, that we may be filled with the

---

[1] Here may the minister take the plate in his hands.
[2] Here may the minister take the cup in his hands.

fullness of his life, may grow into his likeness, and may evermore dwell in him, and he in us. Amen.

Then shall the minister first receive the Holy Communion in both kinds himself, after which he shall proceed to deliver the same to other ministers in like manner, if any be present. After this, the minister shall administer the Holy Communion to the people, while they are devoutly kneeling.

Before giving the bread, the minister shall say:

Jesus said, "This is my body, which is given for you." Take and eat this in remembrance that Christ died for you, and feed on him in your heart by faith, with thanksgiving.

Likewise before giving the cup he shall say:

Jesus said, "This cup is the new covenant in my blood, which is shed for you." Drink this in remembrance that Christ died for you, and be thankful.

When all have communed, the minister shall place upon the Lord's Table what remains of the consecrated elements, covering the same with the linen cloth.

Then shall the minister and people say:

O Lord, our heavenly Father, we, thy humble servants, desire thy fatherly goodness mercifully to accept this our sacrifice of praise and thanksgiving; most humbly beseeching thee to grant that, by the merits and death of thy Son Jesus Christ, and through faith in his blood, we and thy whole Church may obtain forgiveness of our sins, and all other benefits of his passion. And here we offer and present unto thee, O Lord, ourselves, our souls and bodies, to be a reasonable, holy, and living sacrifice unto thee; humbly beseeching thee that all we who are partakers of this Holy Communion may be filled with thy grace and heavenly benediction. And although we be unworthy, through our manifold sins, to offer unto thee any sacrifice, yet we beseech thee to accept this our bounden duty and service; not weighing our merits, but pardoning our offenses; through Jesus Christ our Lord; by whom, and with whom, in the unity of the Holy Spirit, all honor and glory be unto thee, O Father Almighty, world without end. Amen.

Then shall be said or sung the Gloria in Excelsis, *the people standing:*

Glory be to God on high, and on earth peace, good will toward men. We praise thee, we bless thee, we worship thee, we glorify thee, we give thanks to thee for thy great glory, O Lord God, heavenly King, God the Father Almighty!

O Lord, the only-begotten Son Jesus Christ; O Lord God, Lamb of God, Son of the Father, that takest away the sins of the world, have mercy upon us. Thou that takest away the sins of the world, have mercy upon us. Thou that takest away the sins of the world, receive our prayer. Thou that sittest at the right hand of God the Father, have mercy upon us. For thou only art holy; thou only are the Lord; thou only, O Christ, with the Holy Ghost, art most high in the glory of God the Father. Amen.

Then shall the minister let the people depart with this blessing:

The peace of God, which passeth all understanding, keep your hearts and minds in the knowledge and love of God, and of his Son Jesus Christ our Lord; and the blessing of God Almighty, the Father, the Son, and the Holy Spirit, be among you, and remain with you always. **Amen.**

An Order for the Administration of the Sacrament of the Lord's Supper or Holy Communion II

The Lord's Table should have upon it a fair linen cloth.

Let the pure, unfermented juice of the grape be used.

It is our custom to receive the Sacrament of the Lord's Supper kneeling, but if persons so desire, they may receive the elements while seated or standing.

Upon entering the church let the communicants bow in prayer and in the spirit of prayer and meditation approach the blessed Sacrament.

The minister shall read one or more of these sentences, during the reading of which the stewards shall take up the offering for the needy.

Let your light so shine before men, that they may see your good works, and glorify your Father which is in heaven.

Lay not up for yourselves treasures upon earth, where moth and rust doth corrupt, and where thieves break through and steal: but lay up for yourselves treasures in heaven, where neither moth nor rust doth corrupt, and where thieves do not break through nor steal.

Whatsoever ye would that men should do to you, do ye even so to them: for this is the law and the prophets.

Not everyone that saith unto me, Lord, Lord, shall enter into the kingdom of heaven; but he that doeth the will of my Father which is in heaven.

Zacchaeus stood, and said unto the Lord; Behold, Lord, the half of my goods I give to the poor; and if I have taken anything from any man by false accusation, I restore him fourfold.

He which soweth sparingly shall reap also sparingly; and he which soweth bountifully shall reap also bountifully. Every man according as he purposeth in his heart, so let him give; not grudgingly, or of necessity: for God loveth a cheerful giver.

As we have therefore opportunity, let us do good unto all men, especially unto them who are of the household of faith.

Godliness with contentment is great gain. For we brought nothing into this world, and it is certain we can carry nothing out.

Charge them that are rich in this world, that they be ready to distribute, willing to communicate; laying up in store for themselves a good foundation against the time to come, that they may lay hold on eternal life.

God is not unrighteous to forget your work and labor of love, which ye have showed toward his name, in that ye have ministered to the saints, and do minister.

To do good and to communicate forget not: for with such sacrifices God is well pleased.

Whoso hath this world's good, and seeth his brother have need, and shutteth up his bowels of compassion from him, how dwelleth the love of God in him?

He that hath pity upon the poor lendeth unto the LORD; and that which he hath given will he pay him again.

Blessed is he that considereth the poor: the LORD will deliver him in time of trouble.

Then shall the minister read this invitation:

Ye that do truly and earnestly repent of your sins, and are in love and charity with your neighbors, and intend to lead a new life, following the commandments of God, and walking from henceforth in his holy ways; draw near with faith, and take this holy Sacrament to your comfort; and make your humble confession to Almighty God, meekly kneeling upon your knees.

Then shall this general confession be made by the minister and all those who are minded to receive the Holy Communion, both he and they humbly kneeling, and saying:

Almighty God, Father of our Lord Jesus Christ, Maker of all things, Judge of all men; we acknowledge and bewail our manifold sins and wickedness, which we from time to time most grievously have committed, by thought, word, and deed, against thy divine majesty, provoking

most justly thy wrath and indignation against us. We do earnestly repent, and are heartily sorry for these our misdoings; the remembrance of them is grievous unto us. Have mercy upon us, have mercy upon us, most merciful Father; for thy Son our Lord Jesus Christ's sake, forgive us all that is past; and grant that we may ever hereafter serve and please thee in newness of life, to the honor and glory of thy name; through Jesus Christ our Lord. Amen.

Then shall the minister say:

O Almighty God, our heavenly Father, who of thy great mercy hast promised forgiveness of sins to all them that with hearty repentance and true faith turn to thee; have mercy upon us; pardon and deliver us from all our sins; confirm and strengthen us in all goodness; and bring us to everlasting life; through Jesus Christ our Lord. **Amen.**

The Collect

Almighty God, unto whom all hearts are open, all desires known, and from whom no secrets are hid; cleanse the thoughts of our hearts by the inspiration of thy Holy Spirit, that we may perfectly love thee, and worthily magnify thy holy name; through Christ our Lord. Amen.

Then shall the minister say:

It is very meet, right, and our bounden duty, that we should at all times and in all places give thanks unto thee, O Lord, holy Father, almighty, everlasting God.

Therefore with angels and archangels, and with all the company of heaven, we laud and magnify thy glorious name, evermore praising thee, and saying: Holy, holy, holy, Lord God of hosts, heaven and earth are full of thy glory. Glory be to thee, O Lord most high! Amen.

Then shall the minister say:

We do not presume to come to this thy table, O merciful Lord, trusting in our own righteousness, but in thy manifold and great mercies. We are not worthy so much as to gather up the crumbs under thy table. But thou art the same Lord whose property is always to have mercy. Grant us therefore, gracious Lord, so to eat the flesh of thy Son Jesus Christ, and to drink his blood, that our sinful souls and bodies may be made clean by his death, and washed through his most precious blood, and that we may evermore dwell in him, and he in us. Amen.

Then the minister shall say the prayer of consecration as followeth:

Almighty God, our heavenly Father, who of thy tender mercy didst give thine only Son Jesus Christ to suffer death upon the cross for our redemption; who made there (by his oblation of himself once offered), a full, perfect, and sufficient sacrifice, oblation, and satisfaction for the sins of the whole world; and did institute, and in his holy gospel command us to continue, a perpetual memory of his precious death until his coming again: hear us, O merciful Father, we most humbly beseech thee, and grant that we, receiving these thy creatures of bread and wine, according to thy Son our Saviour Jesus Christ's holy institution, in remembrance of his death and passion, may be partakers of his most blessed body and blood; who in the same night that he was betrayed took bread; and when he had given thanks, he brake it, and gave it to his disciples, saying, Take, eat; this is my body, which is given for you; do this in remembrance of me. Likewise after supper he took the cup; and when he had given thanks, he gave it to them, saying, Drink ye all of this; for this is my blood of the New Testament, which is shed for you, and for many, for the remission of sins; do this, as oft as ye shall drink it, in remembrance of me. **Amen.**

Then shall the minister first receive the Holy Communion in both kinds himself, and then proceed to deliver the same to the other ministers in like manner, if any be present.

Then shall he say the Lord's Prayer, the people still kneeling and repeating after him every petition:

Our Father who art in heaven, hallowed be thy name; thy kingdom come; thy will be done on earth as it is in

heaven. Give us this day our daily bread. And forgive us our trespasses, as we forgive those who trespass against us. And lead us not into temptation, but deliver us from evil. For thine is the kingdom, and the power, and the glory, forever. Amen.

Then a hymn may be sung, and the communicants shall be invited to the Lord's Table. The minister shall deliver both kinds to the people into their hands.

When he delivereth the bread, he shall say:

The body of our Lord Jesus Christ, which was given for *thee,* preserve *thy soul* and *body* unto everlasting life. Take and eat this in remembrance that Christ died for *thee,* and feed on him in *thy heart* by faith with thanksgiving.

And the minister that delivereth the cup shall say:

The blood of our Lord Jesus Christ, which was shed for *thee,* preserve *thy soul* and *body* unto everlasting life. Drink this in remembrance that Christ's blood was shed for *thee,* and be thankful.

When all have communed, the minister shall return to the Lord's Table, and place upon it what remaineth of the consecrated elements, covering the same with a fair linen cloth.

Then shall the minister and people say:

O Lord, our heavenly Father, we, thy humble servants, desire thy fatherly goodness mercifully to accept this our sacrifice of praise and thanksgiving; most humbly beseeching thee to grant that, by the merits and death of thy Son Jesus Christ, and through faith in his blood, we and thy whole Church may obtain remission of our sins, and all other benefits of his passion. And here we offer and present unto thee, O Lord, ourselves, our souls and bodies, to be a reasonable, holy, and lively sacrifice unto thee; humbly beseeching thee that all we who are partakers of this Holy Communion may be filled with thy grace and heavenly benediction. And although we be unworthy, through our manifold sins, to offer unto thee any sacrifice, yet we beseech thee to accept this our bounden duty and service; not weighing our merits, but pardoning our offenses; through Jesus Christ our Lord; by whom, and with whom, in the unity of the Holy Spirit, all honor and glory be unto thee, O Father Almighty, world without end. Amen.

Then may be said or sung:

Glory be to God on high, and on earth peace, good will toward men. We praise thee, we bless thee, we worship thee, we glorify thee, we give thanks to thee for thy great glory, O Lord God, heavenly King, God the Father Almighty!

O Lord, the only-begotten Son Jesus Christ; O Lord God, Lamb of God, Son of the Father, that takest away the sins of the world, have mercy upon us. Thou that takest away the sins of the world, have mercy upon us. Thou that takest away the sins of the world, receive our prayer. Thou that sittest at the right hand of God the Father, have mercy upon us. For thou only art holy; thou only art the Lord; thou only, O Christ, with the Holy Ghost, art most high in the glory of God the Father. Amen.

Then the minister, if he see it expedient, may offer an extempore prayer; and afterward shall let the people depart with this blessing:

The peace of God, which passeth all understanding, keep your hearts and minds in the knowledge and love of God, and of his Son Jesus Christ our Lord; and the blessing of God Almighty, the Father, the Son, and the Holy Spirit, be among you, and remain with you always. **Amen.**

PROPER PREFACES TO PRECEDE THE SANCTUS IN THE SERVICE OF HOLY COMMUNION

Christmas

Because thou didst give Jesus Christ thine only Son to be born as at this time for us, that by taking flesh of our humanity he might make us partakers of the divine glory. Therefore with angels, etc.

Epiphany

Through Jesus Christ our Lord; who, in substance of our mortal flesh, manifested forth his glory, that he might bring us out of darkness into his own glorious light. Therefore with angels, etc.

Easter Day

But chiefly are we bound to praise thee for the glorious resurrection of thy Son Jesus Christ our Lord, who by his death hath destroyed death, and by his rising to life again hath restored to us everlasting life. Therefore with angels, etc.

Whitsunday

Through Jesus Christ our Lord; according to whose most true promise, the Holy Spirit came down as at this time from heaven as a mighty rushing wind and in tongues of fire, whereby we have been brought out of darkness into the clear light and true knowledge of thee, and of thy Son Jesus Christ. Therefore with angels, etc.

A LECTIONARY OF SUGGESTED LESSONS FOR THE HOLY COMMUNION

First Sunday in Advent	Rom. 13:4-14	Mark 13:1-13
Second Sunday in Advent	Rom. 15:4-13	Matt. 25:1-13

Third Sunday in Advent	I Cor. 4:1-5	Matt. 11:2-15
Fourth Sunday in Advent	Phil. 4:4-7	Luke 3:2-18
Christmas	Heb. 1:1-12	John 1:1-14
	Titus 2:11-14	Luke 2:1-14
The New Year	Rev. 21:1-7	Luke 9:57-62
Epiphany	Eph. 3:1-12	Matt. 2:1-12;
	Acts 13:42-49	28:16-20
Ash Wednesday, or Day of Fasting and Prayer	I Cor. 9:24-27	Matt. 6:16-21
First Sunday in Lent	II Cor. 6:1-10	Matt. 4:1-11
Second Sunday in Lent	I John 2:7-17	Matt. 5:17-20
Third Sunday in Lent	Eph. 5:1-14	Matt. 5:13-16
Fourth Sunday in Lent	Heb. 12:22-29	John 3:16-21
Fifth Sunday in Lent, or Passion Sunday	Heb. 9:11-15	Mark 10:32-45
Sixth Sunday in Lent, or Palm Sunday	Phil. 2:5-11	Mark 11:1-11
Maundy Thursday	I Cor. 11:23-28	John 13:1-17
Good Friday	Heb. 10:1-25	John 19:1-37
Easter Day	Col. 3:1-4	John 20:1-18
	I Pet. 1:3-25	Matt. 28:1-10
Festival of the Christian Home	Eph. 6:1-4	Mark 10:2-16
Ascensiontide	Acts 1:1-11	Luke 24:44-53
	Rev. 5:1-14	
Whitsunday, or Pentecost	Acts 2:1-11	John 14:15-31
Trinity Sunday	Rev. 4	John 3:1-15
	Eph. 2:13-22	
All Saints Day	Rev. 7:9-17	Matt. 5:1-12
Thanksgiving Day	Gal. 6:6-10	Luke 12:13-34

The Order for the Baptism of Infants

Let the parents of every child to be baptized have the choice of sprinkling, pouring, or immersion.

It is proper and desirable that this Sacrament should not only be accompanied by prayer, admonition, and the reading of Scripture, as herein provided, but that it should be administered in the presence of the people, and most suitably in the house of God.

Dearly beloved, forasmuch as all men are heirs of life eternal and subjects of the saving grace of the Holy Spirit; and that our Saviour Christ saith, Suffer the little children to come unto me, and forbid them not, for of such is the kingdom of God; I beseech you to call upon God the Father, through our Lord Jesus Christ, that of his bounteous goodness he will grant unto *this child,* now to be baptized, the continual replenishing of his grace that *he* become a worthy *member* of Christ's holy Church.

Then shall the minister say:

Let us pray.

Almighty and everliving God, we beseech thee that of thine infinite goodness thou wilt look upon *this child* and grant that by the aid of thy Holy Spirit *he* may be steadfast in faith, joyful through hope, and rooted in love, and that *he* may so live the life which now is, that *he* may enter triumphantly the life which is to come; through Jesus Christ our Lord. **Amen.**

Then shall the minister address the parents or sponsors as follows:

Dearly beloved, forasmuch as *this child* is now presented by you for Christian Baptism, and *is* thus consecrated to God and to his Church, it is your part and duty to see that *he* be taught, as soon as *he* shall be able to learn, the meaning and purpose of this holy Sacrament; that *he* be instructed in the principles of our holy faith and the nature of the Christian life; that *he* shall be trained to give reverent and regular attendance upon the public and private worship of God and the teaching of the Holy Scripture; and that in every way, by precept and example, you shall seek to lead *him* into the love of God and the service of our Lord Jesus Christ.

Do you solemnly promise to fulfill these duties so far as in you lies, the Lord being your helper?

We do.

Then shall the people stand, and the minister shall say:

Hear the words of the Gospel written by St. Mark:

And they brought young children to him, that he should touch them: and his disciples rebuked those that brought them. But when Jesus saw it, he was much displeased, and said unto them, Let the little children come unto me, and forbid them not: for of such is the kingdom of God. Verily I say unto you, Whosoever shall not receive the kingdom of God as a little child, he shall not enter therein. And he took them up in his arms, put his hands upon them, and blessed them.

Then shall the minister, who may here take the child in his arms, say to the parents or sponsors:

What name shall be given to this child?

And then, repeating the name, he shall baptize the child, saying:

N., I baptize thee in the name of the Father, and of the Son, and of the Holy Spirit. **Amen.**

Then shall the minister say:

Let us pray.

O God, our heavenly Father, grant that *this child,* as *he grows* in years, may also grow in grace and in knowledge of the Lord Jesus Christ, and that by the restraining and renewing influence of thy Holy Spirit *he* may ever be *a true child* of God, serving thee faithfully all *his* days; through Jesus Christ our Lord. **Amen.**

Almighty God, fount of all love and wisdom, source of all power; so guide and uphold the parents [or sponsors] of *this child* that, by loving care, wise counsel, and holy example, they may lead *him* into that life of faith whose strength is righteousness and whose fruit is everlasting joy and peace; through Jesus Christ our Lord. **Amen.**

Or the minister may offer extempore prayer.

Then may the minister and the people say:

Our Father who art in heaven, hallowed be thy name; thy kingdom come; thy will be done on earth as it is in heaven. Give us this day our daily bread. And forgive us our trespasses, as we forgive those who trespass against us. And lead us not into temptation, but deliver us from evil. For thine is the kingdom, and the power, and the glory, forever. Amen.

Then may be sung a hymn, such as:
406—"Friend of the home: as when in Galilee."
407—"See Israel's gentle Shepherd stand."
440—"I think when I read."

Then may the minister say:

Now unto him that is able to keep you from falling, and to present you faultless before the presence of his glory with exceeding joy, to the only wise God our Saviour, be glory and majesty, dominion and power, both now and evermore. **Amen.**

The Order for the Baptism of Children and Youth

Let every person to be baptized have the choice of sprinkling, pouring, or immersion.

It is proper and desirable that this Sacrament should not only be accompanied by prayer, admonition, and the reading of Scripture, as herein provided, but that it should be administered in the presence of the people, and most suitably in the house of God.

The minister, coming to the font, shall say:

Hear the words of the Gospel written by St. Matthew, in the twenty-eighth chapter, beginning at the sixteenth verse.

Then the eleven disciples went away into Galilee, into a mountain where Jesus had appointed them. And when they saw him, they worshiped him; but some doubted. And Jesus came and spake unto them, saying, All power is given unto me in heaven and in earth. Go ye therefore, and make disciples of all nations, baptizing them in the name of the Father, and of the Son, and of the Holy Spirit: teaching them to observe all things whatsoever I have commanded you: and lo, I am with you alway, even unto the end of the world. **Amen.**

Then shall the minister say:

Let us pray.

Almighty and everliving God, whose most dearly beloved Son Jesus Christ gave himself for our salvation, and did command his disciples that they should go teach all nations, and baptize them in the name of the Father, and of the Son, and of the Holy Spirit; regard, we beseech thee, the supplications of thy congregation; and grant that *these persons* now to be baptized may so open *their hearts* to thee that *they* may receive the fullness of thy grace, and may ever remain in the number of thy faithful children; through Jesus Christ our Lord. **Amen.**

Then the minister shall say to the persons to be baptized:

Well beloved, who are come hither, desiring to receive holy Baptism, you have heard how the congregation hath prayed that God would assist you to open your *hearts* to his love and direction, that you may be faithful *disciples* of our Lord.

Wherefore, for your part, it is needful that in the presence of Almighty God, and the hearing of this congregation, you should now make known your purpose to accept the obligations of this holy Sacrament by answering the following questions:

Will you faithfully put away from you every known sin, of thought, word, or deed, and accept and confess Jesus Christ as your Saviour and Lord?

God helping me, I will.

Will you diligently study the Bible as God's Holy Word, and in all things strive to make it the rule of your life?

God helping me, I will.

Having been taught how the Spirit of our Lord separates right from wrong, will you faithfully endeavor to live so as to be pleasing unto him?

God helping me, I will.

Will you be baptized in this faith?

This is my desire.

Then shall the minister ask each person his name, and shall baptize him, saying:

N., I baptize thee in the name of the Father, and of the Son, and of the Holy Spirit. **Amen.**

Here the minister shall offer an extempore prayer

The Order for the Baptism of Adults

Let every person to be baptized have the choice of sprinkling, pouring, or immersion.

It is proper and desirable that this Sacrament should not only be accompanied by prayer, admonition, and the reading of Scripture, as herein provided, but that it should be administered in the presence of the people, and most suitably in the house of God.

The minister, addressing the people, shall say:

Dearly beloved, forasmuch as our Saviour Jesus Christ sent forth his disciples to teach all nations and baptize them in the name of the Father, and of the Son, and of the Holy Spirit, and wherefore *these persons* come now to be baptized, I beseech you to call upon God the Father that of his bounteous goodness he will grant unto *them* the renewing power of the Holy Spirit and enable *them* by divine grace to attain unto the fullness of salvation in Jesus Christ our Lord.

Let us pray.

Almighty and immortal God, the aid of all that need, the helper of all that flee to thee for succor, the life of them that believe, and the resurrection of the dead; we call upon thee for *these persons* now to be baptized. May *they* be filled with thy Holy Spirit and may *they* find in thee *their* refuge, *their* strength, *their* wisdom, and *their* joy. May *they* be faithful to thee all the days of *their* life and finally come to the eternal kingdom which thou hast promised; through Jesus Christ our Lord. **Amen.**

Then may the minister read one or more of the following lessons:

Peter said unto them, Repent, and be baptized every one of you in the name of Jesus Christ for the remission of sins, and ye shall receive the gift of the Holy Spirit. For the promise is unto you, and to your children, and to all that are afar off, even as many as the Lord our God shall call. And with many other words did he testify and exhort, saying, Save yourselves from this untoward generation. Then they that gladly received his word were baptized: and the same day there were added unto them about three thousand souls. And they continued stead-fastly in the apostles' doctrine and fellowship, and in breaking of bread, and in prayers.

And it came to pass, that, while Apollos was at Corinth, Paul having passed through the upper coasts came to Ephesus: and finding certain disciples, he said unto them, Have ye received the Holy Spirit since ye believed? And they said unto him, We have not so much as heard whether there be any Holy Spirit. And he said unto them, Unto what then were ye baptized? And they said, Unto John's baptism. Then said Paul, John verily baptized with the baptism of repentance, saying unto the people that they should believe on him which should come after him, that is, on Christ Jesus. When they heard this, they were bap-tized in the name of the Lord Jesus. And when Paul had laid his hands upon them, the Holy Spirit came on them.

There was a man of the Pharisees, named Nicodemus, a ruler of the Jews: the same came to Jesus by night, and said unto him, Rabbi, we know that thou art a teacher come from God: for no man can do these miracles that thou doest, except God be with him. Jesus answered and said unto him, Verily, verily, I say unto thee, Except a man be born again, he cannot see the kingdom of God. Nicodemus saith unto him, How can a man be born when he is old? can he enter the second time into his mother's womb, and be born? Jesus answered, Verily, verily, I say unto thee, Except a man be born of water and of the Spirit, he cannot enter into the kingdom of God. That which is born of the flesh is flesh; and that which is born of the Spirit is spirit. Marvel not that I said unto thee, Ye must be born again. The wind bloweth where it listeth, and thou hearest the sound thereof, but canst not tell whence it cometh, and whither it goeth: so is every one that is born of the Spirit.

For this cause I bow my knees unto the Father of our Lord Jesus Christ, of whom the whole family of heaven and earth is named, that he would grant you, according to the riches of his glory, to be strengthened with might by his Spirit in the inner man; that Christ may dwell in your hearts by faith; that ye, being rooted and grounded in love, may be able to comprehend with all saints what is the breadth, and length, and depth, and height; and to know the love of Christ, which passeth knowledge, that ye might be filled with all the fullness of God.

Then shall the minister say to the persons to be baptized:

Dearly beloved, who have come hither desiring to receive holy Baptism, the congregation gives thanks to God for your coming, and prays that the Holy Spirit may dwell within you, and that your faith may not fail. In the hearing of this congregation you should now make known your purpose to accept the obligations of this holy Sacrament.

Do you truly repent of your sins and accept and confess Jesus Christ as your Saviour and Lord?

I do.

Will you earnestly endeavor to keep God's holy will and commandments?

I will.

Do you desire to be baptized in this faith?

I do.

Here the persons shall kneel, and then the minister shall pray:

O merciful God, grant that all sinful affections may die in *these persons,* and that all things belonging to the Spirit may live and grow in *them.* **Amen.**

Almighty, ever-living God; regard, we beseech thee, our supplications and grant that *these persons* may receive the fullness of thy grace and ever remain in the number of thy faithful and beloved children; through Jesus Christ our Lord. **Amen.**

Then the minister, asking the name of each person, shall baptize him, repeating the name and saying:

N., I baptize thee in the name of the Father, and of the Son, and of the Holy Spirit. **Amen.**

Then may the minister offer extempore prayer. Then may the minister and the people say:

Our Father who art in heaven, hallowed be thy name; thy kingdom come; thy will be done on earth as it is in heaven. Give us this day our daily bread. And forgive us our trespasses, as we forgive those who trespass against us. And lead us not into temptation, but deliver us from evil. For thine is the kingdom, and the power, and the glory, forever. Amen.

Then may be sung one or more stanzas of a hymn, such as:

> 223—"Blessed Master, I have promised."
> 226—"O Jesus, I have promised."
> 257—"My gracious Lord, I own thy right."

Then shall the minister say:

Now unto him that is able to keep you from falling, and to present you faultless before the presence of his glory with exceeding joy, to the only wise God our Saviour, be glory and majesty, dominion and power, both now and evermore. **Amen.**

The Order for Receiving Persons as Preparatory Members

The use of this form is optional.

Those who are to be received as preparatory members shall be called forward by name, and the minister, addressing the people, shall say:

Dearly beloved, that none may be admitted hastily into the Church, we receive persons who seek fellowship with us into a preparatory membership, in which they may be properly instructed, and also give proof, both to themselves and to the Church, of the sincerity and depth of their convictions and of the strength of their purpose to lead a new life.

Then, addressing the persons seeking admission as preparatory members, the minister shall say:

Beloved in the Lord, you have by the grace of God made your decision to follow Christ and to serve him. Your confidence in so doing is not to be based on any notion of fitness or worthiness in *yourselves,* but on the gracious promise of God, through our Lord Jesus Christ, who loved us and gave himself for us.

That the Church may know your purpose, you will answer the following questions:

Have you an earnest desire to be saved from your sins?

I have.

Will you guard yourself against all things contrary to the teachings of God's Word, and endeavor to lead a holy life, following the commandments of God?

I will.

Will you give reverent attendance upon the private and public worship of God and the teaching of the Word?

I will.

Then shall the minister say:

On behalf of the Church, and in the hope that you will go forward to complete membership therein, I give you a cordial welcome.

Then may the minister offer extempore prayer.

The Order for Receiving Persons into the Church

On the day appointed, all that are to be received into the Church shall be called forward, and the minister, addressing the people, shall say:

Dearly beloved, the Church is of God, and will be preserved to the end of time, for the promotion of his worship and the due administration of his word and ordinances, the maintenance of Christian fellowship and discipline, the edification of believers, and the conversion of the world. All, of every age and station, stand in need of the means of grace which it alone supplies.

Into this holy fellowship the *persons* before you, who *have* received the Sacrament of Baptism, who *have* learned the nature of these privileges and these duties, and who *have* also been instructed in the teachings and the aims of The Methodist Church, *come* seeking admission. We now propose in the fear of God to question *them* as to *their* faith and purpose, that you may know that *they are* proper *persons* to be admitted into this church.

Then, addressing those seeking admission, the minister shall say:

Beloved in the Lord, you are come hither seeking union with the Church of God. We rejoice that you are minded to undertake the privileges and the duties of membership in the Church. Before you are fully admitted thereto, you should here publicly renew your vows, confess your faith, and declare your purpose, by answering the following questions:

Do you here in the presence of God and this congregation renew the solemn promise and vow that was made at your baptism?

I do.

Do you confess Jesus Christ as your Saviour and Lord and pledge your allegiance to his Kingdom?

I do.

Do you receive and profess the Christian faith as contained in the New Testament of our Lord Jesus Christ?

I do.

Will you be loyal to The Methodist Church, and uphold it by your attendance, your prayers, your gifts, and your service?

I will.

Then those to be received shall kneel, and the minister, who may lay his hand upon the head of every one severally, shall say:

N., the Lord defend thee with his heavenly grace and by his Spirit confirm thee in the faith and fellowship of all true disciples of Jesus Christ. **Amen.**

Here the following form may be used:

Those being received shall rise, and the minister, addressing the people, shall say:

Brethren, I commend to your love and care *these persons* whom we this day recognize as members of the Church of Christ. What is your mind to them?

Whereupon the people shall say:

We rejoice to recognize you as *members* of the Church of Christ, and bid you welcome to all its privileges. Your peace, joy, and welfare are now our own. With you we renew our pledge to God and this church. The LORD bless *you*, and keep *you*: the LORD make his face to shine upon *you*, and be gracious unto *you*: the LORD lift up his countenance upon *you*, and give *you* peace. Amen.

Or the following alternative form may be used:

The minister shall say to the candidates:

We rejoice to recognize you as *members* of the Church of Christ, and bid you welcome to all its privileges; and in token of our brotherly love we give you the right hand of fellowship, and pray that you may be numbered with his people here, and with his saints in glory everlasting.

And the minister shall say to the congregation:

Brethren, I commend to your love and care *these persons* whom we this day recognize as *members* of the Church of Christ. Do all in your power to increase *their* faith, confirm *their* hope, and perfect *them* in love.

Then may be sung one or more stanzas of a hymn, such as:
379—"I love thy kingdom, Lord."
380—"Jesus, with thy Church abide."
383—"How lovely is thy dwelling place."

Then may the minister say:

The blessing of God Almighty, the Father, the Son, and the Holy Spirit, be among you, and remain with you always. **Amen.**

The Order for Receiving Children and Youth into the Church

After the minister previously shall have formed the children into a class (baptizing any whose baptism may have been delayed or neglected), and shall have instructed them in the things necessary for them to know as to the doctrines and rules of the Church, he shall cause them to be conveniently placed before the congregation, and, after inviting their parents and teachers to stand with them on either hand, he shall say:

Brethren of the household of faith, let our hearts be lifted up in thanksgiving to Almighty God, who by the Holy Spirit hath inclined *these children*[1] to desire and ask for membership in the Church. As *they have* arrived at the years of discretion, and now of *their* own accord *appear* before this congregation to take upon *themselves* the vows and enter upon the privileges and duties of the Church, let us with one mind and heart most earnestly invoke in *their* behalf the blessings of Father, Son, and Holy Spirit.

Then shall the minister say:

Let us pray.

Almighty and everliving God, giver of every good and perfect gift; accept our hearty thanks for *these children* whom thou hast committed to our love and care. As thou didst bring *them* into the world, now renew in thy servants, *their* parents, pastors, and teachers, wisdom to train *them* in the way *they* should go. Grant unto *these* thy *children* that from this day forth *they* may grow in grace, and wisdom, and in favor with God and man; through Jesus Christ our Lord. **Amen.**

Then shall the minister address the parents or sponsors:

Dearly beloved, let this be to you a day of peculiar joy and

---

[1] The minister may use the words "youth" or "young people" at his discretion in place of the word "children" here and at other appropriate places in this order.

thanksgiving, in that *these* who *are* your own *have* also entered into a holier spiritual kinship with you in Jesus Christ. While the Church will continue to share with you the duty and privilege of bringing up *these children* in the nurture and admonition of the Lord, it renews its solemn injunction to you, by God's help, faithfully to continue both to teach and to train *them,* by example and precept, in the way of the Lord. Will you accept this duty, in the fear and favor of God, and here and now, in the presence of Almighty God and this congregation, renew the vows made by you in the baptism of *these children?*

With God's help, I will.

Then shall the minister address the children who are candidates and say:

Beloved *children,* our Lord Jesus, by his holy Word, hath expressly given to everyone who believes in him a place in his Kingdom and Church. Before you are admitted into the Church, it becomes my duty to inquire of you as to your purpose of mind and heart:

Do you, *each of you,* believe in God as your heavenly Father?

I do.

Do you accept Jesus Christ as your personal Saviour?

I do.

Do you believe in the Bible as God's holy Word?

I do.

Will you be loyal to The Methodist Church, and uphold it by your attendance, your prayers, your gifts, and your service?

I will.

Here the minister may offer an extempore prayer. Then those to be received shall kneel, and the minister, laying his hands upon every one of them severally, shall say:

I receive you into the Church of Christ and pray God to confirm you in the faith and fellowship of all true disciples of Jesus Christ. **Amen.**

Then shall the minister, the people, and the children say:

Our Father who art in heaven, hallowed be thy name; thy kingdom come; thy will be done on earth as it is in heaven. Give us this day our daily bread. And forgive us our trespasses, as we forgive those who trespass against us. And lead us not into temptation, but deliver us from evil. For thine is the kingdom, and the power, and the glory, forever. Amen.

The Order for Receiving Members by Transfer

or on

Reaffirmation of Faith

or in

Affiliate Membership

The minister shall say:

The following *persons present certificates* of transfer commending *them* to the fellowship of this church: [names].

The following *persons* who *have* been *members* of the Church *desire* to present *themselves* for reaffirmation of *their* faith and reception into the fellowship of this church: [names].

The following *persons,* while retaining *their* membership in *other churches, are* to be welcomed as *affiliate members* in the fellowship of this church: [names].

The *persons* named will now present *themselves* for public reception into the fellowship of this church.

When they have come forward, the minister shall say:

Dearly beloved, you have already confessed your faith in Christ and given *yourselves* to the service of God. As you come to join this church, will you renew your vows previously taken, and will you labor and pray for its upbuilding, and live with this people of God in Christian fellowship?

I will.

The members of this church bid you welcome, and on their behalf I give you the right hand of fellowship. We pray that, as all of us are united in faith and brotherhood, we may grow into the likeness of Christ, being fruitful in every good work and increasing in the knowledge of God; through Jesus Christ our Lord.

The LORD bless *you,* and keep *you:* the LORD make his face shine upon *you,* and be gracious unto *you:* the LORD lift up his countenance upon *you,* and give *you* peace. **Amen.**

The Order for the Solemnization of Matrimony

At the time appointed, the persons to be married—having been qualified according to the law of the state and the standards of the church—standing together facing the minister, the man at the minister's left hand and the woman at the right, the minister shall say:

Dearly beloved, we are gathered here in the sight of God, and in the presence of these witnesses, to join together this man and this woman in holy matrimony; which is an honorable estate, instituted of God, and signifying unto us the mystical union which exists between Christ and his Church; which holy estate Christ adorned and beautified with his presence in Cana of Galilee. It is therefore not to be entered into unadvisedly, but reverently, discreetly, and in the fear of God. Into this holy estate these two persons come now to be joined.

Speaking to the persons to be married, the minister shall say:

I require and charge you both, as you stand in the presence of God, to remember that love and loyalty alone will avail as the foundation of a happy and enduring home. No other human ties are more tender, no other vows more sacred than those you now assume. If these solemn vows be kept inviolate, and if steadfastly you endeavor to do the will of your heavenly Father, your life will be full of joy, and the home which you are establishing will abide in peace.

Then shall the minister say to the man, using his Christian name:

N., wilt thou have this woman to be thy wedded wife, to live together in the holy estate of matrimony? Wilt thou love her, comfort her, honor and keep her, in sickness and in health; and forsaking all other keep thee only unto her, so long as ye both shall live?

The man shall answer:

I will.

Then shall the minister say to the woman, using her Christian name:

N., wilt thou have this man to be thy wedded husband, to live together in the holy estate of matrimony? Wilt thou love him, comfort him, honor and keep him, in sickness and in health; and forsaking all other keep thee only unto him, so long as ye both shall live?

The woman shall answer:

I will.

Then may the minister say:

Who giveth this woman to be married to this man?

The father of the woman, or whoever giveth her in marriage, shall answer:

I do.

Then the minister (receiving the hand of the woman from her father or other sponsor) shall cause the man with his right hand to take the woman by her right hand, and say after him:

I, *N.,* take thee, *N.,* to be my wedded wife, to have and to hold, from this day forward, for better, for worse, for richer, for poorer, in sickness and in health, to love and to cherish, till death us do part, according to God's holy ordinance; and thereto I plight thee my troth.

Then shall they loose their hands; and the woman, with her right hand taking the man by his right hand, shall likewise say after the minister:

I, *N.,* take thee, *N.,* to be my wedded husband, to have and to hold, from this day forward, for better, for worse, for richer, for poorer, in sickness and in health, to love and to cherish, till death us do part, according to God's holy ordinance; and thereto I plight thee my troth.

Then shall they again loose their hands; and the man may give unto the woman a ring, on this wise: the minister, taking the ring, shall say:

This ring is an outward and visible sign of an inward and

spiritual grace, signifying unto all the uniting of this man and this woman in holy matrimony, through the Church of Jesus Christ our Lord.

Then the minister may say:

Let us pray.

Bless, O Lord, the giving of this ring, that he who gives it and she who wears it may abide forever in thy peace, and continue in thy favor; through Jesus Christ our Lord. **Amen.**

The minister shall then deliver the ring to the man to put upon the third finger of the woman's left hand. The man, holding the ring there, shall say after the minister:

In token and pledge of the vow between us made, with this ring I thee wed; in the name of the Father, and of the Son, and of the Holy Spirit. Amen.

In case of a double-ring ceremony, the minister shall deliver the other ring to the woman to put upon the third finger of the man's left hand; and the woman, holding the ring there, shall say after the minister:

In token and pledge of the vow between us made, with this ring I thee wed; in the name of the Father, and of the Son, and of the Holy Spirit. Amen.

Then shall the minister say:

Let us pray.

O eternal God, creator and preserver of all mankind, giver of all spiritual grace, the author of everlasting life; send thy blessing upon this man and this woman, whom we bless in thy name; that they may surely perform and keep the vow and covenant between them made, and may ever remain in perfect love and peace together, and live according to thy laws.

Look graciously upon them, that they may love, honor, and cherish each other, and so live together in faithfulness and patience, in wisdom and true godliness, that their home may be a haven of blessing and a place of peace; through Jesus Christ our Lord. **Amen.**

Then shall the minister join their right hands together and with his hand on their united hands shall say:

Forasmuch as *N.* and *N.* have consented together in holy wedlock, and have witnessed the same before God and this company, and thereto have pledged their troth each to the other, and have declared the same by joining hands (and by giving and receiving *a ring*); I pronounce that they are husband and wife together, in the name of the Father, and of the Son, and of the Holy Spirit. Those whom God hath joined together, let not man put asunder. **Amen.**

Then, the husband and wife kneeling, the minister shall say:

Let us pray.

Our Father who art in heaven, hallowed be thy name; thy kingdom come; thy will be done on earth as it is in heaven. Give us this day our daily bread. And forgive us our trespasses, as we forgive those who trespass against us. And lead us not into temptation, but deliver us from evil. For thine is the kingdom, and the power, and the glory, forever. Amen.

Then shall the minister add this blessing:

God the Father, the Son, and the Holy Spirit, bless, preserve, and keep you; the Lord graciously with his favor look upon you, and so fill you with all spiritual benediction and love that you may so live together in this life that in the world to come you may have life everlasting. **Amen.**

The Order for the Burial of the Dead

The minister shall begin the service by reading one or more of the following sentences:

Jesus said, I am the resurrection, and the life: he that believeth in me, though he were dead, yet shall he live: and whosoever liveth and believeth in me shall never die.

The eternal God is thy refuge, and underneath are the everlasting arms.

The LORD is my light and my salvation; whom shall I fear? the LORD is the strength of my life; of whom shall I be afraid?

The righteous live forever, and the care of them is with the most High: with his right hand he shall cover them, and with his arm shall he shield them.

For we know that if our earthly house of this tabernacle were dissolved, we have a building of God, an house not made with hands, eternal in the heavens.

Then shall the minister say:

Let us pray.

Here may the minister offer one or both of the following prayers, ending with the Lord's Prayer.

Almighty God, fount of all life; thou art our refuge and strength; thou art our help in trouble. Enable us, we pray thee, to put our trust in thee, that we may obtain comfort, and find grace to help in this and every time of need; through Jesus Christ our Lord. **Amen.**

Almighty God, our Father, from whom we come, and unto whom our spirits return; thou hast been our dwelling place in all generations. Thou art our refuge and strength, a very present help in trouble. Grant us thy blessing in this hour, and enable us so to put our trust in thee that our spirits may grow calm and our hearts be comforted. Lift our eyes beyond the shadows of earth, and help us to see the light of eternity. So

413

may we find grace and strength for this and every time of need; through Jesus Christ our Lord. **Amen.**

Our Father who art in heaven, hallowed be thy name; thy kingdom come; thy will be done on earth as it is in heaven. Give us this day our daily bread. And forgive us our trespasses, as we forgive those who trespass against us. And lead us not into temptation, but deliver us from evil. For thine is the kingdom, and the power, and the glory, forever. Amen.

Here may be read one or more of these lessons from the Old Testament:

The LORD is my shepherd; I shall not want.

He maketh me to lie down in green pastures: he leadeth me beside the still waters.

He restoreth my soul: he leadeth me in the paths of righteousness for his name's sake.

Yea, though I walk through the valley of the shadow of death, I will fear no evil: for thou art with me; thy rod and thy staff they comfort me.

Thou preparest a table before me in the presence of mine enemies: thou anointest my head with oil; my cup runneth over.

Surely goodness and mercy shall follow me all the days of my life: and I will dwell in the house of the LORD forever.

LORD, thou hast been our dwelling place in all generations.

Before the mountains were brought forth, or ever thou hadst formed the earth and the world, even from everlasting to everlasting, thou art God.

For a thousand years in thy sight are but as yesterday when it is past, and as a watch in the night.

Thou carriest them away as with a flood; they are as a sleep: in the morning they are like grass which groweth up.

In the morning it flourisheth, and groweth up; in the evening it is cut down, and withereth.

So teach us to number our days, that we may apply our hearts unto wisdom.

Let thy work appear unto thy servants, and thy glory unto their children.

And let the beauty of the LORD our God be upon us: and establish thou the work of our hands upon us; yea, the work of our hands establish thou it.

I will lift up mine eyes unto the hills, from whence cometh my help.

My help cometh from the LORD, who made heaven and earth.

He will not suffer thy foot to be moved: he that keepeth thee will not slumber.

Behold, he that keepeth Israel will neither slumber nor sleep.

The LORD is thy keeper: the LORD is thy shade upon thy right hand.

The LORD shall preserve thy going out and thy coming in from this time forth, and even for evermore.

The LORD is my light and my salvation; whom shall I fear? The LORD is the strength of my life; of whom shall I be afraid?

Though an host should encamp against me, my heart shall not fear; though war should rise against me, in this will I be confident.

For in the time of trouble he shall hide me in his pavilion: in the secret of his tabernacle shall he hide me; he shall set me up upon a rock.

Teach me thy way, O LORD, and lead me in a plain path.

I had fainted, unless I had believed to see the goodness of the LORD in the land of the living.

Wait on the LORD: be of good courage, and he shall strengthen thine heart: wait, I say, on the LORD.

Here may be said or sung the Gloria Patri:

Glory be to the Father, and to the Son, and to the Holy Ghost; as it was in the beginning, is now, and ever shall be, world without end. Amen.

Here shall be read one or more of these lessons from the New Testament:

Let not your heart be troubled: ye believe in God, believe also in me. In my Father's house are many mansions: if it were not so, I would have told you. I go to prepare a place for you. And if I go and prepare a place for you, I will come again, and receive you unto myself; that where I am, there ye may be also. I am the way, the truth, and the life. If ye love me, keep my commandments. And I will pray the Father, and he shall give you another Comforter, that he may abide with you forever; even the Spirit of truth; whom the world cannot receive, because it seeth him not, neither knoweth him; but ye know him; for he dwelleth with you, and shall be in you. I will not leave you comfortless: I will come to you. Because I live, ye shall live also.

Peace I leave with you, my peace I give unto you: not as the world giveth, give I unto you. Let not your heart be troubled, neither let it be afraid.

As many as are led by the Spirit of God, they are the sons of God. For ye have not received the spirit of bondage again to fear; but ye have received the Spirit of adoption, whereby we cry, Abba, Father. The Spirit itself beareth witness with our spirit, that we are the children of God: and if children, then heirs; heirs of God, and joint heirs with Christ; if so be that we suffer with him, that we may be also glorified together.

For I reckon that the sufferings of this present time are not worthy to be compared with the glory which shall be revealed in us.

And we know that all things work together for good to them that love God.

What shall we then say to these things? If God be for us, who can be against us? Who shall separate us from the love of Christ? shall tribulation, or distress, or persecution, or famine, or nakedness, or peril, or sword? Nay, in all these things we are more than conquerors through him that loved us. For I am persuaded, that neither death, nor life, nor angels, nor principalities, nor powers, nor things present, nor things to come, nor height, nor depth, nor any other creature, shall be able to separate us from the love of God, which is in Christ Jesus our Lord.

Now is Christ risen from the dead, and become the firstfruits of them that slept.

But some man will say, How are the dead raised up? and with what body do they come? Thou fool, that which thou sowest is not quickened, except it die: but God giveth it a body as it hath pleased him.

So also is the resurrection of the dead. It is sown in corruption; it is raised in incorruption:

It is sown in dishonor; it is raised in glory: it is sown in weakness; it is raised in power:

It is sown a natural body; it is raised a spiritual body. There is a natural body, and there is a spiritual body.

And as we have borne the image of the earthy, we shall also bear the image of the heavenly.

For this corruptible must put on incorruption, and this mortal must put on immortality. So when this corruptible shall have put on incorruption, and this mortal shall have put on immortality, then shall be brought to pass the saying that is written, Death is swallowed up in victory. O death, where is thy sting? O grave, where is thy victory? The sting of death is sin; and the strength of sin is the law. But thanks be to God, who giveth us the victory, through our Lord Jesus Christ. Therefore, my beloved brethren, be ye steadfast, unmovable, always abounding in the work of the Lord, forasmuch as ye know that your labor is not in vain in the Lord.

And I John saw the holy city, new Jerusalem, coming down from God out of heaven, prepared as a bride adorned for her husband. And I heard a great voice out of heaven saying, Behold, the tabernacle of God is with men, and he will dwell with them, and they shall be his people, and God himself shall be with them, and be their God. And God shall wipe away all tears from their eyes; and there shall be no more death, neither sorrow, nor crying, neither shall there be any more pain: for the former things are passed away.

And he showed me a pure river of water of life, clear as crystal, proceeding out of the throne of God and of the Lamb. In the midst of the street of it, and on either side of the river, was there the tree of life, which bare twelve manners of fruits, and yielded her fruit every month: and the leaves of the tree were for the healing of the nations. And there shall be no more curse: but the throne of God and of the Lamb shall be in it; and his servants shall serve him: and they shall see his face; and his name shall be in their foreheads. And there shall be no night there; and they need no candle, neither light of the sun; for the Lord God giveth them light: and they shall reign for ever and ever.

For this cause I bow my knees unto the Father of our Lord Jesus Christ, of whom the whole family in heaven and earth is named, that he would grant you, according to the riches of his glory, to be strengthened with might by his Spirit in the inner man; that Christ may dwell in your hearts by faith; that ye, being rooted and grounded in love, may be able to comprehend with all saints what is the breadth, and length, and depth, and height; and to know the love of Christ, which passeth knowledge, that ye might be filled with all the fullness of God. Now unto him that is able to do exceeding abundantly above all that we ask or think, according to the power that worketh in us, unto him be glory in the church by Christ Jesus throughout all ages, world without end. **Amen.**

Here may follow music and an address, closing with extempore prayer, or one of the following prayers:

Eternal God, who committest to us the swift and solemn trust of life; since we know not what a day may bring forth, but only that the hour for serving thee is always present, may we wake to the instant claims of thy holy will, not waiting for tomorrow, but yielding today. Consecrate with thy presence the way our feet may go; and the humblest work will shine, and the roughest places be made plain. Lift us above unrighteous anger and mistrust into faith and hope and love by a simple and steadfast reliance on thy sure will. In all things draw us to the mind of Christ, that thy lost image may be traced again, and that thou mayest own us as at one with him and thee. **Amen.**

O God, who art the strength of thy saints, and who redeemest the souls of thy servants; we bless thy name for all those who have died in the Lord, and who now rest from their labors, having received the end of their faith, even the salvation of their souls. Especially we call to remembrance thy lovingkindness and thy tender mercies to this thy servant. For all thy goodness that withheld not *his* portion in the joys of this earthly life, and for thy guiding hand along the way of *his* pilgrimage, we give thee thanks and praise. Especially we bless thee for thy grace that kindled in *his* heart the love of thy dear name, that enabled *him* to fight the good fight, to endure unto the end, and to obtain the victory, yea, to become more than conqueror, through him that loveth us. We magnify thy holy name that, *his* trials and temptations being ended, sickness and death being passed, with all the dangers and difficulties of this mortal life, *his* spirit is at home in thy presence, with whom dwelleth eternal peace. And grant, O Lord, we beseech thee, that we who rejoice in the triumph of thy saints may profit by their example, that, becoming followers of their faith and patience, we also may enter with them into an inheritance incorruptible and undefiled, and that fadeth not away; through Jesus Christ our Lord. **Amen.**

O God, the Lord of life, the Conqueror of death, our help in every time of trouble, who dost not willingly grieve or afflict the children of men; comfort us who mourn, and give us grace, in the presence of death, to worship thee, that we may have sure hope of eternal life and be enabled to put our whole trust in thy goodness and mercy; through Jesus Christ our Lord. **Amen.**

Father of spirits, we have joy at this time in all who have faithfully lived, and in all who have peacefully died. We thank thee for all fair memories and all living hopes; for the sacred ties that bind us to the unseen world; for the dear and holy dead who compass us as a cloud of witnesses, and make the distant heaven a home to our hearts. May we be followers of those who now inherit the promises; through Jesus Christ our Lord. **Amen.**

O Lord and Master, who thyself didst weep beside the grave, and art touched with the feeling of our sorrows; fulfill now thy promise that thou wilt not leave thy people comfortless, but wilt come to them. Reveal thyself unto thy sorrowing servants, and cause them to hear thee say, I am the resurrection, and the life. Help them, O Lord, to turn to thee with true discernment, and to abide in thee through living faith, that, finding now the comfort of thy presence, they may have also a sure confidence in thee for all that is to come; until the day break, and the shadows flee away. Hear us for thy great mercy's sake, O Jesus Christ our Lord. **Amen.**

O Thou who hast ordered this wondrous world, and who knowest all things in earth and heaven; so fill our hearts with trust in thee that, by night and by day, at all times and in all seasons, we may without fear commit those who are dear to us to thy never-failing love for this life and the life to come. **Amen.**

O Lord, we pray thee, give us thy strength, that we may live more bravely and faithfully for the sake of those who are no longer with us here upon earth; and grant us so to serve thee day by day that we may find eternal fellowship with them; through him who died and rose again for us all, Jesus Christ our Lord. **Amen.**

Almighty God, who art leading us through the changes of time to the rest and blessedness of eternity; be thou near to comfort and uphold. Make us to know and feel that thy children are precious in thy sight, that they live evermore with thee, and that thy mercy endureth forever. Thankful for the life which thou hast given us for these seasons, we pray thy help now to resign it obediently unto thee. Assist us to return to the scenes of our daily life, to obey thy will with patience, and to bear our trials with fortitude and hope. And when the peace of death falls upon us, may we find our perfect rest in thee; through Jesus Christ our Lord. **Amen.**

Then may the minister say:

The LORD bless you, and keep you: the LORD make his face shine upon you, and be gracious unto you: the LORD lift up his countenance upon you, and give you peace. **Amen.**

At the grave, when the people are assembled, the minister shall say:

Our help is in the name of the LORD, who made heaven and earth.

Like as a father pitieth his children, so the LORD pitieth them that fear him.

Say to them that are of a fearful heart, Be strong, fear not: behold, your God will come and save you.

The mercy of the LORD is from everlasting to everlasting upon them that fear him, and his righteousness unto children's children.

Then the minister may say:

Forasmuch as the spirit of the departed has entered into the life immortal, we therefore commit *his* body to its resting place, but *his* spirit we commend to God, remembering how Jesus said upon the cross, "Father, into thy hands I commend my spirit."

Or the minister may say:

Forasmuch as Almighty God hath received unto himself the soul of our departed *brother,* we therefore tenderly commit *his* body to the ground, in the blessed hope that as *he* hath borne the image of the earthly so also *he* shall bear the image of the heavenly.

Or the minister may say:

Forasmuch as the spirit of the departed hath returned to God who gave it, we therefore commit *his* body to the ground, earth to earth, ashes to ashes, dust to dust; looking for the general resurrection in the last day, and the life of the world to come, through our Lord Jesus Christ; at whose coming in glorious majesty to judge the world, the earth and the sea shall give up their dead; and the corruptible bodies of those who sleep in him shall be changed and made like unto his own glorious body; according to the mighty working whereby he is able to subdue all things unto himself.

Then may be said:

I heard a voice from heaven, saying unto me:

Blessed are the dead who die in the Lord from henceforth: Yea, saith the Spirit, that they may rest from their labors; and their works do follow them.

Lord, have mercy upon us.

Christ, have mercy upon us.

Lord, have mercy upon us.

Here may the minister and people unite in the Lord's Prayer:

Our Father who art in heaven, hallowed be thy name; thy kingdom come; thy will be done on earth as it is in heaven. Give us this day our daily bread. And forgive us our trespasses, as we forgive those who trespass against us. And lead us not into temptation, but deliver us from evil. For thine is the kingdom, and the power, and the glory, forever. Amen.

Then the minister may say one or more of the following prayers:

Almighty God, with whom do live the spirits of those who depart hence in the Lord, and with whom the souls of the faithful after death are in strength and gladness; we give thee hearty thanks for the good examples of all those thy servants who, having finished their course in faith, do now rest from their labor. And we beseech thee that we, with all those who have finished their course in faith, may have our perfect consummation and bliss in thy eternal and everlasting glory; through Jesus Christ our Lord. **Amen.**

O merciful God, the Father of our Lord Jesus Christ, who is the resurrection and the life, in whom whosoever believeth shall live, though he die, and whosoever liveth and believeth in him shall not die eternally; we meekly beseech thee, O Father, to raise us from the death of sin unto the life of righteousness, that when we shall depart this life we may rest in him, and may receive that blessing which thy well-beloved Son shall pronounce to all that love and fear thee, saying, Come, ye blessed of my Father, receive the kingdom prepared for you from the foundation of the world. Grant this, we beseech thee, O merciful Father, through Jesus Christ our Mediator and Redeemer. **Amen.**

O God of infinite compassion, who art the comforter of thy children; look down in thy tender love and pity, we beseech thee, upon thy servants. In the stillness of our hearts we entreat for them thy sustaining grace. Be thou their stay, their strength, and their shield, that trusting in thee they may know thy presence near, and in the assurance of thy love be delivered out of their distresses; through Jesus Christ our Lord. **Amen.**

Then may the minister say:

The grace of the Lord Jesus Christ, and the love of God, and the communion of the Holy Spirit, be with you all. **Amen.**

The Order for the Burial of a Child

The minister shall begin the service by reading the following sentences:

Jesus said, I am the resurrection, and the life: he that believeth in me, though he were dead, yet shall he live: and whosoever liveth and believeth in me shall never die.

He shall feed his flock like a shepherd: he shall gather the lambs with his arm, and carry them in his bosom.

Blessed are the pure in heart: for they shall see God.

Then shall the minister say:

Let us pray.

Here may the minister offer one or both of the following prayers:

Our heavenly Father, look upon us in our sorrow, and abide with us in our loneliness. O thou who makest no life in vain, and who lovest all that thou hast made, lift upon us the light of thy countenance and give us peace; through Jesus Christ our Lord. **Amen.**

O God our Father, we pray that thou wilt keep in tender love the life which we shall hold in blessed memory. Help us who continue here to serve thee with constancy, trusting in thy promise of eternal life, that hereafter we may be united with thy blessed children in glory everlasting; through Jesus Christ our Lord. **Amen.**

Here may be read:

The Lord is my shepherd; I shall not want.

He maketh me to lie down in green pastures: he leadeth me beside the still waters.

He restoreth my soul: he leadeth me in the paths of righteousness for his name's sake.

Yea, though I walk through the valley of the shadow of death, I will fear no evil: for thou art with me; thy rod and thy staff, they comfort me.

Thou preparest a table before me in the presence of mine enemies: thou anointest my head with oil; my cup runneth over.

Surely goodness and mercy shall follow me all the days of my life: and I will dwell in the house of the LORD forever.

I will lift up mine eyes unto the hills; from whence cometh my help.

My help cometh from the LORD, who made heaven and earth.

He will not suffer thy foot to be moved: he that keepeth thee will not slumber.

Behold, he that keepeth Israel shall neither slumber nor sleep.

The LORD is thy keeper: the LORD is thy shade upon thy right hand.

The LORD shall preserve thy going out and thy coming in from this time forth, and even for evermore.

Here shall be read these lessons from the Gospel:

At the same time came the disciples unto Jesus, saying, Who is the greatest in the kingdom of heaven? And Jesus called a little child unto him, and set him in the midst of them, and said, Verily I say unto you, Except ye be converted, and become as little children, ye shall not enter into the kingdom of heaven. Whosoever therefore shall humble himself as this little child, the same is the greatest in the kingdom of heaven. And whoso shall receive one such little child in my name receiveth me.

Take heed that ye despise not one of these little ones; for I say unto you, That in heaven their angels do always behold the face of my Father which is in heaven.

Let not your heart be troubled: ye believe in God, believe also in me. In my Father's house are many mansions: if it were not so, I would have told you. I go to prepare a place for you. And if I go and prepare a place for you, I will come again, and receive you unto myself; that where I am, there ye may be also. I am the way, the truth, and the life. If ye love me, keep my commandments. And I will pray the Father, and he shall give you another Comforter, that he may abide with you forever;

even the Spirit of truth; whom the world cannot receive, because it seeth him not, neither knoweth him; but ye know him; for he dwelleth with you, and shall be in you. I will not leave you comfortless: I will come to you. Because I live, ye shall live also.

Peace I leave with you, my peace I give unto you: not as the world giveth, give I unto you. Let not your heart be troubled, neither let it be afraid.

Here may follow music and an address, after which the minister shall say:

Let us pray.

Here may the minister offer extempore prayer or one or more of the following prayers:

O God, who art the Father of the families of the earth; look with compassion upon this bereaved family, and pour thy heavenly comfort into their hearts. Help them by faith to see this child, over whom they grieve, safe in that home where sin and sorrow cannot enter. Enrich with thy presence those who mourn; abide in their home; lift up their hearts; bless them with thy favor, which is better than life; and so guide them through the trials and temptations of this world that their re-united family may know fullness of joy in thy presence for evermore. Grant this through him who loved little children and blessed them, even thy Son Jesus Christ our Lord. **Amen.**

O merciful Father, whose face the angels of thy little ones do always behold in heaven; grant us steadfastly to believe that this thy child hath been taken into the safe keeping of thine eternal love; through Jesus Christ our Lord. **Amen.**

O God, who healest the broken in heart, and bindest up their wounds; look down in tender pity and compassion upon thy servants whose joy has been turned into mourning. Leave them not comfortless, but grant that they may be drawn closer to one another by their common sorrow. As thou hast given them this new tie to bind them to the world unseen, so grant unto them that where their treasure is, there may their hearts be also.

Fill their souls with the light and comfort of thy presence. Grant unto them such a vision of that life wherein all mysteries shall be revealed, and all tears be wiped away, that they may be able to endure as seeing thee who art invisible. So dwell with them and be their God, until the day break and the shadows flee away; through Jesus Christ our Lord. **Amen.**

Then may the minister say:

The LORD bless you, and keep you: the LORD make his face shine upon you, and be gracious unto you: the LORD lift up his countenance upon you, and give you peace **Amen.**

At the grave, when the people are assembled, the minister shall say:

Jesus saith to his disciples, Ye now therefore have sorrow: but I will see you again, and your heart shall rejoice, and your joy no man taketh from you.

Forasmuch as the departed has entered into the life immortal, we therefore commit *his* body to its resting place, but *his* spirit we commend to God, remembering how Jesus said upon the cross, "Father, into thy hands I commend my spirit."

Then shall the minister say:

Almighty God, Father of our Lord Jesus Christ, who gave his life for our redemption, and who promised the Holy Spirit, the Comforter; strengthen, we beseech thee, the faith of these bereaved ones, that they may contemplate with peace the blessedness of that eternal home which thou hast prepared for all who love and serve thee. Grant that they, and all others whose joy is turned into mourning, cleaving more closely unto him who is the resurrection and the life, may be led by thy spirit through this uncertain life, till the day break and the shadows flee away. **Amen.**

O God, whose most dear Son did take little children into his arms and bless them; give us grace, we beseech thee, to entrust the soul of this child to thy never-failing care and love, and bring us all to thy heavenly kingdom; through the same thy Son, Jesus Christ our Lord. **Amen.**

Almighty God, Father of mercies and giver of all comfort; deal graciously, we pray thee, with all those who mourn, that, casting every care on thee, they may know the consolation of thy love; through Jesus Christ our Lord. **Amen.**

Here the minister and the people may unite in the Lord's Prayer:

Our Father who art in heaven, hallowed be thy name; thy kingdom come; thy will be done on earth as it is in heaven. Give us this day our daily bread. And forgive us our trespasses, as we forgive those who trespass against us. And lead us not into temptation, but deliver us from evil. For thine is the kingdom, and the power, and the glory, forever. Amen.

Then may the minister say:

The grace of the Lord Jesus Christ, and the love of God, and the communion of the Holy Spirit, be with you all. **Amen.**

The Order for the Ordination of Deacons

When the day appointed by the bishop is come, there shall be a sermon or exhortation declaring the duty and office of such as come to be admitted deacons, how necessary that order is in the Church of Christ, and also how the people ought to esteem them in their office; after which one of the elders shall present unto the bishop all who are to be ordained, and say:

I present unto you *these persons* present to be ordained *deacons:* [names].

Their names having been read aloud, the bishop shall say to the people:

Brethren, *these are they* whom we purpose, God willing, this day to ordain *deacons*. For, after due examination, we find that *they are* lawfully called to this office and ministry, and that *they are persons* meet for the same. But if there be any of you who knoweth any valid reason for which *any one of them* ought not to be received into this holy ministry, let him come forth in the name of God, and disclose what the impediment is.

If any impediment be alleged, the bishop shall desist from ordaining that person until he shall be found to be innocent.

Then shall be read the Collect:

Almighty God, who by thy divine providence hast appointed divers orders of ministers in thy Church, and didst inspire thine apostles to choose into the order of deacons thy first martyr, St. Stephen, with others; mercifully behold *these* thy *servants,* now called to the like office and administration; so replenish *them* with the truth of thy doctrine, and adorn *them* with innocency of life, that by both word and good example *they* may faithfully serve thee in this office, to the glory of thy name and the edification of thy Church; through the merits of our Saviour Jesus Christ, who liveth and reigneth with thee and the Holy Spirit, now and forever. **Amen.**

Then shall be read the Epistle:

Likewise must the deacons be grave, holding the mystery of the faith in a pure conscience. They that have used the office of a deacon well purchase to themselves a good degree, and great boldness in the faith which is in Christ Jesus.

See then that ye walk circumspectly, not as fools, but as wise. Wherefore be ye not unwise, but understanding what the will of the Lord is. Giving thanks always for all things unto God and the Father in the name of our Lord Jesus Christ; submitting yourselves one to another in the fear of God. Finally, my brethren, be strong in the Lord, and in the power of his might. Put on the whole armor of God, that ye may be able to stand against the wiles of the devil. For we wrestle not against flesh and blood, but against principalities, against powers, against the rulers of the darkness of this world, against spiritual wickedness in high places. Wherefore take unto you the whole armor of God, that ye may be able to withstand in the evil day, and having done all, to stand. Stand therefore, having your loins girt about with truth, and having on the breastplate of righteousness; and your feet shod with the preparation of the gospel of peace; above all, taking the shield of faith, wherewith ye shall be able to quench all the fiery darts of the wicked. And take the helmet of salvation, and the sword of the Spirit, which is the word of God; praying always with all prayer and supplication in the Spirit, and watching thereunto with all perseverance and supplication for all saints.

Then shall the bishop, in the presence of the people, examine every one of those to be ordained, after this manner:

Do you trust that you are inwardly moved by the Holy Spirit to take upon you the office of the ministry in the Church of Christ, to serve God for the promoting of his glory and the edifying of his people?

I trust so.

Do you unfeignedly believe the Scriptures of the Old and New Testaments?

I do believe them.

Will you diligently read and expound the same unto the people whom you shall be appointed to serve?

I will.

It appertaineth to the office of a deacon to conduct divine worship and to assist the elder when he ministereth the Holy Communion, to help him in the distribution thereof; to read and expound the Holy Scriptures; to instruct the youth; and to baptize. And, furthermore, it is his office to search for the needy, that they may be visited and relieved. Will you do this gladly and willingly?

I will so do, by the help of God.

Will you apply all your diligence to frame and fashion your own *lives* and the lives of your *families* according to the teachings of Christ?

I will, the Lord being my helper.

Will you reverently heed them to whom the charge over you is committed, following with a glad mind and will their godly admonitions?

I will so do.

Then those to be ordained shall kneel, and the bishop, laying his hands severally upon the head of every one of them, shall say:

Take thou authority to execute the office of a deacon in the Church of God; in the name of the Father, and of the Son, and of the Holy Spirit. **Amen.**

Then shall the bishop deliver to every one of them the Bible, saying:

Take thou authority to read the Holy Scriptures in the Church of God, and to preach the Word. **Amen.**

Then shall the bishop, or one appointed by him, read the Gospel:

Let your loins be girded about, and your lights burning; and ye yourselves like unto men that wait for their lord, when he will return from the wedding; that when he cometh and knocketh, they may open unto him immediately. Blessed are those servants, whom the lord when he cometh shall find watching: verily I say unto you, that he shall gird himself, and make them to sit down to meat, and will come forth and serve them. And if he shall come in the second watch, or come in the third watch, and find them so, blessed are those servants.

Then shall the bishop pray:

Almighty God, giver of all good things, who of thy great goodness hast vouchsafed to accept *these* thy *servants* into the office of deacon in thy Church; make *them,* we beseech thee, O Lord, to be modest, humble, and constant in *their* ministration, and to have a ready will to observe all spiritual discipline; that *they,* continuing ever stable and strong in thy Son Jesus Christ, may so well behave *themselves* in this office that *they* may be found worthy to be called into the higher ministry in thy Church; through thy Son our Saviour Jesus Christ, to whom be glory and honor, world without end. **Amen.**

Direct us, O Lord, in all our doings, with thy most gracious favor, and further us with thy continual help, that in all our works, begun, continued, and ended in thee, we may glorify thy holy name, and finally, by thy mercy, obtain everlasting life; through Jesus Christ our Lord. **Amen.**

Then may the bishop say:

The peace of God, which passeth all understanding, keep your hearts and minds in the knowledge and love of God, and of his Son Jesus Christ our Lord; and the blessing of God Almighty, the Father, the Son, and the Holy Spirit, be among you, and remain with you always. **Amen.**

The Order for the Ordination of Elders

When the day appointed by the bishop is come, there shall be a sermon or exhortation declaring the duty and office of such as come to be admitted elders, how necessary that order is in the Church of Christ, and also how the people ought to esteem them in their office; after which one of the elders shall present unto the bishop all who are to be ordained, and say:

I present unto you *these persons* present to be ordained *elders:* [names].

Their names having been read aloud, the bishop shall say to the people:

Brethren, *these are they* whom we purpose, God willing, this day to ordain *elders.* For, after due inquiry, we find that *they are* lawfully called to this office and ministry, and that *they are persons* meet for the same. But if there be any of you who knoweth any valid reason for which *any one of them* ought not to be received into this holy ministry, let him come forth in the name of God, and disclose what the impediment is.

If any impediment be alleged, the bishop shall desist from ordaining that person until he shall be found to be innocent.

Then shall be read the Collect:

Almighty God, giver of all good things, who by thy Holy Spirit hast appointed divers orders of ministers in thy Church; mercifully behold *these* thy *servants,* now called to the office of elder, and so replenish *them* with the truth of thy doctrine, and adorn *them* with innocency of life, that by both word and good example *they* may faithfully serve thee in this office, to the glory of thy name and the advancement of thy Church; through the merits of our Saviour Jesus Christ, who liveth and reigneth with thee and the Holy Spirit, world without end. **Amen.**

Then shall be read the Epistle and the Gospel:

I was made a minister, according to the gift of the grace of God given unto me by the effectual working of his power. Unto me, who am less than the least of all saints, is this grace given, that I should preach the unsearchable riches of Christ; and to make all men see what is the fellowship of the mystery, which from the beginning of the world hath been hid in God, who created all things by Jesus Christ. And he gave some, apostles; and some, prophets; and some, evangelists; and some, pastors and teachers; for the perfecting of the saints, for the work of the ministry, for the edifying of the body of Christ: till we all come in the unity of the faith, and of the knowledge of the Son of God, unto a perfect man, unto the measure of the stature of the fullness of Christ.

Jesus said, I am the door: by me if any man enter in, he shall be saved, and shall go in and out, and find pasture. The thief cometh not, but for to steal, and to kill, and to destroy: I am come that they might have life, and that they might have it more abundantly. I am the good shepherd: the good shepherd giveth his life for the sheep. But he that is an hireling, and not the shepherd, whose own the sheep are not, seeth the wolf coming, and leaveth the sheep, and fleeth; and the wolf catcheth them, and scattereth the sheep. The hireling fleeth, because he is an hireling, and careth not for the sheep. I am the good shepherd, and know my sheep, and am known of mine. As the Father knoweth me, even so know I the Father: and I lay down my life for the sheep. And other sheep I have, which are not of this fold: them also I must bring, and they shall hear my voice; and there shall be one fold, and one shepherd.

Then shall the bishop say unto the persons to be ordained elders:

Dearly beloved, you have heard of what dignity and of how great importance is this office whereunto you are called. And now again we exhort you, in the name of our Lord Jesus Christ, that you are to be *messengers, watchmen,* and *stewards* of the Lord; to teach and to admonish, to feed and to provide for the Lord's family; to seek for Christ's sheep that are dispersed abroad, and for his children who are in the midst of this evil world, that they may be saved through Christ forever.

Have always, therefore, in your remembrance how great a treasure is committed to your charge. For they unto whom you are to minister are the sheep of Christ, for whom he gave his life. The Church which you must serve is his Bride and his Body. And if it shall happen the Church, or any member thereof, do take any hurt or hindrance by reason of your negligence, you know the greatness of the fault. Wherefore see that you never cease your labor, your care, and your diligence until you have done all that lieth in you, according to your bounden duty, to bring all such as shall be committed to your charge unto perfectness in Christ,

Forasmuch, then, as your office is both of so great excellency and of so great difficulty, consider how you ought to forsake, as much as you can, all worldly cares, and be studious in learning the Scriptures, and in acquiring such knowledge and skill as may help you to declare the living Word of God.

We hope that you have weighed and pondered these things with *yourselves* long before this time, and that you have clearly determined, by God's grace, to give *yourselves* wholly to this work whereunto it has pleased God to call you. Also that you will continually pray that the Holy Spirit may assist you to order the lives of you and yours after the rule and doctrine of Christ, that you may grow riper and stronger in ministry and be godly and wholesome *examples* for the people to follow.

And now, that this congregation of Christ here assembled may also understand your purpose in these things, and that this your promise may the more move you to perform your duties, you shall answer plainly to these things which we, in the name of God and his Church, shall ask of you touching the same:

Do you believe in your heart that you are truly called, according to the will of our Lord Jesus Christ, to the ministry of elders?

I do so believe.

Are you persuaded that the Holy Scriptures contain all truth required for eternal salvation through faith in Jesus Christ? And are you determined out of the same Holy Scriptures so to instruct the people committed to your charge that they may enter into eternal life?

I am so persuaded and determined, by God's grace.

Will you give faithful diligence duly to minister the doctrine of Christ, the Sacraments, and the discipline of the Church, and in the spirit of Christ to defend the Church against all doctrine contrary to God's Word?

I will so do, by the help of the Lord.

Will you be diligent in prayer, in the reading of the Holy Scriptures, and in such studies as help to the knowledge of God and of his Kingdom?

I will, the Lord being my helper.

Will you apply all your diligence to frame and fashion your own *lives* and the lives of your *families* according to the teachings of Christ?

I will, the Lord being my helper.

Will you maintain and set forward, as much as lieth in you, quietness, peace, and love among all Christian people, and especially among them that shall be committed to your charge?

I will so do, the Lord being my helper.

Will you reverently heed them to whom the charge over you is committed, following with a glad mind and will their godly admonitions?

I will so do.

Then shall the bishop say:

Almighty God, who hath given you this will to do all these things, grant also unto you power to perform the same, that he may accomplish his work which he hath begun in you; through Jesus Christ our Lord. **Amen.**

Then the people shall be requested to make their earnest supplications in silent prayer to God for those who are to be ordained as elders, and silence shall be kept for a space; after which shall be said the Veni, Creator Spiritus, *the bishop beginning, and all others answering as followeth, both the bishop and the people uniting in the final couplet.*

Come, Holy Ghost, our souls inspire,
And lighten with celestial fire.
Thou the anointing Spirit art,
Who dost thy sevenfold gifts impart.
Thy blessed unction from above
Is comfort, life, and fire of love.
Enable with perpetual light
The dullness of our blinded sight.
Anoint and cheer our soilèd face
With the abundance of thy grace.
Keep far our foes; give peace at home;
Where thou art Guide, no ill can come.
Teach us to know the Father, Son,
And thee, of both, to be but One;
That through the ages all along
This may be our endless song:
Praise to thy eternal merit,
Father, Son, and Holy Spirit. Amen.

Then shall the bishop say:
Let us pray.

Almighty God, our heavenly Father, we bless and magnify thy holy name for the gift of thy most dearly beloved Son Jesus Christ our Redeemer, and for all his apostles, prophets, evangelists, teachers, and pastors, whom he hath sent abroad into the world. For these here present whom thou hast called to the same holy office and ministry, we render unto thee our most hearty thanks. And now, O Lord, we humbly beseech thee to grant that by *these* thy *ministers,* and by those over whom *they* shall be appointed, thy holy name may be forever glorified, and thy blessed Kingdom enlarged; through thy Son Jesus Christ our Lord, who liveth and reigneth with thee in the unity of the Holy Spirit, world without end. **Amen.**

Then shall the bishop and the elders present lay their hands severally upon the head of every one that receiveth the order of elder, the receivers kneeling, and the bishop saying:

The Lord pour upon thee the Holy Spirit for the office and work of an elder in the Church of God, now committed unto thee by the authority of the Church through the imposition of our hands. And be thou a faithful dispenser of the Word of God, and of his holy Sacraments; in the name of the Father, and of the Son, and of the Holy Spirit. **Amen.**

Then shall the bishop deliver to every one of them, kneeling, the Bible into his hands, saying:

Take thou authority as an elder in the Church to preach the Word of God, and to administer the holy Sacraments in the congregation. **Amen.**

Then shall the bishop pray:

Most merciful Father, we beseech thee to send upon *these* thy *servants* thy heavenly blessings, that *they* may be clothed with righteousness, and that thy Word spoken by *them* may never be spoken in vain. Grant also that we may have grace to receive what *they* shall deliver out of thy Word as the means of our salvation, and that in all our words and deeds we may seek thy glory, and the increase of thy Kingdom; through Jesus Christ our Lord. **Amen.**

Direct us, O Lord, in all our doings, with thy most gracious favor, and further us with thy continual help, that in all our works, begun, continued, and ended in thee, we may glorify thy holy name, and finally, by thy mercy, obtain everlasting life; through Jesus Christ our Lord. **Amen.**

Then may the bishop say:

The peace of God, which passeth all understanding, keep your hearts and minds in the knowledge and love of God, and of his Son Jesus Christ our Lord; and the blessing of God Almighty, the Father, the Son, and the Holy Spirit, be among you, and remain with you always. **Amen.**

If on the same day the order for deacon be given to some and that of elder to others, the deacons shall be first presented and then the elders. The Collect shall be said and the Epistle read, immediately after which they who are to be ordained deacons shall be examined and ordained as is above described. Then, the Gospel having been read, they who are to be ordained elders shall likewise be examined and ordained, as in this office before appointed.

The Order for the Consecration of Bishops

When the time appointed for the consecration of bishops is come, the service shall begin with a hymn, after which the Collect shall be read:

Almighty God, who by thy Son Jesus Christ didst give to thy holy apostles, elders, and evangelists many excellent gifts, and didst charge them to feed thy flock; give grace, we beseech thee, to all the ministers and pastors of thy Church, that they may diligently preach thy Word and duly administer the godly discipline thereof; and grant to the people that they may faithfully follow the same, that they may receive the crown of everlasting glory; through Jesus Christ our Lord. **Amen.**

Then shall one of the elders read the Epistle:

And from Miletus he sent to Ephesus, and called the elders of the church. And when they were come to him, he said unto them, Ye know, from the first day that I came into Asia, after what manner I have been with you at all seasons, serving the Lord with all humility of mind, and with many tears, and temptations, which befell me: how I kept back nothing that was profitable unto you, but have showed you, and have taught you publicly, and from house to house, testifying both to the Jews, and also to the Greeks, repentance toward God, and faith toward our Lord Jesus Christ. And now, behold, I go bound in the spirit unto Jerusalem, not knowing the things that shall befall me there: save that the Holy Spirit witnesseth in every city, saying that bonds and afflictions abide me. But none of these things move me, neither count I my life dear unto myself, so that I might finish my course with joy, and the ministry, which I have received of the Lord Jesus, to testify the gospel of the grace of God. Take heed therefore unto yourselves, and to all the flock, over which the Holy Spirit hath made you overseers, to feed the church of God, which he hath purchased with his own blood. For I know this, that after my departing shall grievous wolves enter in among you, not sparing the flock. Also of your own selves shall men arise, speaking perverse things, to draw away disciples after them. Therefore watch, and remember, that by the space of three years I ceased not to warn everyone night and day with tears. And now, brethren, I commend you to God, and to the word of his grace, which is able to build you up, and to give you an inheritance among all them which are sanctified.

Then shall another elder read the Gospel:

So when they had dined, Jesus saith to Simon Peter, Simon, son of Jonas, lovest thou me more than these? He saith unto him, Yea, Lord; thou knowest that I love thee. He saith unto him, Feed my lambs. He saith to him again the second time, Simon, son of Jonas, lovest thou me? He saith unto him, Yea, Lord; thou knowest that I love thee. He saith unto him, Feed my sheep. He saith unto him the third time, Simon, son of Jonas, lovest thou me? Peter was grieved because he said unto him the third time, Lovest thou me? And he said unto him, Lord, thou knowest all things; thou knowest that I love thee. Jesus said unto him, Feed my sheep.

And Jesus came and spake unto them, saying, All power is given unto me in heaven and in earth. Go ye therefore, and teach all nations, baptizing them in the name of the Father, and of the Son, and of the Holy Spirit: teaching them to observe all things whatsoever I have commanded you: and, lo, I am with you alway, even unto the end of the world. **Amen.**

Then shall the elected person be presented by two elders unto the bishop, the elders saying:

We present unto you this elder chosen to be consecrated a bishop.

Then shall the bishop call upon the people present to pray, saying:

Dearly beloved, it is written in the Gospel of St. Luke that our Saviour Christ continued the whole night in prayer before he chose and sent forth his twelve apostles. It is written also in the Acts of the Apostles that the disciples who were at Antioch did fast and pray before they laid hands on Paul and Barnabas and sent them forth on their first mission to the Gentiles. Let us therefore, following the example of our Saviour Christ and his apostles, give ourselves to prayer before we admit and send forth *this person* presented to us, to the work whereunto we trust the Holy Spirit hath called *him*.

Then shall the bishop pray:

Almighty God, giver of all good things, who by thy Holy Spirit hast appointed divers offices in thy Church; graciously behold *this* thy *servant* now called to the office and ministry of a bishop. So replenish *him* with the truth of thy doctrine, and so adorn *him* with innocency of life, that by both word and deed *he* may faithfully serve thee in this office, to the glory of thy name and the edifying and well governing of thy Church; through the merits of our Saviour Jesus Christ, who liveth and reigneth with thee and the Holy Spirit, world without end. **Amen.**

Then shall the bishop say to him that is to be consecrated:

Brother, forasmuch as the Holy Scriptures command that **we** should not be hasty in admitting any person to government in the Church of Christ, before you are admitted to this ministration, you will, in the fear of God, give answer to these questions:

Are you persuaded that you are truly called to this ministration, according to the will of our Lord Jesus Christ?

I am so persuaded.

Are you persuaded that the Holy Scriptures contain sufficiently all truth required for eternal salvation through faith in Jesus Christ? And are you determined out of the same **Holy Scriptures** so to instruct the people committed to your charge that they may enter into eternal life?

I am so persuaded and determined, by God's grace.

Will you then faithfully exercise *yourself* in the Holy Scriptures, and call upon God through study and prayer for the true understanding of the same?

I will so do, by the help of God.

Are you ready with all faithful diligence to seek and to promote the truth of Christ and to defend the Church against all doctrine contrary to God's Word?

I am ready, the Lord being my helper.

Will you live soberly, righteously, and devoutly in this present world, that you may show *yourself* in all things an example of good works unto others, to the honor and glory of God?

I will so do, the Lord being my helper.

Will you show *yourself* gentle, and be merciful for Christ's sake to poor and needy people, and to all strangers destitute of help?

I will, by the help of God.

Will you maintain and set forward, as much as lieth in you, quietness, love, and peace among all men; and faithfully exercise such discipline in the Church as shall be committed unto you?

I will so do, by the help of God.

Will you be faithful in ordaining and appointing others; and will you ever seek to deal justly and kindly with your brethren of the ministry over whom you are placed as chief pastor?

I will so do, by the help of God.

Then shall the bishop pray:

Almighty God, our heavenly Father, who hath given you a good will to do all these things, grant also unto you wisdom and power to perform the same, that he may accomplish in you the good work which he hath begun, that you may be found blameless; through Jesus Christ our Lord. **Amen.**

Then the people shall be requested to make their earnest supplications in silent prayer to God for those who are to be consecrated as bishops, and silence shall be kept for a space; after which shall be said the Veni, Creator Spiritus, *the bishop beginning, and all others answering as followeth, both the bishop and the people uniting in the final couplet.*

Come, Holy Ghost, our souls inspire,
And lighten with celestial fire.

**Thou the anointing Spirit art,
Who dost thy sevenfold gifts impart.**

Thy blessed unction from above
Is comfort, life, and fire of love.

**Enable with perpetual light
The dullness of our blinded sight.**

Anoint and cheer our soilèd face
With the abundance of thy grace.

**Keep far our foes; give peace at home;
Where thou art Guide, no ill can come.**

Teach us to know the Father, Son,
And thee, of both, to be but One;

**That through the ages all along
This may be our endless song:**

*Praise to thy eternal merit,
Father, Son, and Holy Spirit. Amen.*

Then shall the bishop say:

Let us pray.

Almighty and most merciful Father, who of thine infinite
goodness hast given thine only and dearly beloved Son Jesus
Christ to be our Redeemer, and hast made some apostles, some
prophets, some evangelists, some pastors and teachers, to the
edifying and making perfect of thy Church; grant, we beseech
thee, to *this* thy *servant* such grace that *he* may evermore be
ready to spread abroad thy gospel, the glad tidings of reconciliation with thee, and to use the authority given *him,* not to
destruction, but to salvation; not to hurt, but to help; so that as
a wise and faithful *servant,* giving to all their portion in due
season, *he* may at last be received into everlasting joy; through
Jesus Christ our Lord, who, with thee and the Holy Spirit,
liveth and reigneth, one God, world without end. **Amen.**

Then the bishops and elders present shall lay their hands upon the head of the elected person kneeling before them, the consecrating bishop saying:

The Lord pour upon thee the Holy Spirit for the office and work of a bishop in the Church of God, now committed unto thee by the authority of the Church through the imposition of our hands, in the name of the Father, and of the Son, and of the Holy Spirit. And remember that thou stir up the grace of God which is in thee; for God hath not given us the spirit of fear, but of power, and of love, and of a sound mind. **Amen.**

Then shall the bishop deliver to him the Bible, saying:

Give heed unto reading, exhortation, and teaching. Think upon the things contained in this Book. Be diligent in them, that the increase coming thereby may be manifest unto all men. Take heed unto thyself and to thy teaching; for by so doing thou shalt save both thyself and them that hear thee. Be to the flock of Christ a shepherd. Hold up the weak, heal the sick, bind up the broken, bring again the outcast, seek the lost; faithfully minister discipline, but forget not mercy; that the Kingdom of God may come upon the earth and, when the Chief Shepherd shall appear, that you may receive the never-fading crown of glory; through Jesus Christ our Lord. **Amen.**

Then shall the bishop pray:

Most merciful Father, we beseech thee to send down upon *this* thy *servant* thy heavenly blessing, and so endue *him* with thy Holy Spirit that *he,* preaching thy word, not only may be earnest to reprove, beseech, and rebuke with all patience and doctrine, but also may be to such as believe a wholesome example in word, in conversation, in love, in faith, in chastity, and in purity; that, faithfully fulfilling *his* course, at the latter day *he* may receive the crown of righteousness laid up by the Lord, the righteous judge, who liveth and reigneth, one God with the Father and the Holy Spirit, world without end. **Amen.**

Direct us, O Lord, in all our doings, with thy most gracious favor, and further us with thy continual help, that in all our works, begun, continued, and ended in thee, we may glorify thy holy name, and finally, by thy mercy, obtain everlasting life; through Jesus Christ our Lord. **Amen.**

Then may the bishop say:

The peace of God, which passeth all understanding, keep your hearts and minds in the knowledge and love of God, and of his Son Jesus Christ our Lord; and the blessing of God Almighty, the Father, the Son, and the Holy Spirit, be among you, and remain with you always. **Amen.**

An Order for the Admission of Candidates to Full Membership in an Annual Conference

HYMN *The people standing.*

CALL TO PRAYER

Bishop: The Lord is nigh unto all them that call upon him in truth.

People: Our help is in the name of the Lord, who made heaven and earth. Amen.

INVOCATION *The bishop.*

Let us pray.

Direct us, O Lord, in all our doings, with thy most gracious favor, and further us with thy continual help, that in all our works, begun, continued, and ended in thee, we may glorify thy holy name, and finally, by thy mercy, obtain everlasting life; through Jesus Christ our Lord. **Amen.**

PRAYER FOR UNITY IN FAITH *Here let the people unite with the bishop in prayer.*

O God, who hast joined together divers peoples in the confession of thy name; grant us both to will and to be able to do what thou commandest, that thy people, being called to an eternal inheritance, may hold the same faith in their hearts, and disclose the same godliness in their lives; through Jesus Christ our Lord. Amen.

WORDS OF ASSURANCE *The bishop.*

Who shall ascend into the hill of the LORD? or who shall stand in his holy place? He that hath clean hands, and a

447

pure heart; who hath not lifted up his soul unto vanity, nor sworn deceitfully. He shall receive the blessing from the LORD, and righteousness from the God of his salvation. **Amen.**

COLLECT *Here let all the people unite with the bishop in prayer.*

Almighty and everlasting God, from whom cometh every good and perfect gift; send down upon all ministers, and upon the people committed to their charge, the inspiration of thy Holy Spirit, that they may give themselves with all their powers unto thee, and so bring forward thy Kingdom of righteousness, peace, and good will; through Jesus Christ our Lord. Amen.

DOXOLOGY

THE LESSON FROM THE OLD TESTAMENT *Joshua 1:5-9.*

GLORIA PATRI *Here let all the people arise and sing.*

THE LESSON FROM THE NEW TESTAMENT *John 10:9-16.*

HYMN OF PRAISE *Which may be followed by an address or exhortation by the bishop.*

THE ACT OF DEDICATION *The bishop.*

According to the usage and Discipline of The Methodist Church, you have indicated that you are convinced that you should enter the ministry of Christ's holy Church. You have declared that you are willing to face any sacrifice that may be involved in the consecration of life. You have indicated that you are so situated in life that you can accept the obligations of the itinerant minister. You have affirmed that you will abstain from those acts which may injure your work and influence as a minister of Christ, and that you will keep before you as the one great objective of your life the advancement of the Kingdom of God. Give heed to the words of the gospel of Christ when he said: "If any man will come after me, let him deny himself, and take up his cross, and follow me."

In accordance with the Discipline of The Methodist Church and the historic usages of our communion, you will in the presence of this conference give answer to the following questions:

(1) Have you faith in Christ?

(2) Are you going on to perfection?

(3) Do you expect to be made perfect in love in this life?

(4) Are you earnestly striving after it?

(5) Are you resolved to devote yourself wholly to God and his work?

(6) Do you know the General Rules of our church?

(7) Will you keep them?

(8) Have you studied the doctrines of The Methodist Church?

(9) After full examination do you believe that our doctrines are in harmony with the Holy Scriptures?

(10) Will you preach and maintain them?

(11) Have you studied our form of church discipline and polity?

(12) Do you approve our church government and polity?

(13) Will you support and maintain them?

(14) Will you diligently instruct the children in every place?

(15) Will you visit from house to house?

(16) Will you recommend fasting or abstinence, by both precept and example?

(17) Are you determined to employ all your time in the work of God?

(18) Are you in debt so as to embarrass you in your work?

(19) Will you observe the following directions?

(*a*) Be diligent. Never be unemployed. Never be triflingly employed. Never trifle away time; neither spend any more time at any one place than is strictly necessary.

(*b*) Be punctual. Do everything exactly at the time. And do not mend our rules, but keep them; not for wrath, but for conscience' sake.

After this the formal vote of the conference on admitting the candidates to membership shall be taken. Then shall the bishop say the following, or some other prayer of consecration:

THE PRAYER OF CONSECRATION

O God, our heavenly Father, who didst manifest thy love in sending thine only-begotten Son into the world that all might have life through him; pour out thy Spirit upon thy Church, that it may fulfill thy command to preach the gospel to every creature. Send forth, we beseech thee, laborers into thy harvest; fill them with the Holy Spirit, and with faith; defend them in all dangers and temptations; and hasten the time when the fullness of the nations shall be gathered into thy Kingdom; through the grace of Jesus Christ our Lord. **Amen.**

BENEDICTION

The Order for the Consecration of Deaconesses

When the time appointed is come, a sermon or address may be given declaring what is the office and duty of a deaconess; after which one shall present those to be consecrated deaconesses, saying:

I present unto you *these persons* to be consecrated deaconesses.

Then shall the consecrator say to those present:

Dearly beloved, *these are they* whom we purpose this day to consecrate *deaconesses* in the Church of God. After inquiry and examination we discover that *they have* met the stated requirements of the Church, and believe *them* to be proper *persons* for this work and office.

Then shall the Scripture be read:

When the Son of man shall come in his glory, and all the holy angels with him, then shall he sit upon the throne of his glory: and before him shall be gathered all nations: and he shall separate them one from another, as a shepherd divideth his sheep from the goats; and he shall set the sheep on his right hand, but the goats on the left.

Then shall the King say unto them on his right hand, Come, ye blessed of my Father, inherit the kingdom prepared for you from the foundation of the world: for I was an hungred, and ye gave me meat: I was thirsty, and ye gave me drink: I was a stranger, and ye took me in: naked, and ye clothed me: I was sick, and ye visited me: I was in prison, and ye came unto me.

Then shall the righteous answer him, saying, Lord, when saw we thee an hungred, and fed thee? or thirsty, and gave thee drink? When saw we thee a stranger, and took thee in? or naked, and clothed thee? Or when saw we thee sick, or in prison, and came unto thee?

And the King shall answer and say unto them, Verily I say unto you, Inasmuch as ye have done it unto one of the least of these my brethren, ye have done it unto me.

Then shall the consecrator say to those to be deaconesses:

Dearly beloved, we rejoice that in the providence of God you have been led by the Holy Spirit to devote *yourselves* to Christ-like service under the direction of the Church of Christ. You are to give *yourselves* to the service of the Lord, going about doing good. You are come as your Master to lead the sick and sinning world to the Saviour. Such service lays upon you solemn responsibility.

Do you believe that you are led of God to engage in this work and to assume the duties of this office?

I do.

Do you in the presence of God and of this congregation promise faithfully to perform the duties of a deaconess in the Church of God?

I do.

Will you be diligent in prayer, in the study of the Holy Scriptures, and in such other devotions as will help you to grow in the knowledge and love of God?

I will.

Will you be guided by the will and direction of those whom the Church may place over you in the doing of your work?

I will.

Then shall those to be consecrated kneel for a brief season of silent prayer, after which shall be said:

O eternal God, the Father of our Lord Jesus Christ, who didst call Phoebe and Dorcas into the service of thy Church; look upon *these* thy *servants* who *are* now to be set apart to the office of deaconess. Give to *them,* we pray thee, such understanding of thy holy gospel, such firmness of Christian purpose, such diligence in service, and such beauty of life in Christ, that *they* may be to all whom *they teach* or *serve* a worthy revelation of the meaning and power of the Christian life. May *they* so order *their* time and nourish *their minds* and *hearts* that *they* may constantly grow in grace and in the knowledge of our Lord Jesus Christ, and may steadily increase in power to lead others unto him.

Grant that *they* may have strength of body, mind, and soul for the fulfillment of thy will in the holy task to which thou hast called *them;* and grant *them* thy Holy Spirit, that *they* may worthily discharge the work committed to *them,* to the blessing of mankind and to the praise of Christ our Saviour. **Amen.**

Then the consecrator, laying his hand upon the head of every one severally, shall say:

I admit thee to the office of deaconess in the Church of God, in the name of the Father, and of the Son, and of the Holy Spirit. **Amen.**

Then may a hymn be sung, the deaconesses and the people standing; after which the people shall be dismissed with this blessing:

May Christ dwell in your hearts by faith; that ye, being rooted and grounded in love, may be able to comprehend with all saints what is the breadth, and length, and depth, and height; and to know the love of Christ, which passeth knowledge, that ye might be filled with all the fullness of God. Now unto him that is able to do exceeding abundantly above all that we ask or think, according to the power that worketh in us, unto him be glory in the church by Christ Jesus throughout all ages, world without end. **Amen.**

An Order for the Commissioning of Missionaries and Deaconesses

PRELUDE *The people in devout meditation.*

PROCESSIONAL HYMN *The people standing. If there be no processional, let the first hymn follow the Call to Worship.*

CALL TO WORSHIP

Minister: O magnify the Lord with me, and let us exalt his name together.

People: **With him is the fountain of life: in his light shall we see light.**

Minister: Light is sown for the righteous, and gladness for the upright in heart.

People: **From the rising of the sun unto the going down of the same the Lord's name is to be praised. Amen.**

Here let the people be seated.

INVOCATION *The minister.*

Let us pray.

Everlasting Father, the radiance of faithful souls, who didst bring the nations to thy light and kings to the brightness of thy rising; fill, we beseech thee, the world with thy glory, and show thyself unto all the nations; through him who is the true light and the bright and morning star, Jesus Christ thy Son our Lord. **Amen.**

COLLECT *Here let the people unite with the minister in prayer.*

Almighty God, our heavenly Father, who through thy Son Jesus Christ hast given commandment unto thy people to go into all the world and preach the gospel to every creature; grant us a ready will to obey thy word; and as we have entered into the labors of other

454

men, help us to serve thee, that others may enter into our labors, and that we with them, and they with us, may attain unto everlasting life; through the same Jesus Christ thy Son our Lord. Amen.

Minister: O Lord, open thou our lips.

People: **And our mouth shall show forth thy praise.**

Minister: Praise ye the Lord.

People: **The Lord's name be praised.**

ANTHEM

RESPONSIVE READING *"The Christian Mission"; of which let the paragraphs be read in turn by the minister, those to be commissioned, and the people. Let all stand and remain standing for the Gloria Patri.*

Hear, all ye nations of the earth, the gospel of the unsearchable riches of Christ.

Jesus came, saying: The Spirit of the Lord is upon me, because he hath anointed me to preach the gospel to the poor; and recovering of sight to the blind, to set at liberty them that are bruised, to preach the acceptable year of the Lord.

He came forth and saw a great multitude, and he had compassion on them, for they were as sheep not having a shepherd; and he welcomed them and spoke to them of the kingdom of God, and them that had need of healing he cured.

God, who commanded the light to shine out of darkness, hath shined in our hearts, to give the light of the knowledge of the glory of God in the face of Jesus Christ.

God so loved the world, that he gave his only-begotten Son, that whosoever believeth in him should not perish, but have everlasting life.

For God sent not his Son into the world to condemn the world; but that the world through him might be saved.

Therefore if any man be in Christ, he is a new creature; old things are passed away; behold, all things are become new.

There is no difference between the Jew and the Greek: for the same Lord over all is rich unto all that call upon him.

For whosoever shall call upon the name of the Lord shall be saved.

How then shall they call on him in whom they have not believed? and how shall they believe in him of whom they have not heard? and how shall they hear without a preacher? and how shall they preach, except they be sent?

The gospel of the kingdom shall be preached in all the world, for a witness unto all nations.

The harvest truly is plenteous, but the laborers are few; pray ye therefore the Lord of the harvest, that he will send forth laborers into his harvest.

Also I heard the voice of the Lord, saying, Whom shall I send, and who will go for us?

Then said I, Here am I; send me.

And the King shall say, Inasmuch as ye have done it unto one of the least of these my brethren, ye have done it unto me.

He that hath my word, let him speak my word faithfully, saith the LORD.

Let thy mercy, O LORD, be upon us, according as we hope in thee.

For all things are yours; whether Paul, or Apollos, or Cephas, or the world, or life, or death, or things present, or things to come; all are yours; and ye are Christ's; and Christ is God's.

GLORIA PATRI

THE LESSON FROM THE NEW TESTAMENT *Mark 3:13-15; Matthew 10:38-42.*

SILENT MEDITATION

PRAYER

THE LORD'S PRAYER

OFFERTORY *The dedication of gifts and tithes. An offertory sentence may be said or sung.*

HYMN OF PREPARATION

With thee, our Master and our Lord,
    We greet this wondrous day;
The gates swing open at thy word,
    The paths stretch far away.
The way we take is known to thee,
    Thy footprints there we trace;
Oh, grant us now that we may see
    The radiance of thy face.

We little bring, our gift is small,
    Yet all we are is thine.
Ourselves we give, our life, our all;
    Thy life in ours enshrine.
Oh, lead us forth, with ardor bright
    Enkindled from above;
O Christ, reveal in heaven's own light
    The challenge of thy love.

O living Lord! with courage bless
    This loyal company,
They go to seek the comfortless,
    To find the lost for thee.
Within their hearts they bear thy word,
    They sing with joy thy praise,
Be ever near them, Jesus, Lord,
    Be with them all the days.

Together still! E'en though we part,
    Our life is one in prayer:
Our hearts are ever where thou art,
    And thou art everywhere.

> About the world thy servants stand;
> With them one song we sing,
> Thy conquering love in every land,
> Thy triumph, Christ, our King! Amen.

THE ADDRESS

THE PRESENTATION OF THE MISSIONARIES AND DEACONESSES TO BE COMMISSIONED

THE COMMISSIONING SERVICE

Those to be commissioned shall take their places at the chancel, facing the bishop, who shall say to them:

Hear the words of our Master:

As the Father hath loved me, so have I loved you.

Ye have not chosen me, but I have chosen you, and ordained you, that ye should go and bring forth fruit, and that your fruit should remain: that whatsoever ye shall ask of the Father in my name, he may give it you.

Go ye therefore, and teach all nations, baptizing them in the name of the Father, and of the Son, and of the Holy Spirit: and, lo, I am with you alway, even unto the end of the world.

Your church, in its endeavor to carry out this Great Commission, has declared, "The supreme aim of missions is to make the Lord Jesus Christ known to all people in all lands as their divine Saviour, to persuade them to become his disciples, and to gather these disciples into Christian churches; to enlist them in the building of the Kingdom of God; to co-operate with these churches; to promote world Christian fellowship; and to bring to bear on all human life the spirit and principles of Christ."

Dearly beloved, we rejoice that you have purposed in your *hearts* to devote your *lives* to this task. Your labors may take you to the mountains and the plains, to isolated villages and teeming cities of this country, and to lands across the sea. You are to be among men as *those* who *serve*—teaching, preaching, and healing, ever testifying within the varied activities of our common life to the infinite love of God, shed abroad in Christ Jesus. Such a vocation confers a great privilege; it also lays upon you a solemn responsibility. What you have done alone with God in consecrating your *lives* to this service, we now ask you to do formally and publicly in the presence of this congregation.

Do you believe in your heart that you have been led by the Spirit of God to engage in this work and to assume its responsibilies?

I do so believe.

Will you endeavor, as much as lieth in you, to perform faithfully the duties of *missionaries and deaconesses* in the Church of Christ?

I will endeavor so to do.

Will you be diligent in prayer, in the reading of the Holy Scriptures, and in such studies as help to the knowledge of God and his Kingdom?

I will, the Lord being my helper.

Will you strive so to live that the power of God may be manifest in your life, enabling you to convey the blessed sense of God's presence to those you would serve?

I will, by God's grace.

Will you be loyal to the Church, and accept the authority of those to whom the Church has committed the direction of your work?

I will, the Lord being my helper.

Then shall all bow for a brief period of silent prayer, after which the bishop shall pray:

Almighty God, Father of all mercies; graciously behold *these* thy *servants* now to be commissioned as *deaconesses and missionaries* of thy Church. Endue *them* with thy Holy Spirit; enrich *them* with thy heavenly grace; and strengthen *them* for the tasks which lie ahead, that in all *their* works, begun, continued, and ended in thee, *they* may glorify thy holy name, and advance thy blessed Kingdom; through Jesus Christ our Lord. **Amen.**

Then the bishop, taking the right hand of each one, and repeating the name, shall say:

N., I commission you to take the gospel of our Lord Jesus Christ into all the world, in the name of the Father, and of the Son, and of the Holy Spirit. **Amen.**

To each deaconess the bishop shall say:

N., I commission you a deaconess to take the gospel of our Lord Jesus Christ into all the world, in the name of the Father, and of the Son, and of the Holy Spirit. **Amen.**

When all have been commissioned, the bishop shall turn to the missionaries and deaconesses in the congregation. They shall rise and the bishop, addressing them, shall say:

Beloved in the Lord, once you stood where *these* now *stand,* answering the call of God in your hearts. Obedient to this divine imperative, you have labored at home and abroad, ministering to the needs of men and bringing to them words of life. We are justly proud of your work and are continually thankful for the fullness of your devotion.

These younger *workers* will look to you for help and guidance as *they go* forth to serve with you. I commend *them* to your love and care.

Those who have just been commissioned shall then turn to face these missionaries and deaconesses, who, addressing them, shall say:

We welcome you into our fellowship, and into the joyous service of Christ and his Kingdom. Your peace, joy, and welfare are now our own, and we pledge to you through the days ahead our unfailing support.

With you we renew our dedication to God and to the Church we delight to serve.

Now the God of peace make you perfect in every good work to do his will, working in you that which is well

pleasing in his sight, through Jesus Christ; to whom
be glory for ever and ever. Amen.

*Then shall all the people stand, and the bishop, addressing them, shall
say:*

Members of this congregation, I commend to you *these
men and women* whom we this day have commissioned to
carry into all the world the sacred and imperishable message
of eternal salvation.

In this holy moment we too are called to a renewed consecration of our lives to Christ and his Kingdom. As *these,*
our fellow *workers, go* forth upon *their* mission, let us assure
them that we are with *them* in spirit and are supporting *them*
by word and gift and deed.

*Then all the people, addressing those who have just been commissioned,
shall say:*

We rejoice to recognize you as *missionaries and deaconesses* of our church, and we thank God that you
have dedicated your *lives* to his service throughout all
the world.

We shall follow you with our prayers; we shall support your work with our gifts; and together we shall
strive to minister to the needs of our fellow men and to
bring to them the saving knowledge of our Lord Jesus
Christ.

*Then shall all the people and the newly commissioned missionaries and
deaconesses join in saying:*

We, being many, are one body in Christ, and every
one members one of another.

United we pray: Thy kingdom come; thy will be done
on earth as it is in heaven. And to this end we dedicate ourselves; in the name of the Father, and of the
Son, and of the Holy Spirit. Amen.

SILENT PRAYER *Here let the people be seated and with heads bowed
offer their personal intercessions for those who have just been commissioned and for the missionary enterprise.*

CLOSING PRAYER *The bishop.*

For this cause I bow my knees unto the Father, of whom the whole family in heaven and earth is named, that he would grant you, according to the riches of his glory, to be strengthened with might by his Spirit in the inner man; that Christ may dwell in your hearts by faith; that ye, being rooted and grounded in love, may be able to comprehend with all saints what is the breadth, and length, and depth, and height; and to know the love of Christ, which passeth knowledge, that ye might be filled with all the fullness of God. Now unto him that is able to do exceeding abundantly above all that we ask or think, according to the power that worketh in us, unto him be glory in the church by Christ Jesus throughout all ages, world without end. **Amen.**

RECESSIONAL HYMN

BENEDICTION

POSTLUDE

An Order for the Recognition of Officials in the Church

THIS order may be used as a part of an order of worship when it is desired to recognize those who have been designated by the congregation and the Quarterly Conference as office-bearers in the church. After the sermon the minister may call the trustees, stewards, leaders, and other office-bearers to stand before the chancel or altar.

The minister shall say:

Dearly beloved, we have here met in the presence of God that we may recognize his call, received and acknowledged by these of our fellowship, to the leadership of this church. These persons have been chosen and called to the responsibility of stewardship not merely to be servants of men but primarily to be servants of Christ. They have been duly nominated and elected to these places of responsibility, and now they stand ready to pledge their good will and earnest intent to the carrying out of the duties wherewith the church is now entrusting them. Let us in turn pledge them our support and earnestly pray God's blessing upon them.

Let us pray.

Almighty God, our heavenly Father, we thank thee that thou hast called us into thy Church and hast given us tasks to perform. Bring to us the awareness that thou hast entrusted us with the great plans and duties of thy Kingdom on earth. Send down thy Holy Spirit upon these thy servants whom we, in thy name, call to the work and leadership of this congregation. Endue them with heavenly wisdom, that in counsel they may deal wisely, as those who have the mind of Christ. Grant that these persons now entering upon their duties may obtain thy favor and be successful in the discharge of their responsibilities, that through their devotion and consecration thy Church may be increased and edified; through Jesus Christ our Lord. **Amen.**

Addressing those to be recognized or installed, the minister shall say:

It is the duty of one who has been chosen for a place of leadership in the church to learn to work together with his fellows as a wise counselor and faithful disciple. Though there may be diversity in counsel, there must never be differences in aim or purpose. It is your duty also to be ready to counsel with your minister in his sacred office and to carry a sense of responsibility for the spiritual life of this church. You will have likewise the practical duty of fostering the principle of stewardship and of securing and expending the offerings of the people as these are given to carry on the work of God. Above all, we ask you to be an example yourself, so far as this may prove possible, of one who is loyal and devoted in carrying out the work of the Church.

And now, dearly beloved, having well considered the nature and purpose of these sacred offices to which you have been called, do you accept this holy responsibility, and will you seek to accomplish the work and service it sets before you of our Lord Jesus Christ?

I do, the Lord being my helper.

Then the minister shall say:

May the Lord indeed help you to carry out this sacred trust which you undertake in his name, and grant you power and ability to lead well his people.

Then the minister, speaking to the people, shall say:

We rejoice to recognize these persons as *stewards, trustees, leaders, and office-bearers* of this church. Do all you can, dearly beloved, to assist them in these offices into which they now have been inducted, giving them at all times your co-operation, your counsel, and your prayers.

Then a suitable hymn may be sung, which may be followed by the benediction.

An Order for the Recognition of Church-School Officers and Teachers

THIS order may be used as a part of an order of worship when the work of Christian education is the theme of the day. After the sermon the minister may call the officers and teachers of the church school to stand before the chancel or altar.

The minister shall say:

Dearly beloved, we have here met in the presence of God that we may recognize his call, received and acknowledged by these of our fellowship, to the work of teaching and directing in our church school. As they come in a spirit of devotion to offer themselves to God for this service, it is our obligation to support them by our loyalty and prayers, seeking with them and for them the consecration which is from on high, that they may be enabled to discharge this responsible calling with reverence and faithfulness and to the glory of God.

Then the chairman of the Commission on Education or the minister may read the names of the officers and teachers of the church school. The officers and teachers shall then confess their faith in Christ, responding to the minister as follows:

There is one body, and one Spirit, even as ye are called in one hope of your calling; one Lord, one faith, one baptism, one God and Father of all, who is above all, and through all, and in all.

By grace are we saved through faith; and that not of ourselves: it is the gift of God.

There are diversities of gifts, but the same Spirit. And there are differences of administrations, but the same Lord.

One is our Master, even Christ.

Ye are laborers together with God: ye are God's husbandry, **ye are God's building.**

Other foundation can no man lay than that is laid, which is Jesus Christ.

I beseech you therefore, by the mercies of God, that ye present your bodies a living sacrifice, holy, acceptable unto God, which is your reasonable service.

The love of Christ constraineth us.

Study to show yourselves approved unto God, workmen that need not to be ashamed, rightly dividing the word of truth.

Who is sufficient for these things? Without him we can do nothing.

God is able to make all grace abound toward you; that ye may abound to every good work.

Faithful is he who calleth us, who also will do it.

Now unto him that is able to do exceeding abundantly above all that we ask or think, according to the power that worketh in us,

Unto him be glory in the church by Christ Jesus throughout all ages, world without end. Amen.

Romans 12:1-8 read responsively may be used alternatively.

Here let the people be seated and bow in prayer while the officers and teachers kneel at the altar. Then shall the minister say:

Ye are not your own; ye are bought with a price; therefore glorify God in your body, and in your spirit, which are God's.

Neglect not the gift that is in you. Give heed to reading, to exhortation, to teaching.

If any of you lack wisdom, let him ask of God, who giveth to all men liberally, and upbraideth not. But let him ask in faith, nothing wavering.

Then shall the minister and the officers and teachers unite in prayer.

Eternal and everliving Father, who dost call us to thy service, and dost promise grace and strength for the fulfilling of thy will; look with favor upon us, as we dedicate ourselves to the task of working in this school. Grant

that we may grow in the knowledge and love of thy word, that we may minister to the growing life of thy Church, and to the glory of thy holy name; through Jesus Christ our Lord. Amen.

Then may follow a short extempore prayer of dedication by the minister. Afterward a suitable hymn may be sung, which may be followed by the benediction.

An Order for the Recognition of Choristers

At an appointed time the choir director, with his choristers properly robed, shall stand before the minister, who shall say:

It is a good thing to give thanks unto the LORD, and to sing praises unto thy name, O most High:

To show forth thy lovingkindness in the morning, and thy faithfulness every night.

Then the choir director shall say:

I present these persons to be recognized as choristers in this church.

Then shall the minister say:

Are you convinced that these persons by their integrity of life, good behavior, and knowledge of music will exercise this office to the honor of God and the edifying of the Church?

Then shall the choir director say:

I have inquired of them and have also examined them and commend them for this service in the Church.

Then the minister, addressing the persons who are seeking admission as choristers, shall question them as follows:

Do you desire to become a member of this choir?

I do.

Do you promise obedience to its rules and officers?

I do.

Will you endeavor always to be reverent in the house of God?

I will, with the help of God.

Will you seek to hold your life to the high level that is in accordance with this high office?

468

I will, the Lord being my helper.

Then shall the choir director and candidates kneel, and the minister, calling each by name, shall say:

N., I admit thee into the choir of this church. What thou singest with thy mouth, believe in thy heart; what thou believest in thy heart, practice in thy life. And may our heavenly Father give thee grace to sing his praise and live to his glory both in this world and in the world to come; through Jesus Christ our Lord. **Amen.**

Here let all the people unite in prayer.

Almighty God, unto whom all hearts are open, all desires known, and from whom no secrets are hid; cleanse the thoughts of our hearts by the inspiration of thy Holy Spirit, that we may perfectly love thee, and worthily magnify thy holy name; through Christ our Lord. Amen.

Our Father who art in heaven, hallowed be thy name; thy kingdom come; thy will be done on earth as is it in heaven. Give us this day our daily bread. And forgive us our trespasses, as we forgive those who trespass against us. And lead us not into temptation, but deliver us from evil. For thine is the kingdom, and the power, and the glory, forever. Amen.

Then may the minister say:

The LORD bless you, and keep you: the LORD make his face shine upon you, and be gracious unto you: the LORD lift up his countenance upon you, and give you peace. **Amen.**

An Order for the Laying of the Cornerstone of a Church

At the time appointed the hymn "The Church's one foundation is Jesus Christ her Lord" may be sung, all the people standing, after which the minister shall say:

Our help is in the name of the LORD, who made heaven and earth.

Except the LORD build the house, they labor in vain that build it.

Dearly beloved, we are assembled to lay the cornerstone of a new house for the worship of the God of our fathers. Let us not doubt that he will favorably approve our godly purpose, and let us now devoutly invoke his blessing on this our undertaking.

> *Then shall the minister offer an extempore prayer.*

Then the following lesson from the Old Testament may be read responsively by the minister and the people, the people standing:

The earth is the LORD's, and the fullness thereof; the world, and they that dwell therein.

For he hath founded it upon the seas, and established it upon the floods.

Who shall ascend into the hill of the LORD? or who shall stand in his holy place?

He that hath clean hands, and a pure heart; who hath not lifted up his soul unto vanity, nor sworn deceitfully.

He shall receive the blessing from the LORD, and righteousness from the God of his salvation.

This is the generation of them that seek him, that seek thy face.

Lift up your heads, O ye gates; and be ye lift up, ye everlasting doors.

And the King of glory shall come in.

Who is this King of glory?

The LORD strong and mighty, the LORD mighty in battle.

Lift up your heads, O ye gates; even lift them up, ye everlasting doors.

And the King of glory shall come in.

Who is this King of glory?

The LORD of hosts, he is the King of glory.

Then may the Gloria Patri *be said or sung:*

Glory be to the Father, and to the Son, and to the Holy Ghost. As it was in the beginning, is now, and ever shall be, world without end. Amen.

Then shall be read the lesson from the New Testament, the people being seated:

For we are laborers together with God: ye are God's husbandry, ye are God's building. According to the grace of God which is given unto me, as a wise master builder, I have laid the foundation, and another buildeth thereon. But let every man take heed how he buildeth thereupon. For other foundation can no man lay than that is laid, which is Jesus Christ. Now if any man build upon this foundation gold, silver, precious stones, wood, hay, stubble; every man's work shall be made manifest: for the day shall declare it, because it shall be revealed by fire; and the fire shall try every man's work of what sort it is. If any man's work abide which he hath built thereupon, he shall receive a reward. If any man's work shall be burned, he shall suffer loss: but he himself shall be saved; yet so as by fire. Know ye not that ye are the temple of God, and that the Spirit of God dwelleth in you?

Here may follow a prayer, offering, anthem, address, and hymn.

Then, standing at the side of the cornerstone, the minister may read the following scripture sentences:

The LORD hath chosen thee to build a house for the sanctuary: be strong, and do it. Fear not, nor be dismayed: for the LORD God, even my God, will be with thee; he will not fail thee, nor forsake thee, until thou hast finished all the work for the service of the house of the LORD.

Therefore thus saith the Lord GOD, Behold, I lay in Zion for a foundation a stone, a tried stone, a precious cornerstone, a sure foundation.

According to the grace of God which is given unto me, as a wise master builder, I have laid the foundation.

Other foundation can no man lay than that is laid, which is Jesus Christ.

Then shall the minister offer the prayer of consecration:

Almighty God, the Rock of Ages; on thee we build all our hopes for this life and that which is to come. Other foundation we would not seek to lay than that is laid, which is Jesus Christ; and we are to build upon this cornerstone a holy temple to the living God. Accept the act by which we lay this cornerstone. Bless those whose offerings enable us to build this house of worship. Graciously guard and direct those who labor in erecting it, shielding them from accident and peril. May the walls of this building rise in security and in beauty; and may the hearts of these thy people be fitly joined together into a living temple, builded upon the foundation of the apostles and prophets, Jesus Christ being the chief cornerstone. **Amen.**

Then may the minister and the people recite the Litany for the Laying of a Cornerstone:

To the glory of God our Father, to the service of our dear Master and his Church, and to the abiding presence of the Holy Spirit,

We lay the cornerstone of this church.

For a building of which Jesus Christ is the chief cornerstone, the pillar and ground of the truth,

We lay this cornerstone.

For a building that shall stand as a symbol of the Church Universal, the cornerstone of which is truth, the creed of which is love, and its towers eternal hope,

We lay this cornerstone.

For a church that shall exalt not a religion of creed or of authority, but a religion of saving grace, of personal experience, and of spiritual power,

We lay this cornerstone.

For a church that shall exalt the ministry of the open Bible, with its faithful record of human life, its unfolding of the redeeming grace of God through Jesus Christ, its message of warning, inspiration, comfort, and hope,

We lay this cornerstone.

For a church that shall teach and incarnate the doctrine of the fatherhood of God and the brotherhood of man,

We lay this cornerstone.

For a church that shall fulfill a ministry of social service and be a blessing unto men,

We lay this cornerstone.

For a church that shall be a renewing and cleansing power in the community, and that loves every other communion that exalts Christ in the service of man,

We lay this cornerstone.

For a church with an open door for all people, rich or poor, homeless or desolate, who need the help of God through us,

We lay this cornerstone.

For a church that shall gather the children in its arms and hold them close to Christ, that they may grow up in the Church and never be lost from the fold,

We lay this cornerstone.

For a church which stands for the sacramental truth: "It is more blessed to give than to receive,"

We lay this cornerstone.

For a church which takes hold on two worlds, and stands for the unseen and eternal, and which offers to men the abundant life which now is and which is to come,

We lay this cornerstone in the name of Almighty God.

In loving memory of those who have gone from us, whose hearts and hands have served in this church; with gratitude for all whose faith and consecrated gifts make this house possible, for all who may share this spiritual adventure; and with hope for all who shall worship in this house in years to come,

We lay this cornerstone in the name of Almighty God, Father, Son, and Holy Spirit, unto the ages of ages, world without end. Amen.

Then shall the minister, standing by the stone, exhibit to the people a box to be placed in the stone. It may contain such articles as a Bible, The Methodist Hymnal, *the latest* Discipline, *church periodicals, names of the pastor, Official Board, the building committee of the church, with such other documents as may be desired. The minister may read the list of articles so deposited in the box. Then with the aid of the builder, the minister shall lay the stone in its place.*

Then shall the people sing the following hymn:

On this stone now laid with prayer
Let thy church rise, strong and fair;
Ever, Lord, thy name be known,
Where we lay this cornerstone.

May thy Spirit here give rest
To the heart by sin oppressed,
And the seeds of truth be sown,
Where we lay this cornerstone.

Open wide, O God, thy door
For the outcast and the poor;
May they know this house their own,
Where we lay this cornerstone.

By wise master builders squared,
Here be living stones prepared
For the temple near thy throne,
Jesus Christ its Cornerstone.

Then shall the minister say:

Now unto him that is able to keep you from falling, and to present you faultless before the presence of his glory with exceeding joy, to the only wise God our Saviour, be glory and majesty, dominion and power, both now and evermore. **Amen.**

This order may be abridged according to the needs of the occasion.

An Order for the Dedication of a Church

Let the service of worship begin at the time appointed. Let the people kneel or bow in silent prayer upon entering the sanctuary.

PRELUDE *The people in devout meditation.*

HYMN *The people standing.*

CALL TO WORSHIP

Minister: Serve the Lord with gladness.

People: **Enter into his gates with thanksgiving, and into his courts with praise.**

Minister: O come, let us worship and bow down: let us kneel before the Lord our maker.

People: **He is our God; and we are the people of his pasture, and the sheep of his hand. Amen.**

Here let the people be seated.

INVOCATION *The minister.*

Let us pray.

O God, eternal and ever blessed, who delightest in the assembling of thy people in the sanctuary; receive us graciously as we come into thy house, and grant, we entreat thee, that peace and prosperity may be found within its walls, that the glory of God may be the light thereof, and that we may be satisfied with the goodness of thy house; through Jesus Christ our Lord. **Amen.**

COLLECT FOR DEDICATION DAY *Here let the people unite with the minister in prayer.*

Direct us, O Lord, in all our doings, with thy most gracious favor, and further us with thy continual help, that in all our works, begun, continued, and ended in

thee, we may glorify thy holy name, and finally, by thy mercy, obtain everlasting life; through Jesus Christ our Lord. Amen.

ANTHEM

CANTICLE OF THE CHURCH *To be said responsively by the minister and the people. Here let the people stand and remain standing until after the Affirmation of Faith.*

Arise, shine; for thy light is come, and the glory of the LORD is risen upon thee.

For behold, darkness shall cover the earth, and gross darkness the people.

But the LORD shall rise upon thee, and his glory shall be seen upon thee.

And the nations shall come to thy light, and kings to the brightness of thy rising.

The abundance of the sea shall be turned unto thee; the wealth of the nations shall come unto thee.

Thy gates shall stand always open; they shall not be shut day nor night,

That men may bring unto thee the wealth of the nations, and their kings led with them.

For the nation and kingdom that will not serve thee shall perish; yea, it shall be utterly wasted.

Violence shall no more be heard in thy land, wasting nor destruction within thy borders.

But thou shalt call thy walls Salvation, and thy gates thou shalt call Praise.

The sun shall be no more thy light by day; neither for brightness shall the moon give light unto thee.

But the LORD shall be unto thee an everlasting light, and thy God thy glory.

Thy sun shall no more go down; neither shall thy moon withdraw itself.

For the LORD shall be thine everlasting light, and the days of thy mourning shall be ended.

GLORIA PATRI

AFFIRMATION OF FAITH *The minister and the people.*

I believe in God the Father Almighty, Maker of heaven and earth; and in Jesus Christ his only Son our Lord; who was conceived by the Holy Spirit, born of the Virgin Mary, suffered under Pontius Pilate, was crucified, dead, and buried; the third day he rose from the dead; he ascended into heaven, and sitteth at the right hand of God the Father Almighty; from thence he shall come to judge the quick and the dead. I believe in the Holy Spirit, the holy catholic Church, the communion of saints, the forgiveness of sins, the resurrection of the body, and the life everlasting. Amen.

THE SCRIPTURE LESSON

PRAYER

HYMN

THE SERMON *Which may be followed by prayer.*

THE DEDICATION OF GIFTS AND TITHES

OFFERTORY RESPONSE *The people standing.*

> Praise God, from whom all blessings flow;
> Praise him, all creatures here below;
> Praise him above, ye heavenly host:
> Praise Father, Son, and Holy Ghost. Amen.

Here let the people be seated.

THE ACT OF DEDICATION
Some person authorized shall say to the officiating minister:

We present this building to be dedicated to the glory of God and the service of men.

Then shall the minister say:

By what name shall this church henceforth be known?

To which shall be answered:

It shall be called the *N*. Methodist Church.

Then shall the minister say to all the people:

Beloved in the Lord, we rejoice that God put it into the hearts of his people to build this house to the glory of his name. I now accept this building to be known as *N*. Methodist Church, to dedicate it, and to set it apart for the worship of Almighty God and the service of all men. Let us therefore, as we are assembled, solemnly dedicate this place to its proper and sacred uses.

Then, all standing, the minister shall say, the people responding:

To the glory of God the Father, who has called us by his grace;

To the honor of his Son, who loved us and gave himself for us;

To the praise of the Holy Spirit, who illumines and sanctifies us;

We dedicate this house.

For the worship of God in prayer and praise;

For the preaching of the everlasting gospel;

For the celebration of the holy Sacraments;

We dedicate this house.

For the comfort of all who mourn;

For strength to those who are tempted;

For light to those who seek the way;

We dedicate this house.

For the hallowing of family life;

For teaching and guiding the young;

For the perfecting of the saints;

We dedicate this house.

For the conversion of sinners;
For the promotion of righteousness;
For the extension of the Kingdom of God;
We dedicate this house.

In the unity of the faith;
In the bond of Christian brotherhood;
In charity and good will to all;
We dedicate this house.

In gratitude for the labors of all who love and serve this
church;
In loving remembrance of those who have finished their
course;
In the hope of a blessed immortality through Jesus Christ
our Lord;
We dedicate this house.

Then shall the minister and people together say:

**We now, the people of this church and congregation,
compassed about with a great cloud of witnesses, grateful for our heritage, sensible of the sacrifice of our
fathers in the faith, confessing that apart from us their
work cannot be made perfect, do dedicate ourselves
anew to the worship and service of Almighty God;
through Jesus Christ our Lord. Amen.**

Then shall the minister say:

Accept, O God our Father, this service at our hands, and
bless it to the end that this congregation of faithful people
may make manifest the Church of the living God, the pillar
and ground of truth, and so may this house be the place
where thine honor dwelleth and the whole earth be filled
with thy glory; through Jesus Christ our Lord.

THE SANCTUS *To be sung or said responsively by the minister and
the people.*

Therefore with angels and archangels, and with all the

company of heaven, we laud and magnify thy glorious name, evermore praising thee, and saying:

Holy, holy, holy, Lord God of hosts, heaven and earth are full of thy glory. Glory be to thee, O Lord most high! Amen.

PRAYER *Here the minister may offer an extempore prayer or one or more of the following prayers:*

O eternal God, whom the heaven of heavens cannot contain, much less the walls of temples made with hands; graciously accept the dedication of this house to thy honor and glory. **Amen.**

Grant, O Lord, that all who here share in the Sacraments, the ministry of the Word, and the fellowship of praise and prayer may know that God is in this place, may hear thy voice within their hearts, and may go forth to extend to the uttermost bounds of life the Lord Christ's Kingdom. **Amen.**

Now therefore, O Lord, let thine eyes be open toward this house day and night; and let thine ears be ready toward the prayers of thy children, which they shall make unto thee in this place. And whensoever thy servants shall make to thee their petitions, do thou hear them, and when thou hearest, forgive. Grant, O Lord, we beseech thee, that here and elsewhere thy ministers may be clothed with righteousness, and thy saints rejoice in thy salvation. And may we all, with thy people everywhere, grow up into a holy temple in the Lord, and be at last received into the glorious temple above, the house not made with hands, eternal in the heavens. And to the Father, and the Son, and the Holy Spirit, be glory and praise, world without end. **Amen.**

HYMN

SILENT PRAYER

BENEDICTION

POSTLUDE

An Order for the Opening of a Church for Worship

ACCORDING to the Discipline of The Methodist Church a church cannot be dedicated until it is free of debt. This is not a service of dedication. It is an opening of a church for worship with the expectancy that the congregation of faithful people will make every sacrifice to remove all encumbrance from the House of God.

Let the service of worship begin at the time appointed. Let the people kneel or bow in silent prayer upon entering the sanctuary.

PRELUDE *The people in devout meditation.*

HYMN *The people standing.*

CALL TO WORSHIP

Minister: Our help is in the name of the Lord, who made heaven and earth.

People: **Except the Lord build the house, they labor in vain that build it.**

Minister: Give unto the Lord the glory due unto his name: bring an offering, and come into his courts.

People: **Praise waiteth for thee, O God, and unto thee shall the vow be performed. Amen.**

Here let the people be seated and bow in prayer.

INVOCATION *The minister.*

Let us pray.

O Lord God, almighty and most merciful, whom the heaven, even the heaven of heavens cannot contain, much less temples built with hands, but who also dwellest with men, and delightest thyself in the fellowship of thy people; cleanse our hearts, we beseech thee, from all evil thought and desire, and vouchsafe thy divine presence and blessing, both that those things may please thee which we do at this present, and also that we may at length obtain thy favor with life everlasting in thy heavenly kingdom; through Jesus Christ our Lord. **Amen.**

COLLECT *Here let the people unite with the minister in prayer.*

Direct us, O Lord, in all our doings with thy most gracious favor, and further us with thy continual help, that in all our works, begun, continued, and ended in thee, we may glorify thy holy name, and finally, by thy mercy, obtain everlasting life; through Jesus Christ our Lord. Amen.

THE LORD'S PRAYER

Our Father who art in heaven, hallowed be thy name; thy kingdom come; thy will be done on earth as it is in heaven. Give us this day our daily bread. And forgive us our trespasses, as we forgive those who trespass against us. And lead us not into temptation, but deliver us from evil. For thine is the kingdom, and the power, and the glory, forever. Amen.

ANTHEM

RESPONSIVE PSALM *Here let the people stand and remain standing until after the* Gloria Patri.

The earth is the LORD's, and the fullness thereof; the world, and they that dwell therein.

For he hath founded it upon the seas, and established it upon the floods.

Who shall ascend into the hill of the LORD? or who shall stand in his holy place?

He that hath clean hands, and a pure heart; who hath not lifted up his soul unto vanity, nor sworn deceitfully.

He shall receive the blessing from the LORD, and righteousness from the God of his salvation.

This is the generation of them that seek him, that seek thy face.

Lift up your heads, O ye gates; and be ye lift up, ye everlasting doors.

And the King of glory shall come in.

Who is this King of glory?

The Lord strong and mighty, the Lord mighty in battle.

Lift up your heads, O ye gates; even lift them up, ye everlasting doors.

And the King of glory shall come in.

Who is this King of glory?

The Lord of hosts, he is the King of glory.

GLORIA PATRI

THE SCRIPTURE LESSON

DECLARATION *The minister.*

In the name of God and in the presence of this congregation I now declare this church to be open for the worship of God and the service of men. May it be a house of prayer for all people. Upon you as a congregation there rests the solemn responsibility to see to it that all liability of a financial character resting upon this property be speedily lifted so that this church may be dedicated to God in the name of the Father, and the Son, and the Holy Spirit. Let us join in an act of consecration to God and his Church.

RESPONSIVE PRAYER *Here let the people bow.*

Almighty and everlasting God, in communion with the saints in all the ages, and remembering the heritage that has been given to us, we offer thee our praise and thanksgiving.

O Lord, hear our prayer.

Help us to accept the privilege and responsibility of this

thy fellowship of faith; here may we keep the unity of the spirit in the bond of peace.

So may we fulfill the law of love.

Enable us, by thy grace, to dedicate ourselves this day to the great task which thou dost lay upon our hearts and consciences.

In all that we do, be thou, O Lord, our strength and help.

Reveal to us the beauty of thy perfect law, the joy of our living Lord, so that with glad hearts we may move forward in paths of high devotion and great achievement.

Be thou, O Lord, our guide and help for evermore. Amen.

PRAYER OF THANKSGIVING *The minister.*

Most glorious God, accept through thy beloved Son our thanksgivings for thine unspeakable love and goodness. Thou art the Father of mercies, and God of all comfort, full of compassion, forgiving iniquity, transgression, and sin. We thank thee that thou hast founded thy Church upon the apostles and prophets, Jesus Christ himself being the chief cornerstone. We thank thee that thou hast committed to thy ministers the word of reconciliation. Continue thy loving-kindness unto us, that we may rejoice and be glad in thee all our days. Guide us by thy counsel, and afterward receive us to thy glory; where, with all the blessed host of heaven, we may behold, adore, and perfectly and joyfully praise thee, our most glorious creator, redeemer, and sanctifier, for ever and ever. **Amen.**

ANTHEM

OFFERTORY *The dedication of gifts and tithes. An offertory sentence may be said or sung.*

HYMN

THE SERMON *Which may be followed by prayer.*

AN INVITATION TO CHRISTIAN DISCIPLESHIP

HYMN or DOXOLOGY *The people standing.*

SILENT PRAYER

BENEDICTION

POSTLUDE

An Order for the Dedication of an Organ

DOXOLOGY *The people standing.*

CALL TO WORSHIP

Minister: Surely the Lord is in this place.

People: **This is none other but the house of God, and this is the gate of heaven.**

Minister: Enter into his gates with thanksgiving, and into his courts with praise.

People: **O magnify the Lord with me, and let us exalt his name together. Amen.**

Here let the people be seated.

INVOCATION *The minister.*

Let us pray.

Almighty God, who hast made the heart of man to respond to the touch of thy Spirit as a harp to the hand of a master; give to us the vision of thy glory as we worship thee. We laud thee, we bless thee, we give thanks unto thy great name, for thy lovingkindness and thy truth. Unto thee we bring the obedience of our thanksgiving and the praise of our devotion; through Jesus Christ our Lord. **Amen.**

COLLECT *Here let the people unite with the minister in prayer.*

Almighty God, unto whom all hearts are open, all desires known, and from whom no secrets are hid; cleanse the thoughts of our hearts by the inspiration of thy Holy Spirit, that we may perfectly love thee, and worthily magnify thy holy name; through Christ our Lord. Amen.

ACT OF PRESENTATION *The people standing. The organ may be presented for dedication by one of the trustees, or someone designated for that purpose, in some such words as:*

We present this organ for dedication, [the gift of *N*. for the glory of God, and in loving memory of *N*.]

ACT OF DEDICATION *To be said responsively by the minister and the people.*

In the name of the Father, and of the Son, and of the Holy Spirit, we dedicate this organ to the praise of Almighty God.

Praise God in his sanctuary: praise him in the firmament of his power. Praise him with the sound of the trumpet: praise him with psaltery and harp.

We dedicate this organ to the cultivation of a high art: to the interpretation of the message of the masters of music, to an appreciation of the great doxologies of the Church, and to the development of the language of praise which belongeth both to earth and to heaven.

Praise him with stringed instruments and organs. Let everything that hath breath praise the Lord. Praise ye the Lord.

We dedicate this organ to the wedding march, to thanksgiving on festal occasions, and to such inspiration in the service of song that all people may praise the Lord.

O sing unto the Lord a new song: sing unto the Lord, all the earth, in psalms and hymns and spiritual songs, singing and making melody in your heart to the Lord.

We dedicate this organ to the healing of life's discords, and the revealing of the hidden soul of harmony; to the lifting of the depressed and the comforting of the sorrowing; to the humbling of the heart before the eternal mysteries, and the lifting of the soul to abiding beauty and joy, by the gospel of infinite love and good will.

That at the name of Jesus every knee should bow, of things in heaven, and things in earth, and things under the earth; and that every tongue should confess that

Jesus Christ is Lord, to the glory of God the Father.

PRAYER OF DEDICATION *The minister.*

Let us pray.

Our God and Father, whom the generations have worshiped with concord of sweet sound; be pleased to accept this organ as a song of praise unto thee. **Amen.**

Grant that its music, with accompanying song, may come as a blessed benediction upon all who worship here. **Amen.**

May this organ become undying music in the world as its notes of cheer, comfort, communion, and courage are modulated into human lives for daily task and noble service. **Amen.**

To all organists who shall sound its notes, and to all worshipers who shall be lifted Godward by its voice, may there come at times the sweep of hallelujahs from the throne of the redeemed, until earth below shall be attuned to heaven above, singing hallelujah to him who reigneth, Lord of lords, the King of kings. Hallelujah! **Amen.**

Here may be sung a suitable hymn or anthem, after which may follow a recital or sermon. An offering may then be received, followed by the singing of a hymn.

BENEDICTION

POSTLUDE

An Order for the Dedication of a Church-School Building or Parish House

PRELUDE *The people in devout meditation.*

HYMN *The people standing.*

CALL TO WORSHIP

Minister: Our help is in the name of the Lord, who made heaven and earth.

People: **Except the Lord build the house, they labor in vain that build it.**

Minister: Establish thou the work of our hands upon us; yea, the work of our hands establish thou it.

People: **Blessed be the name of the Lord from this time forth, and for evermore. Amen.**

Here let the people be seated.

INVOCATION *The minister.*

Let us pray.

Almighty and eternal God, whose lovingkindness never faileth, who rulest both in heaven and in earth, keeping mercy for thy people who walk before the presence of thy glory; graciously vouchsafe thy presence as we dedicate this building to thy service; mercifully illumine and brighten it with thine own glory, and pour down thy blessing upon it; through Jesus Christ our Lord. **Amen.**

THE LORD'S PRAYER

Our Father who art in heaven, hallowed be thy name; thy kingdom come; thy will be done on earth as it is in heaven. Give us this day our daily bread. And forgive us our trespasses, as we forgive those who trespass against us. And lead us not into temptation, but deliver

us from evil. For thine is the kingdom, and the power, and the glory, forever. Amen.

HYMN

THE SCRIPTURE LESSON

Hear, O Israel: the LORD our God is one LORD: and thou shalt love the LORD thy God with all thy heart, and with all thy soul, and with all thy might. And these words, which I command thee this day, shall be in thine heart: and thou shalt teach them diligently unto thy children, and shalt talk of them when thou sittest in thine house, and when thou walkest by the way, and when thou liest down, and when thou risest up. And thou shalt bind them for a sign upon thine hand, and they shall be as frontlets between thine eyes. And thou shalt write them upon the posts of thy house, and on thy gates.

The heart of him that hath understanding seeketh knowledge.

In the morning sow thy seed, and in the evening withhold not thine hand.

It is written in the prophets, And they shall be all taught of God. Every man therefore that hath heard, and hath learned of the Father, cometh unto me.

Who hath known the mind of the Lord, that he may instruct him? But we have the mind of Christ. That we may grow up into him in all things, which is the head, even Christ. Master, we know that thou art true, and teachest the way of God in truth.

And the servant of the Lord must not strive; but be gentle unto all men, apt to teach, patient, in meekness instructing those that oppose themselves; if God peradventure will give them repentance to the acknowledging of the truth.

Go ye therefore, and teach all nations, . . . teaching them to observe all things whatsoever I have commanded you: and, lo, I am with you alway, even unto the end of the world.

ANTHEM or HYMN

THE ADDRESS

OFFERTORY *Followed by an offertory response, which may be the Doxology.*

ACT OF PRESENTATION *Here let the Commission on Education stand up before the people, and let the chairman of the commission say to the minister:*

We present unto you this building to be dedicated to the glory of Almighty God and to the purposes of worship, fellowship, study, and service.

ACT OF DEDICATION *Here let the people stand and unite in the responses to the words of the minister.*

Dearly beloved, it is right and proper that buildings erected for such service in the name of our Lord and Saviour Jesus Christ should be formally and devoutly set apart for their special uses. For such a dedication we are now assembled. And, as the dedication of this building is vain without the solemn consecration of those whose gifts and labors it represents, let us now give ourselves anew to the service of God: our souls, that they may be renewed after the image of Christ; our bodies, that they may be fit temples for the indwelling of the Holy Spirit; and our labors and business, that they may be according to God's holy will, and that their fruit may tend to the glory of his name and the advancement of his Kingdom.

In the name of the Father, and of the Son, and of the Holy Spirit, we dedicate this building to the worship of God.

God is a Spirit: and they that worship him must worship him in spirit and in truth.

We dedicate this building to the purpose of Christian education: to the work of the church school, to the study of the Scriptures, and to the development of Christian character.

Whatsoever things were written aforetime were written for our learning. Blessed are they that hear the word of God, and keep it.

We dedicate this building to the broadening of mental horizons and the deepening of knowledge, that young and old may be awakened and informed.

Thy word is a lamp unto my feet, and a light unto my path.

We dedicate this building to Christian fellowship and to recreation of mind and body.

Thou wilt show me the path of life; in thy presence is fullness of joy; at thy right hand there are pleasures for evermore.

We dedicate this building to those tasks and aims in which the Christian serves his place and time: to the cause of missions, of Christian citizenship, and the broad field of social relations.

The kingdoms of this world are become the kingdoms of our Lord, and of his Christ; and he shall reign for ever and ever.

The minister and the people:

We dedicate ourselves anew to that service of our fellow men wherein can best be performed our true service of God, in obedience to the spirit of the Master when he said: Thou shalt love the Lord thy God with all thy heart, and thy neighbor as thyself.

PRAYER OF DEDICATION *The minister.*

Let us pray.

Almighty God, our heavenly Father, whose eyes are ever toward the righteous, and whose ears are ever open unto their cry; graciously accept, we pray thee, this building which we now dedicate to thee, to thy service, and to thy glory, that in it love and wisdom may unite to bring joy and strength to those who gather here; and we beseech thee, receive us thy servants who here dedicate ourselves anew to thee and to those offices of fellowship and good will in which thou art well pleased. Grant that those who come here may be cheered and quickened in mind and body, and that they may be stirred in spirit to serve thee wisely and steadfastly; and the praise shall be thine forever; through Jesus Christ our Lord. **Amen.**

Blessed Lord, who hast caused all holy Scriptures to be written for our learning; grant that we may in such wise hear them, read, mark, learn, and inwardly digest them, that by patience, and comfort of thy holy Word, we may embrace and ever hold fast the blessed hope of everlasting life, which thou hast given us in our Saviour Jesus Christ. **Amen.**

O God, by whom the meek are guided in judgment, and light riseth up in darkness for the godly; grant us, in all doubts and uncertainties, the grace to ask what thou wouldest have us to do, that the spirit of wisdom may save us from all false choices, and that in thy light we may see light, and in thy straight path may not stumble; through Jesus Christ our Lord. **Amen.**

BENEDICTION

POSTLUDE

An Order for the Dedication of a Hospital

SENTENCES OF PRAISE

Minister: Our help is in the name of the Lord,

People: **Who made heaven and earth.**

Minister: O give thanks unto the Lord; for he is good.

People: **For his mercy endureth forever. Amen.**

Here let the people be seated.

DECLARATION *The minister.*

Dearly beloved, this building, which by the favor of God and the labor of man has been so far completed, is a symbol of that care for the sick and the suffering which was supremely exemplified in the Lord Jesus, and which has always inspired those who follow him. We believe that the heavenly Father not only desires, but gladly accepts, the service of comfort and healing for which this building is to provide, and that he looks with favor upon the dedication of the building to himself and to the welfare of his children.

Let us therefore bring to him our praises for his guidance and aid in this undertaking, and our prayers on behalf of those who by their gifts or their service shall unite in fulfilling those purposes of love and skill for which this building is prepared.

HYMN OF PRAISE

THE SCRIPTURE LESSON

The Spirit of the Lord GOD is upon me; because the LORD hath anointed me to preach good tidings unto the meek; he hath sent me to bind up the broken-hearted, to proclaim liberty to the captives, and the opening of the prison to them that are bound; to proclaim the acceptable year of the LORD; to comfort all that mourn; to appoint unto them that mourn in Zion, to give unto them beauty for ashes, the oil of joy for mourning, the garment of praise for the spirit of heaviness.

The wilderness and the solitary place shall be glad for them; and the desert shall rejoice, and blossom as the rose. Strengthen ye the weak hands, and confirm the feeble knees. Say to them that are of a fearful heart, Be strong, fear not: behold, your God will come and save you. Then the eyes of the blind shall be opened, and the ears of the deaf shall be unstopped. Then shall the lame man leap as an hart, and the tongue of the dumb sing.

And the disciples of John showed him of all these things. And John calling unto him two of his disciples sent them to Jesus, saying, Art thou he that should come? or look we for another? And in that same hour he cured many of their infirmities and plagues, and of evil spirits; and unto many that were blind he gave sight. Then Jesus answering said unto them, Go your way, and tell John what things ye have seen and heard; how that the blind see, the lame walk, the lepers are cleansed, the deaf hear, the dead are raised, to the poor the gospel is preached. And blessed is he, whosoever shall not be offended in me.

HYMN OF DEDICATION

ADDRESS

OFFERTORY *Followed by an offertory response, which may be the Doxology.*

RESPONSIVE READING *The minister and the people.*

Bless the LORD, O my soul: and all that is within me, bless his holy name.

Bless the LORD, O my soul, and forget not all his benefits:

Who forgiveth all thine iniquities; who healeth all thy diseases;

Who redeemeth thy life from destruction; who crowneth thee with lovingkindness and tender mercies.

Like as a father pitieth his children, so the LORD pitieth them that fear him.

For he knoweth our frame; he remembereth that we are dust.

As for man, his days are as grass: as a flower of the field, so he flourisheth.

For the wind passeth over it, and it is gone; and the place thereof shall know it no more.

But the mercy of the LORD is from everlasting to everlasting upon them that fear him, and his righteousness unto children's children;

To such as keep his covenant, and to those that remember his commandments to do them.

Bless the LORD, ye his angels, that excel in strength, that do his commandments, hearkening unto the voice of his word.

Bless ye the LORD, all ye his hosts; ye ministers of his, that do his pleasure.

Bless the LORD, all his works in all places of his dominion.

Bless the LORD, O my soul.

GLORIA PATRI

Glory be to the Father, and to the Son, and to the Holy Ghost; as it was in the beginning, is now, and ever shall be, world without end. Amen.

ACT OF PRESENTATION *Here let the Board of Trustees or the proper committee stand up before the people, and let the chairman of the board or some properly designated person say to the minister:*

We present unto you this building, to be dedicated to the service of Almighty God in the relief of the sick and the suffering, [the gift of *N.* for the glory of God, and in loving memory of *N.*]

ACT OF DEDICATION *Here let the people stand and unite in the responses.*

Dearly beloved, it is right and proper that buildings erected for such service in the name of our Lord and Saviour Jesus Christ should be formally and devoutly set apart for their special uses. For such a dedication we are now assembled. And, as the dedication of this building is vain without the solemn consecration of those whose gifts and labors it represents, let us now give ourselves anew to the service of God: our souls, that they may be renewed after the image of Christ; our bodies, that they may be fit temples for the indwelling of the Holy Spirit; and our labors and business, that they may be according to God's holy will, and that their fruit may tend to the glory of his name and the advancement of his Kingdom.

In the name of the Father, and of the Son, and of the Holy Spirit, we dedicate this building as a hospital to the holy ministry of healing.

Blessed are the merciful: for they shall obtain mercy.

We dedicate this building to Christian helpfulness.

Whosoever shall give to drink unto one of these little ones a cup of cold water only, shall in no wise lose his reward.

We dedicate this building to the sustaining power of the Holy Spirit in time of pain and suffering.

In all their afflictions he was afflicted, and the angel of his presence saved them.

We dedicate this building to the skill and wisdom that bring relief and cure, and to the patient research that uncovers fresh resources with which to serve the public health.

Happy is the man that findeth wisdom. Length of days is in her right hand. She is a tree of life to them that lay hold upon her.

The minister and the people.

We dedicate ourselves anew to that service of our fellow men wherein can best be performed our true service of God, in obedience to the spirit of the Master when he said: Thou shalt love the Lord thy God with all thy heart, and thy neighbor as thyself.

PRAYER OF DEDICATION *The minister.*

Let us pray.

Almighty God, our heavenly Father, whose eyes are ever toward the righteous, and whose ears are ever open unto their cry; graciously accept, we pray thee, this building which we now dedicate to thee, to thy service, and to thy glory, that in it skill and tenderness may unite to bring health and cure to those who come for aid; and we beseech thee, receive us thy servants who here dedicate ourselves anew to thee and to those offices of love and good will in which thou art well pleased. Grant that those who come here in weakness may be made strong, that those who come in pain may find relief, and that those who come in sorrow may find joy and gladness; and the praise shall be thine forever; through Jesus Christ our Lord. **Amen.**

O blessed Lord, who hast power of life and death, of health and sickness; give wisdom and gentleness to all thy ministering servants, to physicians and surgeons, nurses and watchers by the sick, that, always bearing thy presence with them, they may not only heal but bless, and shine as lamps of hope in the darkest hours of distress and fear; through Christ our Lord. **Amen.**

O most merciful Father, we look to thee for thy grace on behalf of those who, coming here in grievous illness, may not return to earthly joys and sorrows, but pass from here into that life immortal where thou dost receive all who put their trust in thee. Thou hast said that as the heavens are higher than the earth, so are thy ways higher than our ways, but we know that all thy children are in thy tender and unfailing love which passeth our understanding, and we pray that the blessed ministry of thy Holy Spirit may sustain them, and that light eternal may shine upon them. **Amen.**

And now, O loving Father, we bow before thee, of whom the whole family in heaven and earth is named, praying that thou wouldest grant us, according to the riches of thy glory, to be strengthened with might by thy Spirit in the inner man; that Christ may dwell in our hearts by faith; that we, being rooted and grounded in love, may be able to comprehend with all saints what is the breadth, and length, and depth, and height; and to know the love of Christ, which passeth knowledge, that we might be filled with the fullness of God. **Amen.**

BENEDICTION

An Order for the Dedication of a School, College, or University Building

PRELUDE *The people in devout meditation.*

SENTENCES OF PRAISE

Minister: O worship the Lord in the beauty of holiness: fear before him, all the earth.

People: **They that worship him must worship him in spirit and in truth. Amen.**

DECLARATION *The minister.*

Dearly beloved, this building, which by the favor of God and the labor of man has been so far completed, embodies the obligation of each generation to impart its treasures of wisdom and knowledge to the generation following. For the fulfillment of this task we need, not only the best that men can do, but above all the blessing of Almighty God. Let us therefore bring to him our praises for his aid in this undertaking, and our prayers on behalf of those who by their gifts or their service shall unite in fulfilling the purpose for which this building is prepared.

HYMN OF PRAISE

THE SCRIPTURE LESSON

Happy is the man that findeth wisdom, and the man that getteth understanding. For the merchandise of it is better than the merchandise of silver, and the gain thereof than fine gold. She is more precious than rubies: and all the things thou canst desire are not to be compared unto her. Length of days is in her right hand; and in her left hand riches and honor. Her ways are ways of pleasantness, and all her paths are peace. She is a tree of life to them that lay hold upon her: and happy is everyone that retaineth her. The LORD by wisdom hath founded the earth; by understanding hath he established the heavens. By his knowledge the depths are broken up, and the clouds drop down the dew. My son, let not them depart from thine eyes: keep sound wisdom and discretion: so shall they be life unto thy soul, and grace to thy neck. Then shalt thou walk in thy way safely, and thy foot shall not stumble.

Enter ye in at the strait gate: for wide is the gate, and broad is the way, that leadeth to destruction, and many there be which go in thereat: because strait is the gate, and narrow is the way, which leadeth unto life, and few there be that find it. Therefore whosoever heareth these sayings of mine, and doeth them, I will liken him unto a wise man, which built his house upon a rock: and the rain descended, and the floods came, and the winds blew, and beat upon that house; and it fell not: for it was founded upon a rock. And everyone that heareth these sayings of mine, and doeth them not, shall be likened unto a foolish man, which built his house upon the sand: and the rain descended, and the floods came, and the winds blew, and beat upon that house; and it fell: and great was the fall of it.

HYMN OF DEDICATION

THE ADDRESS

OFFERTORY *Followed by an offertory response, which may be the Doxology.*

RESPONSIVE READING

Wisdom hath built her house, she hath hewn out her seven pillars.

Doth not wisdom cry? and understanding put forth her voice?

She standeth in the top of high places, by the way in the places of the paths.

She crieth at the gates, at the entry of the city, at the coming in at the doors.

Unto you, O men, I call; and my voice is to the sons of man.

O ye simple, understand wisdom: and ye fools, be ye of an understanding heart.

Hear; for I will speak of excellent things; and the opening of my lips shall be right things.

For my mouth shall speak truth; and wickedness is an abomination to my lips.

Receive my instruction, and not silver; and knowledge rather than choice gold.

For wisdom is better than rubies; and all the things that may be desired are not to be compared to it.

But where shall wisdom be found? and where is the place of understanding?

Behold, the fear of the Lord, that is wisdom; and to depart from evil is understanding.

GLORIA PATRI

Glory be to the Father, and to the Son, and to the Holy Ghost; as it was in the beginning, is now, and ever shall be, world without end. Amen.

ACT OF PRESENTATION *Then let the Board of Trustees or the proper committee stand up before the people, and let one of them say unto the minister:*

We present unto you this building, to be dedicated to the service of Almighty God in the enlightenment of his children, [the gift of *N.* for the glory of God, and in loving memory of *N.*].

ACT OF DEDICATION *The minister, the people uniting in the responses.*

Dearly beloved, it is right and proper that buildings erected for such service in the name of our Lord and Saviour Jesus

Christ should be formally and devoutly set apart for their special uses. For such a dedication we are now assembled. And, as the dedication of this building is vain without the solemn consecration of those whose gifts and labors it represents, let us now give ourselves anew to the service of God: our souls, that they may be renewed after the image of Christ; our bodies, that they may be fit temples for the indwelling of the Holy Spirit; and our labors and business, that they may be according to God's holy will, and that their fruit may tend to the glory of his name and the advancement of his kingdom.

In the name of the Father, and of the Son, and of the Holy Spirit, we dedicate this building to the holy ministry of education.

Take fast hold of instruction; let her not go: keep her; for she is thy life.

We dedicate this building to the spiritual enrichment of all who shall come here in pursuit of knowledge.

Happy is the man that findeth wisdom, and the man that getteth understanding.

We dedicate this building to the loyal service of those whose training and devotion have prepared them to lead students toward the truth.

The Lord God hath given me the tongue of the learned, that I should know how to speak a word in season to him that is weary.

We dedicate this building to that ministry of administration upon whose ability and fruitfulness depends the wise conduct of its affairs.

Who then is that faithful and wise steward, whom his lord shall make ruler over his household? Blessed is that servant, whom his lord when he cometh shall find so doing.

The minister and the people.

We dedicate ourselves anew to that service of our fellow men wherein can best be performed our true service of God, in obedience to the spirit of the Master when he said: Thou shalt love the Lord thy God with all thy heart, and thy neighbor as thyself.

PRAYER OF DEDICATION *The minister.*

Let us pray.

Almighty God, our heavenly Father, whose eyes are ever toward the righteous, and whose ears are ever open unto their cry; graciously accept, we pray thee, this building which we now dedicate to thee, to thy service, and to thy glory, that in it love and wisdom may unite to make plain the path of knowledge to those who gather here; and we beseech thee, receive us thy servants who here dedicate ourselves anew to thee and to those offices of fellowship and good will in which thou art well pleased. Grant that those who come here, whether as administrators, teachers, or students, may come with pure minds, upright purpose, and steadfast endeavor, to learn and to do thy holy will; through Jesus Christ our Lord. **Amen.**

God of our Fathers, we offer thee our heartfelt thanks for all thy servants, the parents and teachers, the benefactors and friends, by whose love and devotion we have come into our great inheritance of health, truth, and piety. Help us to guard faithfully this great boon, to profit by it, to augment it, and loyally to pass it on to the coming generation, that they through us may rise up to serve thee; in the name of Jesus Christ our Lord. **Amen.**

BENEDICTION

POSTLUDE

An Order for the Dedication of a Home

SENTENCES OF PRAISE *The minister.*

Peace be to this house.

Beloved, let us love one another; for love is of God; and everyone that loveth is born of God, and knoweth God.

INVOCATION *The minister.*

Let us pray.

Almighty God, who hast mercifully promised to hear the prayers of thy people who call upon thee; we beseech thee graciously to bless this home which we dedicate to thy honor and service, and make it the abode of purity and peace and truth. Watch over thy people in their going out and their coming in, and direct their footsteps ever in the way of thy commandments; through Jesus Christ our Lord. **Amen.**

THE LORD'S PRAYER *Here let the people unite with the minister in prayer.*

Our Father who art in heaven, hallowed be thy name; thy kingdom come; thy will be done on earth as it is in heaven. Give us this day our daily bread. And forgive us our trespasses, as we forgive those who trespass against us. And lead us not into temptation, but deliver us from evil. For thine is the kingdom, and the power, and the glory, forever. Amen.

HYMN

ACT OF DEDICATION *To be said responsively by the minister and the people.*

In the name of the Father, and of the Son, and of the Holy Spirit, we dedicate this home to the glory of God, committing to his loving care this house and all who dwell in it.

Have thou respect unto the prayer of thy servant, O

LORD my God, which thy servant prayeth before thee today; that thine eyes may be opened toward this house night and day.

We dedicate this home to the deep affections of the family circle, and to all friendly hospitalities.

Now God himself and our Father, and our Lord Jesus Christ, make you to increase and abound in love.

We dedicate this home to the courage, patience, and self-control which make life cheerful and serene.

Let patience have her perfect work, that ye may be perfect and entire, wanting nothing.

We dedicate this home to all beautiful things of heart and mind that lead the soul to wider vision and to higher aims.

> Whene'er a noble deed is wrought,
> Whene'er is spoken a noble thought,
>   Our hearts in glad surprise
>   To higher levels rise.

We dedicate this home to happiness, to hopefulness, and to health, that it may ever be, to those whose home it is, a dear haven of peace and joy.

> Serene will be our days and bright,
> And happy will our nature be,
> When love is an unerring light,
> And joy its own security.

PRAYER OF DEDICATION *The minister.*

Let us pray.

O God, our heavenly Father, giver of life; we pray thee, make this home an abode of light and love. May all that is pure, tender, and true grow up under its shelter. May all that hinders godly union and concord be driven far from it. Make it the center of fresh, sweet, and holy influence. Give wisdom for life, and discretion in the guidance of affairs.

Let thy work appear unto thy servants, and thy glory unto their children. And let the beauty of the LORD our God be upon us: and establish thou the work of our hands upon us; yea, the work of our hands establish thou it. And the praise shall be thine forever. **Amen.**

HYMN

BENEDICTION *The minister.*

The LORD bless us, and keep us: the LORD make his face shine upon us, and be gracious unto us: the LORD lift up his countenance upon us, and give us peace, now and for evermore. **Amen.**

An Order for the Dedication of a Memorial

The service shall be conducted in the customary way, and, when the sermon is ended, an appropriate hymn shall be sung; after which the minister, accompanied by those who are to take part with him in the service, shall proceed to that part of the church where the act of dedication is to take place; and, when the music ends, the people still standing, he shall say:

SENTENCES OF PRAISE

Minister: Our help is in the name of the Lord, who made heaven and earth.

People: **Give unto the Lord, O ye kindreds of the people, give unto the Lord glory and strength.**

Minister: Honor and majesty are before him: strength and beauty are in his sanctuary.

People: **Blessed be the name of the Lord from this time forth and for evermore. Amen.**

Here let the people be seated.

INVOCATION *The minister.*

Let us pray.

Blessed and glorious Lord God Almighty, by whose power, wisdom, and love all things are sanctified, enlightened, and made perfect; be merciful unto us and bless us, we beseech thee, and cause thy face to shine upon us, that what we now do may please thee, and show forth the honor of thy name. Let thy work appear unto thy servants, and thy glory unto their children. And let the beauty of the LORD our God be upon us: and establish thou the work of our hands upon us; yea, the work of our hands establish thou it; through Jesus Christ our Lord. **Amen.**

PRESENTATION AND DEDICATION *When that which is to be*

dedicated is a memorial, the minister shall then call upon the person appointed to perform the presentation of the memorial.

We ask *N.* now to present the memorial.

The person making the presentation shall say:

In the name of [or, In memory of] *N.* **we present to this church this memorial, to be dedicated to the glory and praise of God.**

To which the properly designated official shall respond:

We accept this gift as a sacred trust, and shall guard it reverently, in honor of the faithful and devoted life to whose memory it is erected.

Then the minister shall pronounce the words of dedication:

In the faith of our Lord Jesus Christ, I dedicate this memorial to the glory of God, and in memory of his servant *N.*; in the name of the Father, and of the Son, and of the Holy Spirit. **Amen.**

DEDICATORY PRAYER *Let the people unite in the response.*

Give unto the LORD the glory due unto his name: worship the LORD in the beauty of holiness.

We see Jesus, because of the suffering of death, crowned with glory and honor.

Let us pray.

Almighty God, our heavenly Father, without whom no words or works of ours have meaning, but who dost accept the gifts of our hands as the tokens of our devotion; grant thy blessing upon us as we dedicate this gift to thy glory. May this memorial which we now dedicate be an enduring witness before all thy people of the faithful service of thy servant. May our lives, being consecrated unto thy service, be joined with thy faithful ones into that building which groweth unto a holy temple in the Lord. **Amen.**

HYMN

BENEDICTION

POSTLUDE

Prayers

For All Who Are Sick

O Christ our Lord, who art the Great Physician; grant unto all who are sick the aid of heavenly healing. Look upon all faithful people who are in need and who love to call upon thy name, and take their souls into thy keeping, and vouchsafe to deliver them from all sickness and infirmity. Amen.

We thank thee, O Father, for all who hallow suffering, for those who in their thoughts for others leave no room for pity for themselves, for those whose patience inspires others to hold on; and grant, O loving Father, to all who are bound in the mysterious fellowship of suffering, the sense of comradeship with others, and the knowledge of thy love; and give them thy peace which passeth all understanding. Amen.

O Lord, who dost feel the pain of the world; look down upon all sick and suffering persons; enfold them with thy love, that in the midst of pain they may find thy presence; to doctors and nurses grant tender hearts and healing hands; and give health again in body and soul, for thy tender mercy's sake. Amen.

For a Sick Person

O God, be present in thy goodness with this thy servant, that, *his* weakness being banished, and *his* health restored, *he* may live to glorify thy holy name; through our Lord Jesus Christ. Amen.

O Thou who hearest prayer, we pray thee to be very kind and merciful to thy child *N.*, whose body suffers in pain and weakness. Grant unto *him* patience and tranquility of mind; peace, purity, and courage of soul; the strong will to live if it be thy will; and a heart ready to trust thee waking or sleeping. Bless all the means used for *his* recovery, and all who minister to *him* in *his* suffering. Restore *him* speedily to health, if it please thee, but above all things grant *him* that which thou knowest to be best for *him,* and keep *him* thine for evermore: through Jesus Christ our Saviour. Amen.

O God, our refuge and strength, who art a very present help in trouble; we know that thou lookest graciously upon this thy servant. Send *him* patience and comfort in this time of *his* great distress; strengthen *him* with the consolations of thy Holy Spirit; enable *him* to rise above all pain and weakness; through Jesus Christ our Lord. Amen.

Almighty and immortal God, giver of life and health; we beseech thee for thy servant, for whom we implore thy mercy, that by thy blessing upon *him* and upon those who minister to *him* of thy healing gifts, *he* may be restored to soundness of health, and give thanks to thee; through Jesus Christ our Lord. Amen.

O Lord, holy Father, by whose lovingkindness our souls and bodies are renewed; mercifully look upon this thy servant, that, every cause of sickness being removed, *he* may be restored to soundness of health; through Jesus Christ our Lord. Amen.

For a Sick Child

O God, whose dear Son Jesus Christ did heal children who were sick; send thy help to this child. Help *him* to be quiet, and patient, and cheerful. Take away *his* pain, and make *him* well again, that *he* may grow in body, in mind, and in likeness to Jesus Christ our Lord. Amen.

O Lord Jesus Christ, who didst show thy love by restoring to health the little ones who were brought unto thee; give thy blessing, we beseech thee, to the means now used for the healing of this thy child, that *he* may be restored to health and strength, and spared to a life of usefulness. Amen.

For a Family in Sickness and Bereavement

Almighty God, who abidest always, and who art ever near to uphold and bless; hear now our prayer for thy servants bowed down with grief. May they find strength and peace in thee. For all that hath been gracious and helpful in the days past we devoutly thank thee. Visit us with thy comfort, and be thou thyself our companion. Let us be mindful of the many good things which make life dear and sacred. May our hearts be united in a closer bond of love and sympathy; and give us strength to return to the duties of life with increased devotion and with purer and more earnest purpose. May we ever feel that the eternal God is our refuge, and that underneath are the everlasting arms; through Jesus Christ our Lord. Amen.

Thanksgiving for Recovery of a Sick Person

O Lord, whose compassions fail not, and whose mercies are new every morning; we give thee hearty thanks that it hath pleased thee to give to this our *brother* both relief from pain and hope of renewed health. Continue, we beseech thee, in *him* the good work that thou hast begun, that, daily increasing in bodily strength, *he* may so order *his* life as always to think and do such things as shall please thee: through Jesus Christ our Lord. Amen.

Almighty God, the giver of every good gift; we thank thee for the health restored to thy servant. Thou hast been with *him* in sickness; be with *him* still in health and joy. In the hour of returning gladness suffer us not to forget the days of darkness that are gone. Let us not be numbered among those who are forward to ask in time of trouble, but careless to show themselves thankful when mercy is bestowed. Be thou, O God, loved and obeyed with all our strength; through Jesus Christ our Lord. Amen.

Commendatory Prayers

Thou knowest, Lord, the secrets of our hearts; shut not thy merciful ears to our prayers; but spare us, Lord most holy, O God most mighty, O holy and merciful Saviour, thou most worthy Judge eternal, suffer us not at our last hour, for any pains of death, to fall from thee. Amen.

Go forth upon thy journey from this world, O Christian soul,
In the name of God the Father Almighty who created thee. Amen.
In the name of Jesus Christ who suffered for thee. Amen.
In the name of the Holy Spirit who strengthened thee. Amen.
May thy portion this day be in peace, and thy dwelling in the heavenly Jerusalem. Amen.

After the Birth of a Child

Almighty God, who art thyself known as Father; accept the thanks of our hearts for this thy child now given unto these thy servants. Grant, we beseech thee, unto them thy heavenly grace, that they may so nurture this child that *he* may daily increase in wisdom and stature, and grow in thy love and service through all the days of *his* life; through Jesus Christ our Lord. Amen.

For Those Who Care for the Sick

Almighty God, our heavenly Father, who hast power of life and death, of health and of sickness; give strength, wisdom, and gentleness to all thy ministering servants, all physicians and surgeons, nurses and watchers by the sick, that, always bearing thy presence with them, they may not only heal but bless, and shine as lamps of hope in the darkest hours of distress and fear; through Jesus Christ our Lord. Amen.

O God, in whose dearly beloved Son men have seen the glory of self-sacrifice; grant that all who are called to the sacred office of nursing and caring for the sick may ever remember his holy example, and show forth his unfailing tenderness in the beauty and compassion of their daily lives. Amen.

Almighty God, whose blessed Son Jesus Christ went about doing good and healing all manner of sickness and disease among the people; grant to physicians, surgeons, and nurses wisdom, skill, sympathy, and patience, that they may continue his gracious work among us in all hospitals and infirmaries; prosper their work, O Lord, with thy continual blessing; through the same Jesus Christ our Lord. Amen.

Thanksgiving for Deliverance in Time of Epidemic

Merciful God, to whom alone belong the issues of life and death; we bless the goodness which hath preserved so many of us alive in the midst of a great mortality, and hath restored health in our land, and the voices of joy in many homes. Help us now to offer ourselves a living sacrifice to thee, who art worshiped in spirit and in truth. Amen.

To Be Said by the Sick

O God, help me to think of thee in this bitter trial. Thou knowest how my heart is rent with grief. In my weakness, tested so severely in soul by this experience, I cry unto thee, Father of all life, give me fortitude. Forgive the thoughts of my rebellious soul. Pardon me in these first hours of my grief, if I question thee or exercise myself in things too high for me. Grant me strength to rise above this trial, to bear with humility life's sorrows and disappointments. Be nigh unto me, O God. Bring consolation and peace to my soul. Blessed art thou, O God, who comfortest thy children. Amen.

O God my Father, hold me in thy keeping. Be with me when I am bewildered by sickness and by pain, and through all let me trust thy love that does not fail. Give me back, I pray thee, health and vigor, that I may set my hands again with gladness to the tasks of life. May any suffering I must undergo teach me sympathy with all who suffer; and may every gift of life renewed send me forth with a thankful heart to greater consecration; through Jesus Christ my Lord. Amen.

O God, I am sorely stricken; but in my pain let me not forget thee. Thou art long-suffering and patient; and in thy great mercy thou wilt forgive the murmuring lips and the weary soul. In all humility I lay bare my soul before thee and ask thy pardon for my shortcomings. A broken and contrite heart thou wilt not despise. May it be thy will to aid those who would bring me to a speedy recovery. I thank thee for all the dear ones whose sympathy and care have eased my suffering. Mayest thou answer the prayers of our hearts. Heal me, that I may again praise thy name in the congregation. Oh rejoice the soul of thy servant, for unto thee, O Lord, do I lift up mine eyes. Heal me, O Lord, and I shall be healed; save me and I shall be saved, for thou art my praise. Amen.

O living Christ, make us conscious now of thy healing nearness. Touch our eyes that we may see thee; open our ears that we may hear thy voice; enter our hearts that we may know thy love. Overshadow our souls and bodies with thy presence, that we may partake of thy strength, thy love, and thy healing life. Amen.

The Almighty Lord, who is a most strong tower to all those who put their trust in him, to whom all things in heaven, in earth, and under the earth, do bow and obey, be now and evermore my defense, and make me know and feel that there is none other name under heaven given to man, in whom, and through whom, I may receive health and salvation, but only the name of my Lord Jesus Christ. Amen.

We ask thee not, O Lord, to rid us of pain; but grant in thy mercy that our pain may be free from waste, unfretted by rebellion against thy will, unsoiled by thought of ourselves, purified by love of our kind, and ennobled by devotion to thy kingdom; through the merits of thine only Son our Lord. Amen.

Before an Operation

O loving Father, I commit myself with perfect trust into thy loving hands. Watch over me and protect me in my hour of weakness, and grant that as I become unconscious to earthly things my thoughts may be turned to thee. Bless and guide thy servants who shall tend me; give them such success that we may praise thee for thy goodness. And finally grant that I may so bear suffering with cheerful courage that I may be the means, under thy hand, of helping others in their time of trial; for Jesus Christ's sake. Amen.

An Order for the Administration of the Sacrament of the Lord's Supper or Holy Communion for the Sick

And Others Confined to Their Homes

The minister shall read one or more of the following passages of Scripture:

Behold, I stand at the door, and knock: if any man hear my voice, and open the door, I will come in to him, and will sup with him, and he with me.

I will not leave you comfortless. If a man love me, he will keep my words: and my Father will love him, and we will come unto him, and make our abode with him.

Blessed be God, even the Father of our Lord Jesus Christ, the Father of mercies, and the God of all comfort; who comforteth us in all our tribulation, that we may be able to comfort them which are in any trouble, by the comfort wherewith we ourselves are comforted of God. For as the sufferings of Christ abound in us, so our consolation also aboundeth by Christ.

Then shall the minister say:

Let us pray.

Have mercy upon us, O God, according to thy lovingkindness: according to the multitude of thy tender mercies, blot out our transgressions. Wash us thoroughly from our iniquities and cleanse us from our sins. For we acknowledge our transgressions, and our sin is ever before us. Against thee have we sinned, and done that which is evil in thy sight. Create in us clean hearts, O God, and renew a right spirit within us. Cast us not away from thy presence; and take not thy Holy Spirit from us. **Amen.**

May the almighty and merciful Father grant us pardon and the forgiveness of sins through Jesus Christ our Lord. **Amen.**

Then shall the minister offer the Prayer of Consecration and the Prayer of Humble Access:

Almighty God, our heavenly Father, who of thy tender mercy didst give thine only Son Jesus Christ to suffer death upon the cross for our redemption; who made there, by the one offering of himself, a full, perfect, and sufficient sacrifice for the sins of the whole world; and did institute, and in his holy gospel command us to continue, this memorial of his precious death: hear us, O merciful Father, we most humbly beseech thee, and grant that we, receiving this bread and wine, according to thy Son our Saviour Jesus Christ's holy institution, in remembrance of his death and passion, may also be partakers of the divine nature through him, who in the same night that he was betrayed took bread; and when he had given thanks, he brake it, and gave it to his disciples, saying, Take, eat; this is my body, which is given for you; do this in remembrance of me. Likewise after supper he took the cup; and when he had given thanks, he gave it to them, saying, Drink ye all of this; for this is my blood of the new covenant which is shed for you, and for many, for the remission of sins; do this, as oft as ye shall drink it, in remembrance of me. **Amen.**

We do not presume to come to this thy table, O merciful Lord, trusting in our own righteousness, but in thy manifold and great mercies. We are not worthy so much as to gather up the crumbs under thy table. But thou art the same Lord, whose mercy is unfailing. Grant us therefore, gracious Lord, so to partake of these memorials of thy Son Jesus Christ, that we may be filled with the fullness of his life, may grow into his likeness, and may evermore dwell in him, and he in us. **Amen.**

Our Father who art in heaven, hallowed be thy name; thy kingdom come; thy will be done on earth as it is in heaven. Give us this day our daily bread. And forgive us our trespasses, as we forgive those who trespass against us. And lead us not into temptation, but deliver us from evil. For thine is the kingdom, and the power, and the glory, forever. Amen.

Then shall the minister first receive the elements of the Communion him-self, and then shall administer the Holy Communion to those present.

When the minister offers the bread, he shall say:

Jesus said, "This is my body, which is given for you." Take and eat this in remembrance that Christ died for you, and feed on him in your heart by faith, with thanksgiving.

When the minister offers the cup, he shall say:

Jesus said, "This cup is the new covenant in my blood, which is shed for you." Drink this in remembrance that Christ died for you, and be thankful.

Then the minister shall say:

Let us pray.

O Lord, our heavenly Father, we, thy humble servants, desire thy fatherly goodness mercifully to accept this our sacrifice of praise and thanksgiving; most humbly beseeching thee to grant that, by the merits and death of thy Son Jesus Christ, and through faith in his blood, we and thy whole Church may obtain forgiveness of our sins, and all other benefits of his passion. And here we offer and present unto thee, O Lord, ourselves, our souls and bodies, to be a reasonable, holy, and living sacrifice unto thee; humbly beseeching thee that all we who are partakers of this Holy Communion may be filled with thy grace and heavenly benediction. And although we be unworthy, through our manifold sins, to offer unto thee any sacrifice, yet we beseech thee to accept this our bounden duty and service; not weighing our merits, but pardoning our offenses; through Jesus Christ our Lord; by whom, and with whom, in the unity of the Holy Spirit, all honor and glory be unto thee, O Father Almighty, world without end. **Amen.**

Then may the minister say the benediction:

The peace of God, which passeth all understanding, keep your hearts and minds in the knowledge and love of God, and of his Son Jesus Christ our Lord; and the blessing of God Almighty, the Father, the Son, and the Holy Spirit, be among you, and remain with you always. **Amen.**

An Order for Licensing Persons to Preach

At the time appointed, those to be licensed shall be presented by their respective pastors, of whom one shall say:

Brethren, *we* present unto you *these persons* to be licensed to preach the gospel of the Lord Jesus Christ: [names].

Their names having been read aloud, the district superintendent shall say:

Take heed that *these persons* whom you present unto us this day *are* fitted in character and skill for this sacred vocation.

Then shall the pastor say:

Their churches have inquired diligently concerning *them* and *have* examined *them* and found *them* so to be.

The district superintendent shall then say:

Brethren, you have heard the recommendation of *these persons* by *their pastors*. If there be any of you who knows any reason why *any one of them* should not be licensed to preach the gospel, let him arise now and declare the same.

If no impediment be alleged, the district superintendent shall say:

All vocations are sacred in the sight of the Lord, who created all things and sanctified them by the power of his Spirit. Especially precious in his sight is the preaching of his Word.

Then shall the Scripture be read:

Comfort ye, comfort ye my people, saith your God. Speak ye comfortably to Jerusalem, and cry unto her, that her warfare is accomplished, that her iniquity is pardoned: for she hath received of the LORD's hand double for all her sins.

The voice of him that crieth in the wilderness, Prepare ye the way of the LORD, make straight in the desert a highway for our God. Every valley shall be exalted, and every mountain and hill shall be made low: and the crooked shall be made straight, and the rough places plain: and the glory of the LORD shall be revealed, and all flesh shall see it together: for the mouth of the LORD hath spoken it.

The voice said, Cry. And he said, What shall I cry? All flesh is grass, and all the goodliness thereof is as the flower of the field: the grass withereth, the flower fadeth: because the Spirit of the LORD bloweth upon it: surely the people is grass. The grass withereth, the flower fadeth: but the word of our God shall stand for ever.

The district superintendent shall then ask of those being licensed:

Do you believe you are moved by the Holy Spirit to preach the Word of God?

I do.

Will you strive to live a life in keeping with what you preach?

I will.

Then shall the district superintendent say to every one severally:

N., take thou authority to preach the truths of the Old and New Testaments in the Church of God.

Then shall the district superintendent pray:

Almighty God, whose Word is truth, in the keeping of which is eternal life; we thank thee for *these persons* whom this day we set aside in thy name as *preachers* of thy gospel. Prepare *them* in body, mind, and spirit for *their* task, and continue *them* in thy grace, that *they* may increase and bless thy Church through *their* labors; through Jesus Christ our Lord. **Amen.**

Then may the district superintendent say:

The peace of God, which passeth all understanding, keep your hearts and minds in the knowledge and love of God, and of his Son Jesus Christ our Lord; and the blessing of God Almighty, the Father, the Son, and the Holy Spirit, be among you, and remain with you always. **Amen.**

The Order for the Consecration of Directors of Christian Education

IT IS recommended that this order be used at the time of the report of the Conference Board of Education, or other suitable time approved by the program committee of the Annual Conference, but that it not be used in connection with the conference ordination service.

At the time appointed, the bishop shall declare the office and duty of a director of Christian education, as follows:

Dearly beloved, we rejoice that there is a vocation within the Church for those persons who have been called to serve Christ in the field of Christian education. It is the office of a director of Christian education to assist the pastor in guiding the work of Christian education in the local church. It is the duty of a director of Christian education, through personal endeavor and through the service of others, to lead the people to Christ, to inform them of the way of Christ, and to guide their growing understanding of how to live as Christians.

Then the chairman of the Conference Board of Education shall present those to be consecrated, saying:

I present unto you *these persons*, having been duly certified, to be consecrated *directors* of Christian education: [names].

Their names having been read aloud, the bishop shall say to those to be consecrated:

Dearly beloved, we rejoice that you have purposed in your *hearts* to devote *yourselves* to this task. You are to be among those who serve and teach. Such a vocation confers a great privilege; it also lays upon you a solemn responsibility. What you have done alone with God in consecrating *yourselves* to this service, we now ask you to declare publicly in the presence of this congregation.

Do you believe in your heart that you have been led by the

Spirit of God to engage in Christian education and to assume its responsibilities?

I do so believe.

Will you be diligent in prayer, in the reading of the Holy Scriptures, and in other studies necessary to the development of a program of Christian education?

I will, the Lord being my helper.

Will you strive so to live that the power of God may be manifest in your life, enabling you through a program of Christian education to bring others to an awareness of the presence of God and to become disciples of our Lord Jesus Christ?

I will, by God's grace.

Will you maintain and set forward, as much as lieth in you, quietness, peace, and love among all Christian people, and especially among those who shall be committed to your charge?

I will do so, the Lord being my helper.

Will you be loyal to the Church and accept the authority of those to whom the Church has committed the direction of your work?

I will, the Lord being my helper.

Then those being consecrated shall kneel while the bishop says the prayer of consecration:

O eternal God, the Father of our Lord Jesus Christ; look upon *these* thy *servants* whom we this day consecrate *directors* of Christian education. Grant that *they* may have strength of body, mind, and soul for the fulfillment of thy will, that *they* may worthily discharge the work committed to *them,* to the blessing of mankind and the glory of Christ our Saviour. **Amen.**

ACKNOWLEDGMENTS

ACKNOWLEDGMENT is due authors and publishers who have granted permission for use of copyright materials in this book. They are listed below, and specific items in the Index of Titles and Index of First Lines are identified by the initials preceding these sources.

Older materials no longer copyright have been found in many collections; but specific mention should be made of the *Book of Common Prayer* of the Protestant Episcopal Church in America; *A Book of English Collects,* by John Wallace Suter (New York: Harper & Bros., 1941), compiled from the several national editions of the Anglican prayerbook; and *A Chain of Prayer Across the Ages,* by Selina F. Fox (London, 1913; new American ed., New York: E. P. Dutton & Co., 1943).

Many selections, both old and new, have been altered to suit present-day Methodist worship. Such adaptations are covered by the copyright of this book and must not be reproduced without written permission of both The Methodist Publishing House and the owner of the original.

SOURCES

ACF   A. Campbell Fraser, *A Book of Prayers*. Oxford: Basil Blackwell & Mott, 1932.

AFT   A. F. Thornhill, *Family Prayers*. London: Longmans Green & Co.

BCS   *Book of Church Services*. Prepared by a commission of the National Council of Congregational Churches. Boston: Pilgrim Press, 1922.

BOM   *The Book of Offices*. Being the Orders of Service authorized for use in the Methodist Church together with the Order for Morning Prayer. London: Methodist Publishing House, 1936.

BPS   *A Book of Prayers for Schools*. Ed. Hugh Martin. London: Student Christian Movement Press, 1936.

CLW   Henry Bonner and Frederic C. Spurr, *Come, Let Us Worship*. London: Kingsgate Press, 1930.

CMJ   Charles Michael Jacobs, *Helps on the Road*. Philadelphia: United Lutheran Publication House, 1933.

COC   *The Book of Common Order of the United Church of Canada*. Toronto: United Church Publishing House, 1932.

COS   *Book of Common Order of the Church of Scotland*. By Authority of the General Assembly. Oxford: Oxford University Press, 1940.

CSB   *Common Service Book of the Lutheran Church*. Philadelphia: Board of Publication of the United Lutheran Church in America, 1919.

CWC   *Book of Common Worship*. For Use in the Several Communions of the Church of Christ. New York: E. P. Dutton & Co., Inc., 1932.

CWM   Charles W. Merriam, *Church Worship Book*. Boston: Pilgrim Press, 1931.

CWP   *The Book of Common Worship*. Approved by the General Assembly of the Presbyterian Church in the United States of America. Philadelphia: Presbyterian Board of Christian Education, 1942.

DWM   *Divine Worship*. Approved by the Conference for optional use in Methodist Churches. London: Epworth Press, 1935.

EW   Elizabeth Wilson and Helen Thoburn, National Board of the Young Women's Christian Associations of the United States of America.

HA   Canon Harold Anson.

HVD   Henry van Dyke, in CWP.

JB   John Baillie, *A Diary of Private Prayer*. New York: Charles Scribner's Sons, 1936.

JFN   Joseph Fort Newton, *Altar Stairs*. New York: The Macmillan Co., 1928.

JSE   James William Sells.

JTA   James Thayer Addison. Published in *Prayers for the Christian Year*, comp. Charles Morris Addison. New York: The Century Co., 1931.

JWS   John Wallace Suter, *Prayers of the Spirit*. New York: Harper & Bros., 1943.

KPG   *The Kingdom, the Power and the Glory*. Services of Praise and Prayer for Occasional Use in Churches; an American edition of the "Grey" Book. New York: Oxford University Press, 1933.

LRE   Lisgar R. Eckardt.

MW   Quoted as material used at Beloit College in *Modern Worship*, by Von Ogden Vogt. New Haven: Yale University Press, 1927.

PCY   *Prayers for the Christian Year*. By Authority of the General Assembly of the Church of Scotland. Oxford: Oxford University Press.

PD   Percy Dearmer, *The Sanctuary*. London: Rivingtons, 1905.

PNO   *Prayers New & Old*. 5th ed. Sharon, Pa.: Forward Movement of the Episcopal Church, 1943.

SR   *Services of Religion*. For Use in the Churches of the Free Spirit. Boston: Beacon Press, 1937.

UMN   Ursula M. Niebuhr.

UP [18]   *The Union Prayerbook for Jewish Worship*. Rev. ed. Cincinnati: Central Conference of American Rabbis, 1918.

UP [40]   *The Union Prayerbook for Jewish Worship*. Newly rev. ed. Cincinnati: Central Conference of American Rabbis, 1940.

WEO   W. E. Orchard, *The Order of Divine Service for Public Worship*. 2nd ed. Oxford: Oxford University Press, 1926.

WR   Walter Rauschenbusch, *Prayers of the Social Awakening*. Boston: Pilgrim Press, 1909.

WRB   Walter Russell Bowie, *Lift Up Your Hearts*. New York: The Macmillan Co., 1939.

INDEX OF TITLES

INDEX OF FIRST LINES

534

INDEX OF SCRIPTURE REFERENCES

OLD TESTAMENT

APOCRYPHA

INDEX OF SUBJECTS